ENGLISH POETRY AND POETS.

ENGLISH

POETRY AND POETS.

BY

SARAH WARNER BROOKS.

As the special distinction of man is speech, it would seem that there
can be no higher achievement of civilized men, no proof more conclusive
that they are civilized men, than the power of moulding words into such
fair and noble forms as shall people the human mind forever with images
that refine, console, and inspire. — *Lowell.*

Essay Index Reprint Series

BOOKS FOR LIBRARIES PRESS
FREEPORT, NEW YORK

First Published 1890
Reprinted 1972

Library of Congress Cataloging in Publication Data

Brooks, Sarah Warner, 1822-1906.
    English poetry and poets.

    (Essay index reprint series)
    Reprint of the 1890 ed.
    1. English poetry--History and criticism.
I. Title.
PR502.B8 1972   821'.009   72-37511
ISBN 0-8369-2537-8

PRINTED IN THE UNITED STATES OF AMERICA
BY
NEW WORLD BOOK MANUFACTURING CO., INC.
HALLANDALE, FLORIDA 33009

DEDICATED TO THE MEMORY

OF

𝕸𝖞 𝕭𝖊𝖑𝖔𝖛𝖊𝖉 𝕯𝖆𝖚𝖌𝖍𝖙𝖊𝖗,

IN TENDER AND GRATEFUL ACKNOWLEDGMENT OF ALL HER
HELPFUL AND INTELLIGENT SYMPATHY WITH MY
BEST INTELLECTUAL ENDEAVOR,

MARY ISABEL BROOKS,

DIED MARCH 4, 1883.

PREFACE.

IN the hope that a work undertaken without the remotest view to publication, but for the comparatively ephemeral purpose of imparting oral information and entertainment, may prove permanently valuable, I commit to print the result of much delightful reading, with some loving and earnest (though far from scholarly) original criticism.

In my eager and various reading I quoted and transposed — for the benefit of my classes in English Poetry — from many authors. It did not then seem necessary to retain in memory all the sources of my information; consequently I cannot now duly accredit some of my borrowings. In a work like this, such an offence may, I trust, be forgiven. Where much learned and able work has been done by "my betters," I have not hoped to excel; but if I may help to foster a love and appreciation of the good and true in English verse, I shall have attained to my highest end and ambition.

S. W. B.

CAMBRIDGE, March, 1890.

CONTENTS.

X   CONTENTS.

ENGLISH POETRY AND POETS.

CHAPTER I.

ANCIENT BARDS AND MINSTRELS.

POETRY is older than prose. Tracing her pathway down the dim ages, as she comes, slowly at first, but ever surely, to exalt and ennoble the soul of man, and to weave his dreams, imaginations, and ideals into imperishable fabric, we must grope half-blindly backward to a time when papyrus and parchment had not yet been succeeded by paper, and when no prophetic vision of "Carter's Ink" or "Gillott's Best" had ever dawned upon the imagination in its boldest flight.

The only thoughts which men in their first rude state would be prompted to utter in composition of any length would naturally assume the form of poetry, — as praises of their gods and their ancestors, lamentations over their misfortunes, and rehearsal of their warlike exploits.

When thought depended for its perpetuity on verbal repetition, prose composition, having far less hold upon the imagination and memory than verse, could not well have been retained and transmitted by oral tradition, as were our ancient songs and poems, the rude and meagre beginnings of our literature. Thus it will appear that to poetry we owe not only the cultivation and perfection of our composition, but its very birth.

We are told by the historian that a few years before the birth of Christ a nation of Asiatic Goths who possessed that region of Asia which is now called Georgia, and is connected on the south with Persia, alarmed at the progressive encroachments of the Roman armies, retired in vast multitudes under the conduct of their leader Odin, or Woden, into the northern parts of Europe not subject to the Roman Government, settling in Denmark, Norway, Sweden, and other districts of the Scandinavian territory.

These Goths were hospitably received by the natives, who seem to have finally adopted their language, laws, and religion. The superior ability and address of Odin won the admiration of a more savage people, and they readily gave to this Asiatic chief the title of God. In the Scandinavian mythology he is permanently enthroned as " All-father," the supreme of the immortals. The Goths are said to have brought with them many useful arts, among them the knowledge of " Runes," or letters, which Odin, it is claimed, invented. It may be observed that the word " Rune " is by some derived from " runeu," — that is, to make a slight incision or scratch ; by others from the German word " rauneu," — that is, whisper. Hence " Runic" designates a secret mysterious writing belonging to the priests, to whom at one period the art seems to have been wholly confined. The Runic alphabet has but sixteen characters. From the similarity of the Runic signs to corresponding Roman ones, it has been suggested that this alphabet was borrowed from the Romans ; this, however, is said to have been explained from the fact that the Romans themselves received their characters from an Eastern source, as the Asiatic Goths must have done.

Modern travellers report that there are Runic inscriptions now existing in the deserts of Tartary, which would seem to prove that the art or custom of writing on rocks is Asiatic.

The most ancient specimens of the Norse language are the rune-stones, rings, and wooden tablets, with inscriptions in the old Runic characters.

" Their skill in poetry," says the historian, " was among the arts which the Goths implanted in Scandinavia. With their poetry, they imported into Europe a species of poets called Scalds, or ' polishers of language.' "

The Scalds were from the earliest ages held in the highest veneration by our Teutonic ancestors. As the origin of their art was attributed to Odin, their skill was considered as something divine ; their persons were deemed sacred ; their attendance was solicited by kings, whom they accompanied in battle and whose victories they celebrated ; and they were everywhere loaded with honors and rewards. Dr. Blair's fine essay on the " Poems of Ossian " contains this graphic description of the era of the early Scalds :

" There are," he observes, " four great stages of society: the first and earliest is the life of hunters; pasturage succeeds to this as the ideas of property begin to take root; next, agriculture, and lastly commerce. In the first of these periods, during which hunting was the chief employment of men and their principal method of obtaining subsistence, the art of poetry was planted by Odin in the north of Europe. Whatever was beyond the necessaries of life was known to the Goths only as the spoil of the Roman Province. At their feasts the heroes prepared their own repasts; and as they sat round the light of the burning oak, the wind lifted their locks and whistled through their open halls.

" The rudest face of Nature appears, — a country wholly uncultivated, thinly inhabited, and recently settled. The circle of ideas and transactions was no wider than suits such an age. Valor and bodily strength are the admired qualities. Contentions arise, as is usual among savage nations, from the slightest

causes. To be affronted at a tournament, or to be omitted in
the invitation to a feast, kindles a war. Women are carried off,
and the whole tribe, as in the Homeric times, rise to avenge
the wrong. In their battles it is evident the drum, trumpet, or
bagpipe were not known or used. They had no expedient for
giving the military alarm but striking on a shield or raising
a loud cry.

   " Their armies seem not to have been numerous. They
appear to have been destitute of military discipline and skill.
The battles were disorderly, and terminated for the most part
by a personal combat or wrestling between the two chiefs, after
which the ' bards sang the song of triumph, and the battle
ceased along the hills.' Their ideas were all particular. They
had not words to express general conceptions; these were the
consequence of more profound reflection and larger acquaintance with the arts of thought and speech.

   " A public, a community, the universe, were conceptions beyond their sphere, as also was personification as a poetical figure.
Inanimate objects, such as trees, woods, and flowers, they are
supposed to have personified; but those of later poets — Time,
Terror, Fame, Virtue — were modes of expression too abstract
for the age."

   The poetry of the Scalds, containing not only the praises
of their heroes but their popular traditions and religious
rites, was filled with those superstitions which would naturally pervade the fictions of a wild, imaginative Asiatic
people. Some of the superstitions handed down from the
old Goths and Scandinavians are retained to this day in
the English language. Mara, from whom our "nightmare"
is derived, was in the Runic theology a spirit or spectre
of the night, which seized men in their sleep and suddenly deprived them of speech and motion. Among those
boar-feasting, mead-guzzling Goths we can easily imagine
Mara as a resident household fiend. In the days of fable,
poetry, without fear of contradiction, could give what character she pleased to her heroes. Men loved to record their

connection with chiefs so renowned. Bards were employed
to perpetuate their deeds in song ; and thus in process of
time every chief had a bard in his own family, and the
office at last became hereditary. By the succession of
these bards the poems concerning the ancestors of the
family were handed down from generation to generation,
and always alluded to in the new compositions of the bards.
This custom came down to a period not altogether remote
from our own time ; for after the bards were discontinued
a great number in a clan retained by memory or committed
to writing their compositions, and founded the antiquity of
their families on the authority of their poems.

The descendants of the Celts who inhabited Britain and
its Isles were, it is averred, not singular in this method of
preserving the most precious monuments of their nation.
We are told that the Spartans through long habit became so fond of this custom of oral tradition that they
would never allow their laws to be committed to writing.
All the historical monuments of the old Germans were
comprehended in their ancient songs and orally handed
down.   Garcillan is said to have composed his account
of the Incas of Peru from poetical traditions, the Peru-
vians having lost all other monument of their history.
" When we consider," says Dr. Blair, " a college of
men like the Scalds, who, thus cultivating poetry through
a long series of years, had their imaginations continually
employed upon ideas of heroism, who had all the poems
and panegyrics which were composed by their ancestors
handed down to them with care, is it not natural to think
they would contribute not a little to exalt the public
manners ? "

Warton, who had, it is affirmed, distinctly considered
the peculiarities, habits, and manners belonging to the
early Gothic tribes, places the origin of chivalry in Europe

in these early times, and "finds the seeds of elegance among men only distinguished for their ignorance and barbarity. To this people," he says, "we must refer the origin of gallantry in Europe." Even amid the confusion of savage war and among the most incredible cruelties committed by the Goths at their invasion of Europe, they forbore to offer any violence to the women. The Gothic nations dreaded captivity more on account of their women than their own; and the Romans, availing themselves of this apprehension, often demanded their noblest virgins as hostages.

They believed some divine and prophetic quality to be inherent in their women. It is related of Valeda, a German prophetess, who held frequent conferences with the Roman generals, that on some occasions, on account of the sacredness of her person, she was placed at a great distance on a high tower, from whence like an oracular divinity she conveyed her answers by some chosen messenger. Exaggerated ideas of female chastity prevailed among the Northern nations, and the passion of love, controlled by the principles of honor and integrity, acquired a degree of delicacy.

It is related of Regner Lodbrok that, imprisoned in a loathsome dungeon and condemned to be destroyed by venomous serpents, he solaced himself by recollecting and reciting the glorious achievements of his past life. The first which his Ode commemorates is an achievement of chivalry. It was the delivery of a beautiful Swedish princess, whom he afterward married, from an impregnable fortress in which she was forcibly detained.

Boh, a Danish champion, having lost his chin and one of his cheeks by a single stroke from his adversary, only reflected how he should be received, when thus maimed and disfigured, by the Danish girls. He is said to have

instantly exclaimed, " The Danish girls will not now willingly or easily give me kisses if I should perhaps return
home." Harold, one of the most eminent adventurers of
his age, complains in his Ode that the reputation he had
acquired by so many hazardous exploits, by his skill in
single combat, riding, swimming, gliding along the ice,
darting, rowing, and guiding a ship through the rocks,
had not been able to make any impression upon Elisiff, the
beautiful daughter of Janillas, King of Russia. Chivalry,
it must be remembered, existed but in its rudiments at
this early era; later, after the Norman Conquest, it
became a formal institution.

A skill in poetry is said to have become in some measure
a national science among the Scandinavians, and familiar
with almost every order and degree. Their kings and
warriors partook of the epidemic enthusiasm, breaking
forth on frequent occasions into spontaneous songs and
verses.

Asbiorn Pruda, a Danish champion, who lived at the
close of the tenth century, described his past life in nine
strophes while his enemy, Bruce, a giant, was tearing out
his bowels.

" Tell my mother, Suanita of Denmark," he says, " that
she will not this summer comb the hair of her son; I had
promised her to return, but now my side shall feel the
edge of the sword." Longfellow gives a rhymed translation of this song, each stanza beginning with this line,

" Not such those days of yore."

One could almost fancy the regretful burden of Asbiorn's
death-song floating down the centuries to be re-echoed at
last by that peerless bard who sings from the depth of
" the same divine despair " in strains tender and sad as
the complaining song of his own nightingale, " The days
that are no more."

In the latter half of the tenth century, at the court of
Hakon the Good, flourished the Scald Eyvynd, who for his
skill in poetry was called " The Cross of Poets." Eyvynd
was the most celebrated of all the Scalds. His noble ode,
called in the Northern Chronicles " The Eulogium of
Hakon, King of Norway," was composed in a battle in
which the king with eight of his brothers fell; Eyvynd
fought himself in the battle which he celebrated. This
death-song, of which there is a translation in Longfellow's
collection, contains these lofty sentiments, —

> " Hallowed be the day,
>   Praised the year,
>   When a king is born
>   Whom the gods love!
>   By him his time
>   And his land shall be known.

> " Wealth is wasted,
>   Kinsmen are mortal,
>   Kingdoms are parted;
>   But Hakon remains
>   High among the gods,
>   Till the trumpet shall sound."

" These Northern chiefs appear frequently," observes
Warton, " to have hazarded their lives merely in expectation of meeting a panegyric from their bards. Olave,
King of Norway, when his army was prepared for the
onset, placed three Scalds about him and exclaimed aloud,
' You shall not only record what you have heard but what
you have seen.' " We are told that thus incited they each
obligingly delivered an ode on the spot.

It is related in Canute's History that he ordered the
Scald Loftunga to be put to death for daring to compre-
hend his achievements in too concise a poem. The bard,
however, extorted a speedy pardon by producing the next

day at dinner before the king an ode of more than thirty-eight strophes, for which Canute gave him fifty marks of purified silver.

" Brevity " could not have been " the soul of wit " in Canute's day. Young and Pollock would have been "men of mark " at his court, and Wordsworth's entire " Excursion " might there have secured a patient hearing. When in the sixth century the Saxons succeeded to the Britons and became possessors of England, it is presumed that the tales of the Scandinavian Scalds still flourished among them.

The Saxons were originally situated in those territories which have since been called Jutland, Angelan, and Holstein, and were fond of tracing the descent of their princes from Odin. They were therefore a part of the Scandinavian tribes who were literally our progenitors. That they imported with them into England the old Runic language and letters appears from inscriptions on coins, stones, and other monuments.

Runic inscriptions, as we well know, have been discovered in Cumberland and Scotland, and a coin of King Offa, with a Runic legend, is still extant.

The sacredness of the profession seems to have come down to a later period, for it is recorded that in Ireland to kill a bard or to seize his estate, even for the public service in time of national distress, was considered criminal in the highest degree.

In the old Welsh laws whoever even slightly injured a bard was to be fined six cows, one hundred and twenty pence. The murderer of a bard was to be fined one hundred and twenty cows.

The conversion of the Saxons to Christianity, which is placed about the seventh century, abolished the common use of the Runic characters, which were esteemed unhal-

lowed and necromantic; and with their ancient superstitions, their native and original vein of poetic feeling was
in some measure destroyed.

The genuine successors of the Northern Scalds were the
Anglo-Saxon minstrels, or gleemen, — a distinct order of
men who got their livelihood by singing verses at the houses
of the great.   From the decline of the Scalds till many ages
after the Norman Conquest there never was wanting a succession of them to hand down the art.   Much greater
honors had been heaped upon the ancient bards, in whom
the characters of historian, genealogist, poet, musician, were
all united ; so that while the talents of the minstrels were
chiefly calculated to entertain and divert, the Scalds professed to inform and instruct, and were the moralists and
theologists of their countrymen.

Yet the Anglo-Saxon minstrel, or harper, continued to
command no small degree of public favor.   " The arts he
possessed were," says Bishop Percy, "so extremely acceptable to our ancestors that the word ' glee,' which
peculiarly denoted his art, continues still in our own language to be of all others the most expressive of that popular mirth and jollity, that strong sensation of delight,
which is felt by unpolished and simple minds."

About the beginning of the tenth century the Arabian
vein of fiction is supposed to have been introduced into
the poetry of the North.   " Of a more splendid nature,"
says a learned critic, " and better adapted to the increasing civility of the times, less horrible and gross, it
had a novelty, variety, and magnificence unknown to the
earlier Scaldic era ; and afterwards, enriched by kindred
fancies brought from the Crusades, it gave rise to that
singular and capricious mode of imagination which at
length composed the marvellous machineries of the more
sublime Italian poets and of their disciple, Spenser."

The beautiful romantic fiction that King Arthur, after being wounded at the fatal battle of Camlan, was conveyed by an elfin princess into Faeryland to be cured of his wounds; that he reigns there still in all his pristine splendor and will one day return to resume his throne in Britain, — is found only in the compositions of the Welsh bards who flourished after the native vein of British fabling had been tinctured with exotic imagery.

Tennyson's " Morte D'Arthur " is an exquisitely beautiful version of this old Welsh fable.

After the Conquest, which may be considered as favorable to the establishment of the minstrel profession in England, the Normans, who were early distinguished for their musical talent, and to whom a French writer refers the origin of all modern poetry, would listen to no other songs but such as were composed in their own Norman-French. Yet as the great mass of the native gentry and populace could only understand their own tongue, it is supposed that the English harper and songster was still honored among them. The founding of a priory and hospital by one of their order in 1162 is the first mention made of the native harper after the Conquest. In the reign of Henry II. an annuity from the Abbey of Hide was received by a harper as a reward for his music and songs, which, it is hence inferred, were in the English language.

Henry I., called " fine scholar," was fond of poetry; and his queen, Matilda, — daughter of the Scottish king, Malcolm, and the English Margaret, — patronized the minstrel art so liberally that her generosity became universally known; and crowds of foreigners — scholars, equally famed for verse and singing — came to her court, and "happy did he account himself," says the historian, "who by the novelty of his song could soothe the ears of the queen."

Henry's second queen, Alice, is also addressed by several of the Norman and Anglo-Norman troubadours as the patroness of their art. In the reign of the renowned and romantic King Richard I. the minstrel profession acquired additional splendor.

Richard, who was the great hero of chivalry, was also the distinguished patron of poets and minstrels. He was himself of their number, and some of his poems are still extant. "The distinguished service which he received from his minstrel, Blondel, in rescuing him from his cruel and tedious captivity, ought," says Percy, "to be recorded for the honor of poets and their art." It is thus related by an ancient writer : —

" The Englishmen were more than a whole year without hearing any tydings of their king, or in what place he was kept prisoner. He had trained up in his court a rimer, or Minstrell, called Blondel; who being so long without the sight of his lord, his life seemed wearisome to him, and he became confounded with melancholy. Known it was that he came back from the Holy Land; but none could tell in what country he arrived. Whereupon this Blondel resolved to make search for him in many countries, but he would hear some news of him; after expence of divers days in travell, he came to a towne by good help, near to the castell where his lord, King Richard, lay. Of his host he demanded to whom the castell appertained ; and the host told him that it belonged to the Duke of Austria. Then he enquired whether there were any prisoners detained therein or no ; for always he made such secret questionings wherever he came. And the host made answer that there was one only prisoner, but he knew not what he was, and yet he had been detained there more than the space of a year.

" When Blondel heard this, he wrought such means that he became acquainted with them of the castell, as Minstrels do easily win acquaintance anywhere; but see the king he could not, neither understand that it was he.

" One day he sat directly before the window of the castell, and began to sing a song in French which King Richard and Blondel had sometime composed together.

" When King Richard heard the song, he knew that it was Blondel that sang it; and when Blondel paused at halfe of the song, the king began the other halfe and completed it. Thus Blondel won the knowledge of the king, his master, and returning home to England made the barons of the country acquainted where the king was."

These lines are given as the original song. Blondel sings, —

> " Your beauty, lady fair,
>   None views without delight,
> But still so cold an air
>   No passion can excite ;
> Yet this I patient see,
> While all are shunned like me."

Richard completes the song, —

> " No nymph my heart can wound,
>   If favor she divide,
> And smile on all around,
>   Unwilling to decide.
> I 'd rather hatred bear
> Than love with others share."

In the reign of King John it is related that a minstrel, who superadded to his other talents the character of soothsayer, by his skill in medicated drugs and potions was able to rescue a knight from imprisonment. In the reign of King Henry III. mention is made of Master Ricard, the king's harper, to whom in his thirtieth year that monarch gave forty shillings and a pipe of wine, and also a pipe of wine to Beatrice his wife. The title of Magister or Master, — in the Middle Ages equivalent to the modern title of Doctor, — given to this man, shows his respectable standing. This was in 1252. The minstrel, or harper, was at this time a necessary attendant on a royal personage.

Prince Edward, in his crusade to the Holy Land, in 1271, was rescued from a Saracen assassin by his harper, — a fact proving him to have been officially very near the royal person. Though this prince is said in his reign to have treated the Welsh bards with great severity, in his own court the minstrels appear to have been in high favor. The king of the minstrels was, both in England and on the Continent, a usual officer in the court of princes, and was on the same footing with the king at arms. In the reign of Henry IV. the statute-book shows a severe law passed against the Welsh bards. "This act," observes Percy, "shows that, far from being extirpated by the rigorous policy of Edward I., this order of men were still able to alarm the English Government, which attributed to them ' many diseases and mischiefs in Wales,' and prohibited their meetings and contributions." When in 1473 King Henry V. prepared his great voyage to France, an express order was given to his minstrels, fifteen in number, to attend him, and to each of them he allowed 12*d.* per day, when that sum was more than ten times the value it is at present. Yet we are told that at his triumphant entry into London, after the battle of Agincourt, "he would not allow any ditties to be made, and sung by his minstrels of his glorious victory, for that he would wholly have the praise and thanks given altogether to Almighty God."

In the reign of Henry VI. we read of a commission for impressing boys and youths to supply vacancies by death among the king's minstrels; "who shall be elegant in their limbs, and well-instructed in the minstrel art, for the solace of his Majesty."

In all the establishments of royal and noble households

ample provision was made for the minstrels, and their situation is known to have been both honorable and lucrative. In the fourteenth and fifteenth centuries, the name of minstrel was gradually appropriated by the musician only.

In the time of Henry VIII. it was a common entertainment to hear verses recited by a set of men who obtained their livelihood by repeating them, and who intruded without ceremony into all companies, not only in taverns, but in the houses of the nobility themselves; and it is recorded that long after, in the reign of Elizabeth, it was usual in places of assembly for the company to be desirous to hear of "old adventures, and valiances of noble knights in times past," as those of King Arthur, and his Knights of the Round Table.

When the Earl of Leicester entertained Queen Bess at Kenilworth Castle, in 1575, an ancient minstrel was one of the personages introduced into the pageant. Bishop Percy gives us a passage, quoted from a writer there present, which affords a distinct idea of the character, — "a character which," as he remarks, "is far superior to anything we can at present conceive of the writers of old ballads." It may be found in Percy's "Reliques," vol. i. p. 44.

In the thirty-ninth year of Elizabeth — though romances sung to the harp were still the delight of the common people — this class of men, who appear to have lost all credit, and to have become strolling jugglers, had sunk so low in public opinion that a statute was passed, by which minstrels wandering abroad were included among rogues and vagabonds and sturdy beggars, and were adjudged to be punished as such. This act seems to have put an end to the profession. So long as the minstrels subsisted, like the old Scalds, they seem never to

have designed their rhymes for literary publication; and
it is supposed that they never committed them to writing
themselves. What copies were preserved of them were
doubtless taken down from their own mouths. As most
of the minstrels are represented to have been of the
" North Countryee," the old ballads are in the Northern
dialect. " They abound in antique words and phrases,
are extremely incorrect, and run into the utmost license
of metre; they have also a romantic wildness, and are in
the true spirit of chivalry." The heroic song of "Chevy
Chase," which dates as far back as the time of Henry VI.
and had originally some foundation in fact, is perhaps
the most familiar and popular of all the old ballads. "The
Nut-Brown Maid" — an antique ballad, assigned, I think,
to the fourteenth century — has more beauty of sentiment
than can be discovered in any other composition of the
ancient minstrels; and it has been remarked that "if it
had no other merit than having afforded the groundwork
of Prior's ' Edwin and Emma,' this ought alone to preserve
it from oblivion."

The old romantic tale of " Sir Cauline" might be commended as less gross than most of the antique ballads,
which are for the greater part marred by coarse allusions
and indelicate passages, sanctioned by the usage of that
ruder age, yet offensive to modern taste and refinement.
The ballad of "The Cruel Sister," compiled by Sir Walter Scott, from a copy in manuscript, intermixed with a
beautiful fragment transcribed from the memory of an
old woman who had no recollection of the preceding or
concluding stanzas, though savoring of the marvellous,
is highly pathetic, chaste, and musical. It is supposed to
have been very popular, and may be regarded as a fair
specimen of the most refined of the old ballads.

THE CRUEL SISTER.

THERE were two sisters sat in a bower,
    Binnorie,[1] O Binnorie !
There came a knight to be their wooer,
    By the bonny mill-dams of Binnorie.

He courted the eldest with glove and ring,
    Binnorie, O Binnorie !
But he lo'ed the youngest abune a' thing,
    By the bonny mill-dams of Binnorie.

He courted the eldest with brooch and knife,
    Binnorie, O Binnorie !
But he lo'ed the youngest abune his life,
    By the bonny mill-dams of Binnorie.

The eldest she was vexèd sair,
    Binnorie, O Binnorie !
And sore envied her sister fair,
    By the bonny mill-dams of Binnorie.

The eldest said to the youngest one,
    Binnorie, O Binnorie !
" Will ye go see our father's ships come in ?"
    By the bonny mill-dams of Binnorie.

She has ta'en her by the lily hand,
    Binnorie, O Binnorie !
And led her down to the river strand,
    By the bonny mill-dams of Binnorie.

The youngest stude upon a stone,
    Binnorie, O Binnorie !
The eldest came and pushed her in,
    By the bonny mill-dams of Binnorie.

[1] Pronounced Binnōrie.

She took her by the middle sma',
    Binnorie, O Binnorie!
And dashed her bonny back to the jaw,
    By the bonny mill-dams of Binnorie.

"Oh, sister, sister, reach your hand,
    Binnorie, O Binnorie!
And ye shall be heir of half my land,
    By the bonny mill-dams of Binnorie."

"Oh, sister, I'll not reach my hand,
    Binnorie, O Binnorie!
And I'll be heir of all your land,
    By the bonny mill-dams of Binnorie.

"Shame fa' the hand that I should take,
    Binnorie, O Binnorie!
It's twin'd me and my world's make,
    By the bonny mill-dams of Binnorie."

"Oh, sister, reach me but your glove,
    Binnorie, O Binnorie!
And sweet William shall be your love,
    By the bonny mill-dams of Binnorie."

"Sink on, nor hope for hand nor glove!
    Binnorie, O Binnorie!
And sweet William shall better be my love,
    By the bonny mill-dams of Binnorie.

"Your cherry cheeks and your yellow hair
    Binnorie, O Binnorie!
Gau'd me gang maiden evermore,
    By the bonny mill-dams of Binnorie."

Sometimes she sank, and sometimes she swam,
    Binnorie, O Binnorie!
Until she came to the miller's dam,
    By the bonny mill-dams of Binnorie.

" Oh, father, father, draw your dam !
    Binnorie, O Binnorie!
There 's either a mermaid or a milk-white swan,
    By the bonny mill-dams of Binnorie."

The miller hasted and drew his dam,
    Binnorie, O Binnorie!
And there he found a drownèd woman,
    By the bonny mill-dams of Binnorie.

You could not see her yellow hair,
    Binnorie, O Binnorie!
For gowd and pearls that were so rare,
    By the bonny mill-dams of Binnorie.

You could not see her middle sma',
    Binnorie, O Binnorie !
Her gowden girdle was so bra',
    By the bonny mill-dams of Binnorie.

A famous harper passing by,
    Binnorie, O Binnorie !
The sweet pale face he chanced to spy,
    By the bonny mill-dams of Binnorie.

And when he looked that lady on,
    Binnorie, O Binnorie !
He sighed and made a heavy moan,
    By the bonny mill-dams of Binnorie.

He made a harp of her breast-bone,
    Binnorie, O Binnorie!
Whose sounds would melt a heart of stone,
    By the bonny mill-dams of Binnorie.

The strings he framed of her yellow hair,
    Binnorie, O Binnorie!
Whose notes made sad the listening ear,
    By the bonny mill-dams of Binnorie.

He brought it to her father's hall ;
　　Binnorie, O Binnorie!
And there was the court assembled all,
　　By the bonny mill-dams of Binnorie.

He laid his harp upon a stone,
　　Binnorie, O Binnorie !
And straight it began to play alone,
　　By the bonny mill-dams of Binnorie.

" Oh, yonder sits my father, the king,
　　Binnorie, O Binnorie !
And yonder sits my mother, the queen,
　　By the bonny mill-dams of Binnorie.

" And yonder stands my brother Hugh,
　　Binnorie, O Binnorie !
And by him my William, sweet and true ! "
　　By the bonny mill-dams of Binnorie.

But the last tune that the harp played then,
　　Binnorie, O Binnorie !
Was, " Woe to my sister, false Helèn ! "
　　By the bonny mill-dams of Binnorie.

In the reign of Queen Elizabeth, as the old minstrel art
gradually wore out, a new race of ballad-writers succeeded
who wrote narrative songs merely for the press.   " These
later ballads have an exacter measure, a low and subordi-
nate correctness, sometimes bordering on the insipid, yet
often well adapted to the pathetic."   In the reign of
James I. the ballads produced, which were wholly of this
kind, came forth in such abundance that they began to
be collected into little miscellanies, called Garlands.   In
the Pepysian and other libraries are preserved a great
number of these in black-letter, — a term applied to the
old English, or modern Gothic letter, in which the early

manuscripts were written and the first English books were printed ; many of them have the quaint and affected titles peculiar to the age, and as little religious tracts of the same size were called Penny-Godlinesses, this sort of petty publication had anciently the name of Penny-Merriments. With the decline of the minstrels and the establishment of their legitimate successors, the ballad-writers, ends the history of these

" . . . skylarks in the dawn of years,
The poets of the morn."

CHAPTER II.

EARLIEST REMAINS OF ANGLO-SAXON VERSE.

PURSUING the history of the ancient bards and minstrels, we have rambled down to the reign of James
I. Retracing our steps, we return to the seventh century
and begin a formal history of English poetry with the
earliest recorded " Remains of Anglo-Saxon Verse."

" Fragments of mutilated remains," Longfellow calls
them, " which the human mind has left of itself, coming
down to us through the times of old, step by step, and
every step a century. Old men and venerable," he continues, " accompany us through the Past, and pausing at
the threshold of the Present, put into our hands at parting such written record of themselves as they have. We
should receive these things with reverence ; we should
respect old age."

It is conjectured that as schools were established and
maintained throughout the Roman empire in general,
there were doubtless public seminaries in all the principal
towns of Roman Britain, though no account of them in
particular has been preserved.

To the ancient Britons a stirring and adventurous life
had long been habitual. The departure of the Romans
before the spirit of a new and unaccustomed intellectual
activity had been sufficiently diffused among them, left
them in comparative ease and quiet ; and sunk in sloth
and silence, the love of learning was gradually extin-

guished in the island. It is affirmed that at that time "absolute illiteracy, even among the higher classes of the English, was no uncommon thing."

In the sixth century the controversies between the Greek and Latin churches awoke the minds of men to literary activity, and insensibly taught the graces of style and habits of composition. It is to the faint sparks of knowledge kept alive at that time in the monasteries that we owe the preservation of letters and the liberal arts from total extinction.

The first Anglo-Saxon writer of note who composed in his own language, and of whom there are any remains, is Cædmon, a monk of Whitby, who died about 680.

Cædmon was, like Burns, a poet of Nature's own making. The circumstances under which his talents were first developed are thus related : He was, says the historian, so much less instructed than most of his equals that he had not even learned any poetry ; so that he was frequently obliged to retire, in order to hide his shame, when the harp was moved toward him in the hall, where at supper it was customary for each person to sing in turn. On one of these occasions it happened to be Cædmon's turn to keep guard at the stables during the night; and overcome with vexation, he quitted the table and retired to his post of duty, where, laying himself down, he fell into a sound slumber. In the midst of his sleep, a stranger appeared to him, and saluting him by name, said, "Cædmon, sing me something."

Cædmon answered, "I know nothing to sing, for my incapacity in this respect was the cause of my leaving the hall to come hither."

"Nay," said the stranger, "but thou hast something to sing."

"What must I sing?" said Cædmon.

3

"Sing the creation," was the reply.

Thereupon Cædmon began to sing verses which he had never heard before, and which are said to have been as follows, —

> " Now we shall praise
> The Guardian of heaven,
> The might of the Creator,
> And his counsel,
> The Glory-Father of men!
> How He, of all wonders
> The Eternal Lord,
> Formed the beginning.
>
> " He first created
> For the children of men
> Heaven as a roof,
> The Holy Creator!
> Then, the world
> The Guardian of mankind,
> The Eternal Lord,
> Produced afterwards, —
> The earth for men,
> The Almighty Master!"

Cædmon then awoke, and was not only able to repeat the lines he had heard in his sleep, but he continued them in a strain of admirable versification.

In the morning he hastened to the bailiff of Whitby, who carried him before the Abbess Hilda, and there, in the presence of the learned men of the place, he told his story, and they were all of opinion that he had received the gift of song from heaven. They then expounded to him in his mother tongue a portion of Scripture, which he was required to repeat in verse.

Cædmon went home with his task; and the next morning he produced a poem which excelled in beauty all they were accustomed to hear. Afterward, yielding to the solicitations of the Abbess Hilda, he became an inmate of her house, where she ordered him to transfer into verse the whole of the sacred history, " and," continues the narrator, " he was continually occupied in repeating to himself what he had heard, and like a clean animal ruminating it, he turned it into most sweet verse." He thus composed many poems on the Bible history and on miscellaneous subjects, and some of these have been preserved.

Cædmon has been called the father of Anglo-Saxon poetry, because his name stands first in the history of Saxon song-craft; and also the Milton of our forefathers, because he sang of Lucifer and the loss of Paradise. His account of the fall of man resembles that given in "Paradise Lost;" and one passage in it — the harangue of Satan — it is suggested " might almost be supposed to have been the foundation of a corresponding one in Milton's grand epic." The genuineness of these remains of Cædmon's verse has been called in question. This account of him has indeed " a strong cast of the marvellous," but as competent judges have decided in favor of their authenticity, they are still accepted and approved.

The specimen given of Cædmon may serve as a general one of Anglo-Saxon poetry at that age. As will be observed, it is not rhymed, nor in measured Latin feet, and only distinguished from prose by a very regular alliteration.

In Cædmon's " simple and childlike verse " we find here and there striking poetic epithets. He calls the sky "the roof of nations, the roof adorned with stars." His Creator is " the blithe Heart-king." A laugher is " a laughter-smith," and Ethiopians a people " brown with the hot coals of heaven." Longfellow happily observes that " whenever Cædmon has a battle to describe, he enters into the matter with so much spirit that one almost imagines he sees looking from under that monkish cowl

the visage of no parish priest, but a grim war-wolf, as the
brave were called in the days when Cædmon wrote."

The Epic poem of "Beowulf" is an important relic of
Anglo-Saxon poetry.

It is written in forty-three cantos and some six thousand
lines, and is the oldest epic in any modern language. Its
exact age is unknown, but it is supposed to have been
written somewhere between the seventh and tenth centuries. "Beowulf" exists primitively only in a single
manuscript of the tenth century.

The poem is a history of the wonderful adventures of
King Beowulf, the Sea-Goth. It contains an account of
his battles with Grendels and Fire-drakes, and relates
how, after having made the land rich with treasures found
in the Dragon's Cave, he dies of his wounds. Longfellow
esteems it "a poem of great epic merit. . . . In parts,"
he says, "it is strikingly graphic in description. As we
read," he continues, "we can almost smell the brine and
hear the sea-breeze blow and see the mainland stretch out
its jutting promontories — those sea-noses, as the poet calls
them — into the blue waters of the solemn main."

"Judith and Holofernes," another fragment of the poetry
of this period, is much esteemed by Anglo-Saxon scholars.
This noble passage is spoken by an aged vassal over the
dead body of the hero of the poem : —

> "Byrhtwold spoke ; he was an aged vassal.
> He raised his shield ; he brandished his ashen spear ;
> He full boldly exhorted the warriors :
> ' Our spirit shall be the hardier,
> Our heart shall be the keener,
> Our soul shall be the greater
> The more our forces diminish.
> Here lieth our chief all mangled,
> The brave one in the dust ;
> Ever may he lament his shame

> That thinketh to fly
> From this play of weapons!
> Old am I in life,
> Yet will I not stir hence:
> But I think to lie by the side of my lord,
> That much loved man!'"

"The Fight of Finsborough" is another short and less important fragment.

Two others, founded on the lives of saints, are said to exist, though they never have been published.

Of much later date, and in Norman-Saxon, is the "Chronicle of King Lear." It has no merit as a poem, but is important as proof that the story of King Lear is very old, since it refers to a previous account, — "as the book telleth." The Anglo-Saxons had besides these long and elaborate poems their odes and ballads, of which some account has been given in an introductory chapter.

More than eight hundred years ago, as Canute the Dane — the merciless king who used to say, "He who brings me the head of one of my enemies shall be dearer to me than a brother" — was sailing by the Abbey of Ely, he heard the voices of the monks chanting their holy vesper hymn. Whereupon, it is related, he ordered his knights to row nearer the shore, and sang in his best Anglo-Saxon the following rhyme : —

> "Merry sang the monks in Ely,
> As King Canute was steering by;
> Row, ye knights, near the land
> And hear we these monks' song."

This simple song, that like "a leaf blown about by the wind" has come floating down to us from the past, has little merit in itself, yet reading it, as in a fine old picture we see the rough "war-wolf" leaning landward in the dreamy twilight, listening, sobered and softened, while over the sunset-sprinkled waters float the mellow cadences of the distant vesper hymn.

Then we have in the ninth century the "Metres of King Alfred," translated from the Latin of Boethius, and greatly enriched with interspersed original matter. The memory of "Alfred the Truth-Teller," coming down to us through the discords of the semi-barbarous ninth century, is like a strain of purest harmony ; and in all English history there is no sublimer life than his. In his character "the scholar and the man outshone the king."

Thus he writes : " I wished to live honorably while I lived, and after my life to leave to the men who were after me my memory in good works. . . . God has made all men equally noble in their original nature. True nobility is in the mind, not in the flesh." When Alfred was a young man, there were few or none, it is said, among his countrymen who could readily read the Latin language. He was nearly forty years old when he began the study of that language. He died at fifty-three. Many of his translations have come down to us, and he has, it is supposed, executed many that are now lost. It is recorded of King Alfred that he devoted no less than the eighth part of his whole revenue to the support of the school which he founded, to which many of the noblemen repaired "who had far outgrown their youth, but had not begun their acquaintance with books ; " for even the royal charters of that time instead of the names of kings sometimes exhibit their marks ! To this school, in a true spirit of democracy, he sent his own son Ethelward among the sons of the nobility and inferior classes. "Every person of rank or substance, who either from age or want of capacity was unable to learn to read himself, was compelled to send either his son or kinsman, or if he had neither, a servant, that he might be read to by some one."

And " all this time," we are told that " the brave old king bore manfully the pangs of a terrible unknown disease that nothing could relieve," and of which he died, after a glorious reign of thirty years.   " Alfred the king," he says, quaintly prefacing his " Metres," " was translator of this book, and turned it from book-latin into English, as he most clearly and plainly could amid the various and manifold worldly occupations which often busied him in mind and body."   He ends his task with a prayer.

Some of Alfred's " Metres " have been translated into modern English.   The original Anglo-Saxon, in which they are written, is barely intelligible, even to the scholar. " If it is not literally dumb," says Craik, " its voice has for us of the present day entirely lost its music.   When the study of this original form of our national speech," he continues, " was revived in England in the middle of the sixteenth century, it is supposed that at least for three preceding centuries there had been no one able to read it."   With Alfred ends the list of Anglo-Saxon poets of that remote period.   The next three quarters of a century was too troubled to admit of much attention to literature ; but in the year 1066 the Norman influence infused new life into the half-torpid native civilization.   " It was," says Craik, " the intrusion of another system of social organization, and of another language possessing its own literature, to take the place of what was passing away. For the Norman was already recognized as one of the most brilliantly gifted races, and distinguished for superior aptitude, both in the arts of war and peace, of polity and song."

Though the dawn of the revival of letters in England is properly dated from a point about fifty years antecedent to the Conquest, still an English writer almost contemporary with the Conquest, himself educated abroad,

describes his countrymen generally as having been found by
the Normans a rustic and almost illiterate people. The
French imported into England by the Conqueror and his
people has been called " a confused jargon of Teutonic,
Gaulish, and vitiated Latin." The Saxon, though still
spoken in the country, was not without various adulter-
ations from the French. We are told that in the reign
of Henry II. the nobles constantly sent their children
into France, lest they should contract habits of barbarism
in speech. Of the century following the Conquest is a
metrical translation by one Layamon, a priest of Ernley,
written in unmixed but barbarous Saxon.

It may be considered as throwing a valuable light on
the history of our language at what has been called the
most important period of its existence, being composed at
a time when the Saxons and Normans in England began
to unite into one nation, and to adopt a common language.
" How little the English language," observes Craik, " was
really affected by foreign converse, as late as the thirteenth
century, may be shown by the small amount of the French
or Latin element found in Layamon's poetry." He may
also be regarded as the first of a series of writers who
about the end of that century began to be conspicuous in
our early literary history, called " Rhyming Chroniclers."
Layamon's " Brut," as the early chronicles of Britain were
called — some have supposed from Brutus, the great grand-
son of Æneas, who is represented in them as the first king
of the Britains ; others maintain from the construction of
the word, which is rumor, report, and in the secondary
sense a chronicle or history — Layamon's " Brut," or Chronicle of Britain from the arrival of Brutus to the death of
Cadwalader in A. D. 689, is in the main a translation from
the French "Brut" of Wace, which is itself a translation from
the Latin of Geoffrey of Monmouth, which, again, professes,

and it is supposed, with truth, to be translated from a Celtic original of an unknown date, believed now to be lost.

Layamon by original additions has extended his poem to more than double the length of Wace's " Brut." Scholars have affirmed that Layamon's style is beyond comparison the most lofty and animated of any of the rhyming chroniclers of his country, reminding the reader of the splendid phraseology of Anglo-Saxon verse. My ignorance of the old Anglo-Saxon disqualifies me for forming a judgment of this as well as many other early poems ; but scholars of taste, versed both in Anglo-Saxon and Scandinavian literature, and possessing such knowledge of its laws as is now attainable, have pronounced it a work conceived with true poetic life, and not wanting in artistic elegance and pathos. It is supposed to have been completed in the reign of King John, about the year 1205, as it alludes to the resistance of that king and his nobles to the collection of the tax called Rome-Scot or Peter-Pence, — an annual tribute formerly paid by the English people to the Pope ; being a penny for every house, payable at Lammas Day, — the feast of first-fruits, occurring on the first day of August.

The first rhyming chronicler, after a considerable interval from Layamon, was a monk of Gloucester Abbey, usually called from that circumstance " Robert of Gloucester." His chronicle, a poem of considerable length, the history extending from Brutus to the reign of Edward I., as a work of art, or imagination, possesses little merit.

Robert Manning, a Gilbertine canon in the monastery of Brunne, and hence commonly called Robert de Brunne, a poet of this class, occurs in the reign of Edward I. in the year 1303. He informs his readers that he is more studious of truth than ornament, and that aiming to give information rather than pleasure, he has avoided the phraseology then used by the minstrels and harpers. He is thought to have succeeded admirably, as his chronicle, though it was intended to be sung, at least by parts, at public festivals, is as barren of true Parnassian fire as that of his predecessor, Robert of Gloucester. " Uncouth and unpleasing," observes Warton, " and chiefly employed in turning the theology of his age into rhyme, he contributed to form a style to teach expression and to polish his native tongue. In the infancy of language nothing is wanted but writers ; at that period even the most artless have their use."

The immediate predecessors of Chaucer are Lawrence Minot, who about 1350 composed a series of short poems on the victories of Edward III., that have been commended for the ease, variety, and harmony of their versification ; Richard Rolle, a hermit and D.D., who wrote metrical paraphrases of certain parts of Scripture, and a dull original, moral poem entitled " The Pricke of Conscience ; " and Robert Langland, a secular priest, the author of a satirical poem entitled " The Vision of Piers Ploughman." It has been observed that the tendency of our poetical literature from the days of the Provençal troubadours has been anti-Roman. The poem of Langland, though produced nearly two centuries before either Protestantism or Puritanism was ever heard of, is almost a puritanical and Protestant work. The satire and invective in his poem is directed altogether against the clergy and especially against the monks and friars. Piers, or Peter, is represented as a poor ploughman who falls asleep upon Malvern Hills " on a May mornynge," and in his dream or vision is divinely enlightened, and receives that instruction in Christian truth which he had sought for in vain from every order of the Church. The "Vision of

Piers Ploughman" as a poem has no high merit, but is distinguished as being the earliest original work of any magnitude in the present form of the language, and as showing the progress which was made about the middle of the fourteeenth century toward a literary style. As the popular representative of those doctrines which were silently bringing about the Reformation, it is considered in many points of view as one of the most important works that appeared in England previous to the art of printing.

"As we approach Chaucer," says Warton, "let us stand still and take a retrospect of the general manners." It may be well to do so, quoting largely from that learned and elegant though at times tediously minute author, and adding from various sources whatever might seem to illustrate the subject. "The tournaments and carousals of our ancient princes," he observes, "by forming splendid assemblies of both sexes, while they inculcated the most liberal sentiment of honor and heroism, undoubtedly contributed to introduce ideas of courtesy and decorum. Yet the national manners still retained a degree of ferocity, and the ceremonies of the most refined courts in Europe had often a mixture of barbarism which rendered them ridiculous. Their luxury was inelegant, their pleasures indelicate, and their pomp cumbersome and unwieldy;" those powers of the intellect, we might add, which teach elegant feelings and heighten our natural sensibility, lay unawakened, like the spell-bound princess in the fairy tale, awaiting the touch of the fated enchanter Imagination.

It has been observed that the scarcity of valuable books in England was a serious obstruction to the revival of letters.

Toward the close of the seventh century an English abbot, who with incredible labor and immense expense had collected an hundred volumes on theological and fifty on profane subjects, imagined he had formed a splendid library !

Among the constitutions given to the monks of England, in the year 1092, the following injunction occurs : " At the beginning of Lent the librarian is ordered to deliver a book to each of the religious." A whole year is given for the perusal of the book, and at the returning Lent those monks who had neglected to read the books they had respectively received, are recommended to prostrate themselves before the abbot, and to supplicate his indulgence.

In this age of cheap and too often trashy literature, we can hardly believe that when a book was bought in those olden times, it was customary to assemble persons of consequence and character, and to make a formal record that they were present on this occasion. If a person gave a book to a religious house, he believed that so valuable a donation merited eternal salvation, and offered it on the altar with great ceremony.

Living at this favored period in human progress, when book-making is facilitated by inventive genius ; when our clever inventors cunningly devise type-setting machines, that put us in print as deftly as the frost etches his silvery landscapes on our windows in the still winter moonlight, — we can hardly conceive the weary hours of intense labor that must have been given to the production of a single book before the art of printing became known to our ancestors. Take, for example, the Holy Scriptures alone, which so many zealous monks have spent their entire lives in transcribing and illuminating. In Longfellow's " Golden Legend " we find a beautiful and graphic picture of a monk in the scriptorium of his convent, transcribing and illuminating a manuscript of the Gospels, which vividly impresses upon us the arduous labor of such a work, and the fervor with which it may have been pursued.

It is recorded that the library of the University of Oxford, so late as the year 1300, consisted only of a few books chained, or kept in chests, in the choir of St. Mary's church; and though the invention of paper toward the close of the eleventh century contributed to multiply manuscripts and consequently to facilitate knowledge, even so late as the reign of Henry VI., Warton discovers this instance of the impediments to study, which must have been produced by the scarcity of books. "One of the statutes of St. Mary's College is this: 'Let no scholar occupy a book in the library above one hour, or two hours at most, so that others shall be hindered from the use of the same.'"

For three centuries after the decay of the earliest English scholarship, at its height among our Saxon ancestors about the ninth century, owing almost entirely to the efforts of good King Alfred, the principal productions of the most eminent monasteries were incredible legends which discovered no marks of invention, unedifying homilies and trite expositions of the Scripture. Many bishops and abbots began to consider learning as pernicious to true piety, confounding illiberal ignorance with Christian simplicity. In the mean time, from perpetual commotions, the manners of the people had degenerated from that mildness which a short interval of peace and letters had introduced. In the beginning of the eleventh century England at last received from the Normans the rudiments of that cultivation which it has preserved to the present time.

The Conqueror, we are told, was himself a lover and patron of letters. He filled the bishoprics and abbacies of England with the most learned of his countrymen, who had been educated at the University of Paris, at that time the most flourishing school in Europe. Geoffrey, a learned Norman, was invited from that university to superintend the direction of the school of the priory of Dunstable, where he composed a play called "The Play of Saint Katharine," which was acted by his scholars. Warton supposes this to be the first spectacle of the kind ever attempted, and the first trace of theatrical representation which appeared in England. It is related that he borrowed copes from the sacrist of the neighboring abbey of St. Albans to dress his characters.

After the Norman Conquest, though the Conqueror himself was, it is said, far from showing any aversion to the English language, and when he first came over, applied himself to learn it, that he might without the aid of an interpreter understand the causes that were pleaded before him, persevering in his endeavor " till a more iron time of necessity compelled him to give it up," the exclusive language of government and legislation was French. "The whole land," says an old writer, " began to lay aside the English customs and to imitate the manners of the French in many things ; for example, all the nobility in their courts began to speak French, as a great piece of gentility, and to draw up their charters and other writings after the French fashion ; " and he adds that " they [the Normans] held the language of the natives in such abhorrence that to boys in the schools the elements of grammar were taught in French and not in English."

Thus it came to pass that for some ages after the Conquest the French was the only language spoken by kings and the nobility. Ritson affirms that neither William the Bastard, his son, Rufus the Red, his daughter Maud, nor his nephew Stephen, did or could speak the Anglo-Saxon or English language. It is supposed that the two Henrys I. and II. had some knowledge of the English language, though they might not be able to speak it. Richard I. did not know a word of English. We find no important fact relating to this subject in connection with John; but it is asserted that in no instance was Henry III. known to have expressed himself in English. Edward I. constantly spoke the French language; Edward II. married a French princess and himself used the French tongue; and there is on record only a single instance of Edward III.'s use of the English language. He appeared in 1349 in a tournament at Canterbury with a white swan for his impress, and this motto embroidered on his shield, which is so heartily English that one could imagine it the very roar of the old Lion himself: —

> " Hay, Hay, the wythe swan!
> By Godes soul I am thy man!"

" Yet under all these disadvantages, the national tongue," observes Craik, " possessing as it did the one only great advantage of being the ancestral speech of the people, and having a substantial existence in poems and histories, the memory of its old renown could not altogether pass away; and after a time, though in an altered form, we find it again employed in writing."

CHAPTER III.

CHAUCER.

AT the time when Chaucer wrote, in the latter half of
the fourteenth century, the two languages, — French
and English, — like the two nations, had become widely
separated. The French had gone almost entirely out of use
as a medium of common conversation, — though still the
speech of the court, — and the English had, by throwing off
most of its primitive rudeness, become more fit for literary
composition. Chaucer, with true nobility of soul, " made
choice of the people's speech, rather than the Latin of the
learned, or the French of the noble."

" The King's English" he called it. Thus he quaintly
says : " Let then clerkes enditen in Latin, for they have
the property of science, and the knowing of that faculty ;
and let Frenchmen also enditen their queint termes, for it
is kindly to their mouths ; and let us shew our fantasies in
such words as we learnden of our Dame-tongue," — advice
that might not come amiss in our own day.

Langland, whose " Vision of Piers Ploughman" has been
noticed in the preceding chapter, was our earliest original
writer ; yet though his "Vision" is written in verse, it is not
poetry. Langland had but sipped at Helicon ; Chaucer
drank deep and long. He was England's first great poet,
" the true father of our literature, compared with whose
productions all that precedes is barbarism."

" The notion which most people have of Chaucer," says Craik, " is merely that he was a remarkably good poet for his day, but that both from his language having become obsolete, and from the advancement which we have since made in poetical taste and skill, he may now be considered as fairly dead and buried in a literary, as well as in a literal, sense. Now, instead of this, the poetry of Chaucer is really in all essential respects about the greenest and freshest in our language. He may be said to verify the remark of Bacon that ' what we commonly call antiquity was really the youth of the world; ' his poetry seems to breathe of a time when humanity was younger and more joyous-hearted than it now is. The sire of a nation's minstrelsy, he has looked upon the glorious face of Nature unveiled. It is he alone who has conversed with her directly and without an interpreter, and received upon his heart the perfect image of what she is. Succeeding poets are but imitators in a greater or less degree. They are the fallen race, who have been banished from the immediate presence of the divinity; he is the first man, who has seen God walking in the garden, and communed with him face to face."

A serious obstacle to the general appreciation of the works of this great poet is the now obsolete dialect in which he wrote.

It has been remarked, and with truth, that " if Chaucer's poems had been written in Hebrew, they would have been a thousand times better known, for they would have been translated." Many educated persons and scholars are repelled by his antiquarian English, — " that strange costume of diction, grammar, and spelling, in which his thoughts are clothed, and which," it has been aptly said, " flutter about them like the rags upon a scarecrow." Yet to those who have the patience to master the difficulties of the antiquated English, which though not a dead can scarcely be said to be a living language, Chaucer's poems will yield an abundant reward. Chaucer was

4

born in the reign of Edward III., it is supposed about the year 1328, and educated at Oxford, where it is said he made a rapid progress in the scholastic sciences as they were then taught; but " the liveliness of his parts and the native gayety of his disposition soon recommended him to the patronage of that magnificent monarch of whose reign, as well as of that of his successor, Richard II., he was the most illustrious ornament."

Chaucer was a man of the world. He frequently visited France and Italy under the advantages of a public character. Familiar with the practices and diversions of courtly life, he was enabled to enrich his works with those descriptions of splendid processions and gallant carousals with which they abound. Enabled by his travels to cultivate the Italian and Provençal languages, " he polished and enriched his native versification with loftier cadences and a more copious and various phraseology." Since he first taught his countrymen to write English, and by naturalizing words from the Provençal (then the most polished dialect of any in Europe), formed a style, he may claim to be the father of English composition. Chaucer was an universal reader; and it has been remarked that "his learning is sometimes mistaken for genius." His chief sources were the French and Italian poets. His Knight's Tale is a translation, or imitation, from the Italian of Boccaccio. In passing through his hands it has received new beauties. His " Romaunt of the Rose" is from the French, and highly esteemed by them as one of the most valuable pieces of their old poetry. Chaucer is thought greatly to have improved the original, and to have enriched the allegorical figures in the poem, parts of which owe all their merit to the translator. Chaucer's poem on the subject of Troilus and Cressida has been greatly admired. The fine passage in which " Cresside makes an avowal of her

love has been much quoted and praised. His version of
the legend of Ariadne displays in many fine strokes his
delicate poetic insight, as when — Ariadne awakening
from her swoon to find herself forsaken by Theseus — the
poet says of her, —

> " After a time she rose, and kissed with care
> His footmarks on the sand, which she found there."

Poor Ariadne! We rejoice at last when the poet tells us
that —

> " The throned gods on her their pity took ;
> And in the sign of Taurus, if you look,
> You may behold her starry crown shine clear."

For Chaucer's " House of Fame " no foreign original has
been discovered, although Warton supposes it may have
been translated or paraphrased from the Provençal. It is
in three books, comprising in all twenty-one hundred and
ninety lines. The reference which Chaucer is supposed to
make in this poem to the circumstances of his own life
and the various learning and knowledge with which it is
interspersed, — such as an explanation of the doctrine of
gravitation, and a discourse on the production and propa-
gation of sound, — make it an exceedingly interesting poem.
Its strong delineation of crowded and variegated dramatic
life is praised. It is in " The Canterbury tales " of Chaucer
that we behold the fully rounded and ripened poet. This
great work forms the ever-enduring monument of his genius,
and, as has been aptly remarked, " towers above all else
that he has written like some palace or cathedral ascending with its broad and lofty dimensions from among the
common buildings of a city." Chaucer is supposed to have
been about sixty years of age when he composed " The Canterbury tales." Let us then not fear the bugbear age, —
which is but another name for development.

The work has this origin : A company of pilgrims, consisting of twenty-nine, meet together in fellowship at an inn, all being bent on a pilgrimage to the shrine of Thomas à Becket at Canterbury. These pilgrimages are represented as scenes of much enjoyment and hilarity ; the devotees, having at the outset thwarted the Evil One, did not consider it necessary to resist him by the way, and might therefore consistently put aside any religious strictness or restraint. They all sup together, and after great cheer the Landlord proposes that they shall travel together to Canterbury ; and to shorten their way, that each shall tell two tales, both in going and returning, and whoever told the best should have a supper at the expense of the rest.

Mine host, "both bold of speech, wise and well-taught," is appointed judge and reporter of the stories. The work, as we can readily infer from the plan, — which if carried out would have afforded us no less than a hundred and twenty tales, — is unfinished ; but it contains twenty-four tales, including two in rhythmical prose. These tales are interspersed with prologues, besides the prologue to the whole work, in which the pilgrims are severally described. This general prologue has been pronounced " a gallery of pictures almost unmatched for their air of life and truthfulness."

I borrow a few of these pictures from Horne's " Chaucer Modernized," — a work to which Powell, Wordsworth, Leigh Hunt, and Mrs. Browning have contributed. In the antiquated English Chaucer is indeed not generally appreciated, though one of his admirers *has* expressed a wish to retain him in that ancient costume "for himself and a few friends."

OF A CLERK.

A CLERK there was from Oxford, in the press,
Who in pure logic placed his happiness.

His horse was lean as any garden rake;
And he was not right fat, I undertake,
But hollow lookèd, and sober and ill fed.
His uppermost shirt cloak was a bare thread,
For he had got no benefice as yet,
Nor for a worldly office was he fit.
For he would rather have at his bed's head
Some twenty volumes, clothed in black and red,
Of Aristotle and his philosophy,
Than richest robes, fiddle, or psaltery.
But though a true philosopher was he,
Yet had he little gold beneath his key;
But every farthing that his friends e'er lent,
In books and learning was it always spent;
And busily he prayed for the sweet souls
Of those who gave him wherewith for the schools.
He bent on study his chief care and heed ;
Not a word spake he more than there was need,
And this was said with firm and gravest stress,
And short and quick, full of sententiousness.
Sounding in moral virtue was his speech;
And gladly would he learn and gladly teach.

Scott must have found here the model for his Dominie Sampson.

Equally well drawn is this familiar picture of a good parson : —

"A good man of Religion did I see,
And a poor parson of a town was he ;
But rich he was of holy thought and work.
He also was a learned man, a clerk,
And truly would Christ's holy gospel preach,
And his parishioners devoutly teach.
Benign he was, and wondrous diligent
And patient when adversity was sent ;
Such had he often proved, and loath was he
To cruse for tythes and ransack poverty.
But rather would he give, there is no doubt,
Unto his poor parishioners about,

Of his own substance, and his offerings too.
His wants were humble, and his needs were few.
Wide was his parish — houses far asunder —
But he neglected nought for rain or thunder,
In sickness and in grief to visit all
The farthest in his parish, great and small.
Always on foot, and in his hand a stave,
This noble example to his flock he gave,
That first he wrought, and afterwards he taught.
Out of the Gospel he that lesson caught,
And this new figure added he thereto, —
That if Gold rust, then what should Iron do ?
And if a priest be foul, on whom we trust,
No wonder if an ignorant man should rust ;
And shame it is, if that a priest take keep,
To see an obscene shepherd, and clean sheep.
Well ought a priest to all example give,
By his pure conduct, how his sheep should live.
    He let not out his benefice for hire,
Leaving his flock encumbered in the mire,
While he ran up to London, to St. Paul's,
Seeking a well-paid chanterey for souls,
Or with a loving friend his pastime hold ;
But dwelt at home, and tended well his fold,
So that to foil the wolf he was right wary.
He was a shepherd, and no mercenary ;
And though he holy was, and virtuous,
He was to sinful men full piteous.
His words were strong, but not with anger fraught ;
A lore benignant he discreetly taught.
To draw mankind to heaven by gentleness
And good example was his business,
But if that any one was obstinate,
Whether he were of high or low estate,
Him would he sharply check, with altered mien :
A better parson there was nowhere seen.
He paid no court to pomps and reverence,
Nor spiced his conscience at his soul's expense ;
But Jesu's lore, which owns no pride or pelf,
He taught — but first he followed it himself."

Goldsmith, in his " Deserted Village," must have had in mind this parson when he described the village preacher. They have some beautiful traits in common.

In the Friar's Tale, Chaucer thus shrewdly makes Satan acknowledge the beneficence of evil : —

> "A Devil must do God's work, 'twixt you and me ;
> For without him, albeit to our loathing,
> Strong as we go, we devils can do nothing,
> Though to our prayers sometimes he giveth leave
> Only the body, not the soul, to grieve.
> Witness good Job, whom nothing could make wroth.
> And sometimes have we power to harass both ;
> And then again, soul only is possest,
> And body free ; and all is for the best.
> Full many a sinner would have no salvation
> Gat he not it by standing our temptation,
> Though God he knows, 't was far from our intent
> To save the man ; his howl was what we meant."

" In these tales," says Warton, " Chaucer's knowledge of the world availed him in a peculiar degree, and enabled him to give such an accurate picture of ancient manners as no contemporary nation has transmitted to posterity. It is here we view the pursuits and employments, the customs and diversions, of our ancestors, copied from the life, and represented with equal truth and spirit. The figures are all British, and bear no suspicious signatures of classical, Italian, or French imitation."

" What an intimate scene of English life in the fourteenth century," says Campbell, " do we enjoy in these tales, beyond what history displays by glimpses, through the stormy atmosphere of her scenes, or the antiquary can discover by the cold light of his researches ! " Of this national work, which embodies Chaucer's native genius, unassisted and unalloyed, his contemporaries and their suc-

cessors were justly proud. Many copies existed in manuscript ; and when the art of printing first came to England,
one of the first duties of Caxton's press was to issue an
impression of these tales, which first gave literary per-
manence and consistency to the language and poetry of
England.

The versions of Chaucer given by Pope and Dryden are
elaborate and highly finished productions ; but Chaucer
being the most simple and natural of poets, as they were
the most sounding and artificial, they are, properly speaking, paraphrases bearing but the faintest resemblance to
the great poet. Other and inferior poets have grossly mutilated his finest passages of pathos and humor. The most
rational attempt to render Chaucer intelligible is the later
work of Horne, to which allusion has already been made ;
here we have the poet's thought bereft of the obsolete
dialect which naturally repels many lovers of good poetry.

Chaucer was a student, a soldier, and a courtier ; often
employed in public affairs of delicacy and importance ; and
as his fortunes rose and fell with those of his king, he saw
many bitter reverses.   He accompanied the army of Edward III. when it invaded France, and was made prisoner
in the year 1359 at the siege of Retters.

At the age of forty-one he married — after a long and
faithful attachment, which appears to have been as faithfully returned — Philippa de Rouet, one of the queen's
maids of honor, whose duty to her royal mistress prevented her marriage till by the queen's death she was
released from a prior obligation, and left free to follow her
own sweet will.   The union — as we might infer — was a
most happy one.

Chaucer is supposed to have resided, when at home,
in a house granted by the king, near the royal manor at
Woodstock, surrounded with every mark of luxury and

distinction. The venerable oaks yet shade the spot where it is said his morning walk may still be traced.

> " O rock upon their towery tops
> All throats that gurgle sweet!
> All starry culmination drop
> Balm dews to bathe their feet! "

In the reign of Richard II., on the 25th of October, 1400, the poet died in London, and was buried in Westminster Abbey, the first of that illustrious file of poets whose ashes consecrate and enrich the sacred edifice. The character of Chaucer, which may be seen in his works, is thus faithfully portrayed : " He was the counterpart of Shakespeare in cheerfulness and benignity of disposition ; no enemy to mirth and joviality, yet delighting in his books, and studious in the midst of an active life. He was an enemy to superstition and priestly abuse. He retained through life his strong love of the country, and its inspiring and invigorating influences. The month of May was always a carnival in his heart and fancy. ' Hard is his heart,' he sings, ' that loveth nought in May.' "

Critics place Chaucer in the first class of poetry, — the natural. He has masterly execution, but not much invention.

Like Shakespeare, he is remarkable for the variety of the qualities he possesses, excelling equally in the comic and the pathetic.

He has great wit, great humor, strong manly sense, great power of description, perfect knowledge of character, occasional sublimity, and the deepest pathos.

He was the first great English poet, and while the language is spoken, he will be honored as the " father of our literature."

CHAPTER IV.

SOME PREDECESSORS OF SPENSER.

IT has been asserted that if Chaucer had not existed, the poems of John Gower would alone have been sufficient to rescue the reigns of Edward III. and Richard II. from the imputation of barbarism.

Gower is supposed to have been born about the year 1325, and must consequently have been a few years older than Chaucer. His capital production is a poetical work in three parts, which were respectively entitled, " Speculum Meditantis," or, " The Mirror of Meditation," written in French rhymes, in ten books, and never printed ; the " Vox Clamantis," or, " Voice of one Crying in the Wilderness," containing seven books of Latin elegiacs, which was also never printed ; and the " Confessio Amantis," or, " The Lover's Confession," an English poem in eight books, first printed by Caxton in the year 1483.

This poem was written at the command of Richard II., who, meeting Gower rowing on the Thames near London, invited him into the royal barge, and " after much conversation, requested him to book some new thing."

It is on this work that Gower's character and reputation as a poet are almost entirely founded.

The " Confessio Amantis " is a grave discussion on the morals and metaphysics of love, exemplified by a variety of apposite stories extracted from classics and chronicles.

In this degenerate nineteenth century we can hardly imagine an elegant scholar, of Gower's depth and breadth, sitting gravely down to a discussion of the morals and metaphysics of love.

Nowadays if poor Cupid ever dare come into serious learned society, he is fain to fold his arms, hang his head, tuck his abhorred quiver under his wing, and entering with Paul Pry's lowest bow, "hope he don't intrude;" happy if indeed he be not altogether driven out and forced to take shelter between ignoble "yellow covers," where, mutilated by false description, false sentiment, bad manners, and bad morals, from a winged god he dwindles to a vile grub-worm. The age of mechanics is not the age of chivalry; and we read with incredulous wonder of the ridiculous but systematic solemnity with which the passion of love was treated in those days of splendid gallantry.

Chaucer's "Court of Love" contained the twenty statutes which that court observed under the severest penalties, and from which there seems to have been no appeal; and we find in Warton's History this singular account of a Society of the Penitents of Love, established in Languedoc, where enthusiasm was carried to as high a pitch as it ever was in religion. This society presents a curious picture of the times. It was "a contention of ladies and gentlemen who should best sustain the honor of their amorous fanaticism." Their object was to prove the excess of their love by showing with an invincible fortitude and consistency of conduct, with no less obstinacy of opinion, that they could bear extremes of heat and cold.

Accordingly, the resolute knights and esquires, the dames and damsels who had the hardiness to embrace this severe institution, dressed themselves during the heat of summer in the thickest mantles lined with the warmest furs.

In this they demonstrated, according to the ancient

poets, that love works the most wonderful and extraordinary changes.

In winter their love again perverted the nature of the seasons ; they then clothed themselves in the lightest and thinnest stuffs which could be procured.

It was a crime to wear furs on a day of the most piercing cold, or to appear with a hood, cloak, gloves, or muff.

The flame of love kept them sufficiently warm. Fires by this most economical fanaticism were all the winter utterly banished from their houses, and they dressed their apartments with evergreens.

In the most intense frost their beds were covered only with a piece of canvas.

In the mean time they passed the greater part of the day abroad in wandering about from castle to castle ; "insomuch that many of these devotees, during so desperate a pilgrimage, perished by the inclemency of the weather, and died martyrs to their profession."

The solemn sententiousness of Gower's "Confessio Amantis" caused Chaucer to call him the "moral Gower," and he retained the title ever after.

Gower's education was liberal, his course of reading extensive, and his severer studies were tempered with a knowledge of life. By a critical cultivation of his native language, he labored to reform its irregularities, and to establish an English style. His grave and sententious verses lack spirit and imagination ; yet his language is tolerably perspicuous, his versification often harmonious, and he has much good sense, solid reflection, and useful observation. Warton affirms that "no poet before Gower had treated the passion of love with equal delicacy of sentiment and elegance of composition."

Gower was the friend of Chaucer, though in later life it is supposed that they became alienated. The affliction

of Milton and of Homer — blindness — fell upon him in
his later years.   His death took place in 1408.

John Lydgate, the poet who follows Chaucer and Gower
at the shortest interval, in the reign of Henry VI., and
about the year 1430, arrived at his highest eminence.
Lydgate was a monk of the Benedictine Abbey of Bury,
in Suffolk ; but his genius was so lively, and his accomplishments so numerous, that the holy father, St. Benedict,
it has been hinted, would hardly have acknowledged him
for a genuine disciple.   He had travelled in France and
Italy, studying the poetry, and returning a complete master
of the language and literature, of both countries ; and
though his own writings contain only a few good passages,
he is said to have amplified our language and to have been
the first of our writers whose style is clothed with that
perspicuity in which the English phraseology appears at
this day to an English reader.

The fact that he opened a school in his monastery for
the instruction of young persons of the upper ranks in the
art of versification, is cited as a proof that poetry had
become a favorite study among the few who acquired any
tincture of letters in that age.   " Lydgate," observes
Warton, " was not only the poet of the monastery, but
of the world in general, his hymns and ballads having
the same degree of merit."

A fugitive poem of his is curious for the particulars it
gives respecting the city of London in the early part of
the fifteenth century.

The poet has come to town in search of legal redress
for some wrong, and visits in succession the Court of
Common Pleas, the King's Bench, the Court of Chancery,
and Westminster Hall.   He says, —

> " Within the hall, neither rich, nor yet poor
>   Would do for me aught, although I should die ;

Which seeing, I gat me out of the door,
  Where Flemings began on me for to cry,
  'Master, what will you copen or buy?
Fine felt hats, or spectacles to read?
Lay down your silver, and here you may speed.'

"Then to Westminster gate I presently went,
  When the sun was at high prime.
Cooks to me they took good intent,
  And proffered me bread, with ale and wine,
  Ribs of beef, both fat and full fine;
A fair cloth they 'gan for to spread.
But wanting money, I might not be sped.

"Then unto London I did me hie;
  Of all the land it beareth the prize.
'Hot peascods!' one began to cry;
  'Strawberry ripe, and cherries in the rise!'
  One bade me come near and buy some spice;
Pepper and saffron they 'gan me feed;
But for lack of money, I might not speed.

"Then to the Cheap I 'gan me drawn,
  Where much people I saw for to stand.
One offered me velvet, silk, and lawn,
  Another, he taketh me by the hand:
  'Here is Paris thread, the finest in the land!'
I never was used to such things, indeed;
And wanting money, I might not speed.

"Then went I forth by London Stone,
  Throughout all Canwick Street;
Drapers much cloth me offered loane;
  Then comes me one cries 'Hot sheep's feet!'
  One cried mackerel, rushes green, another 'gan greet.
One bade me buy a hood to cover my head;
But for want of money, I might not be sped.

"Then I hied me unto East-Cheap.
  One cries ribs of beef, and many a pie;
Pewter pots they clattered on a heap;

There was harp, pipe, and minstrelsy,
  'Yea, by cock! nay, by cock!' some began cry,
Some sung of Jenkin and Julian for their meed;
But for lack of money, I might not speed.

" Then into Cornhill anon I yode,
  Where was much stolen gear among.
I saw where hung mine own hood
  That I had lost among the throng.
To buy my own hood I thought it wrong;
I knew it well, as I did my creed;
But for lack of money, I could not speed."

" The rise of such men as Chaucer," it has been happily observed, "is the accident of Nature, and whole centuries may pass without producing them." From his death, in 1400, two centuries in the life of England followed, which, though more enlightened than the times of Chaucer, produced no poet comparable to him.

In this long period poets arose who displayed the grace and elevation, if not the creative energy, of true poetry. Eminent among these was Thomas Howard, eldest son of the Duke of Norfolk, and usually denominated the Earl of Surrey. This nobleman, born in 1516, was educated at Windsor in company with a natural son of Henry VIII., and in early life became accomplished in the learning of the time, and in all kinds of courtly and chivalrous exercise.

About the beginning of the sixteenth century, in the reign of Henry VIII., the sonnets of Petrarch were the great models of composition; it has been said of Surrey that with a mistress as beautiful as Laura, and with Petrarch's passion, if not his taste, he led the way to great improvements in English poetry, by a happy imitation of this great master and other Italian poets, of whom he became a devoted student during his travels in Italy. His poetry is chiefly amorous, and in praise of

Geraldine, descendant of the Dukes of Tuscany, maid of honor to Queen Katharine.

A portrait of this lady, who was the object of Surrey's passionate devotion, is still extant, and is said to be sufficiently beautiful to authorize the poetical raptures of her lover, which, however absurd they may appear, accorded with the fashionable system of Platonic gallantry, introduced from Italy, and " approved at that time by the most virtuous and illustrious."

Surrey is said to have made the tour of Europe in the true spirit of chivalry.

The first city which he proposed to visit in Italy was Florence. Passing a few days at the Emperor's court, on his way thither, he became acquainted with Cornelius Agrippa, a celebrated adept in natural magic, who, as the story goes, showed him in a mirror a living image of the fair Geraldine. This incident is beautifully related by Sir Walter Scott, in the " Lay of the Last Minstrel."

> " 'T was All-Souls' eve ; and Surrey's heart beat high.
>   He heard the midnight bell with anxious start
>   Which told the mystic hour, approaching nigh,
>   When wise Cornelius promised, by his art,
>   To show to him the ladye of his heart,
>   Albeit betwixt them roared the ocean grim ;
>   Yet so the sage had hight to play his part,
>   That he should see her form in life and limb,
>   And mark if still she loved, and still she thought of him.
>
>   .   .   .   .
>
> " Fair all the pageant, but how passing fair
>   The slender form which lay on couch of Ind !
>   O'er her white bosom strayed her hazel hair ;
>   Pale her dear cheek, as if for love she pined.
>   All in her night-robe loose she lay reclined,
>   And, pensive, read from tablet eburnine
>   Some strain that seemed her inmost soul to find.
>   That favored strain was Surrey's raptured line,
>   That fair and lovely form, the Lady Geraldine."

His imagination inflamed anew, this enthusiastic and romantic lover hastened to Florence, and on his arrival immediately published a defiance against any person who could handle a lance, and was in love, " whether Christian, Jew, Turk, Saracen, or cannibal, who should presume to dispute that his Ladye-Love was superior to all that Italy could vaunt of beauty, — that she was fair beyond the fairest." As the lady was pretended to be of Tuscan origin, the pride of the Florentines was flattered ; and the Grand Duke of Tuscany, says the historian, permitted a general ingress into his dominions of the combatants of all countries, till this important trial should be decided. The challenge was accepted and the earl victorious.

The shield which Surrey presented to the duke before the tournament began, was, it is said, in the possession of the late Duke of Norfolk.   Geraldine, we are sorry to add, with all her beauty and grace, was not worth tilting for.   She was vain, frivolous, and coquettish, and is only interesting from having given the impulse to her lover's genius, exciting him to try his powers in a style of composition no models of which yet existed in his native language.

" Only she that hath as great a share in Virtue as in Beauty, deserves a noble love to serve her, and a true poesie to speak her."

Surrey's poetry is remarkable for its flowing melody, correctness of style, and purity of expression.   The highest qualities in his verse are the facility and general mechanical perfection of his versification, and his delicacy and tenderness.   He was the first to introduce the sonnet and blank verse into English poetry.   Surrey's wit, learning, and military ability, excited the jealousy of Henry VIII.   His actions were misconstrued, and he was even accused of designs upon the crown.

The addition of the escutcheon of Edward the Confessor
to his own, though justified by the authority of the heralds,
was a sufficient foundation for an impeachment for high
treason, and he at length fell a sacrifice to the peevish
injustice of this merciless and ungrateful monarch; notwithstanding his eloquent defence, he was condemned by
a servile jury, and beheaded at Tower Hill in the year
1547, at the early age of twenty-seven, having, it is said,
carried away from all his competitors the laurels of knight-
hood and of song.   This sonnet to a lover who presumed
to compare his " Ladye-Love " to Geraldine is a specimen
of Surrey's style.   It is ingenious and elegant; and the
leading compliment has been copied by later poets.

A PRAISE OF HIS LOUE: WHERIN HE REPROUETHE
   THEM THAT COMPARE THEIR LADIES WITH HIS.

> GEUE place, ye louers, here before
> That spent your bostes and bragges in vaine.
> My Ladies beawtie passeth more
> The best of yours, I dare well sayen,
> Than doth the sonne, the candle light,
> Or brightest day, the darkest night.
>   And thereto hath a trothe as iust,
> As had Penelope the fayre.
> For what she saith, ye may it trust,
> As it by writing sealed were ;
> And vertues hath she many moe
> Than I with pen haue skill to showe.
> I could rehearse, if that I wolde,
>   The whole effect of nature's plaint,
> When she had lost the perfit mold,
>   The like to whom she could not paint.
> With wringyng handes howe she dyd cry,
> And what she said, I know it, I.
> I knowe she swore with ragyng mynd :

Her kingdom onely set apart,
There was no losse by loue of kind
That could haue gone so nere her hart.
And this was chiefly all her payne:
She coulde not make the lyke agayne.
Sith Nature thus gaue her the prayse,
To be the chiefest worke she wrought:
In faith, methinke, some better waies
On your behalfe might well be sought
Than to compare (as ye haue done),
To matche the candle with the sonne.

Sir Thomas Wyatt's poetry, neither so flowery in form nor so gentle in spirit as Surrey's, has perhaps more depth of sentiment as well as more force.

Wyatt's skill in arms, fidelity in the execution of public business, and his learning and lively conversational powers, won the favor of Henry VIII., though he is said to have nearly lost his popularity and his head together by his intimacy with Anne Boleyn, to whom these passionate lines of his are supposed to be addressed.

"Forget not yet the tried intent
Of such a truth as I have meant;
My great travail so gladly spent
Forget not yet!

"Forget not yet when first began
The weary life, ye know since whan;
The suit, the service, none tell can,
Forget not yet!

"Forget not yet the great assays,
The cruel wrong, the scornful ways,
The painful patience in delays,
Forget not yet!

"Forget not! oh, forget not this!
How long ago hath been, and is,
The mind that never meant amiss,
Forget not yet!

> "Forget not then thine own approved,
> The which so long hath thee so loved,
> Whose steadfast faith yet never moved :
> Forget not this ! "

The prudence and integrity of the poet justified his innocence, and restored him to the royal favor. Wyatt died at last of a fever caused by riding too fast on a hot day while engaged on a mission for the king.

Surrey's royal murderer wrote a book of sonnets, — a manuscript edition of which is said to be still extant, and was in the possession of the late Lord Eglinton. An old madrigal of his set to music is supposed to have been addressed to Anne Boleyn when he first fell in love with her. It begins thus, —

> " The eagle's force subdues each bird that flies.
> What metal can resist the flaming fire ?
> Doth not the sun dazzle the clearest eyes,
> And melt the ice and make the frost retire ? "

The sonnets that commemorate the loves of this regal butcher bring to mind that famous couplet in Watts' Catechism : —

> " The cat doth play
> And after slay."

Warton sagely informs us that "if Henry had never murdered his wives, his politeness to the fair sex would have remained unimpeached." Murder, we must all agree, is indeed a breach of etiquette.

In 1471 the first book in the English language ever put to the press was printed at Ghent by William Caxton, who, while acting as agent for English merchants in Holland, made himself master of the art, then recently introduced on the Continent. He afterward established a printing-office at Westminster, and produced the " Game of Chess," which was the first book printed in Britain.

" Caxton was," it is said, " a man of plain understanding, but of great enthusiasm in the cause of literature." He translated, or wrote, about sixty different books, all of which went through his own press before his death, in 1491.

CHAPTER V.

ELIZABETHAN AGE, AND SPENSER.

IT has been fairly observed that " of what is commonly called our Elizabethan literature, the greater portion appertains to the reign, not of Elizabeth, but of James, — to the seventeenth, not to the sixteenth century; but as it sprung up in the reign of Elizabeth, and was mainly the product of influences which belong to that age, the common name is the just and proper one. It was born and ripened by that sunny morning of a new day, — ' Great Eliza's golden time,' — when the growing power and prosperity of England had reassured and elevated the national heart." Let us look musingly backward down the long vista of years, and behold in fancy that " golden time" of " Great Eliza." We may see, as in a gorgeous panorama, the splendid court of England's Virgin Queen: the grand presence-chamber, strewn with rushes and adorned with the costly decorations of the time; the " fair Vestal throned by the West," refulgent in jewels and stately in starch and powder; the courtly throng of knights and ladies; Leicester, shrewd, handsome, and unscrupulous, presuming equally on the admiring tenderness of the woman and the golden favor of the queen, and bending low in courtly gallantry to whisper honeyed flatteries, so near that " his breath thaws her ruff." Essex, too, is here, — blunt, loyal, and brave, and basking in the yet unclouded smile of his royal mistress. Raleigh, young, rash, and impetuous, wearing with careless grace his mud-soiled mantle, still elate with his first draught of regal favor, and " fain to climb," although he " fall," is here. Spenser has but just come modestly up to court under the wing of Sidney. A few books of the " Faery Queen " are singing a sweet under-song to themselves in his doublet. Sidney, " the spirit without spot," the flower of knight-hood and manhood, the wonder of whom it might well be said that " Nature lost the perfect mould," and might never bless the world with a counterpart, graces and adorns the scene.

The pageant fades ; knights, lords, and ladies are but " such stuff as dreams are made of," and have long since mouldered in dust. Good Queen Bess has herself " lain down with kings ; " but her golden age shall be honored from generation to generation till earth is hoar, for then it was that Nature, assaying through long centuries in her mystic laboratory, brought forth at last the wonder of all time ; the immortal bard who foreruns the ages, " antici-pating all that shall be said," — our Shakespeare ! The chief glory of the Elizabethan age is its poetry, which ex-ceeds in quality and quantity that of any other age in the annals of English literature.

In a catalogue of good authority no less than two hun-dred poets are referred to that period.

In the poetry of this age fable, fiction, and fancy pre-dominate, and a predilection for thrilling adventures and pathetic events. The cause of this characteristic distinc-tion is thus explained : —

" When the corruptions of popery were abolished, the fashion of cultivating the Greek and Roman learning be-came universal ; classic literature, being liberally diffused by the press, served to excite a taste for elegant reading in lower branches of society than had ever before felt the general influence of letters. The literary character, now no longer appropriated to scholars by profession, was assumed by the nobility and gentry. An accurate comprehension of the phraseology and peculiarities of the ancient poets was, we are told, an indispensable object in the circle of a gentleman's education. Every young lady of fashion was carefully instructed in classical letters, and the daughter of a duchess was taught, not only to distil strong waters, but to construe Greek." Queen Elizabeth's passion for these acquisitions is well known. Roger Ascham, her preceptor, speaks with rapture of her astonishing progress in the Greek nouns, and boasts that " she was accustomed to read more Greek in a day than some canons of Windsor did Latin in one week."

The books of antiquity being thus familiarized to the great, everything was tinctured with ancient history and mythology. It is said that " when the queen paraded through a country town, almost every pageant was a Pantheon. When she paid a visit at the house of any of her nobility, at entering the hall she was saluted by the Penates, and conducted to her privy chamber by Mercury. At dinner — for even the pastry-cooks were expert mythologists — select transformations of Ovid's ' Metamorphoses ' were exhibited in confectionery ; and the splendid icing of an immense historic plum-cake was embossed with a delicious basso-relievo of the destruction of Troy.

" In the afternoon, when she condescended to walk in the park, the lake was covered with tritons and nereids.

" The pages of the family were converted into woodnymphs, who peeped from every bower, and the footmen gambolled over the lawn in the figure of satyrs.

" The next morning, after sleeping in a room hung with the tapestry of the voyage of Æneas, when her Majesty hunted in the park she was met by Diana, who, pronouncing

the royal prude to be the brightest paragon of unspotted
chastity, invited her to groves free from the intrusion of
Actæon.   When she rode through the streets of Norwich,
Cupid, at the command of the mayor and aldermen, ad-
vancing from a group of gods who had obligingly left
Olympus to grace the procession, gave her a golden arrow,
— the most effective weapon of his well-furnished quiver, —
which, under the influence of such irresistible charms,
was sure to wound the most obdurate heart. . . . A gift,"
says the honest historian, "which her Majesty, now verg-
ing to her fiftieth year, received very thankfully."

This inundation of classic pedantry had an immediate
effect upon English literature, enriching the language by a
greater variety of words from the classic tongues, estab-
lishing better models of thought and style, and allowing
greater freedom to fancy and the powers of observation.
"Our poets," observes Warton, "were suddenly dazzled
with these novel imaginations, and the divinities and heroes
of pagan antiquity decorated every composition." The
translation of the classics, which now employed every pen,
gave a currency and celebrity to these fancies.

In the reign of Queen Elizabeth almost all the poets
were either courtiers themselves or under the immediate
protection of courtiers ; whatever, then, there was, refined, gay, or sentimental, in England at this time came
with its full influence upon poetry. Elizabeth herself,
among her many weaknesses and vanities, is said to have
had the desire of shining as a poetess. The praises which
the courtiers and writers of that age lavished upon her for
her classical attainments she really deserved ; but their
admiration of her royal ditties was probably about as just
as the flatteries bestowed on her beauty.

The queen, being herself addicted to poetical composition, was pleased to fill her court with men qualified to

shine in that department of literature, and hence the poets of that age were constantly receiving the smiles and occasionally the solid benefactions of royalty.

The works brought forth at this period have been aptly compared to the productions of " a soil for the first time broken up, when all indigenous plants spring up at once with a rank and irrepressible fertility, and display whatever is peculiar and excellent in their nature on a scale the most conspicuous and magnificent." " The ability to write, having," says an observing critic, " been, as it were, suddenly created, the whole world of character, imagery, and sentiment lay ready for the use of those who possessed the gift, and was appropriated accordingly." As might be expected where there was less rule of art than opulence of materials, the productions of these writers are often deficient in taste. Yet it has been justly observed " that after every proper deduction has been made, enough remains to fix this era as by far the mightiest in the history of English literature, or indeed of human intellect and capacity." " In point of real force and originality of genius," says Craik, " neither the age of Pericles nor the age of Augustus nor the times of Leo X., nor of Louis XIV., can come at all into comparison with the sixty or seventy years that elapsed from the middle of Elizabeth's reign to the period of the Restoration, for in that short period we find the names of all the very great men England has ever produced, — men not merely of great talents, but of vast compass and reach of understanding, and of minds truly creative and original, not perfecting art by the delicacy of their tastes, or digesting knowledge by the justness of their reasonings, but making vast and substantial additions upon which taste and reason must hereafter be employed." The cultivation of an English style began now to be especially regarded. Roger Ascham was the first English scholar who ventured to " break the shackles of Latinity," and publish in English with a view of giving a pure and correct model of English composition.

" Whoever will write well in any tongue," he quaintly observes, " must follow this counsel of Aristotle, — to speak as the common people do, to think as wise men do ; using such strange words as Latin, French, and Italian, do make all things dark and hard." This learned man, university orator at Cambridge, and at one time preceptor and ultimately Latin secretary to Queen Elizabeth, was the first writer on education in our language ; and many of his views on this subject are thought to be remarkable, according with the most enlightened of modern times.

Living in an age when men of learning were prone to waste their talents in disputes about predestination and original sin, this wise man deserves our admiration for the better use of his acquirements. When he died, in 1568, Queen Elizabeth is said to have remarked that she " would rather have given ten thousand pounds than to have lost him," — a coarse estimate of his worth, but doubtless meant to do him honor. Ascham's writings furnished an improved example of style ; yet in this era our language cannot be said to have assumed that facility and clearness, that fluency and grace, which it afterward acquired.

Thomas Wilson, one of the most accomplished scholars of his time, and privy counsellor to the Queen as well as Secretary of State, thus quaintly discusses the prevailing errors in style peculiar to the time : —

" The fine courtier," he says, " will talk nothing but Chaucer. The mystical wisemen and poetical clerkes will speak nothing but quaint proverbs and blind allegories, delighting much in their own darkness, especially when none can tell what they do say.

" Some will be so fine and poetical withal that to their seeming there shall not stand one hair amiss, and yet every body else shall think them meter for a ladie's chamber than for an earnest matter in an open debate. . . . Some," he adds, " use over-much repetition of one letter — as, pitiful poverty prayeth for a penny, but puffed presumption passeth not a point, pampering his paunch with pestilent pleasure; procuring his passport to post it to hell-pit, there to be punished with pains perpetual.

" Some," he continues, " end their sentences all alike, making their talk rather to appear rhymed metre than to seem plain speech. I heard a preacher delighting much in this kind of composition, who used so often to end his sentences with words like unto that which went before, that in my judgement there was not a dozen sentences in his whole sermon but they ended all in rhyme for the most part. Some, not best disposed, wished the preacher a lute, that with his rhymed sermon he might use some pleasant melodie, and so the people might take pleasure divers ways, and dance if they list."

The poets, as might be expected, ran headlong into errors for which they could plead such respectable example as the grave and learned professions. The court language was for some time during Elizabeth's reign formed on the plan of John Lyly, born in 1554, — a pedantic courtier, who wrote a book entitled " Euphues, or, The Anatomy of Wit," which he makes to consist in the power of hatching unnatural conceits. Lyly exercised a powerful and injurious influence upon the literature of his age.

Alliteration, which was now, it is said, almost as fashionable as punning, seemed in some degree to bring back English composition to the barbarous rules of the ancient Anglo-Saxons, the merit of whose poems consisted not in the ideas, but in the quaint arrangement of the words and the regular recurrence of some favorite sound or letter. However, England had now arrived at that period propitious to the growth of original and true poetry.

General knowledge was increasing with a wide diffusion and rapidity. Books began to be multiplied, and a variety of the most useful and rational topics had been discussed in our own language, though it is still affirmed that the generality of the lower and many even of the middle classes remained to the end of this period almost wholly uneducated. It has been supposed that the father of Shakespeare, an alderman of Stratford, could not write his name. In the reign of Elizabeth some poetical names of importance precede that of Spenser. The first is Thomas Sackville, subsequently Earl of Dorset, and Lord High Chancellor of England, and author of "Gorboduc," the first English tragedy.

In 1557 Sackville formed the design of a poem entitled "The Mirrour for Magistrates." In this poem, the scene of which, in imitation of Dante, he lays in the infernal regions, it was his design to make all the great persons of English history, from the Conquest downward, pass in review, and each tell his own tale as a warning to existing statesmen. Other duties compelled Sackville to break off the poem after he had written a portion, and to commit the completion of the work to two poets of inferior note, Richard Baldwin and George Ferrers. Baldwin and Ferrers called other writers to their aid; and as any narrative belonging to the historical or legendary annals of the nation might be inserted in the work without any regard to connection or adaptation, it became a receptacle for all the ready versifiers of the day, and has been aptly compared to "a sort of growing monument or cairn, to which every man added his stone or little separate specimen of brick and mortar, who conceived himself to have any skill in building the lofty rhyme." Yet for all its many authors it is only of note in the history of English poetry for the portions contributed by its originator.

The work is considered of a remarkable kind for the age, and is thought to contain in some parts a strength of description in allegorical painting of character scarcely inferior to Spenser, whose genius was one of the peculiar glories of the romantic reign of Elizabeth.

Edmund Spenser was, like Chaucer, a native of London, born about 1553. The rank of his parents is not known; he is supposed to belong to the noble and ancient family of Spenser, " who," as Gibbon happily remarks, " should consider the ' Faery Queen ' as the most precious jewel in their coronet."

Spenser took his degree in Cambridge in 1576. In 1579 he first published his " Shepherd's Calendar," dedicated to Sir Philip Sidney, who afterward became his friend and patron at court, and recommended him to his uncle, the powerful Earl of Leicester, Queen Elizabeth's prime favorite. As a dependant upon Leicester and a suitor for court favor, Spenser is supposed to have experienced many reverses at this period of his life, of which comparatively little is known. These lines in " Mother Hubbard's Tale," though not printed till 1581, evidently belong to this period.

> " Full little knowest thou that hast not tried
> What hell it is in suing long to bide, —
> To lose good days that might be better spent;
> To waste long nights in peevish discontent;
> To speed to-day, to be put back to-morrow;
> To feed on hope, to pine with fear and sorrow;
> To have thy princess' grace, yet want her peers;
> To have thy asking, yet wait many years;
> To fret thy soul with crosses and with cares;
> To eat thy heart through comfortless despairs;
> To fawn, to crouch, to wait, to ride, to run,
> To spend, to give, to wait, to be undone !"

Spenser, from recently discovered documents, appears to have been employed in inferior State missions, — a task then often devolved on poets and dramatists. At length, when Lord Grey of Wilton was sent as Lord Deputy to Ireland, he became his secretary. Returning to England with the deputy after two years abroad, the poet received from the crown in June, 1586, a grant of land out of the forfeited domain of the Earl of Desmond in Ireland.

"When we remember," says Craik, "that letters as yet depended to a great extent for encouragement and support upon the patronage of the great, and that Spenser's scheme of life was, first of all, to procure for himself by any honorable means the leisure necessary to enable him to cultivate and employ his poetical powers, we shall not blame him for seeking such a provision as he required from the bounty of the crown. Spenser was not a mere dreamer, but a man of the largest sense and the most penetrating insight, of the most general research and information, capable of achieving any degree of success in any other field as well as in poetry; yet conscious of possessing 'the vision and the faculty divine,' he well knew that so endowed he might return to his country what she gave him a hundredfold, by conferring upon the land, the language, and the people what all future generations would prize as their best inheritance, and what would contribute more than laws or victories or any other glory to maintain the name of England in honor and renown so long as it should be heard among men."

As one of the conditions of the grant was that the poet should reside on his estate, he repaired to Ireland, and took up his abode in Kilcolman Castle, which had been one of the strongholds of the earls of Desmond. This castle, though its towers are now almost level with the ground, must ever be dear to the lovers of genius. It stood in the midst of a large plain, by the side of a lake. The river Mulla ran through the poet's grounds, and a distant chain of mountains seemed to bulwark in the romantic retreat. Here Spenser is supposed to have written most of his "Faery Queen." Here he brought home his wife

Elizabeth, — the proud beauty so long loved and so hardly won, who is said to have been the tenderest and most faithful of wives. Of all the sonnets addressed to her (and their name is legion), his reply when she confesses herself won, yet fears to relinquish her maiden freedom, is the most beautiful.

> " The doubt that ye misdeem, fair one, is vain,
>   That fondly fear to lose your liberty ;
>   When losing one, two liberties ye gain,
>   And make him bound that bondage erst did fly.
>   Sweet be the bands the which true love doth tie,
>   Without constraint, or dread of any ill ;
>   The gentle bird feels no captivity
>   Within her cage, but sings, and feeds her fill.
>   There Pride dare not approach nor Discord spill
>   The league 'twixt them that loyal love hath bound ;
>   But simple truth and mutual good-will
>   Seeks with sweet peace to salve each other's wound.
>   There Faith doth fearless dwell in brazen tower,
>   And spotless Pleasure builds her sacred bower."

About two years after this marriage Spenser was attacked in his castle by the jealous adherents of its former chief during the insurrection following Tyrone's Rebellion. The insurgents plundered and set fire to the castle. Spenser escaped with his Elizabeth, but a new-born infant, left behind in the confusion incident to such a calamity, perished in the flames. Impoverished and depressed by these calamities, the poet arrived in London in 1598, and died in about three months, on the 16th of January, 1599. It has been mistakenly stated that the author of the "Faery Queen" died of poverty and starvation. His death was doubtless the result of accumulated misfortune upon a spirit too finely touched for mortal combat with woe and ill; yet he was not without the certainty of a decent subsistence. " His annual pension," observes Todd, " of fifty pounds, granted by Queen Elizabeth, was a sum by no means inconsiderable in those days ; and we may at least believe that a plundered servant of the crown would not pass unnoticed by the government either in regard to permanent compensation or to immediate relief if requisite." His funeral was ordered at the charge of the Earl of Essex, which mark of that generous nobleman's respect has been erroneously cited as a proof of the poet's extreme indigence. His hearse was attended and the pall upborne by the poets of the time, while mournful elegies and poems, with the pens that wrote them, were thrown into his tomb.

Spenser had that high opinion of his own art without which no man can be a true poet. Poetry was with him the great business of his life ; and it has been remarked of him that "he approached the composition of the 'Faery Queen' with a seriousness of resolve not unlike that solemn mood of mind in which Milton has told us that he himself meditated upon the plan of the 'Paradise Lost.'" His works show him to have been a man of great delicacy of organization, with a magnetic sensitiveness to all impressions of beauty, and clearly evince the purity and elevation of his moral nature and the depth and fervor of his religious principles.

The subject which he selected for his great work, though not in accordance with the formal epic model, was peculiarly adapted to the fanciful and romantic character of his mind. Though he borrowed freely from other poets and drew abundantly from the copious stores of both classical and romantic literature, it may still be said of him that he is strictly original and never a servile imitator.

The "Faery Queen" appeared in January, 1589. Its adaptation to the court and times of the Virgin Queen as well as the intrinsic beauty and excellence of the poem, insured it an enthusiastic reception. It was designed by its author

6

to be taken as an allegory or " dark conceit," as he calls it in his letter to Raleigh, explaining the nature and plan of the work. He states his object to be " to fashion a gentleman or noble person in virtuous and gentle discipline," and that he had chosen Prince Arthur for his hero. He conceives that prince to have beheld the Faery Queen in a dream, and to have been so enamoured of the vision that on awakening he resolved to set forth and seek her in Faeryland.

The poet further devises that the Faery Queen keep her annual feast twelve days, twelve separate adventures happening in that time, and each of them being undertaken by a knight.

The adventures were also to express the same number of moral virtues. The Red-cross Knight expresses Holiness; Sir Guyon, Temperance; Britomartis, Chastity. The adventures of the Red-cross Knight shadow forth the history of the Church of England; the distressed knight is Henry IV., and Envy is intended to glance at the unfortunate Mary Queen of Scots. The Queen Gloriana and the Huntress Belphœbe are both symbolical of Queen Elizabeth, whom, as Belphœbe, Spenser thus daintily describes :

> " Her ivorye forehead full of bountie brave,
>   Like a broad table did itself dispred,
>   For love his loftie triumphes to engrave,
>   And write the battailes of his great god head.
>   All good and honour might therein be red ;
>   For there their dwelling was. And when she spake,
>   Sweet wordes, like dropping honey, she did shed,
>   And 'twixt the perles and rubins softly brake
>   A silver sound, that heavenly musicke seemed to make."

In this extract may be seen the dainty luxuriousness of Spenser as a descriptive poet and his richness of fancy and sweetness of conception ; yet with all due deference to the

best of poets, one cannot refrain from contrasting in imagination with this flowery ideal a matter-of-fact picture of
England's maiden royalty. Behold a stately spinster of
fifty-five; her head adorned with reddish hair, a snow-
storm of powder and a pyramid of crowns towering upward from the vasty depths of a huge ruff, like the Sphinx
asserting itself through the encroaching sands of an Egyptian desert; her tall majesty encased in the stubbornest of
hoops, in comparison with which our modern crinoline is
doubtless undulating, and "yclad in her purple gown of cloth
of gold," tricked out in miscellaneous showers of "gold-
en agulets, tortoise-shaped buttons, enamelled oak-leaves
and acorns," "so indifferently stitched on," says the historian, " that her Highness is said always to have returned
minus a portion, whenever she appeared in public," — which
important loss was thus recorded in the court memorandum,
" Lost from her Majesty's back, on the 14th of May, Anno
21, one small acorn and one leaf of gold, at Westminster."
Behold her thus behind a huge fan of red and white feathers,
"having her Majesty's picture within, and on the reverse a
device with a crow over it," and hear on fit occasions, issuing from the sweet lips among the poet's "dropping honey,
'twixt the perles and rubins," a good round oath or two; behold the "ivory forehead, full of bountie brave," distorted
with rage, the " majestie and awful ire," mounting into
uncontrollable fury till this daughter of Henry VIII. falls
down in a fit, from which only vinegar and stimulants, it
is said, could revive her; and looking on this picture and
then on Spenser's rare portrait, we may at least give the
limner credit for " poetic license." We shall, however, be
less inclined to censure him as a sycophant when we remember that many good and wise men were guilty of the same
folly, for flattery was the current coin at the court of Elizabeth. Yet over the faults and follies of this dead queen
let us kindly throw the veil of charity, since underlying

them all were many virtues which have justly endeared
her to the English nation.   Her maternal regard for
her people and wise political discretion cannot be sufficiently extolled, and more than atone for her many defects
of character.   The first three books of the "Faery Queen"
contain a large proportion of the excellence of the work.
Though the latter books have less continuity of splendor,
they all contain innumerable single stanzas and short passages of exquisite beauty, and a few pictures on a more
extended canvas, which are reckoned among the most remarkable of the work, — such as the prophetic satire in anticipation of the Liberty and Equality philosophy, in the
second canto of the fifth book.   The " Shepherd's Calendar " and " Mother Hubbard's Tale " are the most remarkable works of Spenser, written before the " Faery Queen."
The former work is remarkable for the variety of measures
in which it is composed.   A panegyric on Queen Elizabeth
in the fourth eclogue is the most spirited of its lyric passages.
Spenser's " Epithalàmium " on his own marriage with the
Elizabeth whose wooing is related by him in a series of
eighty-eight sonnets is accounted the most splendid spousal
verse in the language.   He concludes it with the true prophecy that it shall stand a perpetual monument of his happiness.   There is nothing in English poetry more beautiful
than the passage in which he describes his youthful bride :

> " Behold, while she before the altar stands,
>   Hearing the holy priest that to her speaks
>   And blesseth her with his two happy hands,
>   How the red roses flush up in her cheeks,
>   And the pure snow with goodly vermeil stain
>   Like crimson dyed in grain ;
>   That even the angels, which continually
>   About the sacred altar do remain,
>   Forget their service and about her fly,
>   Oft peeping in her face, that seems more fair
>   The more they on it stare."

In fancy and invention Spenser is unrivalled. He displays but little comic talent, occasional visionary sublimity, and a pensive tenderness often approaching to the finest pathos. His versification is to the last degree flowing and harmonious. In the stanza which he first made use of, and which is called by his name and recommended by its fulness and richness, its flowing melody, and the stately cadence with which it closes, it has been asserted that " of the many who have been led to follow his example, no one has equalled and few have approached him." Though never intensely impassioned, he completely holds us by his fancy and invention. In the " Faery Queen," though we are wearied by his " dark conceit," and often fain to drop the allegory altogether, our admiration for its pure poesy never flags.

Spenser is the true poet of chivalry and romance ; to read him is like floating in a gorgeous dream through enchanted Venice, in the mellow noon of an Italian night, showered by silvery moonbeams, fanned by airs that have lingered in orange groves, and serened by rhythmical cadence of rippling oar, and song of gondolier. In youth and in riper years we turn to the " Faery Queen " with ever-new delight, as to an April bank thick-dotted with violets, or a sunny woodland slope redolent of rose-tinged arbutus.

Spenser's faults are truly said to have arisen out of the fulness of his riches. His power of circumstantial description betrayed him into an elaboration which often becomes merely tedious minuteness ; while his wonderful command of musical language led him often to protract his narrative till the attention becomes exhausted. Diffuseness of style was a fault common to the age in which he wrote ; and indeed we find it in all poetical composition antecedent to Shakespeare — who foreran his age — while

Spenser, as has been observed, " leaned towards the olden time," and was censured by his cotemporaries and their successors for introducing " new graftes of old and withered words." Conciseness of style, one of the prime excellencies of poetical composition, we may not look for in the infancy of the art, or even in its lusty youth; it is alone the product of its ripe and rounded maturity. Macaulay, indeed, asserts that " the great works of imagination which have appeared in the Dark Ages most command our admiration;" but let us not admit with him that " as civilization advances, poetry almost necessarily declines." The " poetical *temperament* may indeed decline with civilization;" but the poet, we trust, is the indigenous and unfailing product of all time.

It must be remembered that in Spenser's day life rumbled leisurely along in slow-coaches. The man who could afford to execute eighty-eight elaborate sonnets for the wooing of but one fair lady, had surely not attained to our modern facility in " popping the question;" and we may at least believe him to have had more leisure for both wooing and rhyming than is allotted to a busy poet in this hurried nineteenth century. If he could but have superadded to his marvellous fancy and invention, his flowing harmony, and exquisite sense of beauty, the concise elegance which so captivates us in the verse of Longfellow and of Holmes, the " Faery Queen," certainly not in six books, possibly in *one*, would have been entitled to stand in proud pre-eminence, the eternal master-piece of the art!

Though Spenser presents to us a few pictures over which modern decorum would draw a veil, he offends merely against good taste, never against good morals. And it has been justly and beautifully observed that " such passages in Spenser differ from the covert form in which licentiousness is insinuated in many modern poems, as the naked majesty of Diana differs from the voluptuous undress of Aspasia." The absence of an interesting story, the want of human character and passion in the passages that carry on the story, such as it is, have been pronounced no defects in the " Faery Queen," since the poetry is only left thereby so much the purer. " If Spenser was not the greatest of poets," observes Craik, " we may truly say his poetry is the most poetical of all poetry." Here is a picture from Spenser's allegory, — a masker from the pageant raised by the enchanter, to beguile the sad heart of Amoret : —

> " The first was Fancy, like a lovely boy
> Of rare aspect, and beauty without peer,
> Matchable either to that imp of Troy
> Whom Jove did love, and choose his cup to bear ;
> Or that same dainty lad which was so dear
> To great Alcides that whenas he died,
> He wailed woman-like with many a tear,
> And every wood, and every valley wide,
> He filled with Hylas' name ; the nymphs eke Hylas cried.

> " His garment neither was of silk nor say,
> But painted plumes in goodly order dight,
> Like as the sunburnt Indians do array
> Their tawny bodies in the proudest plight.
> As these same plumes, so seemed he vain and light,
> That by his gait might easily appear ;
> For still he fared as dancing in delight,
> And in his hand a windy fan did bear,
> That in the idle air he moved still here and there."

But half of Spenser's original design of the " Faery Queen" was finished. Six of the twelve adventures and moral virtues were produced ; but length of days was not granted the poet to complete on earth his moral and poetical gallery. It has been conjectured that the remain-

ing half was lost, but this supposition is almost ground-
less. Unfortunately the world saw only some fragments
more of the work. The last touching and prophetic notes
of this sweet singer may be found in the eighth imperfect
canto, broken off abruptly, as if the poet had sung no
further, but gone up to eternal harmonies with these last
words upon his lips : —

> " Then gin I think on that which Nature sayd,
>   Of that same time when no more change shall be,
>   But stedfast rest of all things firmly stayed
>   Upon the pillours of Eternity
>   That is contrayre to mutability ;
>   For all that moveth doth in change delight ;
>   But thenceforth all shall rest eternally
>   With him that is the God of Sabaoth hight.
>   O that great Sabaoth God, grant me that Sabbath's sight ! "

CHAPTER VI.

MINOR ELIZABETHAN POETRY.

BEFORE the close of the sixteenth century the wisest and most productive age of our poetical literature had fairly commenced. Spenser alone had added to the language a world of wealth, — a golden inheritance for all posterity. Of the minor poets of the Elizabethan age, who succeeded him by hundreds, few are altogether without merit; "all have caught some echoes of the spirit of music that then filled the universal air."

The minor Elizabethan poetry is for the most part remarkable for ingenuity and elaboration, and for quaintness of thought and expression. It has been observed that "there is often more art in it than nature, yet if it is sometimes unnatural, it is very seldom simply insipid, like much of the well-sounding verse of more recent eras."

Cotemporary with Spenser is Sir Philip Sidney, who in 1554–86 takes his rank in English literary history both as a poet and a prose-writer. What Surrey was in the court of Henry VIII., Sidney was in the court of Elizabeth, who counted him "the jewel of her times." Generous, gallant, and accomplished, we associate him with all the fascinations of chivalry and romance. The brightest ornament of his age, he is still handed down to us as a model of knighthood and manhood. His bravery and chivalrous magnanimity, his grace and polish of manner, the purity of his morals, his learning and refinement,

won for him universal love and esteem ; and it is even
said that in 1585 he was named one of the candidates for
the crown of Poland, at that time vacant, when Elizabeth,
being unwilling to lose him, " threw obstacles in the way
of his election." His military exploits were highly honorable. He died of a wound received at Zutphen in October,
1586, at the early age of thirty-two. Every school-boy
is familiar with the beautiful story of his abnegation in
favor of the dying soldier, — the brightest and greenest
leaf in the immortal bays that encircle the memory of
this darling of fame, of whom it has been said, " he trod
from his cradle to his grave amid incense and flowers,
and died in a dream of glory ! "

The poetry of Sidney, though it is now comparatively
but little read, was extravagantly admired in his own
time. His graces are rather those of artful elaboration
than of vivid natural expression. His style, according
to the fashion of the day, runs into conceits, and has
also some want of animation ; yet it is always harmonious,
and rises often into great stateliness and splendor. As is
the man, so is the poet; and it has been happily observed
that " a breath of beauty and noble feeling exhales from
his productions like the fragrance from a garden of flowers." Sidney's sonnets to Stella — the Philoclea of his
" Arcadia " — have been much admired. His writings are
now less read than they deserve, and undoubtedly for the
same reason that the poetry of Shelley (who, lineally descended from the same noble house, was in many respects
the counterpart of Sidney) is not widely appreciated ; they
" lack" — as Willis expresses it — " flesh and blood ; "
they are too refined and impalpable for human nature's
daily food.

Cooper has called Sidney " a warbler of poetic prose ;"
his " Arcadia " may indeed be styled a prose poem. Modern

critics disagree as to its merits. The personal fame of its author, and the scarcity of works of fiction in the reign of Elizabeth, are supposed in some degree to have contributed to the admiration it excited in his own time. A modern critic has observed that " a work so extensively perused, must have contributed not a little to fix the English tongue, and to form that vigorous and imaginative style which characterizes the literature of the beginning and middle of the seventeenth century." The work was not intended for the press, but was written chiefly for the amusement of his sister; and he gave it the title of "The Countess of Pembroke's Arcadia." The "Arcadia" is an uncompleted work, and appeared only after its author's death. The Puritans of Sidney's age, in their mistaken crusade against poetry and art, had contemptuously denominated poets " Caterpillars of the Commonwealth; " to repel their objections to the poetic art he wrote his tract entitled "The Defence of Poesy." It has been justly admired for the beauty of its style; and though written with the partiality of a poet, it has been commended for the general soundness of its reasoning.

The Stella whom Sidney addresses was the eldest sister of the favorite Essex, and intended from her childhood for his bride. For reasons which do not appear, the projected marriage was broken off by their families, and the lady was married by her guardian to Lord Rich, her declared aversion. She is described as a woman of exquisite beauty, on a grand and splendid scale. Passionately beloved to the last by Sidney, whose love should have " set her high in heaven as any star," one can hardly believe that this woman's after-life was not above reproach. This sonnet, addressed to one who has lately left the presence of Stella, and of whom he inquires of her welfare, " will," says Mrs. Jameson, " commend itself for truth and beauty to all who have known the agony of separation from one beloved."

> " Be your words, good Sir, of Indian ware,
>   That you allow them at so small a rate ?
> When I demand of Phenix Stella's state,
> You say, forsooth, you left her well of late.
> O God ! think you that satisfies my care ?
> I would know whether she doth sit or walk, —
> How clothed, how waited on ? Sighed she, or smiled ?
> With what pastime Time's journey she beguiled ?
> If her lips deigned to sweeten my poor name ?
> Say all, and all well said, still say the same ! "

This sonnet to " Sleep " is one of Sidney's best, and may be regarded as a fairer specimen of his style.

> " Come, Sleep, O Sleep, — the certain knot of peace,
> The baiting place of wit, the balm of woe,
> The poor man's wealth, the prisoner's release,
> The indifferent judge between high and low.
> With shield of proof, shield me from out the press
> Of those fierce darts Despair at me doth throw ;
> O make me in those civil wars to cease.
> I will good tribute pay, if thou do so.
> Take thou of me smooth pillows, sweetest bed ;
> A chamber deaf to noise, and blind to light ;
> A rosy garland, and a weary head.
> And if these things, as being thine by right,
> Move not thy heavy grace, thou shalt in me
> Livelier than elsewhere Stella's image see."

Sir Walter Raleigh, born in 1552, though he has left us much more prose than verse, deserves for the excellence of his few short poems a place among the poets of Elizabeth's reign. In the character of this noble knight we have the brave and chivalrous soldier, the elegant scholar, the man of practical energy, and the sage philosopher singularly united. " Being educated," observes Hume, " amidst naval and military enterprises, he surpassed in the pursuits of literature even those of the most recluse and sedentary lives." Of an ancient family in Devonshire, Raleigh became a soldier at seventeen ; at twenty-eight we find him in London. The loyal surrender of his gay plush mantle for the protection of Elizabeth's immaculate shoes from the soiling mud in her pathway, is a well-known incident. This ready gallantry, by which the young soldier won the favor of his queen, forcibly illustrates his chivalry and tact. It has been aptly said that "this cloak was the means of procuring him many a good suit."

Of an adventurous and restless disposition, Raleigh became, in 1585, a principal abettor of the unsuccessful attempt to colonize Virginia. This expedition was the means of introducing into England that disreputable plant, tobacco. Elizabeth knighted him, and granted him many solid marks of her favor, in return for which he engaged zealously in her service. On the accession of James, Raleigh's prosperity came to an end. Through the malignant scheming of his political enemies, he was accused of conspiring to dethrone the king and place the crown on the head of Arabella Stuart, of attempting to excite sedition, and to establish popery by the aid of foreign powers. A trial for high treason ensued ; "and though he defended himself," says his historian, "with such temper, eloquence, and strength of reasoning that some even of his enemies were convinced of his innocence, and all parties were ashamed of the judgment pronounced," Raleigh was, upon the paltriest evidence, condemned by a servile jury to death. He was, however, reprieved, and committed to the Tower. During the twelve years of his imprisonment — in which his wife was permitted to bear him company — Raleigh wrote most of his works, of which his "History of the World" is the most considerable. This work was considered, both in style and matter, superior to all previous English historical productions. In 1615 — for the furtherance of some sordid scheme of James — Raleigh was set at liberty. In 1618 he was again arrested, and fell a sacrifice to the selfish policy of his king. He was, upon the old sentence, beheaded in the Tower, October 29.

On the scaffold, Raleigh justified his character and conduct to the people, and was brave and firm to the last. Taking up the axe, he said to the sheriff, " This is a sharp medicine, but a sound cure for all diseases," and bade the executioner " fear not, but strike home! " In one of Raleigh's poems occurs this striking couplet: —

> " Passions are likened best to floods and streams ;
> The shallow murmur, but the deep are dumb."

This sonnet of Raleigh's, prefixed to the "Faery Queen," 1590, is a specimen of his art, and illustrates his high estimation of the work: —

> " Methought I saw the grave where Laura lay,
> Within that temple where the vestal flame
> Was wont to burn ; and passing by that way,
> To see that buried dust of living fame
> Whose tomb fair Love and fairer Virtue kept,
> All suddenly I saw the Faery Queen,
> At whose approach the soul of Petrarch wept.
> And from thenceforth those Graces were not seen,
> For they this Queen attended ; in whose stead
> Oblivion laid him down on Laura's hearse.
> Hereat the hardest stones were seen to bleed,
> And groans of buried ghosts the heavens did pierce,
> Where Homer's sprite did tremble all for grief,
> And cursed th' access of that celestial thief."

A whole sermon on the vanity of human ambition is condensed into these six lines composed by Raleigh just before his execution : —

" Even such is Time, that takes on trust
   Our youth, our joys, our all we have,
   And pays us but with age and dust;
   Who in the dark and silent grave,
   When we have wandered all our ways,
   Shuts up the story of our days."

Raleigh introduced Spenser to Queen Elizabeth, and otherwise benefited him by his patronage and encouragement. Spenser became his friend and confidant, and to him the poet explained the " dark conceit " of his " Faery Queen."

It has been affirmed of Raleigh that " had he made poetry a serious pursuit he would have excelled in that, as he has in other departments of learning."

Daniel, born in 1562, — after the death of Spenser, — was in the reign of James, 1603, appointed Master of the Revels, and afterward preferred to be a groom of the chamber to Queen Anne.

Toward the close of his life Daniel retired from court, and died in October, 1619.

His extremely dull works fill two considerable volumes ; yet it is only by virtue of some of his minor pieces and sonnets that he retains his place among the English poets.

One of the most voluminous poets of the time is Michael Drayton, supposed to have been born in 1563, and dying in 1631. Drayton has the fancy and feeling of the true poet. He is the author of many minor compositions, and of three works of great length. His "Barons' Wars " was published in 1596, his " England's Heroical Epistles " in 1598. His " Polyolbion " — a poetical description of England, the work on which his fame principally rests, — contains thirty books. Its publication was completed in 1622.

It has some poetic merit, but is thought to be most remarkable for the learning it displays. The information contained in this work is in general so accurate that it is quoted as an authority. Drayton's most graceful poetry may be found in some of his shorter pieces. His account of the equipage of the Queen of the Fairies, when she set out to visit her lover, Pigwiggen, is a specimen of his lighter style, and " may," observes Craik, " compare with Shakespeare's description of Queen Mab, in ' Romeo and Juliet.' "

" Her chariot straight is ready made,
   Each thing therein is fitting laid,
   That she by nothing might be stay'd,
      For nought must be her letting.
   Four nimble gnats the horses were,
   Their harnesses of gossamere,
   Fly Cranium, her charioteer,
      Upon the coach-box getting.

" Her chariot of a snail's fine shell,
   Which for the colours did excel.
   The fair Queen Mab becoming well,
      So lively was the limning.
   The seat the soft wool of the bee,
   The cover (gallantly to see)
   The wing of a py'd butterflee,
      I trow, 't was simple trimming.

" The wheels composed of cricket's bones,
   And daintily made for the nonce :
   For fear of rattling on the stones,
      With thistle-down they shod it.
   For all her maidens much did fear,
   If Oberon had chanced to hear
   That Mab his queen should have been there,
      He would not have abode it.

" She mounts her chariot in a trice,
 Nor would she stay for no advice,
 Until her maids, that were so nice,
  To wait on her were fitted,
 But ran herself away alone ;
 Which when they heard, there was not one
 But hasted after to be gone,
  As she had been diswitted.

" Hop and Mop and Drab, so clear,
 Pip and Trip and Skip, that were
 To Mab their sovereign dear,
  Her special maids of honour ;
 Fib and Tib and Pink and Pin,
 Tick and Quick and Jill and Fin,
 Tit and Nit and Wap and Win,
  The train that wait upon her.

" Upon a grasshopper they got,
 And what with amble and with trot,
 For hedge or ditch they spared not,
  But after her they hie them.
 A cobweb over them they throw,
 To shield the wind, if it should blow,
 Themselves they wisely could bestow
  Lest any should espy them."

The most eminent translators of foreign poetry belonging to this period are Harrington and Fairfax.

Sir John Harrington, the first translator of Ariosto into English, was a courtier and godson to Queen Elizabeth. His father, Sir John Harrington the elder, was imprisoned in the Tower with Elizabeth in the reign of Mary, from whence he addressed a satirical sonnet to Gardiner, which it is said so won his admiration as to move him to the release of his prisoner. In sending the order for Harrington's enlargement, he grimly observed that " but for his saucy sonnet, he was worthy to have lain a year longer in the Tower." Harrington's translation from Ariosto is thought to have but little merit. His epigrams are his most successful efforts at composition. They are said to have lashed the leading men of Elizabeth's court so severely that her Highness "signified in outward manner her displeasure with her witty godson, though she did like the marrow of the book." In one of his gossiping letters Harrington pleasantly relates this characteristic anecdote of his whimsical godmother. "On Sunday," he says, "April last, my Lord of London preached to the Queen's Majesty, and seemed to touch on the vanity of decking the body too finely. Her Majesty told the ladies that if the bishop held more discourse on such matters she would fit him for heaven, but he should walk thither without a staff and leave his mantle behind him. . . . Perchance," he shrewdly adds, "the bishop hath not seen her Highness's wardrobe."

Well might his reverend Lordship have shaken in his shoes if after that unlucky sermon a panorama of Elizabeth's "three thousand gowns, and eighty wigs of divers colors" had passed in array before him.

Harrington's talent for epigram may be seen in this, of a precise tailor, —

> "A tailor, thought a man of upright dealing, —
> True, but for lying; honest, but for stealing, —
> Did fall one day extremely sick by chance,
> And on the sudden was in wondrous trance.
> The fiends of hell, mustering in fearful manner,
> Of sundry colored silks displayed a banner
> Which he had stolen, and wished, as they did tell,
> That he might find it all one day in hell.
> The man, affrighted with this apparition,
> Upon recovery grew a great precisian.
> He bought a Bible of the best translation,
> And in his life he showed great reformation.

He walked mannerly; he talked meekly;
He heard three lectures and two sermons weekly;
He vowed to shun all company unruly,
And in his speech he used no oath but truly;
And zealously to keep the Sabbath's rest,
His meat for that day on the eve was drest;
And lest the custom which he had to steal
Might cause him sometimes to forget his zeal,
He gives his journeyman a special charge
That if the stuff, allowance being large,
He found his fingers were to filch inclined,
Bid him to have the banner in his mind.
This done (I scant can tell the rest for laughter),
A captain of a ship came three days after,
And bought three yards of velvet and three quarters,
To make Venitians down below the garters.
He that precisely knew what was enough
Soon slipt aside three quarters of the stuff;
His man, espying it, said in derision,
' Master, remember how you saw the vision!'
'Peace, knave!' quoth he, 'I did not see a rag
Of such a colored silk in all the flag.' "

To this period belongs Fairfax, translator of Tasso's " Jerusalem Delivered." Dryden ranked this writer with Spenser as a master of our language, and Waller allowed that he derived from Fairfax the harmony of his numbers. The date of his birth is unknown. It is on record that he was living in 1639.

Dr. John Donne, the famous dean of St. Paul's, wrote most of his poetry before the end of the sixteenth century, though none of it was published till late in the reign of James. Donne may safely be classed with Wilson's " mystical wisemen and poetical clerkes, delighting much in their own darkness, especially when none can tell what they do say." Of this metaphysical poet an able critic observes: "He has used all the resources of the language, not to express thought, but to conceal it; but running through all this bewilderment, a deeper insight detects not only a vein of the most exuberant wit, but often the sunniest and most delicate fancy and the truest tenderness and depth of feeling. Nor can it be questioned that the peculiar construction of Donne's verses was conceived as adapted by choice and system; their harshness was a part of their relish."

Donne was distinguished for his great abilities and the amiability of his character. By a secret marriage with the daughter of Sir George Moore, Lord Lieutenant of the Tower, he fell into trouble and poverty. His domestic trials are said to have comprised every variety of wretchedness except that of separation from his wife, for whom his tenderness was unbounded, and for whose loss his grief is said to have been so overwhelming as to endanger his reason.

Craik observes that " in endeavoring to give expression to his inexpressible passion for her, he has exhausted all the eccentricities of language."

These stanzas from one of his parting songs, though in his own riddling style, are in sentiment exquisitely beautiful.

> " As virtuous men pass mildly away,
>   And whisper to their souls to go,
> ' Whilst some of their sad friends do say,
>   The breath goes now, and some say, no;
>
> " So let us melt, and make no noise,
>   No tear-floods, no sigh-tempests move;
> ' T were profanation of our joys
>   To tell the laity our love.
>
> " Dull sublunary lover's love
>   (Whose soul is sense) cannot admit
> Absence, because it doth remove
>   Those things which alimented it.

" But we 're by love so much refined
    That ourselves know what it is;
Inter-assured of the mind,
    Careless eyes, lips, and hands to miss.

" Our two souls, therefore (which are one),
    Though I must go, endure not yet
A breach, but an expansion,
    Like gold to airy thinness beat.

" If they be two, they are two so
    As stiff twin compasses are two;
Thy soul, the fix'd foot, makes no show
    To move, but doth if th' other do.

"And though it in the centre sit,
    Yet when the other far doth roam,
It leans and hearkens after it,
    And grows erect as that comes home.

" Such wilt thou be to me, who must,
    Like th' other foot, obliquely run;
Thy firmness makes my circles just,
    And makes me end where I begun."

The beautiful little song of Donne's, beginning " Send home my long-strayed eyes to me," has far more harmony and elegance than his other pieces, and has been set to music. These four lines are from one of his most elaborate elegies : —

" Angels did hand her up, who next God dwell,
For she was of that order whence most fell.
Her body 's left with us, lest some had said
She could not die, except they saw her dead."

Donne is also the author of these beautiful and often quoted lines : —

" The pure and eloquent blood
Spoke in her cheeks, and so distinctly wrought,
You might have almost said her body thought."

Donne died at the age of fifty-eight, in 1631.

The intimate friend of Dr. Donne was "Holy George Herbert." Herbert was of noble birth, descended from the earls of Pembroke, and born in Montgomery Castle, Wales, though he is best known as a pious country clergyman. He was educated at Cambridge, and in the year 1619 was chosen orator for the University. Lord Bacon entertained such a high regard for his learning and judgment that he is said to have submitted to him his works before publication. The death of King James deprived him of a lucrative court office, which had formerly been given by Elizabeth to Sir Philip Sidney. He entered into sacred orders, and was made rector of Bemerton in Wiltshire, where he passed the remainder of his life. Herbert's strength was unequal to the self-imposed tasks of his profession. With saint-like zeal and purity he discharged his clerical duties, but died at the early age of thirty-nine. His principal production is entitled "The Temple, or, Sacred Poems and Private Ejaculations." It was not printed till a few years after his death, and was so well received that two thousand copies are said to have been sold in a few years after the first impression. Herbert was a musician, and sang to the lute or viol his own flowing and musical hymns. Many of them are in sentiment exquisitely beautiful, though marred by the absurd conceits and unpoetical similes, which, however intolerable to us, were the fashion of the age. A preacher, cotemporary with Herbert, harangued the University of Oxford, and was, it is said, highly applauded by that learned body for his eloquence, in this style: "Arriving," said he, "at the mount of St. Mary's, in the stony stage where I now stand, I have brought you some fine biscuits, baked in the oven of charity, carefully conserved for the chickens of the Church, the sparrows of the spirit, and the sweet swallows of salvation, — which way of preaching," says the reporter of this homily, "was then commended by the generality of scholars." It is to be inferred that the chickens of the Church throve mightily under this culinary shepherd of souls. In Herbert's well-known lines to Virtue, considered the best in his collection, "the rose is angry and brave, and bids the rash beholder wipe his eye." The spring is compared to a box, and the soul to seasoned timber. The lyric genius of the poet still charms us, in spite of these tasteless conceits ; and the warm and sincere piety which breathes through all his writings gives to them an enduring charm. These stanzas are finely conceived, and are among Herbert's best. The piece is somewhat absurdly called by its author —

THE PULLEY.

WHEN God at first made man,
　　Having a glass of blessings standing by,
" Let us," said he, " pour on him all we can;
　　Let the world's riches which dispersed lie
　　　　Contract into a span."

So strength first made away;
　　Then beauty flowed, then wisdom, honor, pleasure.
When almost all the rest was out, God made a stay,
　　Perceiving that alone of all his treasure
　　　　Rest in the bottom lay.

" For if I should," said he,
　　" Bestow this jewel also on my creature,
He would adore my gifts instead of me,
　　And rest in Nature, not the God of Nature,
　　　　So both should losers be.

> " Yet let him keep the rest,
> But keep them with repining restlessness.
> Let him be rich and weary; that, at least,
> If goodness lead him not, yet weariness
> May toss him to my breast."

George Wither, a cotemporary poet of little power, has some true poetical feeling and expression. He was born in 1588, and died 1667. His fame as a poet is derived chiefly from his early productions, written before he had become a Puritan. During the struggles of that period he was made prisoner by the Royalists, and his life was, it is said, only saved by a joke of his brother bard, Denham, who interfered in his behalf, alleging that as long as Wither lived he (Denham) would not be considered the worst poet in England. Wither is sometimes harsh and obscure, and often affected. It must have been before he imbibed the sectarian gloom of the Puritans that he wrote, —

> "Hang sorrow! Care will kill a cat,
> And therefore let's be merry."

Francis Quarles is a religious poet of this time. He was born in 1592, and died 1644. His " Divine Emblems " were published in 1645, and may still be seen in the cottages of the English peasantry, among whom they were exceedingly popular. He was in his day for this reason called " the darling of our plebeian judgments." Quarles is an ascetic poet, and some of his homilies in verse, on the " Shortness of Life," and the " Vanity of the World," etc., suggest dyspepsia. His style is marred by the most absurd conceits, but he has some true wit and poetic conception. This little poem, on the " Decay of Life," is a specimen of his style, and is one of his best.

"The day grows old, the low-pitched lamp hath made
No less than treble shade;
And the descending damp doth now prepare
To uncurl bright Titan's hair,
Whose western wardrobe now begins to unfold
Her purples, fringed with gold,
To clothe his evening glory, when the alarms
Of rest shall call to rest in restless Thetis' arms.

"Nature now calls to supper, to refresh
The spirits of all flesh.
The toiling ploughman drives his thirsty teams
To taste the slippery streams:
The droiling swineherd knocks away, and feasts
His hungry whining guests:
The box-bill ousel and the dappled thrush
Like hungry rivals meet at their beloved bush."

William Habington, born in 1605, of an ancient Roman Catholic family in Worcester, is one of the most graceful of the minor poets of the time. His poems consist of " The Mistress," " The Wife," and " The Holy Man." These titles each include several copies of verses. Habington's poetry is studded with the conceits of the metaphysical school of his day, and is deficient in power and pathos, yet these faults are redeemed by a delicacy of expression uncommon at that time. He is said to have been entirely untainted by the prevailing licentiousness, and his sentiments on love are pure and noble. Habington claims for himself the honor of being the first conjugal poet in the language. He married Lucy Powis, a grand-daughter of the Duke of Northumberland, whom he celebrates as " Mistress " and " Wife," under the name of Castara. Habington gives us this sweet picture of his Lucy; —

"Such her beauty as no arts
Have enriched with borrowed grace;

Her high birth no pride imparts
For she blushes in her place.
Folly boasts a glorious blood ;
She is noblest being good !

" She her throne makes reason climb,
While wild passions captive lie .
And each article of time
Her pure thoughts to heaven fly .
All her vows religious be,
And her love she vows to me."

His poem entitled " To Roses, in the bosom of Castara,"
is in the graceful style of Waller, but pure and natural
in sentiment. He died in 1654, — the first year of the
Protectorate.

Robert Herrick is one of the most gifted of our early
lyrical poets, born in 1591. His " Hesperides, or, Works
both Human and Divine of Robert Herrick," was published in 1648. Herrick was " one of the jovial spirits
who quaffed the mighty bowl with rare Ben Jonson," and
though a Devonshire vicar for twenty years, many of his
rhymes confer but little credit on the sacred profession.
Gayety was the natural element of Herrick. His philosophy seems to have been epicurean. He bids us
" gather the rosebuds ; to-morrow we die." His poems
abound in lively conceits, playful fancy, natural feeling,
and the sweetest pathos, that wins its way to the heart.
His language is chastely beautiful and picturesque, and
it has been observed of his versification that it is harmony itself.

Herrick's shorter lyrics, some of which have been set
to music, are sung, quoted, and admired by all lovers of
song. The most exquisite are those entitled " To Blossoms," " To Daffodils," " To Primroses," and " Gather the
Rosebuds while ye may.". Among Herrick's lyrics this

latter is not only sweet with the rare grace of the poet,
but highly characteristic of the man.

> " Gather the rosebuds while ye may,
>   Old time is still a-flying ;
> And this same flower that smiles to-day,
>   To-morrow will be dying.

> " The glorious lamp of heaven, the sun,
>   The higher he 's a-getting,
> The sooner will his race be run,
>   And nearer he 's to setting.

> " That age is best which is the first,
>   When youth and blood are warmer ;
> But being spent, the worse and worst
>   Time shall succeed the former.

> " Then be not coy, but use your time,
>   And while ye may, go marry ;
> For having lost but once your prime,
>   You may forever tarry."

This to " Primroses filled with Morning Dew," is in
Herrick's happiest vein, and exhibits the dainty beauty
of his style, and his tender pathos, that is sometimes
like a sob or a quick gush of tears.

> " Why do ye weep, sweet babes ?   Can tears
>   Speak grief in you
>   Who were but born
>   Just as the modest morn
>   Teemed her refreshing dew?
> Alas ! you have not known that shower
>   That mars a flower,
>   Nor felt the unkind
>   Breath of a blasting wind ;
> Nor are ye worn with years,
>   Or warped as we,
>   Who think it strange to see
> Such pretty flowers like to orphans young,
> Speaking by tears before ye have a tongue.

> " Speak, whimp'ring younglings, and make known
>   The reason why
>   Ye droop and weep ;
>   Is it for want of sleep,
>   Or childish lullaby?
> Or that ye have not seen as yet
>   The violet ?
>   Or brought a kiss
>   From that sweetheart to this ?
>   No, no ; this sorrow shown
>   By your tears shed,
>   Would have this lecture read :
> That things of greatest, so of meanest worth,
> Conceived with grief are, and with tears brought forth."

Unfortunately Herrick has bequeathed us verses far less
circumspect than these, for which reckless productions he
penitently craves divine forgiveness ; and when we remember that Falstaff's bane, — canary-sack, — rather than de-
liberate coarseness, was the cause of these unhappy lapses
from propriety, we must charitably accord him our own.
Thus he repents him of his errors : —

> " For these my unbaptized rhymes,
>   Writ in my wild unhallowed times,
>   For every sentence, clause, and word,
>   That 's not inlaid with thee, O Lord !
>   Forgive me, God, and blot each line
>   Out of my book that is not thine !
>   But if, 'mongst all, thou findest one
>   Worthy thy benediction,
>   That one of all the rest shall be
>   The glory of my work and me."

Belonging to this period is Richard Crashaw, a religious
poet of high genius.   The date of his birth is not known.
He died about the year 1650.   Crashaw was an accomplished scholar ; and his translations from the Latin
and Italian have been much praised for freedom, force,

and beauty. He became a proselyte to the Roman Catholic faith, and subsequently a canon of the Church of Loretto.

Crashaw is mystical in style and thought. His verse abounds in metaphor and conceit; yet he is seldom dull, and his versification is often highly musical. He has genuine poetic genius, and after Donne, may be considered the greatest religious poet of the age. In one of his poems occurs the well-known conceit relative to the miracle of water being turned to wine : —

> "The conscious water saw its God, and blushed."

These fine lines are also his : —

> "A happy soul, that all the way
> To heaven hath a summer day."

This extract is from Crashaw's " Temperance, or, The Cheap Physician : " —

> "Age? Wouldst see December smile?
> Wouldst see nests of new roses grow
> In a bed of reverend snow;
> Warm thoughts, free spirits flattering
> Winter's self into a Spring?
> In sum, wouldst see a man that can
> Live to be old, and still a man?
> Whose latest and most leaden hours
> Fall with soft wings, stuck with soft flowers;
> And when life's sweet fable ends,
> Soul and body part like friends, —
> No quarrels, murmurs, no delay;
> A kiss, a sigh, and so away.
> This rare one, reader, wouldst thou see?
> Hark, hither! and thyself be he."

Among the miscellaneous poets of this period we have Sylvester and Barnwell and Marlowe the dramatist. Marlowe's " Passionate Shepherd " is a poem of great beauty. Sylvester claims notice as the now generally received author of the " Soul's Errand," an impressive poem long accredited to Raleigh.

Warner, Daniel, and Drayton, are the three poets most conspicuous in the period immediately succeeding Spenser. The two latter have been already noticed, but Warner's " Albion's England " must be noted as a lively and amusing poem, — in form a history of Southern Britain, from the Deluge to the reign of James I. It embraces every striking event or legend which the old chronicles afford. It has force, vivacity, and graphic description, but little of high imaginative art, and is held now to have been especially suitable for a more barbarous age.

Warner was an attorney by profession ; and his style, curt, direct and clear, was in his day much admired. This fable is one of its neatest specimens : —

" An ass, an old man, and a boy did through the city pass;
  And whiles the wanton boy did ride, the old man led the ass.
  ' See yonder doting fool,' said folks, ' that scarce can crawl for age,
  Doth set the boy upon his ass, and makes himself his page.'
  Anon, the blamed boy alights, and lets the old man ride,
  And as the old man did before, the boy the ass did guide.
  But passing so, the people then did much the old man blame,
  And told him, ' Churl, thy limbs be tough ; let ride the boy, for
      shame ! '
  The fault thus found, both man and boy did back the ass and ride ;
  Then that the ass was overcharged each man that met them cried.
  Now both alight, and go on foot, and lead the empty beast ;
  But then the people laugh, and say that one might ride at least.
  The old man, seeing that he could no ways the people please,
  Not blameless then, did drive the ass, and drown him in the seas."

CHAPTER VII.

OLD ENGLISH DRAMA.

IT is not in general versification alone that the poetical strength of the Elizabethan age is chiefly manifested; toward the latter part of Elizabeth's reign arose the dramatic form of composition and representation, and attracted nearly all the poetical genius of England.

" At the dawn of modern civilization," says our historian, " most countries of modern Europe possessed a rude kind of theatrical entertainment, consisting not in those exhibitions of natural character and incident which constituted the plays of ancient Greece and Rome, but in representations of the principal supernatural events in the Old and New Testaments, and of the history of the saints, whence they were denominated ' Miracle plays.' Considered favorable to the diffusion of religious feeling, they were under the immediate management of the clergy, by whom they appear also to have been acted."

The Miracle play of Saint Katharine, to which allusion has already been made, was acted at Dunstable in 1119, and was the first theatrical representation in England of which we have any account; though how long such entertainments may have existed there, is not known.

The most sacred persons, not excluding the Deity himself, were introduced into these plays; yet judged by the traces of them which remain, they appear to have been profane and indecorous in the highest degree.   " In the

reign of Henry Sixth," says the same writer, " persons
representing sentiments and abstract ideas, being introduced into the Miracle plays, gave birth to a new and
improved form of dramatic compositions, entirely or
chiefly composed of such characters, and called ' Moral
plays.' "

As it required some poetical and dramatic ingenuity to
image forth the characters and assign appropriate speeches
to each, the " Moral plays " may be considered as a great
advance upon the " Miracles." The only scriptural character retained in them was the Devil. As this distinguished personage was painted as black as he should be,
amply furnished with the popular hoof and horns, and
supplied with a tail of becoming length, and was also
perpetually beaten about the stage by an attendant character called the " Vice," it is to be inferred that he not
only served to enliven these sober entertainments, but
conveyed the sound moral lesson which was intended.
However this may have been, the Devil was then the
darling of the multitude.

" My husband, Timothy Tattle," says the good gossip
in Ben Jonson's play, " was wont to say that there was
no play without a fool and a devil in it. He was for the
Devil still, God bless him ! The Devil for *his* money, he
would say ; I would fain see the Devil."

Moral plays appear to have been at the height of popularity in the reign of Henry VIII., in whose reign acting
first became a distinct profession, both Miracle and Moral
plays having previously been represented by clergymen
and school-boys, and only brought forth occasionally as
a part of some public or private festivity.

" It was soon found," continues our informant, " that
a real human being, with a real name, was better calculated to move the audience, to hold their attention, and

to impress them with moral truths than a being who only represented a notion of the mind ; and in the early part of the sixteenth century the substitution of these for the symbolical characters gradually took place ; and thus, with some aid from the Greek dramatic literature which now began to be studied, and from the improved theatres of Italy and Spain, the genuine English drama took its rise.

"The regular drama was from its commencement divided into Comedy and Tragedy, the elements of both being found quite distinct in the rude entertainments we have described."

The Interlude — so called from its being acted in the intervals of a banquet — preceded the modern comedy, and generally represented some familiar incident in the style of the broadest, coarsest farce.

John Heywood, supported as a wit, musician, and writer of plays in the court of Henry VIII., was a distinguished writer of interludes, and is considered the inventor of this species of writing.

The earliest specimen of comedy that can now be found, was the production of Nicolas Udall, master of the Westminster School. It bears the uncouth title of "Ralph Royster Doyster," and is supposed to have been written not later than 1551. The scene is in London, and the characters exhibit the manners of the middle class of that day. It is divided into five acts, and the plot is amusing and well constructed.

The next is "Gammer Gurton's Needle," supposed to have been written about 1565, or still earlier. Tragedy, of later origin than comedy, came directly from the more elevated portions of the Moral plays, and from the pure models of Greece and Rome. The earliest known specimen of this kind of composition is the tragedy of "Ferrex

8

and Porrex," composed by Thomas Sackville—afterward Earl of Dorset—and Thomas Norton, and played before Queen Elizabeth at Whitehall, by the members of the Inner Temple, in January, 1561.

It is founded on a fabulous incident in early British history, and is full of slaughter and civil broils. It is, however, written in regular blank verse, consists of five acts, and bears resemblance to the classic drama of antiquity in the introduction of a chorus; that is, a group of persons whose sole business it is to intersperse the play with moral observations and inferences expressed in lyrical stanzas.

Not long after the appearance of this tragedy, "Damon and Pythias"—the first English tragedy on a classical subject—was acted before the queen at Oxford, in 1566. It was composed by Richard Edwards, a learned member of the University, written in rhyme, and inferior to "Ferrex and Porrex." "Tancred and Gismunda," the first English play taken from an Italian novel, was presented before the queen in 1568.

The first regularly licensed theatre in London was opened at Blackfriars in 1576. It was there that Shakespeare's immortal dramas first saw the light; and there he unwillingly — to borrow his own words — "made himself a motley to the view," in his character of an actor.

The first theatres were composed of wood, of a circular form, and open to the weather, excepting over the stage, which was covered with a thatched roof. Outside, on the roof, a flag was hoisted during the time of performance, — which commenced at three o'clock, at the third sounding or flourish of trumpets.

"The cavaliers," says the historian, "and fair dames of the court of Elizabeth sat in boxes below the gallery, or were accommodated with stools on the stage, where some of the young gallants also threw themselves at length on the rush-strewn floor, while their pages handed them pipes and tobacco, — then a fashionable and highly prized luxury.

" Into the pit, or yard, which was not furnished with seats, the middle classes were crowded.

" Actresses were not seen on the stage till after the Restoration ; the female parts were played by boys, or delicate young men." It has been observed that " while this palliates the grossness of some of the language put into the mouth of females in the old plays, it serves to point out more clearly that innate sense of beauty and excellence which prompted the exquisite loveliness and perfection exhibited in Shakespeare's ideals of woman-hood." Movable scenery was not, it is supposed, in-troduced until after the Restoration.

Rude imitations of towers, woods, animals, or furniture, served to illustrate the scene. To point out the place of action, a board containing the name, written or printed in large letters, was hung out during the performance.

Anciently, an allegorical exhibition, called the " Dumb Show," was exhibited before every act, and gave an out-line of the action to follow. Before dismissing the au-dience, the actors knelt in front of the stage and offered up a prayer for the queen. In " Midsummer Night's Dream," Shakespeare, in the rehearsal of " Pyramus and Thisbe," seems to have caricatured the rude arrangements of the first theatres. It has been observed that " the decline of the drama may in a great measure be attributed to the splendid representations of external nature in our modern theatres, where the attention of the audience is directed rather to the efforts of the painter than to those of the actor, who is lost amid the marvellous effect of light and shade on our gigantic stages." This assertion is not without weight; yet we must, I think, ascribe the decay of dramatic literature to other and weightier causes, on which time will not allow us to dwell.

The English drama, which rose so suddenly and brilliantly on the Elizabethan age, grew as rapidly. Between the years 1568 and 1580 no less than fifty-two dramas were acted at court under the superintendence of the Master of Revels; and in ten years from the opening of the first theatre there were two hundred players in or near the metropolis.

Nearly all the dramatic authors preceding or cotemporary with Shakespeare were men of learning and ability, and a profusion of classic imagery abounds in their plays, though they did not copy the severe and correct taste of the ancient models.

Among the immediate predecessors of the great poet are some worthy of separate notice, though, as has been aptly said, " they must not be thought of along with him, when he appears before us, like Prometheus, moulding the figures of men and breathing into them the animation and all the passions of life." As these dramatists wrote to supply the popular demand for novelty and excitement, in their comedies we are introduced to the coarse raillery and comic incidents of low life, and their tragedies abound in bloodshed and horror; yet nearly all of them, as has been noted, have poetical imagery, bursts of passion, beautiful sentiments, traits of nature, and touches of that happy poetic diction which gives a permanent value and interest to these elder masters of English poetry.

Preceding Shakespeare, and most worthy of notice, are Lyly, Kyd, Greene, Lodge, and Marlowe; Marlowe is by far the greatest of Shakespeare's precursors.

He is supposed to have been born about the year 1562,

and though he had a learned education, is said to have
been the son of a shoemaker. Marlowe was a fiery, imaginative genius, and lived as wildly as he wrote. Condemned by the serious, and stained with follies, while his
genius was rapidly maturing and developing its magnificent resources, he fell a victim to an obscene and disgraceful brawl. A lady to whom he was attached, favored
another lover; finding them in company one day, the poet
in a fit of jealous rage attempted to stab the man with
his dagger. His antagonist seized him by the wrist, and
turning the dagger, gave him a mortal wound. He died
in June, 1593. Marlowe excels in scenes and passages of
terrific grandeur and thrilling agony. One of his most
characteristic features is his high-sounding blank verse
which Ben Jonson aptly calls " Marlowe's mighty line."
The tragedy which exhibits this writer's widest range of
dramatic power is entitled " The Life and Death of Dr.
Faustus." Marlowe's other dramas are, " Tamburlaine
the Great," " Lust's Dominion," " The Jew of Malta,"
" The Massacre at Paris," and " Edward II." Charles
Lamb affirms that the death-scene in this historical drama
(" Edward II.") " moves pity and terror beyond any scene
ancient or modern." This is, however, exaggerated praise;
it is far surpassed by some of Shakespeare's scenes. In
addition to these dramatic productions, Marlowe assisted
Nash in the " Tragedy of Dido," and translated part of
" Hero and Leander " (afterward completed by Chapman)
and the elegies of Ovid. The latter work was, for its
licentiousness, burned by order of the Archbishop of
Canterbury. Marlowe's " Faustus," which may challenge
comparison with Goethe's " Faust," has the same hero,
who, having made a solemn disposal of his soul to Lucifer,
on condition of having a familiar spirit at his hand, and
unlimited enjoyment for twenty-four years, calls up spirits

from the vasty deep, visits different countries, and revels in luxury and splendor. At length the time expires; the bond becomes due; and a party of spirits enter amid thunder and lightning to claim his forfeited life and person. When he stands on the brink of ruin, waiting for the fatal moment, imploring yet distrusting repentance, a scene of enchaining interest proclaims the full triumph of the tragic poet. A short extract from this powerful tragedy will but faintly convey to the reader the grandeur of Marlowe's conception.

FAUSTUS *alone. — The clock strikes eleven.*

FAUST. — O Faustus!
Now hast thou but one bare hour to live,
And then thou must be damned perpetually.
Stand still, you ever-moving spheres of heaven,
That time may cease and midnight never come!
Fair Nature's eye, rise, rise again, and make
Perpetual day! or let this hour be but
A year, a month, a week, a natural day,
That Faustus may repent and save his soul.
O lente, lente currite, noctis equi,
The stars move still, time runs, the clock will strike,
The Devil will come; and Faustus must be damned.
Oh, I will leap to heaven: who pulls me down?
See where Christ's blood streams in the firmament:
One drop of blood will save me: Oh, my Christ!
Rend not my heart for naming of my Christ.
Yet will I call on him. Oh, spare me, Lucifer!
Where is it now? 'T is gone!
And see a threatening arm and angry brow.
Mountains and hills, come, come, and fall on me,
And hide me from the heavy wrath of Heaven!
No? then I will headlong run into the earth.
Gape, earth! Oh, no, it will not harbor me.
You stars that reigned at my nativity,
Whose influence have allotted death and hell,
Now draw up Faustus like a foggy mist

Into the entrails of yon laboring cloud;
That when you vomit forth into the air,
My limbs may issue from your smoky mouths;
But let my soul mount and ascend to heaven!

The scene from which this is taken has seldom been surpassed in interest, passion, and pathos; and though superstition no longer gives its horrors the literal force they are meant to convey, its picture of the worth and indestructibility of the soul, as shown by its capacity for suffering, still holds color.

Cotemporary with Shakespeare, and his fellow-worker in the cultivation of England's early dramatic literature, is Ben Jonson, who was born in 1574, ten years after the bard of Avon, and in his twentieth year appeared as a writer for the stage.

Jonson's early life was full of vicissitudes. His father, a Scottish clergyman, died before the poet's birth. His mother gave her boy a bricklayer for his stepfather, and he was brought home from Westminster School and put to the same uninteresting employment. Ben escaped from this distasteful occupation by enlisting as a soldier. He is said to have reverted in after-life with pride to his conduct as a soldier, — having killed an enemy in single combat in full view of both armies, and otherwise distinguished himself for youthful bravery.

Returning to England, he entered St. John's College, Cambridge, where his stay is supposed to have been shortened on account of straitened circumstances.

At the age of twenty, we find him married, and an actor in London.

At the same time he was engaged in writing for the stage, either by himself, or conjointly with others.

As an actor he is said to have completely failed. In 1596 Jonson produced his play, " Every Man in his

Humor." It was brought out at the Globe Theatre, and Shakespeare was one of the performers in the play. Queen Elizabeth patronized the new poet, and ever afterward it is said that he was "a man of mark and likelihood."

In 1619 Jonson was appointed poet laureate; that is, a poet attached to the king's household, whose business is to compose annually an ode for the king's birthday, and for the New Year. This title was first given in the time of Edward IV. Jonson's compensation was a pension of a hundred marks. In early life he contracted habits of intemperance which never left him; he is said to have prided himself immoderately on his classical acquirements, and to have slighted and contemned his less literary associates. Capable of a generous warmth of friendship, and just in his discrimination of genius and character, with a love of conviviality and high colloquial powers, Jonson became the centre of that band of wits called the Mermaid Club, founded by Sir Walter Raleigh, where Shakespeare, Beaumont and Fletcher, Herrick and other poets are said to have "exercised themselves with wit combats more bright and genial than their wine."

Jonson died in 1637, and was buried in Westminster Abbey. A square stone, marking the spot, was long afterward shown, inscribed only with the words, "O rare Ben Jonson!" His works, all together, consist of about fifty dramatic pieces. By far the greater part of them are masques and interludes. His principal comedies are "Every Man in his Humor," "Volpone," "The Silent Woman," and "The Alchemist." The strong delineation of character is the most striking feature in them.

His comic portraits are often coarse and repulsive, and so exaggerated as to appear like caricatures or libels on humanity; and it has been observed that "his humor will be most relished by those who are most amused by dancing bears, and shows of that class."

His Roman tragedies are considered literal impersonations of classic antiquity. Craik observes that "the effect produced by the most arresting passages in them is the most undramatic that can be; namely, a greater sympathy with the performance as a work of art than anything else."

Both comedies and tragedies exhibit an acute and vigorous intellect, the labor of an artist, possessing rich resources, great knowledge of life down to its lowest descents, coarse wit, lofty declamation, and a power of dramatizing his knowledge and observation with singular skill and effect. He was the founder of a style of regular English comedy, massive, well compacted, and fitted to endure, yet not very attractive in its materials.

"Jonson," it has been remarked, "presents us with two natures, — one hard, rugged, gross, and sarcastic, the other, airy, fanciful, and graceful as if its possessor had never combated with the world and its bad passions, but nursed his understanding and his fancy in poetical seclusion and contemplation." In his lyrics he turns to us this finer side of his nature, as in the well-known song to Celia, — "Drink to me only with thine eyes." Jonson's lines on the portrait of Shakespeare, opposite the frontispiece to the first edition of his works, 1623, are happily conceived, and are interesting as attesting the fidelity of the first engraved likeness of the poet.

> "This figure that thou here seest put,
> It was for gentle Shakespeare cut,
> Wherein the graver had a strife
> With nature, to outdo the life.
> O could he but have drawn his wit
> As well in brass as he hath hit

His face, the print would then surpass
All that was ever writ in brass !
But since he cannot, reader, look
Not on his picture, but his book."

In Jonson's best vein are these lines on the "True worth
of Life" : —

"It is not growing like a tree
In bulk doth make man better be,
Or standing long, an oak, three hundred year
To fall a log at last, dry, withered, sere.
A lily of a day
Is fairer far in May,
Although it fall and die that night ;
It was the plant and flower of light !
In small proportions we just beauties see ;
And in short measures life may perfect be."

To this period belongs the drama of Beaumont and
Fletcher, of whom it has been said that if they were not
great dramatists, they would still be great poets.

The two names must be regarded as indicating one
poet rather than two, since it is impossible to make out
their respective shares in the plays published in their
conjoint names.

John Fletcher was born in 1576, and was ten years older
than his friend Francis Beaumont. They lived together
ten years, writing in union a series of dramas, passionate,
romantic, and comic, blending thus their genius and fame.

The drama of Beaumont and Fletcher, though not in so
high a style as Shakespeare's, is poetical and imaginative.
They are fertile in the invention of plot and incident ; and
for keeping the attention of an audience awake, and their
expectation suspended throughout the whole course of the
action, they approach Shakespeare (who, however, had
higher ends and purposes) ; for this reason, in the great days
of the stage, and so long as the public manners tolerated

their license and grossness, their plays were much greater favorites in the theatres than his. Dryden tells us that two of theirs were acted in his time for one of Shakespeare. The lyrical pieces scattered throughout their plays are among the sweetest in the language; and after Shakespeare, they have left us the richest drama we have. This " To Sleep," from " Valentinian," is one of the most elevated specimens of their verse, and less quoted than their lyrics.

> " Care-charming Sleep, thou easer of all woes,
> Brother to Death, sweetly thyself dispose
> On this afflicted prince : fall like a cloud
> In gentle showers ; give nothing that is loud
> Or painful to his slumbers ; easy, light
> And as a purling stream, thou son of Night,
> Pass by his troubled senses, sing his pain
> Like hollow murmuring wind, or silver rain.
> Into this prince, gently, oh, gently slide,
> And kiss him into slumbers like a bride ! "

The most noted of Shakespeare's successors are Chapman, Dekker, Webster, Middleton, Marston, Taylor, Rowley, Massinger, Ford, Heywood, and Shirley. Among these, Massinger is pre-eminent as a tragic poet. He was born about the year 1584. His life was spent in obscurity and poverty; and one morning in March, 1640, he was found dead in his bed, dying almost unknown, and buried with no other inscription than the melancholy note in the parish register : " Philip Massinger, a stranger."

He wrote a great number of pieces, of which eighteen have been preserved. "The Virgin Martyr," "The Bondman," "The Fatal Dowry," "The City Madam," and "The New Way to pay Old Debts," are his best-known productions. The last-mentioned play has kept possession of the stage chiefly on account of the effective and original character of Sir Giles Overreach, — a character which the genius of Kean has made immortal.

Massinger has greater power as a tragic poet than any writer of the time of James. His tragedies have a calm, proud seriousness that impresses the imagination. His genius was more eloquent and descriptive than impassioned or inventive. His pictures, rather than his sentiments, touch the heart. His versification was smooth and mellifluous. In his comedy he has the same rugged strength that characterizes Ben Jonson. Genuine humor and sprightliness he had none ; and his dialogue, like Jonson's, is often coarse and indecent. His characters are often too depraved to be real. He is not a quotable dramatist, having less sentiment than portrayal of character to commend him. Here is a short but striking passage from " The New Way to pay Old Debts " : —

> " Some undone widow sits upon mine arm,
>   And takes away the use of it; and my sword,
>   Glued to my scabbard with wronged orphan's tears,
>   Will not be drawn."

Ford, Massinger's cotemporary, was born 1586, and died 1639. He is characterized by a tone of pensive tenderness, and a peculiarly soft and musical style of blank verse. His morbid, diseased imagination led him to devote some of his best effort to the description of incestuous passion. The scenes in his " Brother and Sister," describing the criminal loves of Arabella and Giovanni, contain his finest poetry and expression. Charles Lamb ranks Ford with the first order of poets. More impartial critics have admitted his sway over the tender passions and the occasional beauty of his language, but have found him wanting in the elevation of great genius. His cotemporary, Thomas Heywood, the date of whose birth is unknown, but who wrote for the stage as late as 1640, and "had an entire hand," as he tells us, "or at least a main finger," in two hundred and twenty plays, besides attending to his business as an actor, as a dramatist has poetical fancy and an abundance of classic imagery; but as his business was to cater to the play-goer's craving for novelty, scenes of low buffoonery, "merry accidents, intermixed with apt and witty jests," deform his pieces.

Of his twenty-three plays that have come down to us, the best are, "A Woman Killed with Kindness," "A Challenge for Beauty," "The English Traveller," "The Royal King and Loyal Subject," "The Lancashire Witches," "The Rape of Lucrece," and "Love's Mistress." It has been remarked that "there is a natural repose in Heywood's scenes which is in pleasant contrast with the excitement that prevails in those of most of his cotemporaries." The songs scattered through his now neglected plays are often easy and flowing. He informs us in one of his Prologues that —

> "To give content to this most curious age,
>   The gods themselves we 've brought down to the stage,
>   And figured them in planets; made even hell
> Deliver up the Furies, by no spell
> Saving the Muse's rapture. Further we
> Have trafficked by their help; no history
> We have left unrifled; our pens have been dipped
> As well in opening each hid manuscript
> As tracks more vulgar, whether read or sung
> In our domestic or more foreign tongue.
> Of fairies, elves, nymphs of the sea and land,
> The lawns, the groves, no number can be scanned
> Which we have not given feet to."

Heywood impresses one rather as a playwright than a poet; but when we think of his "finger in the pie" of two hundred and twenty plays, and the "several prose works" that he wrote, we must at least praise his industry.

John Marston, writing from 1600 to 1634, some of whose miscellaneous poetry was ordered to be burned for its licentiousness, is the author of "Malcontent," a comedy, "Antonio and Mellida," a tragedy, "The Insatiate Countess," "What you Will," and other plays.   Marston was a rough and vigorous writer.   "His forte," says Hazlitt, "was not sympathy either with the stronger or softer emotions, but an impatient scorn and bitter indignation against the vices and follies of men, which vented itself either in comic irony or lofty invective."   This humorous sketch of a scholar and his dog is not unworthy of Shakespeare : —

> "I was a scholar; seven useful springs
> Did I deflower in quotations
> Of crossed opinions 'bout the soul of man.
> The more I learnt, the more I learnt to doubt.
> Delight, my spaniel, slept, whilst I baused leaves,
> Tossed o'er the dunces, pored on the old print
> Of titled words ; and still my spaniel slept,
> Whilst I wasted lamp-oil, baited my flesh,
> Shrunk up my veins ; and still my spaniel slept.
> And still I held converse with Zabarell,
> Aquinas, Scotus, and the musty saw
> Of Antick Donate ; still my spaniel slept.
> Still on went I ; first, *an sit anima;*
> Then, an it were mortal.   O hold, hold; at that
> They 're at brain buffets, fell by the ears amain
> Pell-mell together ; still my spaniel slept.
> Then, whether 't were corporeal, local, fixt,
> *Ex traduce,* but whether 't had free will
> Or no, hot philosophers
> Stood banding factions, all so strongly propt,
> I staggered, knew not which was firmer part,
> But thought, quoted, read, observed, and pried,

Stufft noting books; and still my spaniel slept.
At length he waked and yawn'd; and by yon sky,
For aught I know, he knew as much as I."

Thomas Middleton was a popular dramatic writer, and the author of about twenty plays. The date of his birth is not given. He was writing for the stage as late as 1624. He died in 1627. A conjecture that an old neglected drama of his, entitled "The Witch," supplied the witchcraft scenery, and part of the lyrical incantations of "Macbeth," has kept alive the name of this poet. It is now, however, thought more probable that the inferior author is the borrower, and it has been aptly said that "the dim, mysterious, unearthly beings that accost Macbeth on the blasted heath, only Shakespeare could have evoked." Middleton's witches, like Shakespeare's, dance about their caldron; and their charm-song is worded not unlike his, but it falls flat in the singing. It is not in the least blood-curdling, but rather suggests "Mother Goose." The witches' moonlight flight is better done. In parts it approaches Shakespeare, but never reaches him. Middleton's witches have no originality. They are of the old common-place type, — a mixture of the ludicrous and uncanny. They are funny, but not awful, — scarcely horrible.

Middleton would seem to have been well known as a dramatic writer, for when in 1617 the Cockpit Theatre was demolished, an old ballad describing the circumstance states, —

"Books old and young on heap they flung,
    And burnt them in the blazes, —
Tom Dekker, Heywood, Middleton,
    And other wand'ring crazys."

John Webster, whom Hazlitt has called "the noble-minded," was united with Dekker in the conjunct authorship then so common. The two dramatists are placed between 1601 and 1641. His plays abound in passages of intense feeling; his subjects are managed with delicacy; and his moral tone is higher than is to be found in most of his cotemporaries, though he could not resist the prevailing appetite for " supernumerary horrors," in which his tragedies abound. His " White Devil," and " Duchess of Malfy " are almost equally admired by critics. The last scenes in the latter play are finely conceived, and in a spirit which students of our elder dramatic literature have admired as belonging peculiarly to Webster.

The Duchess is in prison; Bosola, her captor, enters disguised as a bellman, — usually sent to condemned persons the night before they suffer. In their conversation occurs this fine and often-quoted passage, —

> " Glories, like glow-worms, afar off shine bright;
> But looked to near, have neither heat nor light."

After a coffin, cords, and a bell have been produced, Bosola sings this dirge : —

> " Hark! now everything is still;
> This screech-owl and the whistler shrill
> Call upon our dame aloud,
> And bid her quickly don her shroud.
> Much you had of land and rent;
> Your length in clay 's now competent.
> A long war disturbed your mind;
> Here your perfect peace is signed.
> Of what is 't fools make such vain keeping?
> Sin their conception; their birth weeping·
> Their life a general mist of error;
> Their death a hideous storm of terror.
> Strew your hair with powders sweet,
> Don clean linen, bathe your feet;
> And — the foul fiend more to check —

A crucifix let bless your neck.
'T is now full tide 'tween night and day ;
End your groan, and come away."

The Duchess now addresses her maid, Cariola, —

Farewell, Cariola.
I pray thee look thou giv'st my little boy
Some syrup for his cold ; and let the girl
Say her prayers ere she sleep. — Now what you please.
What death ?
Bosola. — *Strangling.* Here are your executioners.
Duch. I forgive them.
The apoplexy, catarrh, or cough o' the lungs
Would do as much as they do.
Bos. Doth not death fright you ?
Duch. Who would be afraid on 't,
Knowing to meet such excellent company
In th' other world?
Bos. Yet methinks the manner of your death should much afflict
you.
This cord should terrify you.
Duch. Not a whit.
What would it pleasure me to have my throat cut
With diamonds, or to be smothered
With cassia, or to be shot to death with pearls ?
I know death hath ten thousand several doors
For men to take their exits ; and 't is found
They go on such strange geometrical hinges
You may open them both ways. . . .
. . . Tell my brothers
That I perceive death — now I am well awake —
Best gift is they can give or I can take.
I would fain put off my last woman's fault :
I 'd not be tedious to you.
Pull, and pull strongly, for your able strength
Must pull down heaven upon me.
Yet stay ; heaven's gates are not so highly arched
As princes' palaces ; they that enter there
Must go upon their knees. Come, violent death,

9

Serve for mandragora to make me sleep.
Go tell my brothers, when I am laid out,
They then may feed in quiet.   [*They strangle her, kneeling.*

Her brother, Ferdinand, to whom she has given mortal offence by indulging in a generous but infatuated passion for her steward, and at whose instance she is strangled, now enters.

   Ferd. Is she dead?
   Bos. She is what you would have her.
Fix your eye here.
   Ferd. Constantly.
   Bos. Do you not weep?
Other sins only speak; murder shrieks out.
The element of water moistens the earth,
But blood flies upwards, and bedews the heavens.
   Ferd. Cover her face: mine eyes dazzle: she died young.
   Bos. I think not so; her infelicity
Seemed to have years too many.
   Ferd. She and I were twins:
And should I die this instant, I had lived
Her time to a minute.

James Shirley, born in 1594, and dying in 1666, was a voluminous writer, thirty-nine plays proceeding from his prolific pen. As a dramatist, he lacks originality, force, and pathos; but his mind was poetical, and his style and language polished and refined. He is much commended for " the airy touches of his expression, the delicacy of his sentiments, and the beauty of his similes." He is best kept in repute by that fine production, " Death's Final Conquest," which occurs in his play entitled " The Contention of Ajax and Ulysses." These verses were greatly admired by Charles II. : —

> " The glories of our birth and state
>   Are shadows, not substantial things;
> There is no armor against fate;
>   Death lays his icy hand on kings.

Sceptre and crown
Must tumble down
And in the dust be equal made
With the poor crooked scythe and spade.

" Some men with swords may reap the field,
And plant fresh laurels where they kill ;
But their strong nerves at last must yield,
They tame but one another still.
Early or late,
They stoop to fate,
And must give up their murmuring breath,
When they, pale captives, creep to death.

" The garlands wither on your brow,
Then boast no more your mighty deeds ;
Upon Death's purple altar now,
See where the victim bleeds.
All heads must come
To the cold tomb ;
Only the actions of the just
Smell sweet and blossom in the dust."

Shirley is last on the list of this race of dramatists. Taking them all in all (without even including Shakespeare),

" We ne'er shall see their like again."

Had Shakespeare never existed (imagination shudders at such a possibility) we might still exhibit the roll of our elder dramatists with some pride.

With Shirley the production of the Elizabethan drama and the popularity of the stage came to an end.

By an act of the Long Parliament, passed on the 2d of September, 1642, theatrical entertainments were permanently suppressed.

Theatres were demolished by the city authorities, and convicted players were openly whipped ; yet these severe measures did not entirely suppress stage plays. In the country strolling players still continued to set the law at defiance, and in London the players still kept together, and by connivance of the commanding official at Whitehall sometimes represented privately a few plays at a short distance from town. In the mean time, the players, thus cut off from their regular gains, resorted to the sale of their dramatic productions to the booksellers, which in the craving of the public for their customary enjoyment were eagerly sought for. Heretofore the most favorite acting plays had been carefully withheld from the press by the theatrical companies whose property they were ; and the only way in which a reading of them could be obtained was by paying a considerable sum for the loan of the manuscript or a transcript of it.

In a preface to the plays of Beaumont and Fletcher, published in 1647, the reader is thus exhorted : "Congratulate thy own happiness that in the silence of the stage thou hast a liberty to read these inimitable plays, to dwell and converse in these immortal groves which were only showed to our fathers as in a conjuring-glass, as suddenly removed as represented."

CHAPTER VIII.

SHAKESPEARE.

DOUBT and fable, it has been well observed, surround the few incidents in Shakespeare's life; and in our loving reverence for this great soul we are not unwilling that it should be so, for as Emerson happily expresses it, " we are not the friends of his buttons, but of his thought, and are willing that he should be a stranger in a thousand particulars that he may come nearer in the holiest ground, poetic, pure, and universal."

We know that he was born at Stratford-on-Avon in April, 1564, and tradition dates his birth on the 23d of the month, the anniversary of St. George, the tutelar saint of England. His father, John Shakespeare, was a woolcomber, and his mother, Mary Arden, a rustic heiress. Though John Shakespeare by this marriage must have elevated his social position, as he afterward rose to be high bailiff of Stratford, he is found in 1578 mortgaging his wife's inheritance, and from entries in the town books is supposed to have fallen into comparative poverty.

William, being the eldest of six surviving children, was after some education at the grammar school brought home to assist at his father's business. How much education Shakespeare received at this school is not known. His friend, Ben Jonson, allows him " little Latin and less Greek." Yet it must be remembered that with more than ordinary attainments Shakespeare would have been unlearned in the estimation of Jonson, — a man of vast erudition and proportionate self-esteem. The extent of the literary acquirements of the bard of Avon has been thus fairly estimated : " He had what would now be considered a reasonable proportion of Latin. He was not wholly ignorant of Greek. He had a knowledge of the French, so as to read it with ease, and not less of the Italian. He had no ordinary facility in the classics, and had deeply imbibed the Scriptures."

His father, unable to subsist by his original trade, is said at one time to have had recourse to the inferior occupation of a butcher. Aubrey suggests that Shakespeare then began to exhibit his dramatic propensities, and " when he killed a calf would do it in a high style and make a speech." With the author of " Macbeth " for its executioner, an appreciative calf might well have been "half in love with easeful death."

Shakespeare married at the immature age of eighteen Anne Hathaway, the daughter of a substantial yeoman in the neighborhood of Stratford, eight years older than himself. It is conjectured that the poet lived to repent the indulgence of a boyish fancy, an affection too much misgrafted in respect of years ; and this familiar passage in " Twelfth Night " is thought to apply to himself.

> " Let still the woman take
> An elder than herself; so wears she to him,
> So sways she level in her husband's heart.
> For, boy, however we do praise ourselves,
> Our fancies are more giddy and unfirm,
> More longing, wavering, sooner lost and worn,
> Than women's are. . . .
> Then let thy love be younger than thyself,
> Or thy affection cannot hold the bent;
> For women are as roses, whose fair flower,
> Being once displayed, doth fall that very hour."

All this, however, is mere conjecture, as the only writings Shakespeare has left through which we can trace anything of his personal feelings and affections, are his sonnets ; and out of the hundred and fifty-four, — the number he has written, — only twenty-eight can be called love-sonnets. All the others are inscribed to some beloved friend of his own sex, whom the poet addresses in a strain of affection and idolatry, remarkable even in the reign of Elizabeth for its enthusiasm and extravagance.

It has been suggested that these twenty-eight love-sonnets may after all have been written impersonally, and are merely dramatic in expression ; but the general supposition is that they were inspired by the real object of a real affection, however disloyal, blind, and misplaced. Mrs. Jameson infers from them that the beloved lady was " dark-haired and dark-eyed," and that she belonged to "that class of women who do not always, in losing all right to our respect, lose also their claim upon the admiration of the other sex." In our deep and tender veneration for Shakespeare, we cannot conceive him to have been permanently enslaved by mere sensuous beauty unallied to purity and worth. Let us rather trust that, soon disenchanted and disenthralled, he penitently turned from his unlawful love to his sacred conjugal allegiance, and lived ever after in tender friendship with middle-aged Anne Hathaway Shakespeare, who duly made his posset, darned his hose, and knitted up for him the ever-ravelling sleeve of life as only a woman can ; while the poet's foregone ecstasy of love, transmuted at last into a divine aspiration, a blameless craving for ideal beauty and excellence, expressed itself in the white chastity of Imogen, the winsome grace of Rosalind, the tenderness of Juliet, the cloistered innocence of Miranda, the touching sweetness of Ophelia, the modesty of Viola, the gentle dignity of Catherine, the pious sincerity of Cordelia, the holy constancy of Hermione, and the inimitable grace and beauty of the divine Desdemona.

> " A maiden never bold ;
> Of spirit so still and quiet that her motion
> Blush'd at herself."

It is supposed that early in life Shakespeare may have unsuccessfully applied himself to an occupation for which youth and natural gayety unfitted him, — tuition. Tradition also asserts that about this time he fell into ill company, and was led into excesses. Doubtless " Wild Will " had many a lark with the Stratford lads, who, as the story goes, were now and then o'er free with grim Sir Thomas Lucy's deer and conies ; but it must be remembered that in these ruder days when " the spirit of Robin Hood was yet abroad," deer-stealing was looked upon rather as a hazardous exploit than as a crime ; and then, too, —

> " Sir Thomas was too covetous
> To covet so much deer ! "

In his wild youth, Shakespeare is said to have been o'er liberal in his potations, and to have " addicted himself to ale as lustily as Falstaff to his sack." It is not pleasant to imagine the author of "Hamlet" "half-seas over ; " but to err is human, and we can well believe what has been affirmed of the gentle Shakespeare, — " though the ebullitions of high spirits might mislead him, the principles and affections never swerved from what was right." When little more than twenty, Shakespeare had a wife and two children to maintain. Sir Thomas Lucy, a stiff Puritan, and rigid upholder of the game laws, vengefully attacked with the penalties of the law the youth who had no doubt already made the butt of his unripe wit the man who yet survives in the character of Justice Shallow as the laughing-stock of posterity. By his persecutions he at last drove Shakespeare to the metropolis, where Destiny, who shapes our rough-hewn ends, had in store for him not only an asylum, but friends, wealth, and fame.

About the year 1587, in the twenty-third year of his age, the poet is supposed to have arrived in London. His natural taste for theatricals led him at once to the theatre. Some of his townsmen were distinguished performers on the stage, and he seems easily to have secured a some-what menial occupation there. One tradition places him as call-boy, or prompter's attendant, whose employment it is to give the performers notice to be ready to enter whenever they are required on the stage. Another is that Shakespeare's first expedient was to wait at the door of the playhouse and hold the horses of those who rode to the theatre and had no servants to take charge of them during the performance.

It is said that " he became so conspicuous in this office for his care and readiness that in a short time every man as he alighted called for Will Shakespeare, and scarcely any other waiter was trusted with a horse while Will could be had." This was the dawn of better fortune. Shake-speare, finding more horses put into his hands than he could hold, hired boys to wait under his inspection, who when Will Shakespeare was summoned were imme-diately to present themselves : *I am Shakespeare's boy, sir*. And in time, when Shakespeare found higher and more fitting employment, the waiters who held the horses, so long as the practice of riding to the playhouse con-tinued, retained the appellation of " Shakespeare's boys." This story, which Dr. Johnson credits, if it be true, only increases our respect for Shakespeare, who, liberally en-dowed by nature, might well spare a modicum of genius for the by-play of life, and still have more than enough for the grand action. The very fact of his success in horse-holding shows " the myriad-minded man." Shakespeare's talents were not long buried in obscurity. From this inferior station he soon rose to the highest occupation in the theatre, and by the power of his genius raised the national dramatic literature from its infancy to the highest state of perfection which it is perhaps capable of reaching.

Very early in his dramatic career he is said to have attained to a principal share in the direction and emoluments of the theatres to which he was attached. His name stands second in the list of proprietors of the Globe and Blackfriars in the license granted to them by James I. in 1603 ; and his industry in supporting these establishments is said to have been indefatigable. " Titus Andronicus " — the earliest dramatic effort of Shakespeare's pen, according to its date — must have been produced immediately after his arrival in London. The accumulated horrors of its plot, and the dissimilarity of its style from the other efforts of Shakespeare's genius, have caused the critics to doubt that this play is really his own. It was a great favorite at its first performance ; and though it is a heavy and monotonous play, full of barbarities that shock our more refined taste, and bears no resemblance to his divine after-thoughts, — " Othello," " Hamlet," " Macbeth," and "Lear," — it must ever excite our interest as the tragedy on which the immortal master " tried his 'prentice han'."

The fortunes of the poet rose ; the smiles of royalty at length shone upon him. Queen Elizabeth rewarded him with her favor ; and it is related that she was so delighted with the character of Falstaff that she desired the poet to continue it in another play and exhibit him in love. To this command we owe the " Merry Wives of Windsor." It is further related that so eager was the queen to see it acted that she commanded him to finish it in fourteen days, and was " well pleased with the performance." With her successor, James I., Shakespeare was a favorite. The " Tempest" was written for the festivities that attended the marriage of his daughter, the Princess Elizabeth, Miranda, the Island Princess, being designed as a poetic representative of the high-born bride ; and in the royal and learned Prospero a complimentary allusion to the literary character and learned studies of her royal father has been traced.

Shakespeare, like his friend Ben Jonson, was an actor as well as an author. There are some doubts as to his merits as a performer. He is thought to have been but indifferently skilled in the inferior half of his double vocation, as it is said he never attempted a part superior to the ghost in " Hamlet." Reed relates that one of his brothers used to come to London, to visit his brother Will, and be a spectator of him as an actor in some of his plays.

It is pleasant to picture that portion of Shakespeare's life when, honored and applauded, sunned by the smiles of royalty, and relieved by a timely competency from feverish solicitude for daily bread, he was enabled to give the fullest and freest play to that heaven-born genius that " stooped to touch the loftiest thought," and to chisel grandly into life the gorgeous shapes of light and loveliness that floated through his dreams, countless as the airy motes that crowd a sunbeam ; when, at the Mermaid Club, he skirmished in wit with " rare Ben Jonson," talked over new drama plots with Beaumont and Fletcher, or listened with unenvying admiration to the graceful verses of Habington and the dainty conceits of metaphysical Donne, or heard with moistened eye the baby-lyrics of April-mooded Herrick, singing silvery through tears.

Tradition says that a few years before Shakespeare's

death, in possession of an income of about one thousand pounds, — a sum fully adequate to his modest views of happiness, — he retired to his native Stratford to spend his remaining days in ease, retirement, and the conversation of his friends. This event appears to have taken place about the close of the year 1613, when, his wife and family about him, surrounded by familiar scenes and faces, and "bearing his blushing honors thick upon him," in the full splendor of unclouded glory this great sun "made a golden set."

On his birthday, the 23d of April, 1616, his spirit "shuffled off this mortal coil." On the north side of the chancel of the great church at Stratford, he sleeps well. There stands a monument to his memory, containing his bust. He is represented under an arch, — "a fitting emblem of that eternal halo of glory that spans his name."

In 1751, one hundred and thirty-five years after his death, a costly monument was erected to Shakespeare's memory in Westminster Abbey ; the expenses of the statuary were defrayed by a benefit at each of the London theatres.

To Shakespeare's disposition and moral character tradition has ever borne a favorable testimony ; and his gentle and benevolent heart may be seen in almost every page of his works. "Worthy," "gentle," and "beloved," the epithets uniformly coupled with his name, prove the serenity of his temper and the sweetness of his manners. "He was," says Aubrey, "very good company, and of a very ready, pleasant, and smooth wit." Says Rowe, "He was indeed honest, and of an open and free nature, that every one who had a true taste of merit and could distinguish men, had generally a just value and esteem for him." "I loved the man," says Ben Jonson, "and do honor to his memory this side idolatry, as much as any man." His lofty conceptions of purity and goodness are indices to a superior moral nature.

Though Shakespeare retired to ease and plenty while he was yet but little "declined in the vale of years," he made no collection of his works. Of the plays which bear his name in the late editions, the greater part were not published till about seven years after his death; and so careless was this immortal bard of future fame that the few plays which appeared during his life bear evidence of having been thrust into the world apparently without the care of the author, and probably without his knowledge. The first edition of Shakespeare was published in 1623; a second in 1632, — the same as the first, except that it was more disfigured with errors of the press; a third edition in 1664, and in 1685 a fourth. The public admiration of this great English classic now demanded that he should receive the honor of a commentary; and Rowe, the poet, gave an improved edition in 1709. Pope, Johnson, Chalmers, Stevens, and others, successively published editions of the poet, with copious notes. The voluminous edition by Malone and Boswell, published in twenty-one volumes, in 1821, is thought by some to be the best of the whole.

The critics of this great poet, both in England and Germany, and even on this side the water, are innumerable; and it has been remarked that "like Banquo's progeny, they bid fair to stretch to the crack of doom." It has been well said that there never was an author, ancient or modern, whose works have been so carefully analyzed and illustrated, so eloquently expounded, or so universally admired. In the words of Milton, —

> "He so sepulchred in such pomp doth lie
> That kings for such a tomb would wish to die."

"Macbeth," "Lear," "Othello," and "Hamlet" are admitted by all to be Shakespeare's four principal trage- dies. "Lear" stands first for profound intensity of the passion, "Macbeth" for the wildness of the imagina- tion and the rapidity of the action, "Othello" for the progressive interest, and powerful alternations of feeling, "Hamlet" for the refined development of thought and sen- timent. "Twelfth Night, or, What you Will" and "All's Well that Ends Well" have been considered the most de- lightful of his comedies. In the "Tempest" — one of the most original and perfect of his productions — Shakespeare has best shown the variety of his powers, in "Midsum- mer Night's Dream" the delicacy and sportive gayety of his imagination. Hazlitt affirms of this play that "it dis- plays more fancy and imagery, more sweetness and beauty of description, than may be found in the whole range of French poetry put together." "Romeo and Juliet" is the only tragedy which Shakespeare has written entirely upon a love-story. "Whatever," observes the same critic, " is most intoxicating in the odor of a southern spring, languishing in the song of the nightingale, or volup- tuous in the first opening of the rose, is to be found in this poem." It is one of the most natural of Shakespeare's tragedies. "Antony and Cleopatra" is a noble play; though not in the first order of the poet's productions, it is thought to be the finest of his historical plays, and presents a grand picture of Roman pride and Eastern magnificence. In "Richard III." Shakespeare has shown his masterly delineation of character. "This play be- longs rather to the theatre than to the closet;" and of all his plays it has been considered most properly a stage play. It is in Richard III. that the genius of Kean, the great English tragedian, has achieved its proudest tri- umphs; and in that and "Othello," he is said to have acquired his fame. In "Julius Cæsar" the truth of history is finely worked up with dramatic effect. It is not equal to "Antony and Cleopatra," but abounds in admirable and affecting passages, and is remarkable for the profound knowledge of human character it displays. In "Henry IV.," "The Merry Wives," "Measure for Measure," and ". As You Like it," we find the ripened poetical imagination, prodigality of invention, contemplative philosophy and inimitable powers of comedy, "revelling as in an atmosphere of joyous life, fresh from the hand of the Creator."

Shakespeare, who was the true child of Nature, has in his drama disregarded classic rules, pursuing at will his airy way through all the labyrinths of fancy and the human heart. That he has deviated from the dramatic unities of time, place, and action, laid down by the ancients and adopted by the stately French drama, is well-known, and on the whole, needs no defence, since "in his tragedies," as has been observed, "he amply fulfils what Aristotle admits to be the end and object of tragedy, — to beget admiration, terror, or sympathy ; and in his comedies, if the mixture of comic with tragic scenes is considered a blemish, Nature must be the poet's apologist, since such blending of events is in accordance with the actual experience and vicissitudes of life."

My unaccustomed pen may not dare attempt to gauge a mind whose myriad powers have been for three hundred years the fond and inexhaustible theme of scholar, poet, and sage ; and here I can but quote literally from Craik : —

"In what other drama do we behold so living a humanity as his? Who has given us a scene either so crowded with diversities of character, or so stirred with the hurry and heat of actual existence? The men and the manners of all ages and countries

are there: the lovers and warriors, the priests and prophetesses
of the old heroic and kingly times of Greece; the Athenians
of the days of Pericles and Alcibiades; the proud patricians
and turbulent commonality of the earliest period of republican
Rome, — Cæsar and Brutus, and Cassius and Antony, and Cleopatra, and the other splendid figures of that later Roman scene;
the kings and queens and princes and courtiers of barbaric Denmark and Roman Britain, and Britain before the Romans, and
those of Scotland in the time of the English Heptarchy; those
of England and France at the era of Magna Charta; all ranks
of the people of almost every reign of our subsequent history
from the end of the fourteenth to the middle of the sixteenth
century; not to speak of Venice and Verona and Mantua and
Padua and Illyria and Navarre, and the forest of Arden, and all
the other towns and lands which he has peopled for us with
their most real inhabitants.

"Not even in his plays is Shakespeare a mere dramatist.
Apart altogether from his dramatic power he is the greatest
poet that ever lived.

"His sympathy is the most universal, his imagination the most
plastic, his diction the most expressive ever given to any writer.
His poetry has in itself the varied power and excellence of all
other poetry. While in grandeur and beauty and passion and
sweetest music, and all the other higher gifts of song, he may
be ranked with the greatest, — with Spenser and Chaucer and
Milton and Dante and Homer, — he is at the same time more
nervous than Dryden and more sententious than Pope, and
more sparkling, and of more abounding conceit, when he
chooses, than Donne or Cowley or Butler.

"In what handling was language ever such a flame of fire as it
is in his? His wonderful potency in the use of this instrument
would alone set him above all other writers."

It has been stated that in the English language the
number of words in ordinary use does not exceed three
thousand. A rough calculation, founded on Mrs. Clarke's
concordance, gives about twenty-one thousand as the number to be found in the plays of Shakespeare, without count-

ing inflectional forms as distinct words. Not more than seven thousand are given for Milton, making, by a fair estimate, his vocabulary not more than half as copious as the Shakespearian.

The revolution that Shakespeare wrought upon the English drama is clearly shown by comparing his earliest plays with the best the language possessed before his time. Characters in which polished manners and easy grace are as predominant as wit, reflection, or fancy, were then as unknown to the stage as to actual life, and are simply the creations of his genius. The honor of creating the English drama itself is indeed not claimed for Shakespeare; but by refining its rudeness, and giving it grace and elevation, he regenerated and wholly transformed it. His comedies have been aptly termed "meteors of wit, filled with a humor that finds the kernel of the ludicrous in everything." What other dramatist could have created for us a Slender, a Dogberry, a Launcelot, a Touchstone, and a Launce, and last but not least, that rare embodiment of wit and humor, huge Falstaff, "larding the lean earth as he walks along"? — a character "whose very vices," it has been said, "seem made for our delight, since he is a liar, a glutton, a braggart, and a coward more for the amusement of others than for the gratification of himself." Justice Shallow is to him "a man made after supper from a cheese-paring." "If to be fat," quoth he, "is to be hated, then Pharaoh's lean kine are to be loved."

Some of Shakespeare's clowns and fools are but mere poetical creations; yet many of them are to be met with in real life, and are familiar as sunshine. Of this sort is Launce, in the "Two Gentlemen of Verona," and those "hempen homespuns," the Athenian clowns, met by moonlight in the fairy-haunted wood to rehearse their grand tragedy of "Pyramus and Thisbe," proposed by them

10

as a part of the festivities attending the marriage of the
Duke of Athens. It has been justly affirmed that of all
poets we must accord to Shakespeare the most unbounded
range of fanciful invention. Who like him has "given to
airy nothing a local habitation and a name"? How his
Ariel, dainty as the down of a thistle, "drinks the air before him"! How perfectly he does his spiriting, — "be 't
to fly, to swim, to dive into the fire, or to ride on the
curled clouds"! Like a "singing gossamer" he floats in
the air, warbling, —

> "Where the bee sucks, there suck I;
> In a cowslip's bell I lie;
> There I couch when owls do cry.
> On the bat's back I do fly
> After summer, merrily:
> Merrily, merrily, shall I live now,
> Under the blossom that hangs on the bough."

Even that strange monster Caliban, moved by concord
of sweet sounds, is charmed by this creature of ethereal
essences; thus he discourses to the tipsy Trinculo, when
startled by Ariel's invisible music, which he calls "the
tune of Our Catch, played by the picture of Nobody," —

> "Be not afeard; the isle is full of noises,
> Sounds and sweet airs that give delight and hurt not.
> Sometimes a thousand twangling instruments
> Will hum about mine ears; and sometimes voices,
> That if I then had waked after long sleep,
> Will make me sleep again: and then in dreaming,
> The clouds methought would open and show riches
> Ready to drop upon me; that when I waked
> I cry'd to dream again."

It has been noted that "Shakespeare has drawn off
from Caliban the elements of whatever is ethereal and refined to compound them in Ariel, thus finely contrasting

the gross and the delicate;" and what a creature he is! "Hag-seed," says Prospero, —

> "Which any print of goodness would not take,
> Being capable of all ill." . . .

> "A thing most brutish, whose vile nature had
> That in 't which good natures could not abide
> To be with."

Critics have considered the character of Caliban one of Shakespeare's master-pieces. His deformity of body and mind is redeemed by the power and truth of the imagination displayed in his creation, and by that rare embodiment of the very essence of grossness without a particle of vulgarity. One of Shakespeare's German critics has observed that "Caliban is a poetical character, and always speaks in blank verse;" and it will be remembered that he first appears in the play with this rhythmical malediction on his lips: —

> "As wicked dew as e'er my mother brushed
> With raven's feather from unwholesome fen,
> Drop on you both! A south-west blow on ye,
> And blister you all o'er."

"In contrast with Trinculo and Stephano, the vulgar drunken sailors, with their coarse sea-wit, the figure of Caliban," says Hazlitt, "acquires a classical dignity."

"What have we here?" says Trinculo (Shakespeare's admirable prototype of the "dime showman") "A man, or a fish? Dead, or alive? A fish: a strange fish. Were I but in England now (as once I was), and had but this fish painted, not a holiday fool there but would give a piece of silver: any strange beast there makes a man: when they will not give a doit to relieve a lame beggar, they will lay out ten to see a dead Indian."

Who but Shakespeare could have given us Puck, — funny little Puck? The Ariel of the "Midsummer Night's

Dream," he has been called; yet in the main, how unlike is he to the "sprite of Prospero"! Ariel is tender and human, and touched with pity for those upon whom he brings ill. Puck is a wanton Troll, innately delighting in mischief, and heartily enjoying the discomfiture of his victims. "Lord," he exclaims, "what fools these mortals be!"

> "He bootless makes the breathless housewife churn."

> "Misleads night-wanderers, laughing at their harm."

> "The wisest aunt, telling the saddest tale [he boasts],
>   Sometimes for three-foot stool mistaketh me;
>   Then slip I from her, and down topples she."

When he has culled for Oberon the little western flower, "purple with love's wound," and the Fairy King having squeezed upon the sleepy lids of perverse Titania its charmed juice, she is constrained by that potent liquid to dote insanely on ass-headed Bottom, whose "angelic braying wakes her from her flowery bed," with what infinite relish Puck brings the scandal to Oberon! We seem to hear an ethereal chuckle as he declares, —

> "When in that moment (so it came to pass),
>   Titania wak'd and straitway loved an ass!"

And Titania and her train, how exquisite are they, floating like very flower-petals in the summer moonlight! Daintily they sprite it —

> "Over hill, over dale,
>   Thorough bush, thorough brier,
>   Over park, over pale,
>   Thorough flood, thorough fire."

When the Fairy Queen couches upon that bank "where the wild thyme blows," how softly the attendant fairies sing her to sleep! Hear the chorus of their song, steeped

in the juice of poppies, and rhythmical as the rain on
the roof : —

> " Philomel, with melody,
>   Sing in our sweet lullaby ;
> Lulla, lulla, lullaby ; lulla, lulla, lullaby ;
>   Never harm, nor spell, nor charm,
>   Come our lovely lady nigh ;
>   So, good-night, with lullaby."

The devotion of dainty Titania to the donkey of her
heart is conceived in that fine vein of philosophical insight
which often runs like a thread of gold through the gayest
web from the loom of Shakespeare's fancy, and her fairy-
like devices for purging away the mortal grossness of
Bottom are true to the life. Who has not seen similar and
equally futile attempts made by misplaced mortal love,
striving to idealize its indifferent object ?

In fine contrast to Shakespeare's fairies are the Weird
Sisters in " Macbeth," —

> " So withered and so wild in their attire ;
>   That look not like the inhabitants o' the earth,
>   And yet are on 't. . . .
>   Each at once her choppy fingers laying
>   Upon her skinny lips."

" The hags of Shakespeare," says Hazlitt, " are foul anom-
alies, of whom we know not whence they are sprung, nor
whether they have beginning or ending. As they are without
human passions, so they are without human relations. They
come with thunder and lightning, and vanish to airy music.
This is all we know of them. Except Hecate, they have no
names, which heightens their mysteriousness. The names and
some of the properties which Middleton has given to his witches
excite smiles.

" The Weird Sisters are serious things. Their presence cannot co-exist with mirth."

Hear their diabolical croon, —

> " Fair is foul, and foul is fair,
> Hover through the fog and filthy air ! "

Blood-curdling indeed is the simmer of that "double trouble," steaming in their charmed caldron. One look into it is a sup of horror.

> " Toad that under coldest stone
>   Days and nights hast thirty-one !
>   Sweltered venom sleeping got,
>   Boil thou first i' the charmèd pot !
>   Double, double toil and trouble ;
>   Fire, burn ; and cauldron, bubble.

> " Fillet of a fenny snake,
>   In the cauldron boil and bake :
>   Eye of newt, and toe of frog,
>   Wool of bat, and tongue of dog,
>   Adder's fork, and blind worm's sting,
>   Lizard's leg, and owlet's wing
>   For a charm of powerful trouble ;
>   Like a hell-broth boil and bubble.
>   Double, double toil and trouble ;
>   Fire, burn ; and cauldron, bubble.
>   .   .   .   .

> " Nose of Turk, and Tartar's lips ;
>   Finger of birth-strangled babe
>   Make the gruel thick and slab.
>   .   .   .   .

>   Cool it with a baboon's blood,
>   Then the charm is firm and good."

And with what malignant relish the vengeful hag, gossiping with her sister-witch, gloats over her punishment of that frugal sailor's wife who —

> " . . . had chestnuts in her lap
> And mounched, and mounched, and mounched,"

and gave her none! With a cold shiver, one fancies the doomed " master o' the Tiger " crushed " like a rat without a tail," in the hard hand of her vengeance!

When our staid Puritans had their one freak of fancy, — witch-making, — they must here have caught their inspiration. And indeed Banquo's affirmation in respect to the component parts of these chimeras —

> "The earth hath bubbles as the water hath,
> And these are of them " —

would seem to suggest the direct descent of our New England witches from the Weird Sisters of Shakespeare.

In the reign of sober reality who can " hold a candle " to this great dramatist? Compare the best-drawn characters of his brother artists — Jonson, Beaumont and Fletcher, Marlowe, and others — with his passion-tossed Othello, his philosophical, refined Hamlet, his sinning and repenting Macbeth, his pitiable, white-haired Lear, or his greedy, hating Shylock, his " cold-blooded, bottled spider," Richard III., and that subtle, detested villain, Iago; and you will see that even when they are at their best, he is a thousand times better than any of them.

The comedies of these dramatists smack of the " hempen homespuns " to whose level they were written. Shakespeare's, though they sometimes stoop, are pitched in another key, and all ablaze with genuine Attic wit. By some divine instinct he sounded all the mysterious depths of our nature, and like a cunning musician played upon every string of that complex instrument, — the human heart.

Every woman should plant her sprig of rosemary on the grave of Shakespeare; for of all dramatists he has most commended our sex by his lofty ideals of womanhood. His are the truest and yet the noblest of women, — not rose-scented specimens of diluted sentimentality, nor

yet strong-minded Amazons, but women all instinct with
the real beauty of perfect womanhood, — "the sense of
weakness leaning on the strength of affection for support."
Their tenderness is rich as golden mines, and unalloyed
by affectation or disguise. Their purity is like the snow
on sky-kissed mountain peaks; their constancy firm as
the everlasting hills. Their piety is native as the air they
breathe, and without cant or hypocrisy. Timid and delicate by nature, they are, by the might of affection, sometimes sublimed and transfigured into martyrs and saints.
They are beautiful as painter's ideals and graceful as
sculptor's dreams; yet we often forget their outward
charms in the diviner beauty of their souls, and thus —

> " . . . With flowers, with angel offices,
> Like creatures native unto gracious act,
> And in their own clear element, they move."

" By quoting passages from Shakespeare's second-rate
plays alone, we might," says Hazlitt, " make a volume
rich with his praise as is the oozy bottom of the sea with
sunken wrack and sunless treasures." Of this sort is
King Henry's address to the soldiers at the siege of
Harfleur, and that of Cassius to Brutus, instigating him
to join in the conspiracy against Cæsar, and Mark
Antony's address to the throng of citizens in the Forum,
over Cæsar's corpse.

If space but allowed, page after page might be taken
from his drama to prove that in moral sentiment Shakespeare far foreran his age, as in this divine conception
of mercy : —

> " The quality of mercy is not strained;
> It droppeth as the gentle rain from heaven
> Upon the place beneath : It is twice bless'd;
> It blesseth him that gives, and him that takes :

'T is mightiest in the mightiest; it becomes
The throned monarch better than his crown;
His sceptre shows the force of temporal power,
The attribute to awe and majesty,
Wherein doth sit the dread and fear of kings:
But mercy is above this sceptred sway,
It is enthroned in the heart of kings,
It is an attribute to God himself;
And earthly power doth then show likest God's
When mercy seasons justice."

That Shakespeare is great poet as well as great drama-tist, we realize as we read this exquisite passage from the " Merchant of Venice " : —

"... In such a night as this,
When the sweet wind did gently kiss the trees,
And they did make no noise; in such a night,
Troilus, methinks, mounted the Trojan walls,
And sighed his soul toward the Grecian tents,
Where Cressid lay that night.
                    In such a night
Stood Dido with a willow in her hand
Upon the wild sea-banks, and waved her love
To come again to Carthage.
                    In such a night
Medea gathered the enchanted herbs
That did renew old Æson.
How sweet the moonlight sleeps upon this bank!
Here will we sit, and let the sounds of music
Creep in our ears; soft stillness, and the night,
Become the touches of sweet harmony.
Sit, Jessica! Look how the floor of heaven
Is thick inlaid with patines of bright gold;
There's not the smallest orb which thou behold'st,
But in his motion like an angel sings,
Still quiring to the young-eyed cherubim;
Such harmony is in immortal souls;
But, whilst this muddy vesture of decay
Doth grossly close it in, we cannot hear it."

What poet has ever put more beauty into three or four short lines than we find here : —

> ". . . Daffodils,
> That come before the swallow dares, and take
> The winds of March with beauty ; violets dim,
> But sweeter than the lids of Juno's eyes,
> Or Cytherea's breath."

" Nature," it is affirmed, " is not drained, and is yet potent for marvels ; " yet who may dare hope for another Shakespeare? As we hang entranced upon the music of England's singing-birds, — the richest, fullest choir in any land the sun shines upon, — we may hear, with ever-new delight, Milton, her silver-throated lark, fluting unabashed at celestial altitude, and showering all her pearl-sown meadows with the gracious rain of his song ; but nearer and dearer is the lay of Shakespeare, — her winsome robin, a-tilt among rosy orchard blooms, and warbling in the gay sunshine his " wood-notes wild."   Soothed by " a sober certainty of waking bliss," we listen gratefully to his ever-varying song, full, rich, and tender, yet clear and familiar as the drone of the cricket beside our hearth. Milton niched in cathedral walls, amid gorgeous gloom and divine minster strains, is enshrined for all time. But Shakespeare we set among our Penates ; his shrine is in our hearts and homes. We find him " a creature not too bright and good for human nature's daily food," but fit —

> " For every day's most quiet use
> By sun and candle-light."

He is our story-teller, our jester, our preacher, our doctor (homœopathic too, for has he not said to us, through the great Thane of Cawdor, —

> " Throw physic to the dogs; I 'll none of it "),

our teacher, our poet, our brother, and our friend, — our Shakespeare! Age cannot wither nor custom stale his infinite variety. "Let men then acknowledge his great office; let civilization know and not forget its authors and ornaments."

CHAPTER IX.

POETRY OF THE COMMONWEALTH AND THE RESTORATION.

" DURING the forty years comprehended in the period of the Commonwealth and the reigns of Charles II. and James II., there was less change in the taste and literature of the nation than might have been anticipated, considering the mighty events which had agitated the country, and must have deeply influenced the national feelings, — such as the abolition of the ancient monarchy of England and the establishment of the Commonwealth. Authors were still a select class, and literature, the delight of the learned, had not yet become food for the multitude.

" The spirit of chivalry, even before the death of Elizabeth, had begun to yield to more practical and sober views of life; and the long period of peace under James nourished the spirit of inquiry now rapidly spreading among the people, fostering the reasoning faculties and mechanical powers rather than the imagination."

During the reign of Charles I. — a prince of taste and accomplishments — the style of the Elizabethan era was partially revived, though its lustre extended but little beyond the court and the nobility. During the Civil War and the Protectorate, poetry and the drama were buried under the strife and anxiety of contending factions. Cromwell, whose boast was that he would " make the name of an Englishman as great as ever that of a Roman had been," — a wish which, in England's splendid naval victories and unquestioned foreign supremacy, seemed almost realized, — had neither time nor inclination to patronize poetry. If, as Carlyle affirms, " he that *works* and *does* some *poem*, not he that *says* one, is worthy the name of poet," Cromwell was himself a poet, and shaped the grandest epic of all time.

The severity and exclusiveness of Puritanism, that unwisely sought to put down all works of imagination in England, the lovers of art must forever deplore; yet it cannot be denied that this was but a natural and necessary revolt against the luxury and immorality of the age. "These men," as Carlyle expresses it, "knew in every fibre, and with heroic daring laid to heart, that it is good to fight on God's side and bad to fight on the Devil's side." No wonder, then, that to them the drama was anathema maranatha, and playwrights but panderers to the national appetite for abominations; for with all our admiration for the dramatic genius that has immortalized the Elizabethan age, we must admit that the builders of the old English drama, — Shakespeare excluded, — though in their loftier flights they soared like " Jove's proud bird," wide-eyed and unabashed, to salute the sun, did not scruple to become mere barn-yard fowl, lowering to the level of the pit and catering to the ignoble taste of the gross and the depraved, thus debasing their finest plays by passages which good morals must forever ignore. An age that delighted in bear-baiting and bull-fighting as polite recreation cannot altogether be judged by our own standard of decorum; yet when we read that Shirley's " Gamester " — the plot of which was taken from a corrupt Italian novel and given to the author by King Charles himself — was acted at court, and that the king said it was " the best play he had seen for seven years " (a play of which Macaulay has said, " It is difficult to say whether it indicates a lower standard of courtesy and purity in the poet or in the audience who endured it "), we must allow that when gentles and commons had alike become thus vitiated, Puritanism, though far from Attic in its savor, was undoubtedly the only salt that could save already-tainted England from utter social corruption.

Yet this public degeneracy had not infected the whole atmosphere of genius, since to this period belongs one of the proudest triumphs of English poetry. In the reign of Charles II., — a king who, though by birth and education better fitted than Cromwell for a patron of the arts, was rendered by a perverted taste and an indolent, sensual disposition as injurious to art and literature as to the public morals, — in this reign, which has been termed "the age of servitude without loyalty, and sensuality without love, of dwarfish talents and gigantic vices, the paradise of cold hearts and narrow minds, the golden age of the coward, the bigot, and the slave," Milton produced his divine epic; thus proving that "Virtue could see to do what Virtue would, by her own radiant light," and that "Infinite Goodness has never for a long time left a nation without some good and great mind to guide and illuminate the onward course of humanity."

In the times of Charles I. and of the Commonwealth our modern English poetry first evinced a disposition to imitate the French poetry, the distinguishing characteristic of which (and indeed of French art generally) is "the art of making art itself seem nature." The French school of poetry is characterized by a decided preference for what is brilliant rather than what is true and deep, and while it does not altogether eschew conceits and false thoughts, is still in subordination to the principles and laws of good writing, and always reduces conceit to fair rhetorical shape. Waller, Carew, Lovelace, and Suckling, who all began to write about this time, first exemplified in our lighter poetry, by the French neatness in the dressing of the thought, what may be done by correct and natural expression and smoothness of flow, without high imagination or depth of thought. Waller, of the four, was first in the field, but he did not rise to his greatest celebrity till after the Restoration. Carew, Lovelace, and Suckling all belong exclusively to the reign of Charles I. and of the Commonwealth.

Carew was a courtier, and loose and reckless in life. The Celia whom he celebrates in his verse is said to have repaid his flatteries by falsehood ; and thus disappointed, he plunged madly into pleasure, and thereby hastened his end. Before his death he is said to have bitterly and sincerely repented the license of his past life. At the time he wrote, the passionate and imaginative verse of the Elizabethan period was not wholly exhausted, and it has been observed that the genial and warm tints that still colored the landscape were in some measure reflected back by Carew. His short pieces and songs, now the only productions of his that are read, are graceful in sentiment and style, and were, in his day, exceedingly popular.

Lovelace, " whose fate and history would form the groundwork for a romance," wrote a volume of poems dedicated to Lucy Sacheverel, to whom he was betrothed. Her poetical appellation, according to the affected taste of the day, was Lucasta. When the civil wars broke out, Lovelace devoted his life and fortunes to the service of his king, and on joining the army, he wrote to his Lucy this beautiful song, which has been so often quoted, and has more true feeling and correct sentiment than any piece of his time : —

> "Tell me not, sweet, I am unkind,
>   That from the nunnery
> Of thy chaste breast and quiet mind,
>   To war and arms I fly.

" True, a new mistress now I chase,
   The first foe in the field ;
 And with a stronger faith embrace
   A sword, a horse, a shield.

" Yet this inconstancy is such
   As you, too, shall adore ;
 I could not love thee, dear, so much,
   Lov'd I not honour more."

Commanding a regiment at the siege of Dunkirk, Lovelace was severely, and it was supposed mortally, wounded. False tidings of his death were brought to England, and he returned to find his idolized Lucy married to another, — a blow from which he never recovered. He became utterly reckless, wandering about London in obscurity and poverty ; and the accomplished Lovelace, fearlessly brave, handsome in person, a polished high-born courtier and an elegant scholar, in his thirty-seventh year died miserably in an obscure lodging in Shoe Lane. " Lucy Sacheverel," says Mrs. Jameson, " was of noble blood ; but her lover has bequeathed her to posterity forever as faithless and heartless, light as air, false as water, and rash as fire." Lovelace's best poem is addressed " To Althea from Prison."

Sir John Suckling, who, as has been aptly said, " moved gayly and thoughtlessly through his short life, as through a dance or a merry game, died in 1641, at the age of thirty-two. He is the author of a small collection of poems, as well as of four plays. His poetry, though he is classed with the adherents of the French school of propriety and precision, is characterized by a more impulsive air and more impetuosity of manner than that of Waller, Lovelace, or Carew ; he has, moreover, a sprightliness and buoyancy which is all his own.   His famous ballad of " The Wedding " is quoted by critics

as the very perfection of gayety and archness in verse.
This one familiar stanza has in its way never been excelled : —

> " Her feet beneath her petticoat
>   Like little mice stole in and out,
>   As if they feared the light ;
>   But oh ! she dances such a way
>   No sun upon an Easter-day
>   Is half so fine a sight ! "

In Brand's " Popular Antiquities " this verse is quoted
in illustration of the popular notion in former times that
the sun danced on Easter-day, — a superstition still held
by many of the Irish peasantry.

Inferior to Suckling in natural feeling, yet excelling him
in correctness and in general powers of versification, is
Edmund Waller, born in 1605. His mother was a sister
to the celebrated John Hampden, but is said to have been
so violent a Royalist that Cromwell made her a prisoner to
her own daughter in her own house. Her son, the poet,
who was witty and accomplished, but cold and selfish, and
destitute of high principle and deep feeling, was either a
Roundhead or a Royalist as the time served. At twenty-
five a widower, gay and wealthy, he became a suitor to Lady
Dorothea Sidney, eldest daughter of the Earl of Leicester,
who, unmoved by all the poetry in which the heartless
wit celebrates her under the name of Sacharissa, gave her
hand to the Count of Sunderland. It is said that Waller,
meeting her long afterward when she was far advanced
in years, the lady asked him playfully when he would
again write such verses upon her. " When you are as
young, Madam, and as handsome as you were then," was
his heartless reply.

Waller's political course was throughout mean and ab-
ject ; while a member of Parliament under Cromwell, he

11

plotted the return of Charles, for which he was tried, imprisoned a year, and heavily fined. He celebrates Cromwell in one of his most vigorous odes, and no sooner is the king restored to the throne, than he is ready with a congratulatory address.

Charles, who admitted the poet to terms of courtly intimacy, remarked to Waller the inferiority of the royal offering to the panegyric on Cromwell; as ever, witty and self-possessed, he replied, " Poets, Sire, succeed better in fiction than in truth." Waller's wit and sagacity made him the delight of the House of Commons. He served in all the parliaments of Charles's reign ; and at the accession of James II., in 1685, we find him re-elected at the venerable age of eighty. He died on the 21st of October, 1687. Waller in early manhood devoted his muse to the world of fashion and taste, and he wrote in the same strain till he was upward of fourscore. He was styled by his cotemporaries the " maker and model of melodious verse." Pope and Dryden — poets who had not sufficiently studied the excellent models of versification furnished by the old poets and their rich poetical diction — have both confirmed this eulogium. More discerning critics have allowed him sportive sparkling wit, elegance of fancy and style, and easiness of versification, which, in *our* interpretation of the divine meaning of *poet,* but poorly atone for lack of genuine feeling and the royal power of interpreting Nature to man.

Carew and Waller represent the popular court poets of their school, whose aspirations seem to have been bounded by the narrow circle in which they revolved. " Satisfied," says a discerning critic, " with the empty applause of a court, they asked not to live in future generations, or to sound the depths of the human heart. A panegyric on a fine lady was the loftiest theme of their ambition. The

heart appears to have had nothing to do with the poetical homage offered and accepted."

This poem to Celia — Carew's best — is an example of
this style of poetry : —

> "Ask me no more where Jove bestows
> When June is past, the fading rose;
> For in your beauties, orient deep,
> These flowers, as in their causes, sleep.
>
> "Ask me no more whither do stray
> The golden atoms of the day;
> For in pure love heaven did prepare
> Those powders to enrich your hair.
>
> "Ask me no more whither doth haste
> The nightingale when May is past;
> For in your sweet dividing throat
> She winters, and keeps warm her note.
>
> "Ask me no more if east or west
> The Phenix builds her spicy nest,
> For unto you at last she flies
> And in your fragrant bosom dies ! "

Equally elegant and extravagant is this from Waller, on
" A Girdle : " —

> "That which her slender waist confined
> Shall now my joyful temples bind;
> It was my heaven's extremest sphere,
> The pale which held that lovely deer;
> My joy, my grief, my hope, my love,
> Did all within this circle move !
> A narrow compass ! and yet there
> Dwelt all that 's good, and all that 's fair.
> Give me but what this ribbon bound,
> Take all the rest the sun goes round."

These pretty poetical poesies, dedicated to the Delias
and Celias, the divine Sacharissas and fair Amorets, who,
with their rosy cheeks and coral lips, are as insipid as

waxen dolls, inspire us with but little admiration. It charms us not that like the lovers of gorgeous Eastern climes, these poets talk in flowers, since their nosegays are not pure and fresh, with morning dew upon their fair blossoms, but rather, stale, artificial wired bouquets, whose roses sicken, whose violets faint, and whose lilies, though regal and heavy with odor, are bereft of their snow.

A single short lyric of Robert Burns, beginning thus, —

> " Of a' the airts the wind can blow
>   I dearly like the west,
>   For there the bonnie lassie lives
>   The lass that I lo'e best," —

contains more true sentiment and fresh, natural feeling than may be found in the whole range of the poetry of this school.

Though Waller's poems are chiefly short and incidental, he wrote a poem on " Divine Love," in six cantos. In this higher walk of the muse he seems to have failed. His panegyric to Cromwell has been pronounced " one of the most graceful pieces of adulation ever offered by poetry to power." It was an offering of gratitude for permission to return to England after his banishment, and was probably more sincere than most of his effusions.

This fine passage occurs in one of Waller's late poems ; we may hope that, so near the grave, he has at last bid farewell to feigning : —

> " The soul's dark cottage, battered and decayed,
>   Lets in new lights through chinks that time has made !
>   Stronger by weakness, wiser men become,
>   As they draw near to their eternal home.
>   Leaving the old, both worlds at once they view
>   That stand upon the threshold of the new."

Denham and Cleveland both belong to this period. Denham's " Cooper's Hill " is his principal poem, and the one on which his fame rests. Craik considers it the best classical poem produced down to his date. Denham's shorter pieces are spirited, especially some of his songs. He died in 1668, at the age of fifty-three. Every critic, from Dryden to our own time, has praised the four concluding lines in his address to the Thames from his "Cooper's Hill": —

> "O could I flow like thee, and make thy stream
> My great example, as it is my theme!
> Though deep, yet clear, though gentle, yet not dull,
> Strong without rage, without o'erflowing full."

John Cleveland, though the most neglected of all his cotemporaries, was the most popular verse-writer of his day, and for twenty years, was, it is said, held to be the greatest among living English poets (!).

Cleveland's poems have vivacity and sprightliness, and it has been remarked that they seem to have been thrown off in haste, and never to have been afterward corrected or revised.

Cleveland was a Cavalier poet, and by his satire and invective — sometimes more furious than forcible — is allowed to have done the heartiest and stoutest service to the cause. He was the first writer who came forth as champion of the royal cause in English verse; to that cause he adhered till its ruin. At last, in 1655, after having led for some years a fugitive life, he was caught and thrown into prison. Cromwell on his petition allowed him to go at large. He did not long survive his release, but died in April, 1658, a few months before the Protector whose hated dominion had been so fatal to his fortunes. As he is a poet but little quoted, this epitaph on Ben Jonson, which is a fine specimen of exaggerated praise, may be of interest. It is the most concise and the best of several tributes to the memory of the poet.

> " The Muses' fairest light, in no dark time ;
> The wonder of a learned age ; the line
> Which none can pass ; the most proportioned wit
> To nature ; the best judge of what was fit ;
> The deepest, plainest, highest, clearest pen ;
> The voice most echoed by consenting men ;
> The soul which answered best to all well said
> By others, and which most requital made ;
> Tuned to the highest key of ancient Rome,
> Returning all her music with his own ;
> In whom with Nature Study claimed a part,
> Yet who unto himself owed all his art ;
> Here lies Ben Jonson ; every age will look
> With sorrow here, with wonder on his book."

To this period belongs Samuel Butler, the author of " Hudibras," born in 1612. His father was but an English yeoman of limited circumstances ; yet the poet, who is said to have embraced with great eagerness every opportunity of intellectual improvement, has given us a satire that for felicitous versification and sustained, intense wit has never been excelled in our literature.

Great obscurity rests on all parts of Butler's life, at different periods of which he seems to have been clerk, amanuensis, and tutor. At the Restoration he was made steward of Ludlow Castle ; and in 1663 appeared the first part of " Hudibras." A second part appeared in 1664, and a third fourteen years later. The latter part of his life is said to have been spent in struggling circumstances in London ; and though the poet and his work were the praise of all ranks, from royalty downward, he was himself little benefited by it ; and when the king at last ordered him a present of three thousand pounds, it was insufficient to discharge the debts pressing upon him at the time. He died in 1680, in a mean street near Covent Garden, and was buried at the expense of a friend.

" Hudibras " is a Cavalier burlesque of the ideas and

manners of the English Puritans. The original idea of
the poem is to be found in Cervantes's " History of Don
Quixote," — " a book," observes Dr. Johnson, " to which
a mind of the greatest powers may be indebted without
disgrace." Hudibras is a Presbyterian justice who ranges
the country to suppress superstition and correct abuses,
accompanied by an Independent clerk, disputatious and
obstinate, with whom he debates, but never conquers him.

Butler has more wit than any writer in the English
language, in which " Hudibras" has been pronounced
the best satire. Butler's description of the religion of
Hudibras is a fair specimen of his satire : —

> " For his religion, it was fit
>   To match his learning and his wit.
>   'T was Presbyterian true-blue ;
>   For he was of that stubborn crew
>   Of errant saints, whom all men grant
>   To be the true church militant ;
>   Such as do build their faith upon
>   The holy text of pike and gun ;
>   Decide all controversy by
>   Infallible artillery ;
>   And prove their doctrine orthodox
>   By apostolic blows and knocks ;
>   Call fire, and sword, and desolation,
>   A godly thorough reformation,
>   Which always must be carried on,
>   And still be doing, never done
>   As if religion were intended
>   For nothing else but to be mended.
>   .   .   .   .
>   Compound for sins they are inclined to,
>   By damning those they have no mind to.
>   .   .   .   .
>   Rather than fail, they will defy
>   That which they love most tenderly ;
>   Quarrel with minced pies, and disparage
>   Their best and dearest friend, plum-porridge."

Andrew Marvell, who was born 1620, and died 1678, was associated with Milton in friendship and public service. He is best known as a prose-writer, and his poetical genius has not had its merited share of notice and praise. For elegance and gay extravagance, his " Coy Mistress " has never been excelled.

> " Had we but world enough, and time
> This coyness, lady, were no crime.
> We would sit down and think which way
> To walk and pass our love's long day.
> Thou by the Indian Ganges' side
> Should'st rubies find : I by the tide
> Of Humber would complain.   I would
> Love you ten years before the flood
> And you should, if you please, refuse
> Till the conversion of the Jews.
>
> " My vegetable love should grow
> Vaster than empires, and more slow.
> An hundred years should go
> To praise thine eyes, and on thy forehead gaze ;
> Two hundred to adore thy breast ;
> But thirty thousand to the rest :
> An age at least to every part ;
> And the last age should show your heart.
> For, lady, you deserve this state ;
> Nor would I love at lower rate."

The other minor and less distinguished poets of this date are Sedley, Roscommon, Dorset, Cotton, Davenant, and Philips, none of whom are now widely known or read, though they still appear in rank and file among the English poets.

Roscommon's highest praise is to have been celebrated by Pope as the only moral writer of verse in King Charles's reign.

Among the English poets of that school in which the

memory, the judgment, and the wit are more conspicuous than the imagination, Abraham Cowley, born in London in the year 1618, was one of the most popular of his time.

Cowley was the son of a respectable grocer; his mother's exertions procured him a liberal education. When Oxford was surrendered to Parliament, he followed the Queen-Mother to France, where he remained twelve years, and was employed in such correspondence as the royal cause required, and particularly in ciphering and deciphering the letters that passed between Charles and his queen, — an employment of the highest confidence and honor, that for several years is said to have filled all his days, and two or three nights in each week.

At the Restoration, Cowley expected some royal appointment as the reward of his loyalty; but his claims were overlooked. In some of his youthful writings he had not sufficiently bowed down before the golden image of monarchy; and this was now recalled at court to his disadvantage, and his hopes ended in disappointment. He had passed his fortieth year when he gladly retired from the world, and with a royal provision of three hundred pounds per annum, settled at Chertsey, on the banks of the Thames, where his house still remains.

Here, renewing his acquaintance with the beloved poets of antiquity, he commemorated in verse the charms of a country life and composed his fine prose discourses. The happiness he sought in this retirement seems to have eluded his grasp. Dr. Johnson, who would, it is said, have preferred Fleet Street to all the charms of Arcadia and the Golden Age, dwells with grim satisfaction upon Cowley's falling out with retirement, and holds him up as an awful warning to all who may dare pant for solitude.

He died on the 28th of July, 1667, about seven years after his retirement from court and the world. He was interred with great pomp in Westminster Abbey, and " the King himself," observes Sprat, " was pleased to bestow on him the best epitaph when he declared that Mr. Cowley had not left ' a better man behind him.' "

Cowley is said to have lisped in numbers ; in his tenth year he wrote the " Tragical History of Pyramus and Thisbe," published in his " Poetic Blossoms." He wrote the four books of his unfinished poem, entitled " Davideis," — a heroical poem of the troubles of David, — while a student at Trinity College. His " Miscellanies," his " Mistress, or, Love Verses," and his " Pindaric Odes," complete the list of his poetical compositions.

Cowley's " Mistress," though in imitation of Petrarch, is without passion or real tenderness, and was conceived in this wise : " Poets," he says, " are scarce thought freemen of their company, without paying some duties, and obliging themselves to be true to love." Whereupon he obligingly sets himself to the wooing of an imaginary mistress, and amiably counterfeits that passion of whose power he must have been shockingly ignorant, as it is positively asserted that he was never in love but once, and then never found courage to declare himself !

Cowley's wit, accomplishments, and amiability rendered him exceedingly popular. He has great sense, ingenuity, and learning ; but as a poet his fancy is far-fetched and mechanical. He was, in his own time, considered as of unrivalled excellence ; and some of his cotemporaries have even gone so far as to prophesy that posterity would hold him to have been equalled by Virgil alone among the poets of antiquity.

His " Pindaric Odes," though deformed by conceits, contain some noble lines.

His "Anacreons," which are thought to be the happiest of his poems, abound in images of natural and poetic beauty; this, entitled " Drinking," is worthy of Bacchus himself: —

> "The thirsty earth soaks up the rain,
>   And drinks, and gapes for drink again.
>   The plants suck in the earth, and are
>   With constant drinking fresh and fair.
>   The sea itself, which one would think
>   Should have but little need of drink,
>   Drinks ten thousand rivers up,
>   So filled that they o'erflow the cup.
>   The busy sun (and one would guess
>   By 's drunken fiery face no less)
>   Drinks up the sea, and when he has done,
>   The moon and stars drink up the sun.
>   They drink and dance by their own light;
>   They drink and revel all the night.
>   Nothing in Nature 's sober found,
>   But an eternal health goes round.
>   Fill up the bowl, then, fill it high,
>   Fill all the glasses there, for why
>   Should every creature drink but I,
>   Why, men of morals, tell me why ? "

John Dryden, one of the great masters of English verse, and who may be regarded as founder of the school of critical poets, was born in August, 1631. His father was a strict Puritan, of an ancient family, long established in Northamptonshire. Dryden was the eldest of fourteen children, and received a good education, first at Westminster, and afterward at Trinity College, Cambridge.

The first poetical production of Dryden was a set of heroic stanzas on the death of Cromwell. When Charles was restored, he had done with the Puritans, and wrote poetical addresses to the King and Lord Chancellor.

In 1663 he married the Lady Elizabeth Howard, daughter of the Earl of Berkshire. This match added neither

to his wealth nor his happiness ; and when his wife wished
to be a book that she might enjoy more of his company,
Dryden is said to have replied, " Be an almanac, my dear,
that I may change you once a year."

In 1667 he published a long poem, " Annus Mirabilis,"
being an account of the events of the year 1666. The
amusements of the drama revived after the Restoration ;
and Dryden became a candidate for theatrical laurels.

Charles II. returned from his long exile in France with
the political maxims and social habits of his favorite people ; and it was to please this ignoble monarch, of whom
it has been said that "politeness was his solitary good
quality," that a mortal blow was first dealt to the English
drama by introducing into it rhyming plays. Charles
having adopted the French taste in composition, the good
old dramas of Elizabeth and James were banished from
the stage for the degenerate, fashionable rhyming plays
of France, in which conjugal fidelity and sincerity were
held up for constant ridicule ; till the corruptions of the
stage became so notorious that " a grave lawyer," it is
said, " would have debased his dignity, and a young trader
would have impaired his credit, by appearing in those
mansions of dissolute licentiousness that were the proper
element for a depraved king and a corrupt court."

Dryden unhappily became a panderer to this vitiated
taste, and was the most eminent among the crowd of
authors who courted notoriety and won royal patronage,
by adopting the bombast and meanness of the new style.
Thus while Milton, in blindness and poverty, kept his
pure and lofty muse unspotted from the world, the offspring of Dryden's genius " passed through the fire to
Moloch ; " and to his everlasting shame, he produced those
comedies which, as Macaulay aptly says, " introduce us
into a world where there is no humanity, no veracity, no

sense of shame, — a world for which any good-natured man would gladly exchange the society of Milton's devils; and the tragedies that introduce us to people whose proceedings we can trace to no motives; of whose feelings we can form no more idea than of a sixth sense."

Of Dryden's plays, nearly thirty in number, few have much merit considered as entire works, although there are brilliant scenes and spirited passages in most of them. He was an incomparable reasoner in verse, and the discussions between his heroes are considered by critics his best scenes.   He undertook to write for the king's players no less than three plays a year, for which he was to receive three hundred pounds per annum.   He was afterward made poet laureate and royal historiographer with a salary of two hundred pounds.

In Dryden's plays, debased though they may be, there may be found occasional true sentiment, and now and then a fine simile relieves the huge mass of turgid dramatic verse.   A few of these I subjoin: —

> Love is that madness which all lovers have;
> But yet 't is sweet and pleasing so to rave.
> 'T is an enchantment, where the reason 's bound,
> But Paradise is in the enchanted ground.
>
> *Conquest of Granada.*

> Man is but man; unconstant still, and various;
> There 's no to-morrow in him like to-day.
> Perhaps the atoms rolling in his brain
> Make him think honestly this present hour;
> The next, a swarm of base ungrateful thoughts
> May mount aloft; and where 's our Egypt then?
> Who would trust chance?   Since all men have the seeds
> Of good and ill, which should work upward first.
>
> *Cleomenes.*

> Courage uncertain dangers may abate,
> But who can bear the approach of certain fate?
>
> *Tyrannic Love.*

Men are but children of a larger growth.

All for Love.

That friendship which from withered love doth shoot,
Like the faint herbage on a rock, wants root.
Love is a tender amity, refined:
Grafted on friendship, it exalts the mind;
But when the graff no longer does remain,
The dull stock lives, but never bears again.

Conquest of Granada.

Wordsworth found one of Dryden's highly celebrated dramatic "gems" (a description of Nature, in the "Indian Emperor") "vague, bombastic, and senseless." Its charm undoubtedly consisted in its melody.

In 1681 Dryden published his "Absalom and Achitophel," — a bold political satire, allowed to be the "most vigorous and elastic, the most highly varied and beautiful, which the English language can boast." Its popularity placed the author above all his poetical cotemporaries. It was followed by two other equally vigorous satires, — "The Medal" and "Mac Flecknoe." In his satires Dryden drew from the life, and produced matchless portraits. After the accession of James, the poet declared himself a convert to popery. His change of creed, happening at a time when it suited his interests to become a Catholic, was looked upon with suspicion; but it has been proved that his conduct was not fairly open to the charge of unprincipled selfishness. He brought up his family and died in his new belief, the first published fruit of which was his allegorical poem of "The Hind and Panther." The Church of Rome is the Hind, the Church of England the Panther; the other sects are represented as bears, hares, boars, etc., and the Calvinist as a famished wolf —

"... His rough crest rears,
And pricks up his predestinating ears."

The revolution in 1668 deprived Dryden of the income derived from his office of laureate; and stimulated by the want of an independent income, he produced in the latter years of his life the noblest of his works. The "Ode to St. Cecilia" (supposed to be the inventress of the organ), commonly called "Alexander's Feast," was his next work, and is the loftiest and most imaginative of all his compositions. This immortal poem, though superseded in our recitation-books by poorer pieces, is the most superb example of splendid versification that our language affords. It is too long to be given entire; but a stanza or two may convey to those who do not familiarly know it an idea of its exquisite rhythmical flow: —

> " 'Twas at the royal feast, for Persia won
>   By Philip's warlike son:
>   Aloft in awful state
>   The godlike hero sate
>   On his imperial throne;
>   His valiant peers were placed around,
>   Their orows with roses and with myrtles bound:
>   (So should desert in arms be crowned).
>   The lovely Thaïs by his side
>   Sate like a blooming Eastern bride
>   In flower of youth and beauty's pride.
>   Happy, happy, happy pair!
>   None but the brave,
>   None but the brave,
>   None but the brave deserves the fair.
>   .   .   .   .
>   The mighty master smiled to see
>   That love was in the next degree:
>   'Twas but a kindred sound to move,
>   For pity melts the mind to love.
>   Softly sweet in Lydian measures,
>   Soon he soothed his soul to pleasures;
>   War, he sung, is toil and trouble;
>   Honour but an empty bubble;
>   Never ending, still beginning,

> Fighting still, and still destroying;
> If the world be worth thy winning,
> Think, O think it worth enjoying:
> Lovely Thaïs sits beside thee,
> Take the good the gods provide thee:
>
> . . . .
>
>   Thus long ago
> Ere heaving bellows learned to blow,
>   While organs yet were mute,
>   Timotheus to his breathing flute
> And sounding lyre,
> Could swell the soul to rage, or kindle soft desire.
>   At last divine Cecilia came,
>   Inventress of the vocal frame;
> The sweet enthusiast from her sacred store,
>   Enlarged the former narrow bounds
>   And added length to solemn sounds,
> With Nature's mother-wit, and arts unknown before.
>   Let old Timotheus yield the prize,
>   Or both divide the crown:
> He raised a mortal to the skies;
>   She drew an angel down."

In his sixty-eighth year Dryden published his " Fables," — imitations of Boccaccio and Chaucer, — affording the finest specimens of his happy versification. It has been happily observed that " they shed a glory on the last days of the poet, when his fancy, brighter and more prolific than ever, may be compared to a noble river, that expands in breadth, and fertilizes a wider tract of country ere it is finally engulfed in the ocean." He died on the 1st of May, 1700. His remains, after being embalmed, and lying in state twelve days, were interred with great pomp in Westminster Abbey.

Dryden's genius was debased by the false taste of the age; his moral nature — not of the higher type organically — was vitiated by the bad morals of a corrupt court, and he was innately deficient in the higher emotions of love and tenderness. Critics have allowed him invention, fancy, wit, no humor, immense strength of character, elegance, masterly ease, indignant contempt approaching to the sublime, no tenderness, but eloquent declamation and the perfection of uncorrupted English style and of sounding, vehement, varied versification. Pope thus praises his admirable versification : —

> " Waller was smooth ; but Dryden taught to join
> The varying verse, the full-resounding line,
> The long majestic march, and energy divine."

" Perhaps no nation," says Dr. Johnson, " ever produced a writer that enriched his language with such a variety of models ; to him we owe the improvement of our metre, the refinement of our language, and what was said of Rome adorned by Augustus may be applied to English poetry embellished by Dryden, — he found it brick and he left it marble."

Though habitually a careless writer, and constitutionally averse to labor, Dryden is said to have spent a fortnight in perfecting his masterpiece, the " Ode to St. Cecilia." Warton gives us this account of the occasion and manner of his writing it : —

" Lord Bolingbroke, happening to pay a visit to Dryden, found him in an unusual agitation of spirits, even to trembling. On inquiring the cause, ' I have been up all night,' replied the old bard ; ' my musical friends made me promise to write them an ode for their feast of St. Cecilia. I have been so struck with the subject which occurred to me that I could not leave it till I had completed it ; here it is, finished at one sitting.' And immediately he showed him the ode which places the British lyric poetry above that of any other nation."

In the drama Dryden was completely out of his element. With all his command of language, information,

12

and imagery, he had not art or judgment to construct an interesting or consistent drama, or to preserve himself from extravagance and absurdity. A pure and lofty ideal of womanhood seems to have been entirely beyond his reach. Of the softer passions he could form no conception. His love degenerates into licentiousness, his tenderness into rant and fustian ; and it has been observed that " like Voltaire, he probably never drew a tear from reader or spectator." The staple materials of his tragedy are the bowl and dagger, glory, ambition, lust, and crime. It has little truth of coloring, or natural passion ; its characters are for the most part personages in high life, of transcendent virtue, vice, or ambition. It is crowded with fierce passion, with splendid processions, with superhuman love and beauty, and with long dialogues alternately formed of metaphysical subtlety and the most extravagant and bombastic expression. His comedy exhibits a variety of constantly shifting scenes and adventures, complicated intrigues, and successful disguises ; is false to nature, improbable and ill-arranged, and equally offensive to taste and morality.

The merit of Dryden's drama consists in a wild Oriental magnificence of style, in the richness of his versification, and occasional gleams of true genius. " Don Sebastian " is considered his highest effort in dramatic composition. His " All for Love," founded on the story of Antony and Cleopatra, and avowedly written in imitation of Shakespeare, is the only play Dryden ever wrote for himself; "the rest," he says, " were given to the people." The scene between Antony and his general he is said to have preferred to anything which he had written of that kind. It is thought to contain passages that challenge comparison with Shakespeare. It will only be necessary to compare Dryden's conception of the noble Roman with that of Shakespeare to prove that he cannot even graze in his loftiest flights the heights where Avon's bard " sits thronèd and serene ! "

After Dryden the most eminent dramatic writers of this era are Otway, Lee, Crowne, and Shadwell. Lee is characterized by tenderness, fire, and imagination. Crowne in some of his productions is eminent for poetry, and in others for plot and character. Otway's dramas, though rugged and irregular in versification, far excel those of Dryden in propriety of style and character.

Otway was born at Trotting in Sussex, March 3, 1651. Educated at Oxford, he left college without taking his degree. He afterward appeared as an unsuccessful actor, then as a playwright, and subsequently as a military character in Flanders ; there he was cashiered for irregularities, and returning to England, resumed writing for the stage. His short and eventful life, checkered by want and extravagance, was closed prematurely in 1685. One of his biographers relates that he came to his death by too hastily swallowing, after a long fast, a piece of bread which charity had supplied. Whatever may have been the immediate cause of his death, he is known to have been at the time in circumstances of great poverty.

Otway excels in his delineation of the passions of the heart, the ardor of love, and the excess of misery and despair. His fame now rests upon his two tragedies, " The Orphan," and " Venice Preserved ; " but on these it has been aptly remarked that " it rests as on the Pillars of Hercules." The plot of the " Orphan," from its inherent indelicacy and painful associations, has driven this play from the stage ; but " Venice Preserved " is still deservedly popular.

Otway's power in scenes of passionate affection was thought by Walter Scott to rival and sometimes excel

Shakespeare's; and in his excessive praise of this dramatist he has said, "More tears have been shed, probably,
for the sorrows of Belvidera and Monimia than for those
of Juliet and Desdemona."   This passage from "Venice
Preserved" is a sample of Otway's tender pathos: —

    Jaf. O Belvidera! doubly I'm a beggar:
Undone by fortune, and in debt to thee.
Want, worldly want, that hungry meagre fiend,
Is at my heels, and chases me in view.
Canst thou bear cold and hunger?
    Bel. Oh! I will love thee, even in madness love thee!
Though my distracted senses should forsake me
I'd find some intervals when my poor heart
Should 'suage itself, and be let loose to thine:
Though the bare earth be all our resting-place,
Its roots our food, some cliff our habitation,
I'll make this arm a pillow for thine head;
And as thou sighing liest, and swelled with sorrow,
Creep to thy bosom, pour the balm of love
Into thy soul, and kiss thee to thy rest;
Then praise our God, and watch thee till the morning.
    Jaf. Hear this, you Heavens, and wonder how you made her!
Reign, reign, ye monarchs, that divide the world;
Busy rebellion ne'er will let you know
Tranquillity and happiness like mine;
Like gaudy ships, the obsequious billows fall,
And rise again, to lift you in your pride:
They wait but for a storm, and then devour you!
I, in my private bark already wrecked,
Like a poor merchant, driven to unknown land,
That had, by chance, packed up his choicest treasure
In one dear casket, and saved only that:
Since I must wander farther on the shore,
Thus hug my little, but my precious store,
Resolved to scorn and trust my fate no more.

CHAPTER X.

MILTON.

ABOVE all the poets of his age in genius and purity of life and purpose, and in the whole range of English poetry inferior only to Shakespeare in rank, was John Milton, born in London, Dec. 9, 1608. His father was of an ancient Roman Catholic family. Embracing the Protestant faith, he was disinherited, and as a means of support, followed the profession of a scrivener, and was also distinguished as a musical composer.

Milton has been called " a musical poet," and no doubt he inherited his father's harmonical genius. The poet was carefully educated at Christ's College, Cambridge, and was designed for the Church; but " denying the power arrogated by councils and bishops," he preferred, as he tells us, " a blameless life to servitude and forswearing."

In 1632 Milton took his degree of M. A. and retired from the university to his father's country-house, where he spent five years in studying classic literature. Leaving England in 1638, he travelled fifteen months in France and Italy. The Civil War hastened his return to his native land, where he nobly engaged against the prelates and Royalists, and wrote his pamphlets against the Established Episcopal Church, continuing through the whole period of those troublous times to devote his pen to the service of liberty and truth, defending the boldest measures of his party, even to the execution of the King. In these essays, some of which, that they might be read in foreign countries, are written in Latin, Milton displays his unbounded love of liberty and his strong inflexible principles, both in regard to religion and civil government. Macaulay has observed that "as compositions they deserve the attention of every man who wishes to become acquainted with the full power of the English language." The poet must have been about thirty when, having found it necessary to increase his income, he received into his house a few pupils, who appear to have been sons of his relatives and intimate friends, and "proceeded with cheerful alacrity in the noblest of all employments, that of training up immortal souls in wisdom and virtue." Milton taught Latin, Greek, French, Italian, the chief Oriental tongues, mathematics, and astronomy.

Dr. Johnson has been pleased to scoff at Milton as a school-master; but one of his scholars thus bears testimony to his capacity and fidelity as a teacher. "If his pupils," he says, "had received his documents with the same acuteness of wit and apprehension, the same industry and alacrity and thirst after knowledge as the instructor was endowed with, what prodigies of wit and learning might they have proved!"

In 1649 the poet was, without solicitation, appointed foreign or Latin secretary to the Council of State. For ten years his eyesight had been failing, owing to the wearisome studies and midnight watchings of his youth, and by the close of the year 1652 he was totally blind. By the Restoration Milton was deprived of his public employment. In 1643 he married his first wife, Mary Powell. Her voluntary desertion of her husband, his resolve to repudiate her, — which led to his treatises on divorce, — and their subsequent reconciliation are well known. Our satisfaction in the perfecting of "the

patience of the saints" alone reconciles us to the fact that
this woman embittered Milton's life more than fifteen
long years. Graciously released from her by death, he
married soon after his second and most beloved wife,
Katharine Woodcock, who died within a year after their
marriage. By his first marriage Milton had three
daughters. When the youngest was about fifteen, he
married his third wife, Elizabeth Minshul, a gentlewoman
" of twenty-four, without pretensions of any kind, who
willingly gave her life to cheer his blind and helpless
years;" yet to her tender reverence for his studious
habits, and the peace and comfort she shed over his
heart and home, it is said that we owe the " Paradise
Lost." Milton had attained his sixty-sixth year when, his
mind calm and tranquil to the last, though long suffering
acute physical pain, he passed gently from earth.

His funeral was " honored with a numerous and splendid
attendance," and he was buried next his father, in the
chancel of St. Giles at Cripplegate. There is supposed to
have been no memorial on his grave; his memory was,
however, honored with a tomb in Westminster Abbey in
1737, for which the English nation may take to itself no
credit, as it was erected at private expense.

Milton's poverty has been the darling theme of his
eulogists. Even Macaulay, in his inimitable essay on the
poet, cannot refrain from making capital of it. Thus he
writes: " When having experienced every calamity incident to our nature, old, poor, sightless, and disgraced, he
retired to his *hovel* to die." Milton's " hovel " appears to
have been a small but comfortable house, in one room of
which (" hung decently with rusty green ") the poet is described as sitting, not on a three-legged stool, but in a
commodious armchair, and dressed neatly in a suit of
sober black. There he had his beloved books and his

organ; there received his friends and sometimes " distinguished visitors," possessing apparently the comforts of life ; and philosopher as he was, we can imagine that he well might spare its luxuries.   Milton's worldly estate has been thus fairly estimated: His inheritance from his father was but small, and in the Civil War he lost a considerable sum which he had lent to Parliament.   As Latin secretary to the council he enjoyed, while without an associate in the office, the annual sum of nearly three hundred .pounds, — a sum which was lowered when Philip Meadows and Andrew Marvell were his associate secretaries.   He is said to have possessed an estate also, or rather, perhaps, an allowance, of about sixty pounds a year out of the estates which belonged to the plundered Abbey of Westminster.   As it was common during the usurpation to pension individuals out of the lands of deans, chapters, and ecclesiastics, this would seem probable.   Of these revenues, as well as of two thousand pounds which he had placed in the Excise Office, he was deprived at the Restoration.   He had before lost two thousand pounds, by intrusting the sum to a scrivener; and in the fire of London his house in Bread Street was burned.   All these losses he is said to have sustained " with unabated spirit ; " while the frugal management of what he retained, enabled him to live without distress, and even to gratify some of the benevolent impulses of his heart; for when the republican party triumphed, the family of his runaway wife — who were violent Royalists — found in their disgrace and destitution a refuge under his kindly roof, although they had bitterly wronged him by aiding and abetting her desertion of his home.   The three daughters of Mary Powell seem to have inherited the maternal perversity, as Milton complains of their undutifulness and unkindness ; and in the latter years of his life they had left his home.

It was the beautiful theory of Plato that "the soul frames her house in which she will be placed, fit for herself;" and the rare elegance of Milton, both in form and face, would seem to prove this speculation of the grand old Greek. A portrait of the poet at twenty-one is still extant. It has been observed that there could scarcely be a finer picture of pure, ingenuous English youth; "and in this beautiful and well-proportioned body," says quaint Aubrey, "there lodged a harmonical and ingenuous soul."

Milton's deepest fixed idea from his youth upward was that of the necessity of moral integrity to a life of truly great work or endeavor, — an idea which in one of his pamphlets he thus advances, —

"The art of Ovid and Horace I applauded, but the men I deplored; confirmed in this opinion, that he who would not be frustrate of his hope to write well hereafter in laudable things, ought himself to be a true poem; that is, a composition of the best and honorablest things, not presuming to sing high praises of heroic men or famous cities, unless he have in himself the experience of all that is praiseworthy."

With this fine ideal Milton's entire life harmonized. When a mere lad he was nicknamed "The Lady of the College," from his aversion to coarse mirth and riotous living. At that time he carried himself with such proud dignity and high resolve that mistaken tutors, unread in that lettering imprinted by God on the human soul, called him self-willed and obstinate, and as Johnson tells us, undertook to "whip it out of him!" As a graduate, he is still intent on study, and keeps a five years' classic holiday at his father's country-seat in Horton, wearing out, for the sweet sake of his beloved mistress, — Learning, — the bright young eyes that by and by shall no more behold —

"Day, or the sweet approach of even and morn."

Then follow eighteen months of foreign life, and while in Italy he borrows divine conceptions of artistic loveliness and grace to be moulded hereafter into shapes that " not marble shall outlive." At Rome he listens to Leonora Baroni's singing, and better hereafter conceives that accord of the —

> " Seven-fold chorus of hallelujahs
> And harping symphonies."

In the Eternal City the young Englishman receives the admiration of scholars, and is courted by poets and wits. The Civil War calls him home, and like a true patriot he says, " I considered it disgraceful that while my fellow-countrymen were fighting at home for liberty I should be travelling abroad at ease for intellectual purposes." Through all that stormy time we find him the devoted literary champion of infant Liberty in England, leaving in his arguments and appeals that rhythmical prose which is one of posterity's noble inheritances. Macaulay has termed it " a perfect field of cloth of gold, stiff with gorgeous embroidery." The last remains of his eyesight, which for ten years had been failing, were cheerfully sacrificed in the composition of his " Defensio Populi ; " and by the close of the year 1652 Milton was totally blind. The sage has told us that " there is a crack in everything that God has made," and doubtless Milton's character had its imperfections ; but of all our great poets he seems to have best lived according to the standard of the grand old bards, —

> " In the light of the day,
> In the face of the sun."

Though living sagely, soberly, and austerely, like the seers and anchorets of old, he lived cheerfully ; and there was, it is affirmed, no narrowness in his views of what it was lawful to read and study, or even to see and experience; and he thought himself quite at liberty to indulge in his love of art and music and to attend theatrical performances.

With respect to the extent of his information, it has been proved that the poet was without an equal in the whole university; and as he had by nature an intellect of the highest power, so even in youth he jealously asserted his supremacy, assuming that self-confident, almost proud demeanor for which he has been so severely censured, though it was essentially an element of his nature. Critics have accorded to Milton as a poet sublimity in the highest degree; beauty in an equal degree; pathos in a degree next to the highest; perfect character in the conception of Satan, Adam, and Eve; fancy, learning, vividness of description, stateliness, and decorum. His style is elaborate and powerful, and his versification, with occasional harshness and affectation, superior in harmony and variety to all other blank verse. Milton had abundant wit and power of sarcasm, but not much humor. His minor poetry has great beauty, sweetness, and elegance.

Milton's "Elegy on the Death of a Fair Infant Dying in Winter" was written in his eighteenth year. Masson has well said, "Probably in all England at that time could not be found a youth who could pen such verses as these" : —

> "O fairest flower, no sooner blown but blasted,
> *Soft silken primrose*, fading timelessly,
> Summer's chief honour, if thou hadst outlasted
> Bleak Winter's force that made thy blossom dry:
> For he, being amorous, on that lovely dye
> That did thy cheek envermeil, thought to kiss,
> But killed, alas! and then bewailed his fatal bliss."

While yet a student he composed his "Ode on the Nativity," which Hallam pronounces "perhaps the first in

the English language." Five new poems were composed
during his residence at his father's country-seat at Horton, where he retired to study classic literature. Here he
wrote his " Comus " and " Arcades," his " Allegro " and
" Penseroso," and his " Sonnet to the Nightingale." In
" L'Allegro " and " Il Penseroso," Milton has given us
two companion poems on two distinct conditions of mind ;
and the language contains no other twin compositions more
beautiful than these. In the " Allegro " the poet invokes
Mirth — Euphrosyne, the daughter of Zephyr and Aurora
— to bring us —

> " Quips and cranks and wanton wiles,
> Nods and becks, and wreathed smiles
> Such as hang on Hebe's cheek,
> And love to live in dimple sleek ;
> Sport that wrinkled Care derides,
> And Laughter holding both his sides."

As the " Penseroso " is conceived in contrast to the
" Allegro," Milton now invokes Melancholy, the daughter of Saturn and Vesta, —

> " Come, pensive nun, devout and pure,
> Sober, steadfast, and demure,
> All in a robe of darkest grain,
> Flowing with majestic train,
> And sable stole of Cyprus lawn
> Over thy decent shoulders drawn.
> Come, but keep thy wonted state,
> With even step and musing gait,
> And looks commercing with the skies,
> Thy wrapt soul sitting in thine eyes ;
> There, held in holy passion still,
> Forget thyself to marble."

The " Arcades " and " Comus," both written in the
poet's twenty-sixth year, are examples of a form of
literature at that time highly popular, but now obsolete, —

the Masque. The masque originated in the reign of Henry VIII. Primarily, it consisted only of scenery and pantomime, but later, poetical dialogue, songs, and music were added.

In the reign of James and the first Charles the masque had reached its height, and it then employed the first talent of the country in its composition. Masques were generally prepared for some remarkable occasion, as a coronation, the birth of a young prince or noble, or the visit of some royal personage of foreign countries. They usually took place in the hall of the palace, and as Bacon remarks, " being designed for princes, they were by princes played."

The preparation of such pageants, on commission from those who required them, had at last become a regular part of the dramatic profession, and in the hands of such men as Chapman, Fletcher, and Jonson, the literary capabilities of the masque were extended and perfected. " The part of the poet was to seize the meaning of the occasion, to invent some allegory, or adapt some scrap of Grecian mythology or chivalrous legend, in the action of which the meaning could somehow be symbolized, while at the same time room was left for dances, comicalities, and the expected songs and duets. . . . The bit of landscape with which the story opened ; the rocks, grottos, castles, etc., into which the scene changed ; the white clouds descending from the sky, out of which came the resplendent maiden or goddess ; the rain, the thunder, and the bursts of beautiful color ; the appropriate dress for nymphs and nereids, satyrs and sea-gods, negroes or pygmies, or whatever fantastic beings glided or gambolled, spoke or sung," — were elaborated by the machinist. Much depended upon the skill of the masquers and their willingness to spend money beforehand in rich costumes. In this form of composition the dramatic poets exercised their passion for pure sensuous invention.

Though Shakespeare has given us no masques, his " Midsummer Night's Dream " and his " Tempest " may be classed with that order of dramatic fantasies.

The " Arcades " being but a slight composition compared with the " Comus," I pass on to the last-named production. " Comus " was founded on an actual occurrence. Lord Brackley and Mr. Egerton, sons of the Earl of Bridgewater, then President of Wales, with his daughter, Lady Alice, passing through the forest on their way to Ludlow, were benighted, and the lady was for a short time lost; this accident being related to Milton by his friend, Henry Lawes, the musician who taught music at the castle, Milton at his request composed the masque embodying the adventure, and it was acted at Ludlow Castle, before the Earl, on Michaelmas night, 1634. The young lady, the two brothers, and Lawes himself each bore a part in the representation.

It has been aptly said that "in 'Comus' Milton has shown what the pure poetry and pure morality of the masque might be." Much as he wrote afterward, he never has given us anything more poetically perfect than " Comus." Let us glance at a few scenes in this bewitching drama. First, at that of the lady entering the wood, — the dark wood enchanted by Comus, the god of riot and intemperance, the son of Bacchus and Circe, who waylays travellers, and induces them to drink his charmed liquor, which changes their countenances into the faces of beasts.

The lady speaks, —

> " This way the noise was, if mine ear be true,
> My best guide now : methought it was the sound
> Of riot and ill-managed merriment,
> Such as the jocund flute or gamesome pipe

Stirs up among the loose unlettered hinds,
When from their teeming flocks, and granges full,
In wanton dance they praise the bounteous Pan,
And thank the gods amiss. I should be loath
To meet the rudeness and swill'd insolence
Of such late wassailers. . . .
 . . . .
I cannot halloo to my brothers, but
Such noise as I can make to be heard farthest
I 'll venture ; for my new enlivened spirits
Prompt me ; and they perhaps are not far off."

Now comes into the masque the song to Echo. While the lady sings it, Comus listens in admiration, and now, disguised as a shepherd, steps forth and thus hails her, —

" Can any mortal mixture of earth's mould
Breathe such divine, enchanting ravishment ?
Sure something holy lodges in that breast,
And with these raptures moves the vocal air
To testify his hidden residence :
How sweetly did they float upon the wings
Of silence, through the empty-vaulted night,
At every fall smoothing the raven down
Of darkness till it smiled ! I have oft heard
My mother Circe, with the Syrens three,
Amidst the flowery-kirtled Naiades
Culling their potent herbs, and baleful drugs,
Who, as they sung, would take the prison'd soul
And lap it in Elysium ; Scylla wept,
And chid her barking waves into attention,
And fell Charybdis murmured soft applause :
Yet they in pleasing slumber lulled the sense,
And in sweet madness robb'd it of itself ;
But such a sacred and home-felt delight,
Such sober certainty of waking bliss,
I never heard till now."

The brothers, bewildered in the darkness, return at length to find their sister gone ; the younger expresses fear for her safety, and thus the elder reassures him, —

> " Peace, Brother ; be not over exquisite
> To cast the fashion of uncertain ills :
> So dear to Heaven is saintly Chastity,
> That, when a soul is found sincerely so,
> A thousand liveried Angels lackey her,
> Driving far off each thing of sin and guilt."

The attendant spirit in disguise now comes into the masque, and relates to the brothers how, musing on a bank by himself, he hears the barbarous revels of Comus and his crew. Suddenly the roar ceased, and all was silence ; as he listened, at last —

> ". . . A soft and solemn-breathing sound
> Rose like a steam of rich distill'd perfumes,
> And stole upon the air, that even Silence
> Was took ere she was ware, and wished she might
> Deny her nature, and be never more,
> Still to be so displac'd."

It was the lady singing to Echo. He hastens to her relief, knowing by whom the wood is inhabited, but she has been lured away before he reaches the spot. The scene changes to a stately palace, set out with all manner of deliciousness, — soft music, and tables spread with all dainties. Comus appears with his rabble, and the lady, chained as a statue of alabaster, sits in an enchanted chair. He offers the charmed cup ; she cannot rise, but refuses it in disdain, and thus upbraids the sorcerer, —

> " Fool, do not boast ;
> Thou canst not touch the freedom of my mind
> With all thy charms — although this corporal rind
> Thou hast immanacled — while Heaven sees good.
> Hence with thy brewed enchantments, foul deceiver !
> Were it a draught for Juno when she banquets,
> I would not taste thy treasonous offer ; none
> But such as are good men can give good things;
> And that, which is not good, is not delicious
> To a well-governed and wise appetite."

Awed by the superior power of Chastity, but not baffled, Comus again lifts the enchanted cup to her lips; then rush in the brothers with swords drawn, accompanied by Thyrsis, the attendant spirit. They wrest the enchanted glass from Comus, break it, and rout him and his crew; but the lady is still marble-bound to the chair. The motion of the wizard's wand would have released her, but he has escaped with it. Thyrsis, however, has a device in reserve: Sabrina, daughter of Locrene, the son of Brutus, of whom the old British legends tell how, to preserve her honor, she threw herself into the neighboring river, — now the far-famed Severn, — is the goddess of that river. Who so ready to succor maidenhood? Only let her presence be adjured by some suitable song. Thyrsis himself sings, —

> " Sabrina fair,
>   Listen where thou art sitting
> Under the glassy, cool, translucent wave,
>   In twisted braids of lilies knitting
> The loose train of thy amber-dropping hair;
>   Listen for dear honour's sake,
>   Goddess of the silver lake,
>   Listen, and save.

> " By all the nymphs that nightly dance
> Upon thy streams with wily glance,
> Rise, rise, and heave thy rosy head,
> From thy coral-paven bed,
> And bridle in thy headlong wave,
> Till thou our summons answered have.
>   Listen, and save."

Sabrina now rises from under the stage, attended by water-nymphs, and sings, —

> " By the rushy-fringed bank
> Where grows the willow, and the osier dank,
>   My sliding chariot stays,
> Thick set with agate, and the azure sheen

13

> Of turkis blue, and emerald green,
>   That in the channel strays;
> Whilst, from off the vaters fleet
> Thus I set my printless feet
> On the cowslip's velvet head,
> That bends not as I tread;
> Gentle swain, at thy request,
>   I am here."

Sabrina, being duly implored to undo the charm of the vile enchanter, sprinkles drops of pure water on the lady, and disenchanted, she rises from her seat. The spirit then conducts them home; they are presented to their father and mother; songs and dances follow; and at last Thyrsis the spirit — who is till now disguised as a shepherd — resumes his ethereal shape; and slowly ascending and swaying to and fro, he sings the final song, which closes thus: —

> "Mortals that would follow me,
>   Love Virtue; she alone is free:
> She can teach ye how to climb
> Higher than the sphery chime;
> Or, if Virtue feeble were,
> Heaven itself would stoop to her."

Of "Comus" Hallam says: "The subject required an elevation, a purity, a sort of severity of sentiment, which no one in that age could have given but Milton." "Comus" was first published in 1637, not by its author, but by Henry Lawes, the musician, who in his dedication says: "Although not openly acknowledged by its author, yet it is a legitimate offspring, so lovely and so much desired that the often copying it hath tired my pen to give my several friends satisfaction."

"Lycidas," a monody on Milton's college companion, Edward King, who was drowned on his passage from Chester to Ireland, has been ranked with the best ele-

gies in our language. The sounding seas float upon his
" watery bier " the body of this beloved friend, who
" knew himself to sing and build the lofty rhyme," while
his immortal brother poet, transformed in imagination
into a shepherd, gives it in affectionate fancy this sweet
Arcadian burial : —

> " . . . Return, Sicilian Muse,
> And call the vales, and bid them hither cast
> Their bells and flowerets of a thousand hues.
> Ye valleys low, where the mild whispers rise
> Of shades, and wanton winds, and gushing brooks,
> On whose fresh lap the swart-star sparely looks ;
> Throw hither all your quaint enamell'd eyes,
> That on the green turf suck the honied showers,
> And purple all the ground with vernal flowers.
> Bring the rathe primrose that forsaken dies,
> The tufted crow-toe, and pale jessamine,
> The white pink, and the pansy freaked with jet,
> The glowing violet,
> The musk-rose, and the well-attir'd woodbine,
> With cowslips wan that hang the pensive head,
> And every flower that sad embroidery wears :
> Bid amaranthus all his beauty shed,
> And daffodillies fill their cups with tears,
> To strew the laureat hearse where Lycid lies."

" It is somewhat remarkable," observes Hallam, " that
Dr. Johnson has committed his critical reputation by the
most contemptuous depreciation of this poem." When
we consider that in reviewing " Lycidas " Johnson's foot
was miles away from his native heath, we shall not so
much wonder at his blunder. As a critic of the understanding, Johnson was entirely at home ; but pure poesy,
that appeals only to the imagination, was simply unintelligible to him ; and in all his good, useful, but earth-
bounded life, he had never even dreamed of the seraphic
harmonies that made with Milton their familiar home.

And moreover, he could never forgive Milton his politics and principles, or lose an opportunity to vent his spleen upon him. His "Life of Milton" is the least veritable of all the lives, and in parts is meanly malignant. To every man his due; but not till a lumbering elephant can conceive of the *modus operandi* of a humming-bird, will men of Dr. Johnson's mould be divinely commissioned to analyze the delicate "soul-stuff" of poets. Thus it is that he turns from this exquisite elegy, with its description of flowers even surpassing that of Shakespeare in "Winter's Tale," and oracularly pronounces it "disgusting" (!).

Though Milton's minor poetry would alone have rendered his name immortal, the measure of his fame would have still been incomplete without his great epic. "Paradise Lost," or, "The Fall of Man," however improbable and unreasonable the Hebrew account of it may seem to a more enlightened theological age, was undoubtedly regarded by Milton and his cotemporaries as an actual and veritable occurrence. That it had long been familiar to him as a subject for poetry, two draughts of his scheme, preserved among the manuscripts in Trinity College Library, testify. In 1642 the poet, with that calm consciousness of his own high powers which was but natural and becoming to a soul endowed with gifts seldom imparted to our race, and "bound everlastingly," as he says, "in willing homage to the holy and the beautiful," promises to undertake a work that will do honor to his country. "A work," he continues, "not to be obtained but by devout prayer to that Eternal Spirit that can enrich with all utterance and knowledge, and sends out his seraphim, with the hallowed fire of his altar, to touch and purify the lips of whom he pleases." In an epic poem the subject is the most important part. "Milton's subject," says Addison, "was

greater than Homer's or Virgil's; it does not determine
the fate of single persons or nations, but of the whole
species.   The actors are the united powers of hell and the
radiant inhabitants of heaven, man in his greatest perfection, and woman in her highest purity and beauty, — characters not only more magnificent but more new than any
characters in Homer or Virgil, or indeed in the whole
circle of nature.   These actors are not only our progenitors, but our representatives; and we have an actual interest in everything they do, and no less than our utmost
happiness is concerned and lies at stake in their behavior.
These characters, for the most part, lie out of nature, and
were to be formed purely by the poet's own invention."

By the choice of the noblest words which our tongue
could afford him, Milton has carried our language to a
greater height than any of the English poets have ever
done before or after him.   If he has introduced foreign
idioms and transpositions, it has been remarked that " his
sentiments were so wonderfully sublime that it would have
been impossible for him to have represented them in their
full strength and beauty without having recourse to these
foreign assistances.   Our language sunk under him, and
was unequal to that greatness of soul which furnished him
with such glorious conceptions."

In his conceptions of Satan and Eve, Milton has been
accorded " perfect character."   Satan may be regarded
as the grand effort of his genius.   To an enlightened
Christian philosophy evil is not dispensed to man by a
malignant demon, but wisely allotted to him by One, —

> " For whom to live, is still to give,
> And sweeter than our wish His will : "

yet in its cruder conceptions of the control of the universe, the imagination has almost invariably divided its

sway between two distinct agencies, — the one creative, preservative, and beneficent, the other destructive and malignant ; and the popular presentation of each has been somewhat in accordance with the development of the race.

To the old Hebrew, literal and material, both good and evil became incorporate.   Satan, clothed in tangible, substantial matter, went " to and fro in the earth, and walked up and down it."   The age of Milton had scarcely improved upon the Hebrew Devil.   "Nothing less than horns and a tail," says Hallam, "were the orthodox creed." Compare the Satan handed down from the Miracle and Moral plays of England ("a creature without human shape, yet denied the fair proportions of a beast") with Milton's ruined archangel, as in the language of Channing he is thus finely presented, —"Colossal in strength and majesty, repelling us by his transcendent evil, yet almost ennobling the soul by his exhibition of the unsubdued energy of mind triumphing over unutterable physical agony," — and you will at once admit that the poet foreruns his age in the harmony and grandeur of the ideal conception, and allow that the character of Milton's Satan will, so long as the language is·spoken, command our admiration as a sublime poetic effort.

We must observe the wisdom of Milton in investing his hero with form and matter (since pure immaterial essence would have failed to convey to the human mind an adequate image of his attributes), and his delicate sense of fitness and propriety in making that matter in a large degree superior to the natural laws by which we suppose matter to be governed.   It has been well observed that " there is an indefiniteness in the description of the person of Satan which excites without shocking the imagination, and aids us to reconcile in our conception of him a human form with superhuman attributes."   Thus he is first pictured

rising from the burning lake after the nine days' trance succeeding his dreadful overthrow and fall from heaven : —

> " With head uplift above the wave, and eyes
> That sparkling blazed; his other parts besides
> Prone on the flood, extended long and large,
> Lay floating many a rood. . . .
> Forthwith upright he rears from off the pool
> His mighty stature; on each hand the flames
> Driven backward slope their pointing spires, and roll'd
> In billows leave i' th' midst a horrid vale.
> Then with expanded wings he steers his flight
> Aloft, incumbent on the dusky air.
> His spear . . .
> He walked with to support uneasy steps
> Over the burning marle, not like those steps
> On heaven's azure, and the torrid clime
> Smote on him sore besides vaulted with fire."

And here follows that one matchless sentence which gives
us the key-note to Satan's grandeur, — " Natheless he so
indured."

" By merit raised to that bad eminence," with what
" pomp supreme, and godlike imitated state " he takes
possession of hell's gorgeous throne! And with what
cunning policy he thence harangues his subjects : —

> " Powers and dominions, deities of heav'n!
> For since no deep within her gulf can hold
> Immortal vigor, though oppress'd and fallen,
> I give not heaven for lost : from this descent
> Celestial virtues rising will appear
> More glorious and more dread, than from no fall,
> And trust themselves to fear no second fate."

Milton in his delineation of Satan ignores the illogical
and unlovely doctrine of total depravity, since he allows
even to the archangel of evil exalted sentiments and
touches of better feeling; as in the glimmerings of remorse and self-accusation inspired in his mind by the

distant prospect of Eden, before the opening of his noble
address to the Sun, and in his partial relenting after the
contemplation of Adam and Eve in their beauty and innocence in the bowers of Paradise.

> " Ah, gentle pair, ye little think how nigh
> Your change approaches, when all these delights
> Will vanish, and deliver ye to woe:
> And should I at your harmless innocence
> Melt, as I do, yet public reason just,
> Honour and empire with revenge enlarged,
> By conquering this new world, compels me now
> To do what else, though damned, I should abhor."

Witness too, his remorseful burst of tenderness when
beholding —

> " Millions of spirits for his fault amerc'd
> Of heaven, and from eternal splendor flung
> For his revolt, yet faithful how they stood,
> Their glory withered."

He strove to address them and —

> " Thrice he assayed, and thrice in spite of scorn,
> Tears, such as angels weep, burst forth."

Satan's ironic scorn is finely delineated in that passage
where, required to give an account of himself to the patrol-
ling angel, he exclaims, —

> " Know ye not me ?   Ye knew me once no mate
> For you, there sitting where you durst not soar;
> Not to know me, argues yourself unknown,
> The lowest of your throng."

And again, when —

> " . . . On the beach,
> Of that inflamèd sea he stood, and called
> His legions, angel forms, who lay entranc'd
> Thick as autumnal leaves that strow the brooks
> In Vallombrosa. . . .

> He called so loud, that all the hollow deep
> Of hell resounded : Princes, potentates,
> Warriors, the flower of heav'n, once yours, now lost,
> If such astonishment as this can seize
> Eternal spirits ; or have ye chosen this place
> After the toil of battle to repose
> Your wearied virtue, for the ease you find
> To slumber here, as in the vale of heaven ?
> Or in this abject posture have ye sworn
> To adore the conqueror ? . . .
> Awake, arise, or be forever fallen ! "

Thus has the poet's imagination achieved its highest triumph by portraying a character which — to borrow the thought of Coleridge — "is so often seen in little on the political stage, exhibiting all the restlessness, temerity, and cunning of the mighty hunters of mankind, from Nimrod to Napoleon," and by throwing around this character a singularity of daring, a grandeur of sufferance, and a ruined splendor that make him a monarch to whom alone we may accord the throne of hell.

In its universality lies the wonderful power of genius. Turning from the ruined archangel to spotless Eve, new-moulded, dewy and fresh from the hand of God in all her loveliness, we can scarcely conceive her to be a creation of the same mind. Thus she is first pictured by the poet : —

> "For softness formed, and sweet attractive grace ;
> She as a veil down to her slender waist
> Her unadorned golden tresses wore
> Dishevelled, but in wanton ringlets waved.
> So passed she naked on, nor shunned the sight
> Of God or angels, for she thought no ill."

Thus Adam beautifully acknowledges to the angel the superior charm of her mental loveliness, —

> "Neither her outside form so fair
> So much delights me, as those graceful acts

> Those thousand decencies that daily flow
> From all her words and actions. So absolute she seems
> And in herself complete, so well to know
> Her own, that what she wills to do or say
> Seems wisest, virtuousest, discreetest, best:
> All higher knowledge in her presence falls
> Degraded, wisdom in discourse with her
> Loses discountenanced, and like folly shews:
> Authority and reason on her wait,
> As one intended first, not after made
> Occasionally; and, to consummate all,
> Greatness of mind and nobleness their seat
> Build in her loveliest, and create an awe
> About her, as a guard angelic placed."

Dr. Johnson has accused Milton of a " Turkish contempt for woman, as shown in his delineation of Eve;" surely a woman of the above type would ill become an Oriental harem!

Lovely and purely feminine is this picture of our fair mother: —

> " With lowliness majestic from her seat she rose,
> And grace that won who saw to wish her stay
> Rose and went forth among her fruits and flowers,
> To visit how they prospered, bud and bloom,
> Her nursery; they at her coming sprung,
> And touched by her fair tendance, gladlier grew."

This description of Eve's housewifery in anticipation of Raphael at dinner, is finely drawn: —

> " So saying, with despatchful looks in haste
> She turns, on hospitable thoughts intent
> What choice to choose for delicacy best,
> What order, so contrived as not to mix
> Tastes, not well joined, inelegant, but bring
> Taste after taste, upheld with kindliest change;
> Bestirs her then, and from each tender stalk
> Whatever earth, all-bearing mother, yields
> She gathers, tribute large, and on the board
> Heaps with unsparing hand: for drink the grape

> She crushes, inoffensive must, and meathes
> From many a berry, and from sweet kernels pressed
> She tempers dulcet creams, nor these to hold
> Wants her fit vessels pure; then strows the ground
> With rose and odours from the shrub unfumed."

Charlotte Bronte complains that "Milton saw in Eve his *cook*, not the mother of mankind." And why not give to the fair mistress of Eden culinary genius? In that sparsely settled region, the cooking, if not attended to by Eve, must have been assigned to Adam — which Heaven forbid!

Another authoress sees only in Eve "an overgrown baby, with nothing to recommend her but her submission and her fine hair." Let us leave to her undisputed possession that adjunct of beauty so often deplorably missing in her daughters; but as to her "submission," it may be disputed on the best of authority, since Adam himself says, —

> "Authority and reason on her wait,
> As one intended first, not after made
> Occasionally."

This graceful, delicate, and purely feminine creation of Milton is supposed to stand for Nature's first attempt at womankind. Remembering this, and taking into consideration the roundabout way of her production, we may, I think, regard her with some satisfaction. In the "courage of her convictions" she at least surpasses Adam, who somewhat meanly lays at her door his share of the blame, after the "gentle pair" have together undone us all. Hallam says, "If Milton had made Eve a wit or a blue, the Fall might have been accounted for as easily as possible, and spared the serpent the trouble."

In 1671 Milton produced his "Paradise Regained," — a model of the shorter epic, an action comprehending few characters and a brief space of time. The subject was far less capable of calling forth the vast powers of the poet's mind; and though it abounds with passages equal to any of the same nature in " Paradise Lost," it is, as a whole, less ornate, elevated, and imaginative, and cannot at all compare throughout with the greater poem. " Samson Agonistes " succeeded " Paradise Regained." In this his last poem " ebbs the mighty tide of Milton's genius." An air of grandeur pervades it, the vigor of thought remains, but the imagination flags ; and it is not, even with the lovers of poetry, a popular poem, though critics assert that it deserves a higher rank than has been accorded it. " In ' Paradise Lost,' " says Craik, " Milton rises high above all Greek, above all Roman fame." The first book of that poem is held, by the same critic, to be " probably the most perfect and splendid of all human compositions."

Judging it, not from a theological, or even from an ethical standpoint, but purely as a work of art, posterity will, I think, confirm his estimate of this noble poem. It was begun by Milton in 1658, completed in 1665, and put in print in 1667. Simmons, the bookseller, gave five pounds down for it! Five more were to be received from him for two ensuing editions. When the third payment fell due, Milton no longer needed mortal pittances, and it was received by his widow, who outlived him fifty-three years. She sold all her claims on the poem for eight pounds! In thirteen years but three thousand copies had been sold.

CHAPTER XI.

POPE, AND THE MINOR POETS OF THE ARTIFICIAL SCHOOL.

THE reigns of William III., Anne, and George I. produced a class of poets to whom is justly awarded the praise due to a polished style, and a felicity in painting artificial life, — qualities less valued in our own time than the bold originality of style and thought, the vivid imaginative power, and the depth of natural sentiment which characterizes the poets who preceded them. They were sagacious, neat, clear, and reasonable, but for the most part cold, timid, and superficial.

The period of twelve years which comprises the reign of Anne — from 1702 to 1714 — was styled during the whole of the eighteenth century the Augustan era of English literature, on account of its supposed resemblance in intellectual opulence to the reign of the Emperor Augustus. "The present age has not followed or confirmed this opinion."

During the whole thirty-eight years of which this era was the central period, the popular poets either filled high diplomatic and official situations, or were engaged in schemes of ambition, where offices of State, and the ascendency of rival parties, rather than poetical or literary laurels, were the prizes contended for.

"Writing," says an observing critic, "with infinite good sense, grace, and vivacity, and above all, writing for the first time in a tone that was peculiar to the upper ranks of society, and upon subjects that were almost exclusively interesting to them, they naturally figured as the most accomplished, fashionable, and perfect writers which the world had ever seen, and made the wild, luxuriant, and humble sweetness of our earlier poets appear rude and untutored in the comparison. Yet amid all the gayety, polish, and sprightliness of fancy conspicuous in the writers of this period, we look in vain for the lyrical grandeur and enthusiasm which charms us in the elder poets and redeems so many apparent errors."

Though by mixing in courtly society, and enjoying much worldly prosperity and importance, the poets of this time may have gained in taste and correctness, they undoubtedly impaired the native vigor and originality of genius and the steady worship of truth and Nature. "The path of things is silent;" and high thoughts and divine imaginations are most successfully nursed in solitude.

The modish court Muse in hoop and stays, stiff in brocade, and refulgent in jewels, bears little resemblance to the graceful sisterhood of Helicon; yet the age, it must be allowed, produced several writers who, each in his own line, may be called extraordinary. At the head of this, the artificial school of verse, was Alexander Pope, by whom the poetry of elegant and artificial life was exhibited in a perfection never since attained. Pope was born in London, May 21, 1688.

His father, a linen-draper, having acquired an independent fortune, retired to Binfield, Windsor Forest. He was a Roman Catholic, and the young poet was partly educated by the family priest. Subsequently being sent to a Catholic seminary, he lampooned his teacher, was severely punished, and afterward taken home by his parents, and attended no school after his twelfth year. Though self-educated, the whole of Pope's early life is affirmed to have been that of a severe student. He was, even from infancy, a poet, and tells us that —

"As yet a child, and all unknown to fame,
I lisped in numbers, for the numbers came."

Dryden early became the particular object of his admiration, and when not more than twelve years of age, he prevailed upon a friend to introduce him to the coffee-house which Dryden then frequented, that he might have the gratification of seeing the great master of the art, whom he afterward acknowledged to be his instructor in versification; and who, though infinitely less subtile, polished, and refined than Pope (being a homelier and bolder artist, and far more true to Nature), must be regarded as the founder of this school of poetry of which Pope may claim to be the master. At that early age Pope wrote, and afterward destroyed, various dramatic pieces; and at the age of sixteen he composed his pastorals, in imitation of Chaucer.

In 1711 appeared his "Essay on Criticism," — a work which, though composed when the author was only twenty-one, displays a marvellous ripeness of judgment, and is affirmed to be the finest piece of argumentative and reasoning poetry in the English language. This essay, commended by Addison in the "Spectator," immediately rose into great popularity. The style of Pope was now formed and complete. His versification was that of his model, Dryden; but he gave to the heroic couplet a terseness, correctness, and melody all his own.

The essay was shortly afterward followed by the "Rape of the Lock," — the most graceful, ingenious, and delightful of all his compositions. The subject of this poem was the stealing of a lock of hair from a beauty of the day by her lover, whose playful pilfering was taken seriously, and caused an estrangement between the lovers and their respective families. Pope wrote his poem to reconcile them by making a jest of the affair. In this amicable undertaking he did not succeed, though by the effort he added vastly to his poetical reputation.

The machinery of the poem, founded upon the fanciful yet charming theory that the elements are inhabited by sylphs, gnomes, nymphs, and salamanders, was suggested by some of his friends. By blending the most delicate satire with the most lively fancy, in the "Rape of the Lock" Pope has produced a poem which is allowed to be the finest and most brilliant mock-heroic poem in the world. He could scarcely have conceived a more admirable prototype of our modern society belle than his Belinda of the "Rape of the Lock": —

> "Fair nymphs and well-dress'd youths around her shone,
>   But every eye was fix'd on her alone.
> On her white breast a sparkling cross she wore,
> Which Jews might kiss, and infidels adore.
> Her lively looks a sprightly mind disclose,
> Quick as her eyes, and as unfix'd as those.
> Favours to none, to all she smiles extends;
> Oft she rejects, but never once offends.
> Bright as the sun, her eyes the gazers strike,
> And, like the sun, they shine on all alike.
> Yet graceful ease, and sweetness void of pride,
> Might hide her faults, if belles had faults to hide:
> If to her share some female errors fall,
> Look on her face, and you'll forget them all."

Pope's description of the sylphs may compare with Shakespeare's conception of Ariel: —

> "Some to the sun their insect wings unfold
> Waft on the breeze, or sink in clouds of gold;
> Transparent forms too fine for mortal sight,
> Their fluid bodies half dissolved in light.
> Loose to the wind their airy garments flew,
> Thin glittering textures of the filmy dew,
> Dipped in the richest tincture of the skies,
> Where light disports in ever mingling dyes,

While every beam new transient colours flings,
Colours that change whene'er they wave their wings.

. . . .

Some in the fields of purest ether play,
And bask and whiten in the blaze of day.
Some guide the course of wandering orbs on high,
Or roll the planets through the boundless sky :
Some, less refined, beneath the moon's pale light
Pursue the stars that shoot athwart the night,
Or suck the mists in grosser airs below,
Or dip their pinions in the painted bow,
Or brew fierce tempests on the wintry main,
Or o'er the glebe distil in kindly rain.
Others, on earth, o'er human race preside,
Watch all their ways, and all their actions guide."

Pope now commenced the translation of the Iliad.   This gigantic task is said to have at first oppressed him with its difficulty ; but in a short time, as he grew more familiar with Homer's images and expressions, his work became less formidable, and he was soon able to despatch fifty verses a day.   By this translation the poet obtained a clear sum of five thousand three hundred and twenty pounds.   Well might he exclaim, —

" And thanks to Homer, since I live and thrive,
Indebted to no prince or peer alive."

Critics have disagreed in their estimate of this work. Dr. Johnson calls it " the noblest version of poetry the world has ever seen."   The fatal facility of Pope's rhyme, the additional false ornaments which he imparted to the ancient Greek, and his departure from the nice discrimination of character and speech which prevails in Homer, are faults which more modern critics have universally admitted.   Cowper remarks that " the Iliad and Odyssey in Pope's hands have no more the air of antiquity than if he himself had invented them."

14

Pope's genius was certainly most un-Homeric, yet the English Iliad is still allowed by those who have knowledge and skill to estimate its excellence and difficulty, to be a great work. The success of the Iliad led to the translation of the Odyssey; and though to this work the poet called in assistance, the two translations occupied a period of twelve years.

Pope was now enabled to purchase a house and grounds nearer the metropolis, and in 1725 he removed with his father and mother, to whom his affection and reverence was, through life, touchingly constant and undeviating, from the shades of Windsor Forest to his villa at Twickenham, where he resided during the remainder of his life. This classic spot Pope delighted to improve, and the taste with which he laid out his grounds — five acres in all — is said to have had a marked effect on English landscape gardening. The Prince of Wales took the design of his garden from Pope's; and from him Kent, the improver and embellisher of pleasure-grounds, received his best lessons. Here the poet was visited by ministers of State, wits, poets, and beauties.

In 1716 Pope wrote the most highly poetical and passionate of his works, the "Epistle from Eloisa to Abelard." The delicacy of narration, the glow and fervor of passion, the beauty of imagery and description, in this poem, have been highly commended; while the exquisite melody of its versification has been aptly compared to "the rising and falling of the tones of an Æolian harp." Pope has conceived nothing finer than the closing passages of the poem, where the heroine, from the cruel unrest of love and the agony of penitence, rises at last into the highest devotional rapture, and subsides into saintly resignation.

In 1733 Pope published his "Essay on Man," being

part of a course of moral philosophy in verse, which he projected. The poem is perhaps more to be commended for its poetry than its philosophy. Its metaphysical distinctions have been in a measure superseded by broader views of life ; yet it is throughout brilliant with fine passages that will, no doubt, be quoted and admired so long as the language endures. Its morality too is good for all time ; it may be seen in passages like these : —

> " In Faith and Hope the world will disagree,
> But all mankind's concern is charity."

> " Honour and shame from no condition rise ;
> Act well your part, there all the honour lies."

> " A wit's a feather, and a chief a rod ;
> An honest man's the noblest work of God."

> " One self-approving hour whole years outweighs."

Pope's future labors were chiefly confined to satire. Of all his satires the " Dunciad " is the most elaborate and splendid. Though displaying his fertile invention, his variety of illustration, and the unrivalled force and facility of his diction, it has still been regarded rather with pity than admiration, — pity that one so highly gifted should allow himself to descend to personal abuse, and devote the end of a great literary life to a work so mean. Pope as a satirist is surpassed by Dryden. Though he attained to more finished excellence in composition, his satirical portraits, with one or two exceptions, are feeble compared with those of his great master, " who," as has been observed, " drew from the life, and hit off strong likenesses, while Pope, like Sir Joshua Reynolds, refined in his colors, and many of his pictures are faint and vanishing delineations."

Between the years 1733 and 1740 the poet published his inimitable epistles, satires, and moral essays.

The last days of Pope were disturbed by political events ; the anticipated approach of the Pretender led the Government to issue a proclamation prohibiting every Roman Catholic from appearing within ten miles of London.   The poet complied with the proclamation, but was soon afterward too ill to appear in town.

A constant state of excitement, added to a life of ceaseless study and contemplation, operating on a frame naturally delicate and deformed from birth, had completely exhausted his vital energies.   He submitted without a murmur to his sickness, which he terms " this additional proclamation from the Highest of all Powers."   He now complained of his inability to think ; yet a short time before his death he said, " I am so certain of the soul's being immortal that I seem to feel it within me, as it were, by intuition."   The dearest dream of this man's life had been literary fame ; and for that he was even willing to sacrifice the manly virtues of candor and sincerity. The soul, " so long misled by wandering fires," comes home at last ; and these are his dying words : " There is nothing that is meritorious but virtue and friendship."

Pope died on the 30th of May, 1744.   As a poet he will not rank with the great masters of the lyre.   He has neither the creative energy nor the universality of Shakespeare ; he lacks the sublimity of Milton, the wild, luxurious sweetness of Spenser, and the wholesome, hearty fidelity to Mother Nature which so charms us in Chaucer. In a sound and vigorous body his genius would no doubt have developed differently ; as it was, his life seems to have been too introverted and self-centred.   His moral nature was refined and high-toned, but shackled and cramped by an outworn and illiberal creed ; he was a fond and steady friend, yet his extreme sensibility, his hasty and irritable temper, and over-indulged vanity often betrayed him into mean petulance and undignified fierceness. Though not the anointed high-priest of Nature, he was organically the nicest observer and the most accurate describer of the phenomena of the mind. Critics have allowed him wit, fancy, good sense, and an elegance which has never been surpassed, or perhaps equalled, being a combination of intellect, imagination, and taste, under the direction of an independent spirit and refined moral feeling. If he had studied more in the school of Nature, and perhaps less in that of art, he might have strung his lyre to deeper and diviner melodies; but as it is, he is one of our most brilliant and accomplished English poets.

"Pope's epistolary excellence," says Johnson, "had an open field; he had no English rival, living or dead." A notorious publisher of the day, having obtained by surreptitious means a portion of the correspondence of Pope, the poet complied with the general entreaty of the public and gave to the world a collection of his letters, which went through several editions. As literature was the business of Pope's life, and composition his first and favorite pursuit, he wrote always with a view to admiration and fame. Consequently his letters are too carefully and elaborately written for spontaneous effusions of private confidence, yet many of them are exquisitely beautiful in thought and imagery. Nothing could be finer in its way than that description of the death of two lovers by lightning given in a letter to Lady Mary Wortley Montagu in 1718.

The over-curious admirers of Pope may be gratified with the most minute details of his person and peculiarities; for "are they not all to be found in the book of the Chronicles" of Johnson the doctor? They may know how at table, the poet (poor little man!) had his seat raised to bring him on a level with his dinner; how, like Harry Gill, he shivered all the long winter; and wore a doublet of fur under his linen shirt; how he enlarged his slender legs with three pairs of hose, and wore a stiff-laced canvas bodice under his flannel waistcoat, and had recourse to a tie-wig when his hair fell away; how he delighted to heat potted lampreys in a silver saucepan, and at dinner was fain to roll spiced meats as sweet morsels under his tongue. They may learn that he munched biscuits and dry conserves between the courses; that he sometimes nodded in company, and once, when the Prince of Wales was talking of poetry, actually refreshed himself with a short nap! that the maid at my Lord Oxford's deposed that in the frosty winter she was ousted from her blessed bed four times in one night to supply Mr. Pope with paper, lest he should lose a thought! They may be assured that he punctually required his writing-box to be set upon his bed before he rose, and kept the poor maids and footmen trotting about all night, while like Oliver Twist he asked for "more" coffee; that he wrote the Iliad on backs of letters to save paper, and was therefore nicknamed "Paper-Saving Pope;" and that his once-adored Lady Mary contradicted him when they were guests at my Lord Oxford's, and they quarrelled and quarrelled till one or the other left the house.

They may be told how faithful and constant was his love for Mistress Martha Blount; and when in illness and age she neglected him, he excused her " human frailty " as he terms it, and cherished her still in his noble, constant heart; how he delighted in his garden, his " quincunx," and his vines, and made unto himself a grotto adorned with fossils, — a place of silence and retreat from which cares and passions should be excluded, — to the infinite disgust of good, social tea-drinking Dr. Johnson, who, in majestic contempt, has dubbed Pope's grotto an " excavation ; " how tenderly he loved and revered his venerable parents ; how fond and faithful he was to his friends, true and loving to the last, and during his state of helpless decay, was, in his intervals of reason, always saying something kind either of his present or absent friends, so that "his humanity" is said to have "survived his reason;" but let us —

> " No farther seek his merits to disclose,
> Or draw his frailties from their dread abode
> (Where they alike in trembling hope repose)
> The bosom of his Father and his God."

Of the same school, though far inferior to Pope, both in genius and moral aim, was Matthew Prior, born in 1664.

Prior was of humble origin, his father being by trade a joiner. Matthew, by his father's early death, was left to the care of his uncle, a vintner, who sent him for a time to Westminster School, and afterward took him home to assist in the business of the inn, where the Earl of Dorset, a celebrated patron of genius, chanced to find him reading Horace, and was so well pleased with his proficiency that he generously undertook the care and cost of his education ; and in his eighteenth year Prior was entered at St. John's College, Cambridge. At the university the poet distinguished himself; the Earl continued his patronage, invited him to London, and obtained for him an appointment as secretary to the Earl of Berkeley. In this capacity Prior obtained the approbation of King William, who made him one of the gentlemen of his bedchamber.

After many royal honors and appointments he went in 1711, with Lord Bolingbroke, to France, to negotiate a treaty of peace. His public dignity and splendor was now at its height. A favorite of the French monarch, he received at Paris at least all the *honors* of an ambassador, though he is said to have hinted to the Queen, in an imperfect poem, that no service of plate had been allowed him; and it appeared by the debts he contracted that his remittances were not punctually made. Returning to London in 1715, he was committed to prison on charge of high treason; this accusation against the poet appears to have been unjust, and after two years' confinement, he was released without a trial.

Being now left without any other support than his fellowship of St. John's College, he continued his studies, and published by subscription a collected edition of his poems, and thus realized the sum of four thousand pounds. An equal sum was presented to him by the Earl of Oxford, and he was enabled to lay up for old age that provision for comfort and private enjoyment which he desired. These, however, he did not long possess, for he died at fifty-seven in the year 1721.

Prior was not a scrupulous poet, and has sometimes overstepped the bounds of decency. As he wrote, so he lived; and he is said to have been quite willing to descend from the dignity of the poet and statesman to the low delights of mean company. The Chloe whom he celebrates in verse, and at whose request he is said to have written his " Henry and Emma," — a paraphrase on the old ballad of the " Nut-Brown Maid," and not so good as the original, — was anything but a poet's ideal. It is related of Chloe that once, in her lover's absence, she decamped with his plate. Not at all disenchanted by this disreputable proceeding, Prior forgave her, and to the last clung to her with insane tenderness. Having spent the evening " in colloquy sublime " with Lords Oxford and Bolingbroke, Pope and Swift, Prior would, it is said, go and smoke a pipe, and drink a bottle of ale with a common soldier and his wife before going to bed.   Though a wise statesman and an elegant poet, his life was sadly debased by irregularity and sensuality.

As a poet Prior is classed among the agreeable and accomplished, who sport gayly on the surface of existence, but have no power to penetrate its depths.   His works range over a variety of style and subject, — as odes, songs, epistles, epigrams, and tales.   His longest poem, "Solomon," is the most moral, most correctly written, and Cowper has considered it the best of his productions, though his tales and lighter pieces are generally considered his happiest efforts.

He possessed in the highest degree the art of graceful, fluent versification.   His expression was choice and studied, abounding in classical allusions and images, but without any air of pedantry or constraint.   He has been paradoxically termed "the most natural of artificial poets," thus proving the old maxim that "the perfection of art is the concealment of it."   Of Prior's shorter pieces the "Garland," though perhaps not the best, is in sentiment the purest : —

> "The pride of every grove I chose,
>   The violet sweet and lily fair,
> The dappled pink and blushing rose,
>   To deck my charming Chloe's hair.

> "At morn the nymph vouchsafed to place
>   Upon her brow the various wreath ;
> The flowers less blooming than her face,
>   The scent less fragrant than her breath.

> "The flowers she wore along the day,
>   And every nymph and shepherd said,
> That in her hair they looked more gay
>   Than glowing in their native bed.

"Undressed at evening, when she found
  Their odours lost, their colors past,
She changed her look, and on the ground
  Her garland and her eyes she cast.

"That eye dropped sense distinct and clear,
  As any muse's tongue could speak,
When from its lid a pearly tear
  Ran trickling down her beauteous cheek.

"Dissembling what I knew too well,
  'My love, my life,' said I, 'explain
This change of humour; prithee tell —
  That falling tear — what does it mean?'

"She sighed, she smiled, and to the flowers
  Pointing, the lovely mor'list said,
'See, friend, in some few fleeting hours, .
  See yonder, what a change is made.

"'Ah me! the blooming pride of May
  And that of beauty are but one;
At morn both flourish bright and gay,
  Both fade at evening, pale, and gone.'"

In epigram Prior was apt, as here, —

"They never taste who always drink;
  They always talk who never think."

The most artless and best beloved of all the Pope and
Swift circle of wits and poets was John Gay, born in
1688. Gay's father was of an ancient family in Oxford,
but being in reduced circumstances, he apprenticed his
son to a silk-mercer in London. In this mercenary employment he did not long continue. Like most of the
poets of the day, he was an anxious suitor for court
favor; yet though he became secretary to the Duchess of
Monmouth, and subsequently to Lord Clarendon, "his
genius," it is said, "proved his best patron."

Gay has the wit and gayety of Prior, without his elegance. Hazlitt ranks his "Beggar's Opera" with the most refined productions in the language. Its moral tendency can scarcely be commended, as the poet's heroes are thieves and highwaymen; but the songs and music and political satire in the piece gave it great success, and it had a run of sixty-three nights, and was "the rage of town and country."

Gay wrote several other plays, of less merit, though more profitable. His "Polly," the sequel to the "Beggar's Opera," brought him eleven or twelve hundred pounds. The Duchess of Marlborough gave one hundred pounds as her subscription for a copy! Gay's "Shepherd's Week" abounds in humor; and his "Black-Eyed Susan" is one of our finest ballads. His fables, though surpassed by La Fontaine's, are the best in our language. Swift's friendship for Gay was sincere and tender; and Pope held him equally dear, and has thus happily characterized him, —

> " Of manners gentle, of affections mild ;
> In wit a man, simplicity a child."

Of Gay's fables, "The Monkey," "The Fox at the Point of Death," and "The Hare with many Friends," are considered the best. It has been suggested that in the latter he "drew from his own experience."

> " Friendship, like love, is but a name
> Unless to one you stint the flame.
> The child whom many fathers share,
> Hath seldom known a father's care.
> 'T is thus in friendship; who depend
> On many, rarely find a friend.
>   A Hare, who, in a civil way,
> Complied with everything, like *Gay*,
> Was known by all the bestial train
> Who haunt the wood, or graze the plain.
> Her care was never to offend,

And every creature was her friend.
   As forth she went at early dawn
To taste the dew-besprinkled lawn
Behind she hears the hunter's cries,
And from the deep-mouthed thunder flies:
She starts, she stops, she pants for breath;
She hears the near advance of death;
She doubles, to mislead the hound,
And measures back her mazy round;
Till, fainting in the public way,
Half dead with fear she gasping lay;
What transport in her bosom grew,
When first the Horse appeared in view!
' Let me,' says she, ' your back ascend,
And owe my safety to a friend:
You know my feet betray my flight;
To friendship every burden 's light.
The Horse replied : ' Poor honest Puss,
It grieves my heart to see thee thus;
Be comforted; relief is near,
For all your friends are in the rear.'
   She next the stately Bull implored,
And thus replied the mighty lord :
' Since every beast alive can tell
That I sincerely wish you well,
I may, without offence pretend
To take the freedom of a friend.
Love calls me hence; a favorite cow
Expects me near yon barley-mow;
And when a lady 's in the case,
You know all other things give place.
To leave you thus might seem unkind;
But see, the Goat is just behind.'
   The Goat remarked her pulse was high,
Her languid head, her heavy eye;
' My back,' says he, ' may do you harm;
The Sheep 's at hand, and wool is warm.'
   The Sheep was feeble, and complained
His sides a load of wool sustained ;
Said he was slow, confessed his fears,
For hounds eat sheep, as well as hares.

> She now the trotting Calf addressed
> To save from death a friend distressed.
> ' Shall I,' says he, ' of tender age,
> In this important care engage ?
> Older and abler passed you by;
> How strong are those, how weak am I !
> Should I presume to bear you hence,
> Those friends of mine may take offence.
> Excuse me, then.   You know my heart ;
> But dearest friends, alas ! must part.
> How shall we all lament ! adieu !
> For, see, the hounds are just in view ! ' "

Gay died suddenly in 1732.

One of the most remarkable men of this age was Jonathan Swift, born in Dublin, 1667.   The natural force and inventive genius displayed by Swift in his prose writings have in a measure obscured his reputation as a poet, though he is placed by critics in the first rank of agreeable moralists in verse.   Born a posthumous child, and bred up an object of charity, the want and dependence with which he was early familiar appear to have sunk deep into his soul.   He early adopted the custom of keeping his birthday as a day of mourning rather than of joy, reading ever upon its annual recurrence that passage from Scripture in which Job curses the day upon which it was said in his father's house that a man-child was born.

Swift was sent by his uncle to Trinity College, Dublin, which he left in his twenty-first year, and was received into the house of Sir William Temple, a distant relative of his mother.   Here he met King William, and, it is said, indulged hopes of royal preferment which were never realized.   In 1692 he took orders in the Irish Church, and we afterward find him living as an obscure country clergyman on a salary of one hundred pounds, subsequently as chaplain and secretary to the Earl of Berkeley, and later rector of Laracor in Ireland.

The "Man with the Iron Mask" was not more inscru-
table than was Swift in his social and domestic life. His
apparently true attachment to the Stella whom he has
celebrated in verse was rendered weird and unnatural by
his determination — to which it is said he ever strictly
adhered — never to see her except in the presence of a
third person. Worn out at last with the cruel scandal
of the misjudging world that treated her as the mistress
of the man who had secretly, and it would seem grudgingly, married her, this poor lady died under the insane
tyranny of one who, as he said, "loved her better than his
life a thousand millions of times!" "Human nature,"
says one of his critics, "has perhaps never before or
since presented the spectacle of a man of such transcendent powers as Swift involved in such a pitiable labyrinth of the affections."

During his residence in Ireland he had engaged the
affections of another young lady, who, under the name
of Vanessa, rivalled Stella in poetical celebrity and in
personal misfortune. There is nothing, even in fiction,
more steeped in pathos than the sad story of this poor girl.
Beautiful, virtuous, talented, and accomplished, she wor-
shipped at eighteen, in her plain tutor, — "a gown of forty-
four," — her (to use her own words) "guide, instructor,
lover, friend." That she might breathe the same air with
Swift, she removed to Ireland as Stella had done, and
submitting herself to coldness and neglect, lived, like lonely
"Mariana in the moated grange," a life of the deepest
seclusion, varied only by the angel visits of the dean, each
of which she commemorated by planting with her own
hand a laurel in the garden where they met.

After a blameless but ill-judged attachment of eight
years, when all her agonizing remonstrances, her devotion,
and her offerings, — touching beyond expression, — had

failed, she was struck to the heart by the cruel assurance that Swift was already the husband of another. She sent him the reply to her letter of interrogation received from Stella. In a paroxysm of fury, he immediately sought her presence, and flinging at her this letter, rode fiercely to Dublin. This ebullition of fury was her death-warrant. She survived it but a few weeks. In her will she ordered that the poem of " Cadenus and Vanessa," in which Swift had sung their friendship and her praises, should be published.

Alas! since the day when the poet of poets made Titania adore Bottom, women have, now and then, wasted themselves on brutes. Who among us would care to be celebrated as coarsely, and held as cheaply in the public eye, as is Stella in these birthday verses of her clownish-souled husband?

TO STELLA AT THIRTY-SIX.

ALL travellers at first incline
Where'er they see the fairest sign:
And if they find the chambers neat,
And like the liquor and the meat,
Will call again, and recommend
The Angel Inn to every friend.
What though the painting grows decay'd,
The house will never lose its trade.
Nay, though the treacherous tapster, Thomas,
Hangs a new Angel two doors from us.
   .   .   .   .   .
We think it both a shame and sin,
To quit the true old Angel Inn.
  Now this is Stella's case in fact,
An angel's face a little crack'd;
Could poets or could painters fix
How angels look at thirty-six. . . .

Swift, in view of all this, has been unjustly regarded as a diabolical monster of cruelty ; for charity finds the key-note to a life of singular inconsistency in the latent insanity which must then have been lurking in his frame, and which, as we know, overcame him at last. His heart, weaker than his intellect, must have sooner felt its ravages ; and a presentiment of his fate seems to have haunted him through life. After various attacks of deafness and giddiness, his temper became ungovernable, and his reason gave way. "The stage mercifully darkened," says Scott, "before the curtain fell ; " and Swift's almost total silence during the last three years of his life (for the last year he spoke not a word) was the last appalling scene in the strange drama of a life whose frailties and errors seem to have been but the natural result of a diseased mental organization.

Swift died on the 19th of October, 1745, and was buried in St. Patrick's Cathedral, amid the tears and prayers of his countrymen. His fortune, amounting to about ten thousand pounds, he left chiefly to found a lunatic asylum in Dublin ; to use his own words, —

> "He gave the little wealth he had,
> To build a house for fools and mad ;
> And showed by one satiric touch,
> No nation needed it so much."

This description in "Baucis and Philemon" is an example of Swift's Dutch art, and a fair specimen of his smooth versification ; it is a part of the account of the metamorphosis of their cottage : —

> "They scarce had spoke, when fair and soft
> The roof began to mount aloft ;
> Aloft rose every beam and rafter ;
> The heavy wall climbed slowly after.

The chimney widened and grew higher,
Became a steeple with a spire.
    The kettle to the top was hoist,
And there stood fasten'd to a joist,
But with the upside down to show
Its inclination for below:
In vain; for a superiour force
Apply'd at bottom stops its course:
Doomed ever in suspense to dwell,
'T is now no kettle, but a bell.
    A wooden jack, which had almost
Lost by disuse the art to roast,
A sudden alteration feels,
Increas'd by new intestine wheels;
And, what exalts the wonder more,
The number made the motion slower.
The flier, though it had leaden feet,
Turn'd round so quick you scarce could see 't;
But, slacken'd by some secret power,
Now hardly moves an inch an hour.
The jack and chimney, near allied,
Had never left each other's side:
The chimney to a steeple grown,
The jack would not be left alone;
But, up against the steeple rear'd,
Became a clock, and still adher'd;
And still its love to household cares,
By a shrill voice, at noon, declares,
Warning the cookmaid not to burn
That roast meat which it cannot turn.
    The groaning-chair began to crawl
Like a huge snail along the wall,
There stuck aloft in public view,
And with small change, a pulpit grew.
    The porringers, that in a row
Hung high, and made a glittering show,
To a less noble substance chang'd
Were now but leathern buckets rang'd.
    The ballads, pasted on the wall,
Of Joan of France, and English Moll,
Fair Rosamond, and Robinhood,

> The little Children in the Wood,
> Now seem'd to look abundance better,
> Improv'd in picture, size, and letter:
> And, high in order plac'd, describe
> The heraldry of every tribe.
>
>   A bedstead of the antique mode,
> Compact of timber many a load,
> Such as our ancestors did use,
> Was metamorphos'd into pews;
> Which still their ancient nature keep,
> By lodging folks dispos'd to sleep.
> The cottage, by such feats as these
> Grown to a church by just degrees
> The hermits then desir'd their host
> To ask for what he fancied most."

As a poet Swift is faithfully minute in description; in satire he displays rare wit; his versification is easy and flowing. He is often repulsively gross in his style and subject, and always " of the earth, earthy." His verses on his own death are a fine example of his peculiar poetical vein, — a mad play and sparkle of ironic wit blent with a homely and heart-felt pathos. The purity of his prose style renders it a model of English composition. " The Tale of a Tub," and " Gulliver's Travels," rather than his poems, are the chief corner-stones of his fame.

If poetry is indeed but an endeavor of the soul to escape from the persecution of realities into that golden clime, the enchanted land of Fancy, the latter composition is, in conception, a poem. Swift is considered the most masculine genius of his age and the most earnest thinker of a time when there was less earnest and deep thinking in England than in any era of our literature.

Of Addison it may also be said that his prose was the chief source of his fame; he wanted both the fancy and fire of the poet, though through his muse he first won distinction. He was the son of an English dean, and born in

1672. At Oxford he distinguished himself by his Latin poetry, and subsequently, by a poem to his Majesty, presented by the Lord-Keeper, he obtained a pension which enabled him to make the tour of Italy, from whence he wrote his " Poetical Letter," considered the most elegant and animated of all the productions of his muse. The death of King William deprived him of his pension ; but he afterward won court favor by celebrating in verse the battle of Blenheim, and was made Under-Secretary of State, as well as Keeper of the Records in Ireland.

Addison received his highest political honor in 1717, when he was made Secretary of State. Wanting the physical boldness of an effective public speaker, he was unable to defend his measures in Parliament, and his critical nicety and fastidiousness rendered him unfit for the prompt discharge of the ordinary duties of the office. It is said that when, as under-secretary, he was employed to send word to Prince George, at Hanover, of the death of Queen Anne and the vacancy of the throne, he was so distracted by the choice of expression that the task was given to a clerk, who boasted of having done " what was too hard for Addison."

The poet held the office of secretary but a short time, retiring with a pension of fifteen hundred pounds. He died in 1719, " calmly and religiously resigning a life which, though not long, had been well spent." His friend Tickell has thus commended his virtue and worth : —

> " He taught us how to live ; and, oh ! too high
> The price of knowledge ! taught us how to die."

" Addison had," says Steele, " that remarkable bashfulness which is a cloak that muffles and hides true merit." Chesterfield calls him " the most timorous and awkward of men ; " and he himself thus bears testimony to his own backwardness in conversation : "I could draw bills," he says, " for a thousand pounds, yet I had not a guinea in my pocket." In familiar and unrestrained intercourse " his conversation," says Pope, " has in it something more charming than I have found in any other man."

It has been suggested that Addison was first led to excess in wine — his only moral weakness — by a desire to set loose his tongue. This propensity was unfortunately aggravated by his unhappy marriage with the mean Countess of Warwick, who treated him more as a slave than a husband ; and like many another, he at last sought in the wine-cup a Lethe for domestic discontent. It has been justly remarked that " the uniform tendency of all his writings is his best and highest eulogium," and that " the impression made by them is like being recalled to a sense of something akin to that original purity from which man has long been estranged." His hymns, by their unaffected piety and elegance, commend themselves alike to the religious and the critical.

In 1713 his tragedy of " Cato " was brought on the stage. Addison's genius was not dramatic ; and though " Cato " abounds in lofty sentiments, contains passages of great moral beauty and dignity, preserves the unities of time and place, and has been commended for sonorous diction, it is still marble cold, — a graceful and majestic work of art, but lifeless and fair as some fine antique statue. There is more of the fervor and fire of true dramatic genius in a single page of " Othello " than can be found in the entire play of " Cato." In its own way, however, it is probably unrivalled. It is one of the few English tragedies that foreigners have admired. The French have even placed it before " Macbeth." It was translated into that language and performed by the Jesuits in their college at

St. Omers, and also rendered into Italian and German. As a prose-writer Addison may claim the merit of correcting our language, and effecting a revolution in our literature by modelling a pure English style; and he must be allowed the still higher praise of having elevated the taste and increased the piety, philanthropy, and refinement of his age. In Queen Anne's blessed time poetry was not, as now, like virtue, its own reward. It had its solid and tangible emoluments. For this single simile of Addison's in the " Battle of Blenheim," he was made Commissioner of Appeals on the spot, the Lord Treasurer's admiration of the poem being so enthusiastic that he could not even wait for its completion before rewarding the poet for these lucky lines, —

> " So, when an angel, by divine command,
>   With rising tempests shakes a guilty land,
>   Such as of late o'er pale Britannia passed,
>   Calm and serene he drives the furious blast,
>   And, pleased th' Almighty's orders to perform,
>   Rides in the whirlwind, and directs the storm."

Smooth and elegant as these lines are, we have, I think, seen better work of the same sort done for less pay; it is, however, no doubt, reassuring to be informed that our battles are heaven-directed, however questionable we find the assertion.

The dramatic literature of this period was, like its general poetry, polished and artificial. In tragedy the highest name is that of Southerne, who, though his language is feeble compared with that of the great dramatists, and his general style low and unimpressive, may claim with Otway the power of touching the passions. Addison's " Cato," it may be observed, is more properly a classic poem than a drama.

The vigorous exposure of the immorality of the stage

by Jeremy Collier, and the essays of Steele and Addison now improving the taste and moral feeling of the public, a partial reformation took place in the drama, which the Restoration had introduced; but even at the representation of these improved plays it is asserted that ladies still had occasion to wear masks, as they usually did on the first days of acting a new play. In comedy the highest name of this period is that of Congreve, born in Ireland, 1670. He was of a good family, studied law, but began early to write for the stage. His "Old Bachelor," produced in his twenty-first year, was acted with great applause. His life was a happy and prosperous one. A complaint in the eyes afflicted him in his latter days, which finally terminated in blindness. He died in 1729.

Dryden complimented Congreve as "one whom every muse and grace adorned;" and Pope dedicated to him his translation of the Iliad.

We must not omit one remarkable incident in the life of Congreve, — his apparently blameless intimacy with the Duchess of Marlborough, at whose table he sat daily, regaling her Highness with his conversation and amiably assisting in her household management. On his death he left the bulk of his fortune, amounting to about ten thousand pounds, to this eccentric lady. Her Grace laid out her friend's bequest in a superb diamond necklace, which she wore in honor of him; and report says she honored his memory in ways much more extraordinary. It is affirmed that her Ladyship had a statue of the deceased poet in ivory, which moved by clockwork, and was placed daily at her table; and moreover that the good woman had a wax doll made in imitation of him, and that to render the illusion complete, the feet of this doll were regularly blistered and anointed by the doctors, as poor Congreve's feet had been when he suffered from the gout.

Posterity has not awarded to Congreve the high place
in literature which the glittering artificial school allowed
him. Brilliant in dialogue and repartee, exuberant in
dramatic incident and character, he has still but few
charms to the genuine lovers of the natural and the true,
and is not recommended by any moral purpose or sentiment.   One line in his tragedy of the " Mourning Bride "
has been often quoted : —

"Music hath charms to soothe a savage breast."

The age now under notice derives perhaps greater lustre from its essayists than from its poets and dramatists.
Papers containing news had been established in London
and other large cities, since the time of the Civil War, but
the idea of issuing a periodical sheet, commenting on the
events of private life and the dispositions of ordinary
men, was never before entertained either in England or
elsewhere.   The credit of beginning this new and peculiar
kind of literature is due to Sir Richard Steele, who first
conceived the idea of attacking the vices and foibles of
the age through the medium of a lively periodical paper,
and accordingly commenced the publication of the
" Tatler," a small sheet designed to appear three times a
week, a part of each paper — to conciliate the news-lover
— being devoted to public and political intelligence.   The
" Tatler " was in 1711 merged in the more celebrated
" Spectator" (subsequently superseded by the " Guardian "),
which appeared every morning in the shape of a single
leaf and invariably without any admixture of politics,
and was received at the breakfast-tables of most persons
of taste then living in the metropolis.   Steele contributed
the greater part of the light and humorous sketches ; Addison most of the articles in which there is any grave reflection or elevated feeling.   The beneficial influence of

this form of literature on the morality, piety, manners, and intelligence of the British people has been extensive and permanent; and to the circulation of these papers may also be ascribed the beginning of a just taste in the fields of fancy and picturesque beauty. "From the perusal of these essays," says Dr. Drake, " that large body of the people included in the middle class of society first derived their capability of judging of the merits of a refined writer; and the nation at large gradually from this epoch became entitled to the distinguishing appellations of literary and critical."

Notwithstanding the high excellence which must be attributed to the British essayists, we cannot accord to them that philosophic depth, that comprehensiveness and originality which since the age of Queen Anne has come into request. And though the poets of the age may have corrected the indecencies introduced at the Restoration, they are deficient in force or greatness of fancy and in those natural graces of pathos and enthusiasm which are the life-blood of true poetry.

CHAPTER XII.

YOUNG, THOMSON, GOLDSMITH, GRAY, MINOR POETS, AND COWPER.

THE fifty-three years between 1727 and 1780, embracing the reign of George II. and a portion of the reign of George III., was not marked by such striking features of originality or vigor as some of the preceding eras ; yet it produced more men of letters, as well as more men of science, than any epoch of similar extent in the literary history of England. It was also a time during which greater progress was made in diffusing literature among the people at large than had been made perhaps throughout all the ages that went before it.

The publication of Percy's "Reliques" and Warton's "History of Poetry," by directing public attention to the early writers and showing the powerful effects which could be produced by simple narrative and natural emotion in verse, had sown the seed which was to germinate in the next generation, when Cowper should complete what Thomson had begun. A sort of successor, under the reign of Pope, of the Donnes and Cowleys of a former age, was the author of the "Night Thoughts," having "Donne's conceits without his subtle fancy, the quibbles and contortions of Cowley without his elegance, playfulness, and gayety."

Dr. Edward Young, born in 1684, was educated at Oxford ; and in 1712 he commenced public life as a court-

ier and poet, and in both characters he figures till past
eighty. In his youth Young was gay and dissipated.
The dissolute and notorious Duke of Wharton, who was,
it is said, " the scorn and wonder of his day," was his
patron and companion. When upward of fifty he entered
the Church, wrote a panegyric on the King, and was made
one of his Majesty's chaplains, and, as Swift has it, was
thus —

> " Compelled to torture his invention,
> To flatter knaves, or lose his pension."

In 1730 the poet obtained from his college the living of
Welwyn, in Hertfordshire, where he was destined to close
his days. He was, all his life long, an indefatigable
courtier, and was eager to obtain royal preferment; but
having unluckily professed in his poetry a strong love of
retirement, the ministry, it is said, seized upon this as a
pretext for keeping him out of a bishopric.

In 1731 Young married Lady Elizabeth Lee, daughter
of the Earl of Lichfield, and widow of Colonel Lee; this
ambitious alliance proved a happier union than the titled
marriages of Dryden and Addison. By her first marriage
the lady had two children, to whom Young was warmly
attached; both died, and when in 1741, ten years after
their marriage, the mother also followed, Young produced
the " Night Thoughts."

This long poem, founded on family misfortune, colored
and exaggerated for poetical effect, " shows," as has been
remarked, " the poetical artist fully as much as the
humble and penitent Christian." Swift had asserted that
hypocrisy was less mischievous than open impiety, yet
no man had a greater dread of this sin than he; and it
has been said of him that " instead of wishing to seem
better, he contrived ever to seem worse, than he really was,
and not only carefully hid the good he did, but willingly

incurred the suspicion of evil which he did not." The character of Young affords the most striking contrast to that of Swift. In his poetry he is a severe moralist and ascetic divine, yet it can hardly be inferred that he felt the emotions he described, as they seem not to have influenced his conduct. After a youth of dissipation and a manhood of bustling ambition, we find him unweaned from the world till age has incapacitated him for its pursuits. In 1761 he was made Clerk of the Closet to the Princess Dowager of Wales, and died four years afterward, in April, 1765.

Of Young's numerous works, "The Night Thoughts," "The Universal Passion," and the tragedy of "Revenge," are thought to be the best. "This poet," as Hazlitt observes, "has been overrated, from the popularity of his subject, and the glitter and lofty pretensions of his style." He is all art and effort, and though in his "Night Thoughts" we find poetical imagery, sound maxims, and passages of great force, it is a poem that few care to peruse continuously. With all its epigrammatic point and wit, its religious sentiment is morbid and unwholesome; and the gloomy views it presents of life, even Mrs. Gummidge with all her "contrairy" experiences could scarcely be justified in indulging. Its want of plot and progressive interest, combined with its tedious length; the tenacity with which the poet holds on to his illustrations, — only equalled by the twenty-seventhlies in the good old sermons, — are a weariness to flesh and spirit. In epic poetry, where the interest is sustained by action, long stories may be tolerated; but sermons, either poetical or prosaic, lose in pith, as they gain in "linked sweetness long drawn out." "Young," says Hazlitt, "has false ornament, labored conceit, false fancy, false sublimity, and mock tenderness." Yet we must still accord to him

genius and true poetical inspiration. His verse has been
aptly termed, —

> " The glorious fragments of a fire immortal
> With rubbish mixed, and glittering in the dust."

One of the most poetical passages in the " Night
Thoughts " is this apostrophe to Night : —

> " And art thou still unsung,
> Beneath whose brow, and by whose aid, I sing ?
> Immortal silence! where shall I begin ?
> Where end ? or how steal music from the spheres
> To soothe their goddess ?
>   Oh majestic Night !
> Nature's great ancestor ! Day's elder born !
> And fated to survive the transient sun !
> By mortals and immortals seen with awe !
> A starry crown thy raven brow adorns,
> An azure zone thy waist ; clouds, in Heaven's loom
> Wrought through variety of shape and shade,
> In ample folds of drapery divine,
> Thy flowing mantle form, and, heaven throughout,
> Voluminously pour thy pompous train :
> Thy gloomy grandeurs, Nature's most august
> Inspiring aspect ! Claim a grateful verse ;
> And, like a sable curtain starred with gold,
> Drawn o'er my labors past, shall clothe the scene."

This apostrophe has been called " magnificent," and said
" scarcely to be equalled in English poetry since the epic
strains of Milton." This seems now exaggerated praise.
The same fine poetic conception, rendered in simple, natural, and concise style, and irradiated by a hopeful, helpful
philosophy, would have been far more admirable ; as we
shall see by turning to these fine stanzas from Longfellow's
" Hymn to the Night " : —

> " I felt her presence, by its spell of might,
>   Stoop o'er me from above :
> The calm majestic presence of the Night,
>   As of the one I love.
>   .   .   .   .

"O holy Night! from thee I learn to bear
   What man hath borne before:
Thou layest thy finger on the lips of Care,
   And they complain no more."

As Young was all art and effort, Thomson was all neg-
ligence and Nature, pouring forth his "unpremeditated
lay" with the wild luxuriance of the bird in the greenwood, — Nature's thriftless prodigal, showering with lavish
melody the heedless air, careless of a listening ear.

James Thomson was born at Ednam near Kelso, County
of Roxburgh, September, 1700.   His father, then minister
of the parish of Ednam, removed a few years afterward to
that of South-dean in the same county, — a primitive and
retired district situated among the lower slopes of the
Cheviots.   Here the young poet spent his boyish years.
At eighteen he was sent to Edinburgh College.   His
father died when he had passed but two years there, and
the poet proceeded to London, to push his fortunes.   A
friend procured him the situation of tutor to the son of
Lord Binney; and he was now advised to connect some
of his descriptions of winter into one regular poem.   This
was done, and "Winter" (the copyright sold for only
three guineas) was published in March, 1726.

The poem was immediately popular, and a second and
third edition appeared the same year.   In 1727 "Summer" appeared; and the following year Thomson issued
proposals for publishing by subscription the "Four Seasons."   The number of subscribers, at a guinea each
copy, was three hundred and eighty-seven, but many took
more than one copy; and Pope, it is said, showed his generous appreciation of the poet who of all his cotemporaries
was perhaps most directly his antipodes, by taking three
copies.

In 1731 Thomson, in the capacity of tutor, or travelling

companion, had the good fortune to visit France, Switzerland, and Italy.   On his return, he published his poem of "Liberty," and obtained a situation as secretary, which he is said with his characteristic indolence to have lost at last by failing to solicit a continuation of the office.   His circumstances were at length brightened by a yearly pension of one hundred pounds from the Prince of Wales, and an appointment to the office of Surveyor-General of the Leeward Islands, the duties of which he was allowed to perform by deputy, and which brought an annual income of three hundred pounds.

The poet now resided in comparative opulence at Kew-lane, near Richmond, where his domain is said to have been "the scene of social enjoyment and luxurious ease." Thomson appears to have been utterly devoid of that predilection for a garret commonly ascribed to poets.

His cottage at Kewlane — a very Castle of Indolence — is described as elegantly furnished, with spacious grounds, and ample cellar, which after his death was found well-stocked with wines and good Scotch ale.   In this comfortable and elegant retreat, where "retirement and Nature" are said to have "become more and more his passion every day," he died suddenly, in August, 1748.

Thomson is the best of our descriptive poets ; and in the "Seasons" his subject — comprehensible and interesting both to the ignorant and refined — renders him the most popular of poets.   In describing a landscape he transfers to the imagination of his readers the vivid impression which as a whole it makes upon his mind, rather than the minute inventory of objects which, however perfect, cannot fail to weary the mind of the reader.   "Thomson," says Dr. Johnson, "thinks in a peculiar train, and he thinks always as a man of genius ; he looks around on

Nature and on life with the eye which Nature bestows only on a poet, and with a mind that at once comprehends the vast, and attends to the minute." To this well-expressed encomium another critic happily adds : " He looks also with a heart that feels for all mankind. His sympathies are universal. His touching description of the peasant perishing in the snow, the Siberian exile, or the Arab pilgrims, are all marked with that humanity and true feeling which show that the poet's virtues formed the magic of his song." Thomson was a born poet. Critics have allowed him invention, fancy, wit, and humor of the most voluptuous kind. " His faults," it has been aptly said, " were those of his style. He is often inelegant, and his diction is at times too gaudy and ornamental ; but the original genius of the poet, the pith and marrow of his imagination, the fine natural mould in which his feelings were bedded, were too much for him to counteract by neglect or affectation or false ornaments."

In the drama Thomson failed. " Agamemnon," his tragedy, we are told, was " only endured." It struggled with great difficulty through the first night. We have a ludicrous picture of the author on that hapless night appearing in panting haste before some friends with whom he was to sup, and pitiably excusing his delay by relating how at the play the anguish of his soul had broken out in perspiration, and had so disordered his wig as to render him unpresentable till he had been refitted by a barber.

On his poem of " Liberty " Thomson is said to have spent two years, but his best two productions are " The Castle of Indolence " and " The Seasons." " The Seasons" abounds in fine passages ; perhaps the most striking are the description of the contagion among the ships at Carthage and that of the caravan at Mecca. This bit from " Summer " is an example of the poet's happy diction :

> " Among the crooked lanes, on every hedge,
> The glow-worm lights his gem; and through the dark
> A moving radiance twinkles.   Evening yields
> The world to night; not in her winter robe
> Of massy Stygian woof, but loose arrayed
> In mantle dun . . .
> 　　　　　　 . . . leading soft
> The silent hours of love, with purest ray
> Sweet Venus shines. . . . The fairest lamp of night."

Thomson's " Castle of Indolence " has in it more pure
poesy than the " Seasons," and is consequently less
widely popular, though some critics have considered it
his best poem.   The materials of this exquisite poem he
is said to have derived originally from Tasso, though
from the marked similarity between it and the " Faery
Queen," the direct inspiration of the poet might seem to
have been drawn from Spenser.   Thomson, though less
elegant, had the same luxuriant exuberance that characterizes the elder poet, and it is the true source of his
power.   " The Castle of Indolence " was a poem after his
own heart.   Here he finds a subject entirely in unison with
his own listless temper; and the description of this luxurious palace of ease, with its lotos-eating inmates, is
indeed perfect and delightful, doing equal honor to the
genius and the supreme laziness of the poet who has been
seen eating peaches off a tree, with both hands in his
waistcoat pockets!   Thus, in numbers that

> "Softer fall than petals from blown roses on the grass,"

he describes that restful " lovely spot of ground " whereon
he built his " Castle," —

> " Was nought around but images of rest :
> Sleep-soothing groves, and quiet lawns between ;
> And flowery beds that slumb'rous influence kest,
> From poppies breathed ; and beds of pleasant green,

Where never yet was creeping creature seen.
Meantime unnumbered glittering streamlets played,
And hurlèd everywhere their waters' sheen;
That, as they bickered through the sunny glade,
Though restless still themselves, a lulling murmur made.

"Joined to the prattling of the purling rills,
Were heard the lowing herds along the vale,
And flocks loud bleating from the distant hills,
And vacant shepherds piping in the dale:
And now and then sweet Philomel would wail,
Or stock-doves 'plain amid the forest deep,
That drowsy rustled to the sighing gale;
And still a coil the grasshopper did keep;
Yet all these sounds y'blent inclined all to sleep.

"Full in the passage of the vale above,
A sable, silent, solemn forest stood,
Where nought but shadowy forms was seen to move,
As Idlesse fancied in her dreaming mood:
And up the hills, on either side, a wood
Of blackening pines, aye waving to and fro,
Sent forth a sleepy horror through the blood;
And where this valley winded out below,
The murmuring main was heard, and scarcely heard, to flow.

"A pleasing land of drowsy-head it was,
Of dreams that wave before the half-shut eye:
And of gay castles in the clouds that pass,
Forever flushing round a summer-sky:
There eke the soft delights, that witchingly
Instil a wanton sweetness through the breast,
And the calm pleasures, always hovered nigh;
But whate'er smacked of 'noyance or unrest,
Was far, far off expelled from this delicious nest."

Thomson received his highest praise in the prologue to
his posthumous tragedy, "Coriolanus."   "His works,"
said Lord Lyttleton, "contain no line which dying he
could wish to blot."

Worthy of notice among the minor poets of this era is
16

Akenside, author of the " Pleasures of Imagination," a
poet of taste and genius, and Beattie, whose fame rests
upon his unfinished poem, " The Minstrel," — a composition which has been commended for the correctness of its
style and the genius displayed in it, though in our day it
is but little read.

In this age lived and wrote the sacred bard, Dr. Watts,
whose poetry, consisting almost wholly of the fine devotional hymns so well known, will ever give his name a
place in the annals of our literature.   These hymns are, it
is true, unequal in merit, yet the best of them as sacred
lyrics have never been excelled ; and when, inspired by the
grandeur of his subject and elevated by pure religious fervor, he forgets the narrow dogmas of creed in expansive
and sublime conceptions of the Infinite, nothing can excel
in grandeur and majesty his inspired numbers, as in stanzas
like this, —

> " Our lives through various scenes are drawn,
>   And vexed with trifling cares ;
> While Thine eternal thought moves on
>   Thine undisturbed affairs."

In the literary annals of this period few names stand
higher or fairer than Goldsmith's.   In massive force of
understanding, in sagacious knowledge of the world, and
in moral poise of character, he was surpassed by his cotemporary, Dr. Johnson ; yet though in strength and
solidity Johnson bears the palm, Goldsmith far excelled
him in that inimitable grace and poetic elegance that are
part and parcel of the man.   Johnson might perhaps too
demand notice as an excellent reasoner in rhyme, though
one could not disparage the craft by according to him the
title of poet.   In the " Vanity of Human Wishes " he
takes expanded views of human nature, society, and manners, yet the same composition, in his own high-sounding,

sonorous prose, would have been far more admirable.
Nature has been lavish of rhymers, but chary of poets ;
and it is well to remember this wise maxim, " Never sing
your thought when you can *say* it." In the world of letters Johnson was crowned king, and though it must be
allowed that he depressed the literature of imagination
and poetry, he conferred a lasting benefit upon the language by elevating that of the understanding.

Oliver Goldsmith was born at Pallas, a small village in
the county of Longford, Ireland, on the 10th of November, 1728. His father, a poor curate, eked out his scanty
salary by cultivating the soil. Succeeding to a rectory,
he removed to Lissoy, where Goldsmith's youth was
spent, and where he found the materials for his " Deserted
Village."

At Trinity College, where, after a good country education, he was admitted a sizar, it is related of the poet that
— good-natured, thoughtless, and irregular — having un-
expectedly come into possession of thirty guineas, he
provided for the lads and lasses of the neighborhood a
bountiful collation, and made due preparation for an Irish
jig in his own apartment. His tutor, grim and awful,
broke in upon the festivities, and routed the dancers after
beating the host in the very presence of his guests ! Goldsmith fled in mortification from college, and having soon
exhausted his remaining guineas, wandered about the country for some time in the utmost poverty.

He was found by his good brother Henry, clothed, and
carried back to college, and in 1749 was admitted to the
degree of B. A. His father in the mean time had died.
Returning to his home in Lissoy, he idled away two years
among his relatives, spent one year as tutor in a gentleman's family, and then his uncle having given him twenty
pounds to study the law, proceeded to Dublin for that pur-

pose. There he lost the whole sum in a gaming-house. A second contribution was raised, and the poet proceeded to Edinburgh, where he continued a year and a half studying medicine. Time will not permit us to follow through all its vicissitudes the life of Goldsmith.

From his progenitors he inherited a thriftless extravagance, a warm heart, and an open hand, and that simple credulity in human goodness which unfitted him for a skilful part in the great game of life. He delighted in making others happy, yet he was seldom enough at ease in pecuniary matters to be happy himself; and all his life long, while good-naturedly relieving the necessities of others, he was harassed to death by his own. His unwise benevolence, that often did more credit to his heart than his head, is illustrated by this amusing anecdote : —

A friend had invited the poet to breakfast; the appointed hour had passed, and impatient of delay, he repaired to Goldsmith's apartments and found him still in bed, covered, and apparently half smothered, with scattering, unmanageable feathers. On inquiry, he learned that the poet had met, the evening before, a poor woman with her children, soliciting charity. He has not a crown in his purse, but bidding her await him at the gate, he hastens to his room, strips the covering from his bed, and bestows upon her the blankets and a part of his own clothing to enable her to raise funds for her necessities. In the night he awoke, shivering, and feeling the need of the missing blankets, ripped open the feather-bed and patiently crawled inside the ticking for warmth, whence, well befeathered, he issued, to the infinite amusement of his waiting host.

Difficulty and distress clung to Goldsmith to the last. He lived solely by his pen. His name stood foremost among his cotemporaries, and when at the summit of his fame and popularity, his works brought him in from one thousand to eighteen hundred dollars per annum. Yet his careless generosity, his heedless profusion, and extravagance in dress, combined with the attraction of the gaming-table, kept him continually in debt. He continued to write task-work for the booksellers, till worn out by close application and goaded by pecuniary embarrassment, he was attacked by a painful disease, succeeded by a nervous fever which ended his life at the early age of forty-five.

He died two thousand pounds in debt! "Was ever poet so trusted before?" exclaims Johnson. He was laid in the Temple burying-ground, and a monument erected to his memory in Westminster Abbey, next the grave of Gay, to whom, as has been observed, he bore some resemblance in character, though far surpassing him in genius. "Light lie the turf upon thy breast, gentle, loving, childlike heart; beloved with all thy faults and absurdities, thy thoughtless extravagances and innocent vanities, thy blossom-colored coat, rosy and radiant as thine own imagination. Let thy manly independence, generous benevolence, and enlightened zeal for the happiness and improvement of mankind cover the 'failings that ever' leaned to virtue's side."

"Poor Goldsmith!" says Irving, "shall we not feel for him who felt for all? With all his wealth of genius, the victim of his own fatal imprudence, 'struggling,' as he tells us, 'year after year with indigence and contempt, with all those strong passions that make contempt insupportable,' and in his hopeless condition requesting a gaol as a favor!"

Goldsmith may be said to belong to the school of Pope in form and in style. He has the same harmony and grace, and is nearly faultless; yet the earnestness and gentle simplicity of the man give to his poetry a tenderness and

a natural unstudied excellence which Pope never attained.
He is never sublime, seldom insipid or coarse. Johnson,
in his epitaph on the poet, has well characterized him :
" A ruler of our affections, and mover alike of our laughter and our tears, as gentle as he is prevailing."

In December, 1764, appeared Goldsmith's poem of the
" Traveller," which is the chief corner-stone of his fame.
Critics have considered it one of the finest poems in the language. His " Deserted Village " is almost equally meritorious, and there is probably no poem in the English language,
unless it be Gray's " Elegy," more universally popular. Its
best passages — such as the School-master's portraiture, the
description of the Ale House, and that picture of the Village
Preacher for which the poet's father sat — are familiar to
all ; yet so perfect are they in outline and beauty of coloring as never to weary by repetition. One might as soon
call a rose hackneyed ; and indeed we may say of some of
Goldsmith's verses that they have the same consummate
perfection that Nature has given to her floral master-
piece. Of the " Traveller " it has been affirmed that
" it is without one bad line." This is the Preacher's
fine portrait : —

> " A man he was to all the country dear,
> And passing rich with forty pounds a year ;
> Remote from towns he ran his godly race,
> Nor e'er had changed, nor wished to change his place ;
> Unskilful he to fawn or seek for power,
> By doctrines fashioned to the varying hour ;
> Far other aims his heart had learned to prize,
> More bent to raise the wretched than to rise.
> His house was known to all the vagrant train ;
> He chid their wanderings, but relieved their pain.
> The long-remembered beggar was his guest,
> Whose beard descending swept his aged breast ;
> The ruined spendthrift, now no longer proud,
> Claimed kindred there, and had his claims allowed ;

The broken soldier, kindly bade to stay,
Sat by his fire, and talked the night away;
Wept o'er his wounds, or tales of sorrow done,
Shouldered his crutch, and showed how fields were won.
Pleased with his guests, the good man learned to glow,
And quite forgot their vices in their woe;
Careless their merits or their faults to scan,
His pity gave ere charity began.
      Thus to relieve the wretched was his pride,
And e'en his failings leaned to virtue's side;
But, in his duty prompt at every call,
He watched and wept, he prayed and felt for all;
And as a bird each fond endearment tries,
To tempt her new-fledged offspring to the skies,
He tried each art, reproved each dull delay,
Allured to brighter worlds, and led the way.
Beside the bed where parting life was laid,
And sorrow, guilt, and pain by turns dismayed,
The reverend champion stood.   At his control
Despair and anguish fled the struggling soul;
Comfort came down the trembling wretch to raise,
And his last faltering accents whispered praise.
      At church, with meek and unaffected grace
His looks adorned the venerable place;
Truth from his lips prevailed with double sway;
And fools, who came to scoff, remained to pray.
The service past, around the pious man,
With ready zeal, each honest rustic ran;
E'en children followed with endearing wile,
And plucked his gown, to share the good man's smile;
His ready smile a parent's warmth expressed,
Their welfare pleased him, and their cares distressed;
To them his heart, his love, his griefs were given,
But all his serious thoughts had rest in heaven.
As some tall cliff that lifts its awful form,
Swells from the vale, and midway leaves the storm;
Though round its breast the rolling clouds are spread,
Eternal sunshine settles on its head."

Equally perfect is the School-master's picture, in —

    ". . . words of learned length, and thundering sound,"

arguing with the parson before the gaping rustics, till —

> ". . . still the wonder grew
> That one small head could carry all he knew ! "

By his pen Goldsmith has added vastly to the glory
of English literature and given delight to millions. Who
that reads the " Vicar of Wakefield " does not bless the
Providence that gave him to mankind?   The fashion of
this world passeth away, but human nature is eternally
the same, reproducing in one generation the faults and
the virtues of another on and on in endless cycles of being.
For nearly a whole century Moses has continued to go to
the fair, Mrs. Primrose has innocently prided herself upon
her daughters and her gooseberry wine ; poor Olivia, stoop-
ing to folly, still claims a pitying tear ; and not Rosa Bonheur's quadrupeds shall outlive those gratuitous " sheep "
that the obliging artist agreed to " throw in " as abundantly as possible when he undertook the great " family
picture."

Goldsmith produced his popular comedy of the " Good-
Natured Man " in 1768, and in 1773 " She Stoops to Con-
quer " was brought out at Covent Garden Theatre " with
immense applause."   And now, at the summit of his fame,
after his toilsome march, weary and worn, he lay down at
noontide, and slept the sleep that knows no waking.

By far the greatest of the minor poets belonging to the
age of the first two Georges was William Collins, who died
at the early age of thirty-eight, nearly all his poetry having
been written ten years before his death.   The story of his
life is brief and mournful.   Though but the son of a trades-
man, he received a learned education.   His genius was
great and his learning extensive ; and full of high hopes
and magnificent schemes, he repaired from Oxford to
London.

In 1746 he published his "Odes," which were purchased by Millar, the bookseller, but failed to attract the attention they so richly merited.   Nature had tempered Collins of clay too fine for the rough uses of life. The sensitive poet sunk under the disappointment; and already overshadowed by madness, — the fatal malady that overcame him at last, — he wasted in listless indolence or reckless dissipation the fine promise of his youth. The poet Thomson, whom he appears to have known and loved, died in 1748.   Collins " strung his lyre yet once again," and produced in honor to his memory that ode which has been pronounced one of the finest elegiacs in the language.

Now, in the midst of his difficulties his uncle died and left him a sum which he did not live to exhaust, — two thousand pounds.   He repaid the bookseller the loss sustained by the publication of his "Odes," and buying up the remaining copies, committed them to the flames.   The sunshine of fortune came too late.   He had produced works of genius, and the world had regarded them with scorn.   He sunk into a state of nervous imbecility, and his faithful sister, — who tended him till only the faint traces of memory and reason were left, — at last found it necessary to confine him in a lunatic asylum.   One can picture nothing, unless it be Charles Lamb and his poor crazed Mary, more touching than the devotion of this sister to mad, mournful Collins, wandering, as he is said to have done, when set at liberty, day and night among the sombre aisles and cloisters of the cathedral at Chichester, answering the pealing minster music with the loud sobs and moans of a breaking heart.   At last, with every spark of imagination extinguished, he is pictured, clasping with clinging hands only one book, and " that," he says, " is the best," the Bible.   And thus he died : —

> "This poet, who in a golden clime was born
>   With golden stars above,
>   Dowered with the hate of hate, the scorn of scorn,
>   The love, of love."

Peace to his broken heart!

Of Collins it has been justly said that " he had genius enough for anything ; " and all that he has written is full of imagination, pathos, and melody. It has been justly observed that " if there is any defect in his poetry, it is that it has too little of earth in it. In the purity and depth of its beauty it resembles the bright blue sky." Though utterly neglected on their first appearing, his " Odes " in the course of one generation, without any aid to bring them into notice, were acknowledged to be the best of their kind in the language. Silently and imperceptibly they had risen by their own buoyant merit, and their power was felt by every reader of true poetic feeling.

Of Collins's shorter odes this is perhaps the finest : —

> " How sleep the brave who sink to rest,
>   By all their country's wishes blest!
>   When Spring, with dewy fingers cold,
>   Returns to deck their hallowed mould,
>   She there shall dress a sweeter sod,
>   Than Fancy's feet have ever trod.
>
> " By fairy hands their knell is rung,
>   By forms unseen their dirge is sung;
>   There Honour comes, a pilgrim gray,
>   To bless the turf that wraps their clay,
>   And Freedom shall awhile repair,
>   To dwell, a weeping hermit, there."

Gray and Shenstone both outlived Collins, though born before him. Shenstone, born in 1714, and dying in 1763, is remembered for his " School-mistress " and a few pleas-

ing shorter poems. He aimed at political as well as poetical celebrity, and disappointed in his ambition, died in
solitude, but " still," it is said, " a votary of the world."
Two smooth stanzas from Shenstone, conned in the dear
old "English Reader," delighted our tender infant heart:

> " I have found out a gift for my fair,
>   I have found where the wood-pigeons breed:
> But, oh, let me this plunder forbear
>   She will say 't was a barbarous deed;
>
> " For he ne'er can be true, she averred,
>   Who would rob a poor bird of its young;
> And I loved her the more when I heard
>   Such tenderness fall from her tongue."

Ah, hardened indeed in iniquity we deemed the big
head-boy of our reading class who spouted fervently
those melting lines while still cold-bloodedly intent upon
his Saturday's birds'-nesting!

Thomas Gray, author of the far-famed " Elegy in a
Country Churchyard," was born in 1716. His father
had driven his wife and child from him by harsh treatment; and the poet owed to the exertions of his mother
as a needlewoman the advantages of a learned education.
These domestic circumstances are supposed to have given
to the poet that tinge of melancholy and pensive reflection
which is visible in his poetry.

After leaving college, his life affords but little of interest.
He spent a year in Italy with his friend, Horace Walpole.
His father's death now left him a moderate competency;
and being " more intent on learning than on riches," after
taking his degree in civil law he did not care to follow
up the profession, but fixing his residence at Cambridge,
passed amid its noble libraries and learned societies the
greater part of his remaining life. He died in 1771, in

his fifty-fifth year, and was buried, according to his desire, by the side of his good mother at Stoke, near Windsor.

Though Gray's poetry is confined to a few pieces, he may rank in quality with the first order of poets. His two odes, the " Progress of Poetry " and the " Bard," though not as purely poetical, surpass in fire, energy, and boldness of imagination the odes of Collins. The poetry of Gray has been aptly compared to " mosaic-work." In his country rambles he carried with him a plano-convex mirror, which in surveying landscapes gathers into one confined glance the forms and tints of the surrounding scene. A critic has observed that " his imagination performed a similar operation in collecting, fixing, and appropriating the materials of poetry. All is bright, natural, rich, and interesting, but seen only for a moment."

Gray is characterized by the finest classic taste. He studied in the school of the ancient and Italian poets, yet in his translations from the Norse tongue he has given to the wild superstitions of the Gothic nation the natural fire and rude energy of the Scandinavian bards. The highest poetry, addressing itself only to minds of kindred taste, can never be extensively popular. " Gray's classical diction," observes Craik, " his historical and mythological personification, must ever be lost on the multitude ; while his ' Elegy,' dealing with a subject familiar to all, and describing in exquisite harmonious verse what all might feel or imagine, will not lack readers or admirers, and will ever be the main prop of his reputation." There is scarcely a poem in the language more universally approved than Gray's " Elegy." Yet history does record that one solemn old lady conscientiously objected to the poem on this ground, — it was, she affirmed, "altogether too light and trifling !" This fact proves universal popularity to be unattainable. How must this same excellent person have been shocked by the sinful levity of Gray's " Ode on a Favorite Cat Drowned in a Tub of Goldfishes," who —

> " Eight times emerging from the flood,
> Mewed loud to every watery god ! "

In the " Progress of Poetry," less familiar than the " Elegy," we have some of Gray's richest and most majestic strains ; as, for example, the poetical character of Shakespeare, from which our poet, Stoddard, as may readily be observed, has borrowed the leading thought in his fine poem on the same subject.

> " Far from the sun and summer gale,
> In thy green lap was Nature's darling laid ;
> What time, where lucid Avon strayed,
> To him the mighty mother did unveil
> Her awful face ; the dauntless child
> Stretched forth his little arms, and smiled.
> ' This pencil take,' she said, ' whose colors clear
> Richly paint the vernal year :
> Thine too these golden keys, immortal boy !
> This can unlock the gates of Joy ;
> Of horror that, and thrilling fears,
> Or ope the sacred source of sympathetic tears.' "

Of equal excellence is this of Milton, from the same poem : —

> " Nor second he, that rode sublime
>   Upon the seraph-wings of Ecstasy,
>   The secrets of th' abyss to spy.
> He passed the flaming bounds of place and time :
> The living throne, the sapphire-blaze,
> Where angels tremble while they gaze,
> He saw ; but blasted with excess of light,
> Closed his eyes in endless night."

Notwithstanding their varied and complicated versification, Gray's stanzas flow with lyrical ease and perfect harmony. Description he considered a graceful ornament of poetry, but held that it ought never to make the subject, holding no poetry to be admirable that did not contain some weighty moral truth or some chain of reasoning. His standard was not a correct one; but he seems carefully to have practised what he believed and taught. Some profound thought or sentiment mingles with all he describes. As a poet he displays pathos, humor, elegance of diction, purity of aim, and exquisite finish. The "Elegy" has perhaps been inordinately valued. Gray's "Eton College" and "Progress of Poetry," by persons of kindred taste and knowledge, are quite as highly esteemed as that more popularly conceived poem. In 1854 a manuscript copy of the "Elegy," written in the poet's own small neat hand, was sold for the large sum of one hundred and thirty-one pounds! It has been aptly said that "it would be well for those who are disposed to underrate the gift of song to remember that although Gray is said to have been the most learned man of his age (he was certainly the most learned poet since Milton), a laborious student of history, genealogy, antiquities, and natural history, indeed versed more or less in every branch of knowledge except mathematics and theology; though his life was always that of a scholar, and only at intervals that of a poet, — for his fame he is indebted to half a dozen little poems, and not at all to the notes and fragments of criticism and commentary that he left in almost every department of human learning."

Thomas Chatterton, —

> "The marvellous boy,
> The sleepless soul that perished in his pride," —

was born at Bristol, 1752. He was the posthumous son of a school-teacher, and educated at a charity school where nothing but English, writing, and accounts were taught;

yet he was the most remarkable instance of precocious genius that his country and perhaps the world has ever known. "Genius," however, as has been observed, "should be estimated by its magnitude, rather than by its prematureness."

Chatterton attained in early boyhood the full powers of manhood; and if he had lived and failed to produce anything greater, as he might, he would have ceased to be a wonder. Apprenticed to an attorney at fourteen, his irksome duties still left him time to pursue his favorite studies, — poetry, antiquities, and heraldry. A proud ambition was his ruling passion; and by the pretended discoveries of old manuscripts — which were in reality the productions of his own precocious genius — he won at that early age the notice which he desired, and for a time duped the public. Subsequently his poems, which were written in the antique language and diction of the ancient bards, were proved to be forgeries. But this discovery only made him more famous; and great the wonder grew that an indifferently educated boy of sixteen should have produced such works. In poetical power and diction the avowed compositions of Chatterton are far inferior to the forgeries. Sir Walter Scott accounts for this by the fact that the whole powers and energies of the child must at a very early age have been converted to the acquisition of the obsolete language and peculiar style necessary to support this deep-laid deception. Our modern spiritualist would account for the superior excellence of the forgeries in quite another way; for was not this morbid boy cast in very "medium" mould? Where could defunct bards, whose restless ghosts still sigh along the ages for mortal celebrity, have found a readier mouthpiece than in this mesmeric and unscrupulous boy? If Chatterton — poor lad! — had but postponed his advent to this more psychical nineteenth century, what a world of trouble the spiritualists might have saved the antiquarians !

Released from his three years' apprenticeship, Chatterton went to London, where he engaged in various tasks for the booksellers, and wrote for the magazines and newspapers. He was, it is said, but a poor patriot, and wrote on both sides if money was to be got. He made it his boast that " his company was courted everywhere, and that he would settle the nation before he had done." These splendid hopes were early nipped in the bud. Failing to obtain a comfortable subsistence by his pen, Chatterton applied, as a last hope, for the appointment of surgeon's mate to Africa. He was refused the necessary recommendation, and disappointed and discouraged, fell into habits of intemperance, made no further effort at literary composition, and having cast off the restraints of religion, he had but one steady principle to guide him, — his affection for his mother and sister, to whom he sent remittances of money while his means lasted ; yet even this did not redeem him.

Reduced now to actual want, and his constitutional melancholy and pride aggravated by the fatal stimulant to which he resorted, he still maintained a maudlin self-respect, and the very day before his death he is said to have haughtily rejected a dinner offered him by his tender-hearted landlady. Wretched and starving, in his insane misery he tore all his papers, and destroyed himself by taking arsenic. He died in 1770. At the time of his death he was aged but seventeen years and nine months.

" Great geniuses," observes Hazlitt, " like great kings, have too much to think of to kill themselves ; for their mind also to them a kingdom is. . . . I believe," says the same critic, " that he would not have written better had he lived. He knew this *himself*, or he *would* have *lived*."

Malone — somewhat absurdly, I think — considers Chatterton the greatest genius that England has produced since the days of Shakespeare. Whatever may be affirmed of Chatterton's genius as to quantity, it must be insisted upon that in quality it bears not the slightest comparison with that of Shakespeare. Nature fashioned the bard of Avon in her choicest mould ; and a sound mind in a sound body developed in the open air of existence a genius healthy as it was rare. Chatterton's genius, precipitated in the feverish hot-bed of disease, was as morbid and unnatural as it was wonderful. Shakespeare goes to London indigent and obscure. Shall poverty overcome *him?* No. Let him rather overcome *her*. And manly and independent, he holds horses and is clothed and fed, and lives on forever in " Lear " and " Macbeth," in " Hamlet" and " Othello." Chatterton — poor boy ! — carries to the same great swarming hive of humanity his dreams and hopes, his penury and his pride. Poverty and want, like ravening wolves, are upon him ; he will " not dig ; to beg he is ashamed," and in his mad despair he says, " I will curse God and die ; " and *he* lives but in a few poems, flung like mournful driftwood on the shore of Time, — sad mementos of a bark that on its first venture went down, wrecked upon the cruel rocks of passion, penury, and pride !

> " Whatever crazy sorrow saith,
>   No life that breathes with human breath
>   Has ever truly longed for death.

> " 'T is life, whereof our nerves are scant,
>   Oh life, not death, for which we pant ;
>   More life, and fuller, that we want ! "

Chatterton's most distinguishing feature as a poet is his power of picturesque painting. His poems consist of the " Tragedy of Ælla," the " Execution of Sir Charles Baw-

17

din," "Ode to Ælla," "The Battle of Hastings," "The Tournament," one or two dialogues, and a description of Canynge's feast.

As Chatterton concentrated his whole faculties on the herculean task of creating the person, history, and language of an ancient poet, he could have had no time for the study of our modern poets, their rules of verse, or modes of expression ; and writing in his own character, his effusions, though they display a wonderful command of language, vigor, maturity, and freedom of style, are often in bad taste. In maturing his forgeries, he had no confidant in his labors, but toiled on in secret, gratified only by the stoical "pride of talent." Conceiving that the moon added to his inspiration by its immediate presence, he frequently wrote by its beams. He would also, it is said, lie down on the meadows in view of St. Mary's Church, Bristol, fix his eyes upon the ancient edifice, and seem as if he were in a kind of trance ; thus feeding his romantic imagination, he nursed that enthusiasm which at length destroyed him.

The success of Macpherson's "Ossian," then in the high tide of popularity, would appear to have prompted the remarkable forgeries of Chatterton. Macpherson seems to have collected some fragments of ancient Gaelic poetry floating among the Highlands. These he wrought up into regular poems, and gave to the world as the productions of Ossian, — a bard of the third or fourth century, — he, Macpherson, having translated them from the Gaelic. Not at all staggered by the astounding possibility that a people exhibiting the high and chivalrous feelings, and the refined virtues of modern civilization, existed at that early period among the wild, remote mountains of Scotland, or by the idea of the poems being handed down unimpaired by tradition through so many centuries among rude, savage, and barbarous tribes, the public received these forgeries with avidity. "Many doubted," it is said; "others disbelieved; but a still greater number indulged the pleasing supposition that Fingal fought and Ossian sung." The sale of Ossian's poems was immense, and Macpherson realized a handsome fortune. Time and an improved taste have abated the popularity of these poems, once hailed with delight by Gray, Hume, Blair, and others equally eminent, and said to have been the favorite reading of Napoleon; yet we must still accord to them a wild, solitary magnificence, pathos, tenderness, and true poetical power. The lamentations in the "Song of Selma" and the "Desolation of Balclutha" are finely conceived; as, for example, in this description : —

"The daughter of the snow overheard, and left the hall of her secret sigh.
She came in all her beauty, like the moon from the cloud of the east.
Loveliness was around her as light; her steps were like the music of songs."

How much of the published work is ancient, and how much fabricated, cannot now be ascertained. A fierce controversy raged for some time in regard to their authenticity. The Highland Society instituted a regular inquiry into the subject; and in their report the committee state that they have not been able to obtain any one poem the same in title and tenor with the ones published. It has been suggested that after having enjoyed the pleasure of duping so many critics, Macpherson intended one day to claim the poems as his own. His death, somewhat premature and sudden, closed the scene; and he left among his papers not a single line that throws any light upon the controversy. When Macpherson had not the groundwork of the ancient bard to build upon, he was a far more indifferent poet than Chatterton.

Chatterton's minstrel song in "Ælla" is perhaps his best production; it is at least his most poetical.

THE MINSTREL'S SONG IN ÆLLA.

O sing unto my roundelay;
  O drop the briny tear with me;
Dance no more on holiday,
  Like a running river be;
    My love is dead,
    Gone to his death-bed,
    All under the willow-tree.

Black his hair as the winter night,
  White his neck as summer snow,
Ruddy his face as the morning light,
  Cold he lies in the grave below:
    My love is dead,
    Gone to his death-bed,
    All under the willow-tree.

Sweet his tongue as throstle's note,
  Quick in dance as thought was he;
Deft his tabor, cudgel stout;
  Oh! he lies by the willow-tree.
    My love is dead,
    Gone to his death-bed,
    All under the willow-tree.

Hark! the raven flaps his wing,
  In the briered dell below;
Hark! the death-owl loud doth sing
  To the nightmares as they go.
    My love is dead,
    Gone to his death-bed,
    All under the willow-tree.

See! the white moon shines on high;
  Whiter is my true-love's shroud;

Whiter than the morning sky,
  Whiter than the evening cloud.
    My love is dead,
    Gone to his death-bed,
    All under the willow-tree.

Here upon my true-love's grave
  Shall the baren flowers be laid,
Nor one holy saint to save
  All the celness of a maid.
    My love is dead,
    Gone to his death-bed,
    All under the willow-tree.

With my hands I 'll bind the briers,
  Round his holy corse to gre;
Ouphante faery, light your fires,
  Here my body still shall be.
    My love is dead,
    Gone to his death-bed,
    All under the willow-tree.

Come with acorn-cup and thorn,
  Drain my heart's blood all away;
Life and all its good I scorn,
  Dance by night, or feast by day.
    My love is dead,
    Gone to his death-bed,
    All under the willow-tree.

Water-witches, crowned with reytes,
  Bear me to your deadly tide:
I die — I come — my true-love waits. —
  Thus the damsel spake, and died.

William Cowper, whose name cast the greatest lustre upon the latter part of the eighteenth century, though now somewhat neglected by us for the more lofty and splendid poets of our choice, is still dear to our inmost hearts. This gentle and affectionate poet — a sort of rhyming Penates — we still enshrine in our homes, and associate with the familiar joys of daily existence.

Cowper was born in the county of Hereford, 1731, and was descended from some of the noblest families of England on his father's side, and his mother's lineage could be traced, by four different lines, from Henry III. The poet, being God's most royal child, may afford to be "too proud to care from whence he came;" but Cowper's unassuming, childlike character appears the more lovely against this lustrous background. His father, Rev. Dr. Cowper, was chaplain to George II., and held besides the rectory of Great Burkhamstead. In his sixth year the poet lost his mother, and was sent to boarding-school. There, a delicate homesick child, he was for two miserable years subjected to the mean tyranny of an older school-fellow. Subsequently he "served," as he tells us, "a seven years' apprenticeship to the classics" at Westminster School, and at the age of eighteen was removed and articled to an attorney. Having passed through this training, he was, in 1764, called to the bar. In his thirty-second year Cowper found himself, by the death of his father, left with a small patrimony, which was fast growing less. The law was with him but a nominal profession, and in this crisis of his fortunes his kinsman, Major Cowper, presented him with a lucrative and desirable appointment in the House of Lords, which he accepted.

The seeds of insanity already in his brain were rapidly developed by the labor of studying the forms of procedure; and haunted by the dread of an impending examination at the bar of the House, he brooded over this necessity until reason fled, and in his madness he attempted his own life. Fortunately for himself and mankind, this desperate effort

failed. The appointment was of course given up, and
Cowper was removed to a private mad-house. In less
than eight months his reason was restored, but he continued through life a victim to those "hypochondrias"
which Carlyle tells us "all great souls are apt to have,
till the eternal ways and the celestial guiding-stars disclose
themselves, and the vague abyss of life knit itself up into
firmaments for them." His madness was succeeded by a
gentle melancholy, and by a new-born religious zeal, whose
fervor caused his friends to question if it were not a continuation of his madness. He now resolved to withdraw
entirely from the world, ceased corresponding with his
friends, and removing to the town of Huntingdon, near
Cambridge, became first a visitor, then a boarder, and
was afterward adopted into the family of Mr. Unwin, — a
clergyman of the place. After the death of Mr. Unwin, he
still resided with his widow, gentle Mary Unwin, —

"Partaker of his fame, and sad decline," —

removing with her to Olney, which now became their home.
  In 1773 Cowper's melancholy again developed into decided insanity, and in this unhappy state, faithfully attended
by Mary Unwin, about two years of his life were passed.
Cowper's mental disease was at this time greatly aggravated, if not entirely caused, by his hopeless religious
views, which led him to brood almost exclusively over
human depravity and the more awful attributes of his
God. He was associated with Rev. John Newton, to
whose collection of hymns he largely contributed. This
good person was unfortunately the worst of intimates for
a man who needed to be inspired by cheerfulness rather
than terror, yet at this time, with the exception of Mrs.
Unwin, he was his only acceptable friend. After his recovery from this attack our poet's gentle days were passed

beautifully and blamelessly, if not happily ; and what with
his pet hares, his poetry, his drawing and gardening, he
led a busy, useful life.   In 1796 his beloved Mrs. Unwin,
after a long and helpless disease, left him.   " He could
not," says his biographer, " believe her actually dead till
he saw the body in the placid repose of eternity.   Then
with a passionate exclamation of sorrow he flung himself
to the other side of the room, and from that time never
mentioned her name, though he survived her more than
three years."

Cowper's life to the last was shadowed by the dark cloud
of religious despondency.   In April, 1800, he passed beyond the region of clouds in a sleep so gentle and beautiful
that the moment of his departure was imperceptible.

In Cowper's character we have the finest combination
of purity of aim, lofty and unwavering principle, and rich
intellectual power.

In his verse he may be said to have broken through the
conventional forms and usages established by Pope, and
compared with his predecessors may be called a natural
poet.   He was endowed with little fancy and creative imagination ; yet after Thomson, he may be considered the
best of our descriptive poets.   His poetry is of high and
varied excellence, and has in it that simple earnestness
that charms even unpoetical minds.   Critics have allowed
him minute graphical power, tenderness, pathos, fine manly
sense, great simplicity, with terseness of style, wit, humor,
and elegance.

A distinguishing quality of his genius is its power to
blend harmoniously argument, piety, poetry, and common-
sense.   In his earliest poems it was his especial purpose
to make a departure from the old polished uniformity of
Pope and his imitators, and consequently they are purposely rugged.   Later, he acquired an individual freedom

of versification, a variety of pause and cadence, united with easy grace and melody, careful finish, simplicity, and terseness.   It is to be regretted that Cowper's religious melancholy and chronic dejection of mind hindered the habitual exercise of that rich humor which was also a part of his nature.   He says of himself when in the solicitor's office that he and his fellow-clerk, the future Lord Chancellor Thurlow, were "constantly employed in giggling and making giggle; " and we may well believe him.   In the Temple he wrote gay verses, and associated with congenial wits.   Mary Unwin, lovely and devoted as she was, does not seem to have been one to whom the element of mirth was natural and necessary.   Lady Austen, an accomplished and attractive widow who came to reside in the poet's neighborhood, and to whom, in part, we owe the "Task," — as it was she who induced him to write that poem, — appears to have had the happiest mental influence over Cowper.   Their friendship was unfortunately dissolved before that poem was completed.   It is said that she proved too attractive, exacting too much of that time and attention that belonged to Mary Unwin, whom Newton tells us in his diary that Cowper would have married but for his taint of insanity.   Whatever may have been the cause of their alienation, Lady Austen left Olney forever, but not until she had told the poet the "true story of 'John Gilpin,' " on which that inimitable ballad is founded, and which, as his biographer tells us, sprang up like a mushroom in a single night.   The lively lady having related it to Cowper in one of their evening parties, on his return from that cheerful gathering, it was versified in bed and presented to Lady Austen the next morning, in the shape of a ballad.

Of Cowper's long poems, the "Task" and "Table Talk" are considered the best.   The latter has many

fine and familiar passages. One of the best is that on
" Voltaire and the Lace-Weaver." His " Hymns " are
the best in our older collections. Who has not felt their
gentle power, and been inspired by their earnest piety,
as he sings verses like this? —

> " Return, O holy Dove, return !
>   Sweet messenger of rest !
> I hate the sins that made thee mourn,
>   And drove thee from my breast."

Cowper's poem on the receipt of his mother's picture is
full of tender filial pathos, and has been much admired.
His translations of the Iliad and Odyssey are the least
successful of his performances. His beautiful fable of
" The Nightingale and the Glow-Worm " is one of his
happiest productions. Cowper's subjects are not always
poetically chosen, and he is sometimes minutely prosaic
enough to satisfy the soul of the most inveterate realist.
His " Poetical Epistles " and many other shorter poems
are truly in the " pitch of prose ; " and when he begins
by informing

> " Dear Anna " that " between friend and friend
>   Prose answers every common end,"

we most heartily say Amen, and most sincerely regret that
an *un*common end should have induced him to " drop into
poetry." His poem to Mary, addressed to Mrs. Unwin,
old, infirm, and fast fading out of his life, but still divinely
dear to his tender, faithful heart, is one of his most beautiful
productions, and may be given as a specimen of his simple,
earnest pathos.

> " The twentieth year is well-nigh past
>   Since first our sky was overcast,
> Ah, would that this might be the last !
>   My Mary !

"Thy spirits have a fainter flow,
I see them daily weaker grow —
'T was my distress that brought thee low,
         My Mary!

"Thy needles, once a shining store,
For my sake restless heretofore,
Now rust disused, and shine no more,
         My Mary!

"For though thou gladly wouldst fulfil
The same kind office for me still,
Thy sight now seconds not thy will,
         My Mary!

"But well thou play'dst the housewife's part,
And all thy threads, with magic art,
Have wound themselves about this heart,
         My Mary!

"Thy silver locks once auburn bright,
Are still more lovely in my sight
Than golden beams of orient light,
         My Mary!

"For could I view nor them nor thee,
What sight worth seeing could I see?
The sun would rise in vain for me,
         My Mary!

"Partakers of thy sad decline,
Thy hands their little force resign;
Yet gently prest, press gently mine,
         My Mary!

"Such feebleness of limb thou prov'st,
That now at every step thou mov'st,
Upheld by two, yet still thou lov'st,
         My Mary!

"And still to love, though prest with ill,
In wintry age to feel no chill,
With me is to be lovely still,
         My Mary!

"But ah! by constant heed I know,
How oft the sadness that I show,
Transforms thy smiles to looks of woe,
            My Mary!

"And should my future lot be cast
With much resemblance to the past,
Thy worn-out heart will break at last,
            My Mary!"

In 1782 appeared anonymously his famous " History of
John Gilpin." It is one of the most delightfully humorous
poems in the language. To " the man who laughs " what
picture can be more soul-satisfying than that of this "linen-
draper bold," intent upon celebrating his conjugal anniversary, and mounting, with the " caution and good heed " of
an unaccustomed equestrian, the snorting beast, loaned for
the occasion, —

            "Stooping down as needs he must,
            Who cannot sit upright," —

while the frighted horse, clasped by his mane, —

            ". . . which never in that sort
            Had handled been before,
            What thing upon his back had got
            Did wonder more and more!"

But Gilpin, still valiantly clinging to his back, wigless,
hatless, with his long red cloak streaming in the wind,
flies past the Bell at Edmonton, where from thé balcony
his spouse and the already-arrived and waiting participants
of his holiday — " six precious souls, and all agog " —
astonished to behold the Hamlet of their play left out
and tantalizingly scampering away under their very noses,
thus hail him : —

> " ' Stop, stop, John Gilpin ! — Here 's the house ! '
>   They all at once did cry ;
>   ' The dinner waits, and we are tired ! '
>   Said Gilpin : ' So am I ! ' "

But on he goes, the turnpike gates flying open before him,
and the hue and cry behind, the tollmen all thinking that
he " rode a race."

> " And so he did, and won it too,
>   For he got first to town ;
>   Nor stopped till where he had got up
>   He did again get down."

We may well spare from history the august figure of
Alexander the Great trampling down the world on his
Bucephalus ; but doughty John Gilpin, never ! On the
back of the Calendar's runaway, this famous equestrian
hero must forever " drink the wind of his own speed," and
in this sound poetical faith —

> " Now let us sing, long live the king,
>   And Gilpin, long live he."

CHAPTER XIII.

SCOTTISH POETRY AND ROBERT BURNS.

IN the reign of Edward II. (1307–27) — which is thought to be the era of the earlier metrical romances of Scotland — lived Thomas of Ercildoune, noted in Scottish tradition under the appellation of Thomas the Rhymer.

Sir Walter Scott in 1804 published a composition of this poet entitled " Sir Tristrem," which he supposed upon tolerable evidence to have been written in the middle or latter part of the thirteenth century, though the soundness of his theory has since been denied. The romance of " Sir Tristrem" was taken from the Auchinleck manuscript in the Advocates' Library at Edinburgh, — a volume containing in all forty-four pieces of ancient poetry, complete or imperfect, and supposed to have been compiled in an Anglo-Norman convent in the earlier part of the fourteenth century.

The language spoken by the Lowland Scotch in the earlier part of the fourteenth century, which is the age of the birth of Scottish poetry, must have sprung out of the same sources and been affected by nearly the same circumstances as the English of the same age, and is said to have been distinguished from that of the south of England, which acquired the ascendency over that of the northern counties as the literary dialect, by little more than the retention of many vocables which had become obsolete among the English, and a generally broader enunciation of the vowel sounds.

Chaucer had in the latter part of that century a more formidable rival than his friend Gower, in the person of a Scotchman by the name of John Barbour. Of his personal history but little is known. In the year 1320 he is styled Archdeacon of Aberdeen in a passport granted him by Edward III. at the request of King David II. of Scotland, to come into England for the purpose of studying in the university at Oxford. Three other passports are extant; the third, in 1368, secures him protection in coming with two valets and two horses into England, and travelling through the same on his way to France, for the purpose of studying there.

It is to be inferred from this outfit that Barbour was in most prosaically " comfortable circumstances." His death is known to have taken place at an advanced age, in 1395. His sole remaining work, " The Bruce," is a complete history of the memorable transactions by which King Robert asserted the independency of Scotland, and obtained its crown for himself and family.

" The Bruce " is a poem of great length, comprising between twelve and thirteen thousand lines. The main texture of the narrative has always been regarded as an authentic historical monument, and has been received and quoted by all subsequent writers and investigators of Scottish history.

Barbour lacks the grand inventive imagination of Chaucer, and has neither his wit nor humor nor his delicate sense of the beautiful; but his diction is clear, strong, and direct, and his narrative descriptive, animated, and picturesque. And though his poem lacks sweetness and harmony, it is pervaded with generous and dignified sentiment. He paints the injuries of his country with distinctness and force, and celebrates the heroism of her champions and deliverers with admiration and sympathy.

Cotemporary with Barbour, and like him adorning the
language by a strain of versification, expression, and poetical imagery far superior to his age, is Blind Harry, who
about 1460 wrote a heroic poem entitled " The Adventures of Sir William Wallace." Of this author nothing is
known but that he was blind from infancy, and that he
wrote this poem, and made a living by reciting it, or parts
of it, before company. It abounds in marvellous stories of
the prowess of Scotland's grand old hero, whose name will
forever thrill along the chords of the national heart.

Some of Harry's legends are thought to have no foundation in fact, though from the simple unaffectedness of the
narrative it is supposed that the author meant only to state
real facts. Blind Harry's poem has been commended for
elevated sentiment and poetical effect, and a paraphrase of
it into modern Scotch, by William Hamilton, has long been
a popular volume among the Scottish peasantry. Dr.
Currie, in his Life of Burns, affirms that the study of this
book had great effect in kindling the genius of this gifted
son of Scotland.

King James I. of Scotland may be considered as the
most eminent of all her poets of the early part of the
fifteenth century. James was in his eleventh year when
he was carried away to England, in 1405, by Henry IV.;
and it is probable that he still retained some of the peculiarities of his native idiom, though the poem may be regarded as written in English rather than in Scotch. The
difference, however, between the two dialects was not so
great at this early date as it afterward became. The only
certain production of his is a long poem called " The King's
Quhair " (or " book ") in which he describes the circumstances of an attachment formed for a beautiful English
princess while a prisoner in Windsor Castle. This lady,
Joanna Beaufort, he is said first to have beheld walking in

the garden below, from the window of his prison in the
Round Tower. She was afterward married to the king,
and accompanied him to Scotland.

"The King's Quhair" is a serious poem of nearly fourteen hundred lines; the style is in great part allegorical,
and the poet is evidently an imitator of Chaucer. He is
said to have approached nearer to the excellence of his
great model than any poet before the reign of Elizabeth.
It contains descriptive passages of great beauty. Thus
he addresses this beautiful vision, at whose sudden apparition he says, —

> "Anon, astart
> The blood of all my body to my heart.
>
> . . . .
>
> Ah, sweet! are ye a worldly creature,
> Or heavenly thing in likeness of nature?
>
> . . . .
>
> Or are ye God Cupidis own princess,
> And comin are to loose me out of band?
> Or are ye very Nature the goddess,
> That have depainted with your heavenly hand,
> This garden full of flowers as they stand?
> What shall I think, alas! what reverence
> Shall I minister unto your excellence?
>
> . . . .
>
> If ye a goddess be, and that ye like
> To do me pain, I may it not astart:
> If ye be warldly wight, that doth me sike,
> Why list God make you so, my dearest heart,
> To do a seely prisoner this smart,
> That loves you all, and wot of nought but woe?
> And therefore mercy, sweet! sin' it is so."

King James was assassinated at Perth in the year 1437, at
the age of forty-two.

It has been observed that "most of the English poets
immediately succeeding Chaucer seem rather relapsing into
barbarism than availing themselves of those striking orna-

18

ments which his judgment and imagination had disclosed.
Yet during this poetical dearth in England, as if the singular fortunes of James I. were shaped on purpose to transfer
the manner and spirit of Chaucer's poetry into Scotland,
that country produced a race of true poets." One of the
earliest after James I. is Robert Henryson. Of this poet's
era little is known. He was alive and very old about the
close of the fifteenth century, and was at some period of his
life a school-master at Dunfermline. He wrote a series of
fables, some miscellaneous poems, and the beautiful pastoral of "Robyn and Makyne," printed by Bishop Percy
in his " Reliques."

William Dunbar, whom Sir Walter Scott considered a
poet unrivalled by any that Scotland has ever produced,
and who may perhaps be placed on the same line with the
inspired ploughman in comic power and superior depth
of passion, is even said to excel him in strength and
general fertility of invention. His works were, with the
exception of one or two pieces, confined to an obscure
manuscript, from which they were only rescued when their
language had become so antiquated as to render the world
insensible in a great measure to their many excellences.
From this circumstance popular fame has done but little
justice to this gifted poet, who is said to have been alike
master of every kind of verse.

Dunbar flourished at the court of James IV. at the end
of the fifteenth and the beginning of the sixteenth centuries. After taking his degree, in 1479, at St. Andrew's,
he became one of the order of Grey Friars, and travelled
in that capacity for some years in England and France as
well as Scotland, preaching, as was the custom of the order,
and living by the alms of the pious. The poet renounced
at last this sordid profession, which involved a constant
exercise of falsehood, deceit, and flattery.

He is thought to have been afterward employed by King
James in connection with various foreign embassies, and
in this capacity to have visited Italy, Spain, and France,
besides England and Ireland, thus acquiring that knowledge of mankind which is an important part of the education of the poet. For some years ensuing he is said to
have lived at court, receiving a pension from his royal
master, whom he regaled with his compositions and the
charms of his conversation, — a servile life which ill accorded with his manly Scottish spirit, and at which he
repines greatly in his poems. He died about 1520, at
the age of sixty.

Dunbar's poems are of three classes, — the allegorical,
the moral, and the comic. Of his allegorical poem entitled
" The Dance," it has been said that " for strength and
vividness of painting it would stand a comparison with
any poem in the language."

Another of the distinguished luminaries that marked the
restoration of letters in Scotland at the commencement of
the sixteenth century is Gavin Douglas. Descended from
a noble family and born in the year 1475, Douglas was a
scholar of distinguished elegance. His accomplishments
obtained him high promotion in the Church. In the year
1513, to avoid persecution, he fled from Scotland to England, where Henry VIII. received him graciously, and in
consideration of his literary merits allowed him a liberal
pension. He died of the plague in London and was buried
in the Savoy Church in the year 1521.

Douglas was eminent for his cultivation of the vernacular
poetry of his country. His most remarkable production is
the translation of Virgil's Æneid into Scottish heroics, being
the first version of a Latin classic into any British tongue.
Though in too obsolete a language ever to regain popularity, this work is allowed by critics to be a masterly

performance. His principal original composition is a long poem entitled "The Palace of Honour," bearing so strong a resemblance to Bunyan's "Pilgrim's Progress" that it is thought Bunyan could scarcely have been ignorant of it.

Sir David Lyndsay, born about 1490, closes the list of Scottish poets belonging to this period. He was an officer at court and a favorite of James V., and died about the year 1555.

Lyndsay cannot lay claim to any high imaginative power, but his poems are characterized by infinite wit, spirit, and variety in all the familiar forms of poetry. He chiefly shone as a satirical and humorous writer. Aiming his satire at the dissolute clergy, he is said to have lashed up the popular contempt for that venerable but then tottering fabric, the Catholic Church, and thus to have done high service to the Reformation in Scotland.

For nearly the whole of the seventeenth century not even the name of a Scottish poet occurs. The religious austerity of the Covenanters, still hanging over Scotland, had damped the efforts of poets and dramatists ; yet still among her banks and braes, singing low and sweet to itself like a hidden April rill, went many a comic song of broad rustic humor, and many a tear-steeped ballad in "homely westlin jingle," preluding the rich song of that glorious peasant-poet who woke at last among her hills a harp passionate and melodious as that which burning Sappho swept of old in classic Greece.

Allan Ramsay, born in 1686, is accounted the proper successor of Sir David Lyndsay, after the lapse of more than a century and a half. Ramsay belongs to the order of self-taught poets, his original profession being that of a wig-maker. At twenty-six he commenced writing, and was made poet laureate to a convivial society of young men, called the "Easy Club," writing various light pieces, chiefly of a local and humorous description, which were sold at a penny each, and became exceedingly popular. In the year 1712 he married the daughter of an author, Christina Ross, who was his faithful partner for more than thirty years.

Ramsay's continuation of King James's "Christ's Kirk on the Green" was his first published performance, executed with genuine humor, fancy, and a perfect mastery of the Scottish language. In 1712 appeared his "Gentle Shepherd," which was received with universal approbation, and republished both at London and Dublin.

In the mean time, the poet had left off wig-making, and opened a bookseller's shop. Ramsay established the first circulating library in Scotland; and led by the promptings of a taste then rare in his country, expended his savings in the erection of a theatre for the performance of the regular drama, which the Edinburgh magistrates shut up for him, leaving him, it is said, without redress.

Ramsay associated with the leading nobility, lawyers, wits, and literati of Scotland, and was the Pope, or Swift, of the North. He died in 1758. His verse is in general neither very refined nor imaginative; he excels in native humor and in lively, original sketches of Scottish life. His lyrics lack grace and elegance, yet many of them abound in rustic hilarity and humor, and though far inferior to those of Burns, are still favorites with the lovers of Scottish song. Ramsay has taste, judgment, and good sense, and it has been said of him that "though he wrote trash in all departments, he really failed in none." His fame rests upon his "Gentle Shepherd," which is his great work, and has been allowed by a modern critic to be perhaps the finest pastoral drama in the world. Pope greatly admired this poem, and Ramsay was, both with himself and Gay, a favorite.

In his life Ramsay showed that citizen-like good sense which Heaven too seldom bestows upon the poet. With true Scottish thrift he kept his purse well filled, and wisely gave over poetry before age had cooled his fancy, unwilling to risk the reputation he had already acquired, as he thus tells us, like the canny practical Scotchman that he was : —

> " Frae twenty-five to five and forty
> My muse was neither sweer nor dorty ;
> My Pegasus would break his tether,
> E'en at the shagging of a feather,
> And through ideas scour like drift,
> Streaking his wings up to the lift ;
> Then, then my soul was in a low,
> That gart my numbers safely row.
> But eild and judgement gin to say,
> Let be your sangs, and learn to pray."

Burns was immediately preceded by a few native poets of talent and popularity, — Alexander Ross, a school-master in Lochlee, died in 1784 ; John Lowe, from 1750 to 1798, author of the fine pathetic ballad entitled " Mary's Dream," his only work worthy of preservation ; Lady Anne Barnard, who wrote that most perfect and tender of all ballads, " Auld Robin Gray," and kept its authorship a secret for the long period of fifty years ; and Robert Fergusson, born 1751, died 1774. The melancholy story of Fergusson's life, shortened by dissipation, darkened by remorse, and ending in insanity, is of mournful interest, which deepens when we regard him as the immediate forerunner of Burns, rising on Scotland like that —

> " . . . Prophet star,
> That in the dewy trances of the dawn,
> Floats o'er the solitary hills afar,
> And brings sweet tidings of the ling'ring morn."

In Canongate churchyard, where Fergusson had slept unnoticed for many years, Burns, with that loving reverence for kindred genius which marked his noble nature, erected a simple stone above his brother poet's grave.

Fergusson was the poet of Scottish city life. Deficient in energy and passion, yet with a keen perception of the ludicrous, and a copious and expressive flow of language, he excelled in accurate painting of scenes of real life and traits of Scottish character. His pieces, which were chiefly contributed to the "Weekly Magazine," were collected and published in one volume in 1773, and were well received by the public.

Burns, who, like Shakespeare, is said to have sometimes condescended to work after inferior models, copied the style of Fergusson, whose writings he greatly admired, even preferring them to those of Ramsay. "The Farmer's Ingle" of this poet is supposed to have suggested to Burns the "Cotter's Saturday Night;" but Fergusson's poem is a mere inventory of a farm-house. Burns, while he is as faithful in description, has added passion, sentiment, and patriotism to the subject. There is all the difference in the two poems that exists between Dutch and Italian painting. Mere mechanical skill may portray the perfect form, but a higher inspiration can alone hope to grasp the soul in all art.

After the publication of Fergusson's volume of poems, there was a dearth in Scottish poetry for an interval of thirteen years, and then suddenly Burns appeared, and lo! all the land was showered with song, and a world of passion and beauty was laid open to her sons by that rare genius who in his short life added new interest and glory to his country, and enriched and embellished her for all ages.

Robert Burns was born in the parish of Alloway on the 25th of January, 1759. His father was of the north of Scotland, and for the first six or seven years of the poet's life a gardener, to which occupation he was bred. " The dearest wish and purpose of this worthy man was," says Robert, " to keep his children under his eye till they could discern good from evil ; " so with the assistance of his generous master he ventured on a small farm on his estate. There, in his humble dwelling, which was, it is said, literally a " tabernacle of clay," with the exception of a little thatch, and of which he himself was the architect, under the pressure of early and incessant toil, of inferior and often scanty nutriment, was reared that bard whose genius has been for more than half a century the glory of Scotland.

What education he could afford the father gave to his sons. Robert was taught English well, and by the time he was eleven years of age is said to have been a critic in substantives, verbs, and participles. He was also taught writing, had a whole fortnight's French, and was one summer quarter at land-surveying. For the facility of his memory he was greatly indebted to his good father, whose method was to have his instructor make him thoroughly acquainted with the meaning of every word which was to be committed to memory. Thus, at an earlier period than common the boy was taught the arrangement of words in sentences, as well as a varied expression.

Burns, with his small library, which until his twenty-third year consisted of the " Spectator," Pope's works, Allan Ramsay, a collection of English songs, and a few more less considerable works, knew nothing of the dissipation of reading ; and as his attention was not distracted by a multitude of volumes, his mind developed with original and robust vigor.

It has been justly said that "the true elements of poetry were in the life of Burns, no less than in his writings." In bodily frame he rose nearly five feet ten inches; of superior agility and strength, in the various labors of the farm he excelled all his competitors, and his brother, Gilbert Burns, declares that in mowing — the exercise that is said to try all the muscles most severely — Robert was the only man that at the end of a summer's day he was ever obliged to acknowledge his master.

At this period of his life Burns has been thus described: —

"Elevated by a manly integrity of character, which as a peasant he guarded with jealous dignity; a true patriot, loving the very soil of his country, and worshipping the memory of her ancient heroes; exploring every scene and memorial of departed greatness; burning with generous emotions to do something for old Scotland's sake; yet simple, and loving the sentiments and manners of himself and his rustic compeers. The wild upheavings of his ambition; the precocious maturity of his intellect and passions; the sturdy frame linked to the delicate sensibility that mourned the destruction of the 'crimson-tipped' daisy, and wept over the ruined hopes of a 'wee-bit mousie,' — all belong to the true spirit of romantic poetry."

Burns, whose passionate attachment to the society of woman is well known, was from boyhood to manhood, as his brother avers, "constantly the victim of some fair enslaver," though governed ever by the strictest rules of virtue and modesty, from which he never deviated till he reached his twenty-third year. He was at that time betrayed by his heart into an imprudent connection with Jean Armour, afterward Mrs. Burns, a misstep in his life which, though it may deserve our censure, was honorably retrieved by a legal though private and irregular marriage, which in Scotland is more honorable and binding than elsewhere. Burns in his then destitute circumstances dare not undertake the support of a family. It was agreed that he should go to Jamaica to push his fortunes, his bonnie Jean remaining in the mean time with her father till it might please Providence to put in his power the means to maintain his child and herself.

As he had not sufficient money to pay his passage, and the vessel in which he had taken it was not to sail for some time, he was advised to publish his poems in the mean time by subscription, as a likely way of getting a small increase to his funds. Accordingly, subscription bills were issued immediately, and the printing was commenced in Kilmarnock, his preparations going on at the same time for his voyage.

Thus in the summer of 1786 Burns issued his first volume. It contained matter for all minds, — for the lively and the thoughtful, the poetical enthusiast, and the man of the world; and so eagerly was the book sought after that where copies of it could not be obtained, many of the poems were transcribed, and sent round in manuscript among admiring circles. A second edition was published in Edinburgh in 1787, no less than twenty-eight hundred copies being subscribed for by fifteen hundred individuals! Burns, raised by this unexpected good fortune from the most disheartening poverty to comparative independence, gave up the projected voyage to Jamaica, took a farm at Ellisland, and married with all due solemnities his faithful Jean, — "a hale, sprightly damsel, bred among the hay and heather," lacking, it is true, that polish of mind and delicacy of soul which a poet might seek in his ideal, yet endowed with rustic grace, mother-wit, modesty, and a generous, loving nature, united to a sound, healthy frame, and proving through good and ill a fond and faithful wife. In 1788 Burns obtained what he anxiously desired in addition to his means as a farmer, — an appointment in the excise; but the duties of this office and his own convivial habits interfering with the management of his farm, in 1791 he gladly abandoned it, subsisting hereafter entirely upon his excise salary of seventy pounds per annum.

Having acquitted himself to the satisfaction of the board, and hoping to support himself and family (now consisting of a wife and four bairns) on this humble income till promotion arrived, he had disposed of his stock and crop at public auction, and removed to a small house which he had taken at Dumfries. Promotion never came. " The age," says Craik, " was unworthy of such a gift from Heaven as its glorious peasant-poet. His blood was too hot; his pulse beat too tumultuously; and it treated him rather like an untamable, howling hyena that required to be caged and chained, if not absolutely suffocated at once, than as a spirit of divinest song. Never, surely," he adds, " did men so put a bushel upon a light, first to hide, and afterwards to extinguish it." To Mrs. Dunlop, his faithful and admirable friend, Burns thus writes about six months before his death : —

" There had much need be many pleasures annexed to the states of husband and father, for God knows they have many peculiar cares. I cannot describe to you the anxious, sleepless hours these ties frequently give me. I see a train of helpless little folks, me and my exertions all their stay; and on what a brittle thread does the life of man hang! If I am nipt off at the command of fate, even in all the vigor of manhood as I am, — such things happen every day, — gracious God! what would become of my little flock !

" A father on his death-bed taking his last leave of his children, has indeed woe enough; but the man of competent fortune leaves his sons and daughters independency and friends; while I — but I shall run distracted if I think any longer on the subject."

Burns, at the early age of thirteen, was the principal laborer on his father's farm ; and though by nature of robust
frame, the weary buffeting of misfortune, spare diet, and
over-exertion had induced in him at that early age a chronic
depression of spirits, more terrible than the keenest physical pain, with which he was troubled through all his
after-life. " At this time," writes his brother Gilbert,
" he was almost constantly afflicted in the evenings with
a dull headache, which at a future period of his life he exchanged for a palpitation of the heart and a threatening of
fainting and suffocation in his bed in the night-time. . . .
I do not recollect," continues this good brother, " till
toward the end of his commencing author (when his growing celebrity occasioned his being often in company) to
have ever seen him intoxicated ; nor was he at all given
to strong drinking. Every member of the family was allowed ordinary wages for the labor he performed on the
farm. My brother's allowance was seven pounds per
annum. I was intrusted with the keeping of the family accounts, and during this period his expenses never
in any one year exceeded his slender income. His temperance and frugality were everything that could be
wished."

At first the poet, though addicted to excess in social
parties, still abstained from the habitual use of strong
liquors ; but poverty, misfortune, and that cruel neglect
which his own conscious genius, as well as honest integrity, told him was unmerited, led him at last into constant
excess. That predisposition to hypochondria which ease
of mind, temperate habits, and sound sleep, with the old
salutary ploughman's exercise, might have overcome, was
now aggravated by the steady use of stimulants. The in-
ordinate action of the circulating system became at length
habitual ; the process of nutrition was unable to supply

the waste, and the powers of life began to fail.   As the strength of his body decayed, his resolution became feebler ; and though to bonnie Jean he acknowledged his transgressions and promised amendment again and again, it was too late.   The circles in that awful vortex of ruin were fast engulfing that glorious soul that might have soared and sung with cherubim, such harmony was in it !

On his death-bed poverty and anxiety still pursued Burns ; and when Reason at length forsook her noble throne, the horrors of a visionary jail tortured the poor delirious victim to the last.   " His affecting exclamations," says his biographer, " were now heart-rending." On the fourth day of this fever-dream, God in mercy released from mortal suffering this great and ill-fated genius.

Scotland, after digging the grave of her poet, might at least undertake to lay him becomingly therein.   And now a grand funeral, military honors, and a fine procession were the laggard distinctions paid to the cold clay of her proudest son.   During this stately burial service poor Jean bode wofully at home, and " as if Nature were in a bustle to fill a gap in the universe," another man-child was on that day born under that desolate roof.

Burns died in great poverty, but free from debt ; and his family were placed above immediate want by the generous subscription made in the neighborhood, of seven hundred pounds.   Thus the melancholy forebodings of the husband and father were happily disappointed.

Lacking that polish which early association with refined society might have given him, Burns's appearance and manner were said to have been somewhat peculiar in the high circles into which his genius gave him a free passport ; yet such was his irresistible power of fascination that he never failed to delight and to excel.

" None," says his friend, Mrs. Dunlop, a lady of high birth and gentle culture, " ever outshone Burns in the charms — the sorcery, I would almost call it — of fascinating conversation.

" The rapid lightnings of his eye were always the harbingers of some flash of genius; his voice alone could improve upon the magic of his eye, — sonorous, replete with the finest modulations, it alternately captivated the ear with the melody of poetic numbers, the perspicuity of nervous reasoning, the keenness of satire, the ardent sallies of enthusiastic patriotism, or the sportiveness of humor."

As the wild passionate nature of Burns made him a true lover, it also made him, what Dr. Johnson so much admires, " a good hater; " his resentment, however, was easily allayed by calm reflection and the ascendency of his better nature ; and his manly and candid avowal of error was, to a generous mind, doubly enhanced from its never being attended with servility.   Incapable of any pecuniary meanness, he carried his unsordid disregard of money to a blamable excess.   The mean barter of selfish publishers for his poet-craft he proudly disdained to accept, though furnishing his beautiful lyrics to the " Museum " of Johnson, as well as to the greater work of Thomson, without fee or reward, while the justice and generosity of the latter was constantly pressing upon him some recompense.

Poverty never bent his honest dignity of spirit ; even in the midst of distress he bore himself loftily to the world, and received with a jealous reluctance every offer of friendly assistance.   " Light lie the turf upon his breast," he writes, " who wrote ' Reverence thyself ; ' " and again, " when I am laid in my grave, I wish to be stretched at full length, that I may occupy every inch of ground which I have a right to."

The character of Burns was naturally religious, though his reckless effusions seem often to give the lie to this as-

sertion. From a letter written to his father at an early
period of his life, and when in great poverty, this passage
may be cited as an example of his seriousness : —

"My only pleasurable employment is in looking backwards
and forwards in a moral and religious way. 'The soul, uneasy
and confined at home, rests and expatiates in a life to come,' and
I would not exchange the noble enthusiasm with which three
verses in the seventh chapter of Revelation inspire me for all
that this world has to offer.

"P. S. My meal is nearly out, and I am going to borrow
until I get some."

Here is a portion of God's message of comfort to Burns,
poor, hungry, and depressed: "For the Lamb which
is in the midst of the throne shall feed them, and shall
lead them unto living fountains of waters : and God shall
wipe away all tears from their eyes."

The poetry of Burns is more fraught with matter and
meaning than with invention. His inspiration is that of
passion rather than of imagination, and hence its universal
popularity. The name of Burns had, even before his death,
become a household word in his country. "Of great natural sagacity," observes Craik, "his logical faculty and
judgment of the first order, no man ever had a more substantial intellectual character ; and though he is the greatest peasant-poet that has ever appeared, his poetry is so
remarkable in itself that the circumstances in which it was
produced hardly add anything to our admiration."

What Shakespeare was to the English drama, Robert
Burns was to the poetry of Scotland. The lips of the
Scottish muse, touched with a burning coal from that altar
kindled by Nature's own hand in the soul of her passion-
child, thrilled with a new and intenser life, and woke to a
tenderer and diviner song that shall echo among her heath-

clad hills as long as "rivers roll and woods are green."
While in England Cowper was bringing poetry from the
narrow artificial canals into which Pope and his school had
trained it, into the broader and deeper channels of truth
and Nature, Burns came as a co-worker in Scotland. "It
seemed," says one of his critics, "as if a new realm had
been added to the dominions of the British muse, — a new
and glorious creation, fresh from the hand of Nature.
There was the humor of Smollett, the pathos and tenderness of Sterne or Richardson, the real life of Fielding, and
the description of Thomson, all united in delineations of
Scottish scenery by an Ayrshire ploughman."

We cannot fail to observe that the peculiar dialect of
Burns, being a composite of Scotch and English, which he
varied at will, generally reserving the Scotch for the comic
and tender, and the English for the serious and lofty, renders his diction remarkably rich and copious. It has been
aptly remarked that "the Scottish language possesses advantages somewhat akin to that possessed by the Greek in
the time of Homer; that from having been comparatively
but little employed in literary composition, and only imper-
fectly reduced under the dominion of grammar, many of its
words have several forms which are not only convenient
for the exigencies of verse, but are used with different
effects or shades of meaning. To those unfamiliar with
the dialect, it is impossible to convey a sufficient notion of
the aptness of the poet's language, or to give the effect of
the diminutives in which the Scottish language is almost
as rich as the Italian. For example, while the English
has only its 'mannikin,' the Scotch has its 'mannie,'
'mannikie,' 'bit mannie,' 'bit mannikie,' 'wee bit
mannie,' 'wee bit mannikie,' 'little wee bit mannie,'
'little wee bit mannikie,' and so with 'wife' and many
other terms, while almost every substantive noun has at

least one diminutive form, such as ' mousie,' ' housie,' etc."

In English, Burns has sometimes violated purity of diction ; but his Scotch is as uniformly natural and correct as it is appropriate and expressive.   His picturesque expression, which so charms us, is said to have been equally the result of accurate observation, careful study, and strong feeling.   In description he is literal, energetic, and true. His views of real life and manners are finely moralized. His range of subjects was widely diversified, including the romantic landscape, the customs and superstitions of his country, the delights of convivial society, and the delicate and fervent emotions of our nature.   In no kind of composition does he fail, unless perhaps in his epigrams, Nature having gifted him more largely with humor than wit.

It has been affirmed that " the 'Tam O'Shanter' of Burns alone, had he never written another syllable, would have been sufficient to have transmitted his name proudly to posterity."   In the introductory part of this poem, where Tam beside the ale-house ingle tipples with his cronies, oblivious of the " mony lengthened sage advices " of his gude-wife Kate, who " sits at hame like gathering storm, nursing her wrath to keep it warm," character and nature are delineated with perfect truth and humor ; and in this troublous world one might be forgiven a sigh of envy on beholding Tam " unco fou," o'er all the ills of life victorious.   And who will not confess to an illicit longing for that same foamy draught in which —

> " Care, mad to see a man so happy
> E'en drowned himself amang the nappy ! "

Scarcely excelled in power of imagination by Shakespeare himself is Burns's weird description of the orgies

of the witches, and the infernal scenery in which they
are exhibited, —

> " Coffins stood round like open presses
> That shaw'd the dead in their last dresses;
> And by some devilish cantrip slight,
> Each in its cauld hand held a light
> By which heroic Tam was able
> To note upon the haly table,
> A murderer's banes in gibbet airns;
> Twa span-lang wee unchristened bairns;
> A thief, new-cutted from a rape,
> Wi' his last gasp his gab did gape;
> Five tomahawks wi' bluid red-rusted;
> Five scymetars wi' murder crusted;
> A garter, which a babe had strangled;
> A knife, a father's throat had mangled,
> Whom his ain son o' life bereft,
> The gray hairs yet stack to the heft;
> Three lawyers' tongues turned inside out,
> Wi' lies seamed like a beggar's clout,
> Wi' mair o' horrible and awfu'
> Which e'en to name would be unlawfu'."

The introduction of a *young* witch among the wrinkled
withered beldames in " the core " is a happy and original
idea, bringing, as it does, transported Tam entirely into the
spirit of the scene, and rendering him through her fascinations utterly oblivious of the horrors of his situation ; and it
has been happily observed that Burns's " conceit of bringing even Satan himself within the sphere of her charms is
unique, and adds greatly to the merit of the composition."
The only fault found in this poem is that at the conclusion
it falls off in interest.   This is said to be owing to Burns
having stuck to the popular tale of this hero ; for Tam
was not a creation of fancy, but a real person.   He was
known in plain prose as Thomas Reid, laborer ; and it
is recorded that he died at Lochwinnock on the 9th of

August, 1823, borne down, it is said, by the many ills of age and disease, and though for months before his death incapable of labor, retaining to the last the desire of being " fou for weeks thegither." Rare Tam ! it is good to know that thou hast in verity surmounted "the lang Scots miles " and " won the key-stone of the brig." Fair blow the gowans on thy grave !

Burns considered " Tam O'Shanter " his master-piece, and many critics have regarded it in the same light; yet it does not perhaps embody what is brightest and best in his poetry. His address to a mouse on turning up her nest with a plough in November is richer in true poetic light and color. Its companion poem is that to a daisy. In these and in the " Cotter's Saturday Night " it has been happily remarked that " the poet is seen in his happiest inspiration, his brightest sunshine, and his tenderest tears." The latter poem is familiar to all, and in true and touching description is almost unrivalled.

As a picture of manners " Halloween " is Burns's greatest performance. Written with easy vigor, in execution perfect, for fulness of varied life, for truth, reality, and flashing sun-lighted humor, it has been pronounced unequalled. Nothing finer than this description of a stream seen by moonlight is to be found in descriptive poetry :

> " Whyles o'er a linn the burnie plays,
>   As thro' the glen it wimpl't ;
> Whyles round a rocky scar it strays;
>   Whyles in a wiel it dimpl't ;
> Whyles glittered to the nightly rays,
>   Wi' bickering, dancing dazzle ;
> Whyles cookit underneath the braes,
>   Below the spreading hazel,
>   Unseen that night."

Who that reads it does not bless Burns for writing in the mother-tongue ? No English words could have given it

such witchery. The more considerate part of Burns's nature, his sagacity and good sense, his large heart and understanding, speaks in some of his epistles. The one
addressed to Andrew Aiken is said to have been more
salutary in a moral sense to the young men of Scotland
than any sermon ever published in that country. That
to his brother poet Davie is equally good.

More elevated and impassioned is the poem entitled
" The Vision," which has been termed " the finest revelation ever made of the romantic hope and ambition of
a youthful poet." In the last stanza we may observe
that Burns rises in his inspiration into the most graceful
English.

> " And wear thou this, — she solemn said, —
> And bound the Holly round my head :
> The polished leaves and berries red,
>   Did rustling play ;
> And, like a passing thought, she fled
>   In light away."

The poet's happiest and richest humor may be seen in
the " Twa Dogs." Never were dogs (" who," as some
one observes, " since the days of Æsop have seemed of all
brutes most entitled to the privilege "), sitting down to
moralize on human affairs, such downright dogs ! Cæsar,
of foreign extraction, whose —

> " . . . letter'd braw brass collar
> Shew'd him the gentleman and scholar,"

though not unmindful of his high degree, is still full of
condescension to plebeian Luath, the ploughman's collie,
whose —

> " Honest sonsie, baws'nt face,
>   Ay gat him friends in ilka place."

In their long discussion of " the lords o' the creation,"
neither the character nor the different conditions of the dogs

is ever lost sight of; and after recounting the follies of the
superior brutes, with what inimitable self-complacency —

> " They each get up and shake their lugs,
> Rejoiced they are na men, but dogs ! "

Many of Burns's brilliantly comic pieces are unfortunately
marred by indelicate and reckless touches, as in the " Holy
Fair," " Death and Dr. Hornbook," and " Holy Willie's
Prayer."   One of the poet's best productions, whimsically
comic, with touches of the terrific and the tender, is his
fanciful "Address to the De'il."   It will be remembered that
the worthy Covenanters of Scotland, in their blind unco'
goodness, had felt themselves divinely commissioned to
crop the lusty fancy of the peasantry as closely as they
sheared their own solemn pates.   Of brownies, spunkies,
bogles, kelpies, warlocks, and witches, they would have
none ; yet one awful being of supernatural mould they still
suffered to go at large, —

> " Whiles ranging like a roaring lion
> For prey a' holes and corners tryin'."

The Devil they considered a strictly scriptural apparition,
and eminently salutary to the souls of the peasantry as
well as to their own.

Burns evidently accepted the popular conception of the
person and attributes of Satan, however ludicrous it may
have seemed to his superior sense, while his fancy and
imagination purged its grossness, and touched it with
poetic beauty.   This awful and harmful personage, stray-
ing in a lonely glen beneath the glimmering moon, is en-
countered by the poet, who, nothing daunted, deems it
incumbent upon him to undertake that novel duty, —
the lecturing of Satan for his sins !   This in all the droll
familiarity of sly humor he at once proceeds to do.   This

concluding stanza of the poem, in which pity for the fate of Satan is blended with a forlorn hope for his ultimate salvation, is inimitable.

> " But fare ye weel, auld Nickie-ben !
> O wad ye tak a thought an' men'
> Ye aiblins might — I dinna ken —
> Still hae a *stake :*
> I 'm wae to think upo' yon den,
> Ev'n for *your* sake ! "

Well might stout John Knox have arisen wrathfully from his grave to cuff the ears of this recreant Presbyterian (as he is said to have done those of his beautiful, contumacious queen, Mary of Scotland) for this stretch of " effectual calling."

And we must not forget those verses suggested by a certain unique decoration on a " Lady's Bonnet " (which shall be nameless). What a world of sharpened, sly philosophic inspection is contained in this last often-quoted stanza, —

> " O wad some Power the giftie gie us
> To see oursels as ithers see us !
> It wad frae monie a blunder free us
> And foolish notion :
> What airs in dress and gait wad lea'e us —
> And ev'n devotion ! "

No truer poetry than Burns's songs and ballads exists in any country. They are always the expression of real feeling and passion, never labored and ingenious performances, like some of the English lyrics, but simple and natural as a shout of laughter or a gush of tears, the poet's thought at the moment finding vent in musical words.

Moore informs us that he became a writer of lyrics that he might express what music conveyed to himself. Burns

is said to have had no technical knowledge of music, and
the pleasure he derived from his native airs (some of which
are conjectured to have been preserved in the wilds and
mountains of Scotland with the native race, and to have
descended from remote ages) was mainly the result of
association.

The Scottish peasantry had long been in possession of
many songs composed in their native dialect, and sung to
these ancient airs.   These songs, though rustic, have been
commended for truth of character, the language of Nature,
and as pictures of real Arcadian life.   "Though Knox
and his disciples," as has been said, "might influence the
Scottish Parliament, with her rural muse they contended
in vain."   Clear Highland voices still woke the wild
echoes, and the plaintive melodies of love, sweet as the
south wind sighing amid the silver birks, went singing
softly among the Lowland homes.   "These airs were not
all plaintive ; many of them were lively and humorous,
suited to an energetic and sequestered people in their
hours of mirth and festivity, though to us some of them
might appear coarse and indelicate."

Burns, whose soul was of finest harmony and easily
stirred into lyric melody, has by his compositions in this
line immortalized some of his native airs.   Lyric composition was peculiarly suited to his genius ; and in his songs
his language and imagery, always the most appropriate,
musical, and graceful, has been deemed "a greater marvel
than the creations of Handel or Mozart."   Of these songs,
universally familiar, "Highland Mary" may perhaps be
considered most excellent.   Though not of the smooth-
est versification, every line and cadence of this poem is
steeped in inimitable pathos, and it has the rare merit of
being addressed from the heart to the real object of the
poet's tender and undying regret.   The song "To Mary

in Heaven," as a simple, natural outburst of tenderness, has never been excelled.

The songs written in honor of bonnie Jean are all admirable and familiar. Of the truest lyric ring is " Their Groves of Sweet Myrtle." This one inimitable stanza one could fancy not to have been framed of mere words, but of the viewless vibrations of harmonious sound : —

> " Their groves o' sweet myrtle, let foreign lands reckon,
>   Where bright beaming summers exalt the perfume,
> Far dearer to me yon lone glen o' green breckan,
>   Wi' the burn stealing under the lang yellow broom :
> Far dearer to me are yon humble broom bowers,
>   Where the blue-bell and gowan lurk lowly unseen :
> For there, lightly tripping amang the wild flowers,
>   A-listening the linnet, aft wanders my Jean."

Of these songs, of which Burns has written above two hundred, among the best are " John Anderson," " Mary Morrison," " Sweet Afton," " Bonnie Doon," and the far-famed " Bannockburn," the noblest heroic ode in the Scottish language. We must not forget " Bonnie Leslie," " which contains in one verse," observes Walter Scott, " the essence of a thousand love-tales."

> " But to see her is to love her,
>   And love but her forever ;
> For nature made her what she is
>   And ne'er made sic anither."

And there, too, is " Green Grow the Rashes, O," in which Burns has thus given us his very self, —

> " The warly race may riches chase,
>   And riches still will fly them, O ;
> An' tho' at last they catch them fast,
>   Their hearts can ne'er enjoy them, O !

> " There's nought but care on every han',
>   In ev'ry hour that passes, O ;
> What signifies the life o' man,
>   An' 't were na for the lasses, O ! "

The influence of such a poet on the popular mind of Scotland cannot be estimated.

"The tendency of some things," observes Craik, "both in the character of the people and their peculiar institutions, demanded such a check or counteraction as was supplied by this frank, generous, reckless poetry, springing so singularly out of the iron-bound Calvinistic Presbyterianism of the country, like the flowing water from the rock in Horeb.   In any country, among any people, such a poet would help to sustain whatever nobleness of character belonged to them, — for whatever there may be to disapprove of in the license or indecorum of some things that Burns has written, there is at least nothing mean-souled in his poetry any more than there was in the man.   It is never for a moment even vulgar or low in expression or manner; it is wonderful how a native delicacy of taste and elevation of spirit in the poet has sustained him here, with a dialect so soiled by illiterate lips, and often the most perilous subject."

In his songs especially has the genius of Burns interwoven itself with every fibre of the national heart.   Among Scotland's heathery hills and flowery wilds his memory is still green as the slopes —

"Where summer first unfolds her robes."

To his countrymen, estranged from their native soil and toiling in foreign wilds, or trafficking with keen " inspection " in alien marts of trade, his ballads come singing in the dear old idiom, welcome as a breath of their native air, and sweet as the sound of " burnies wimpling through the glens " of their native land.   Let them ever bless and commemorate the day that gave to Scotland Robert Burns, — one who though not immaculate (the sun himself hath shown us spots upon his golden disk) was true bard and every inch a man.

CHAPTER XIV.

WORDSWORTH AND THE LAKE SCHOOL.

FROM the Queen Anne poets grew up that taint in our diction which has been denounced as " technically poetic language," — sound without sense, signifying nothing.   Although the poets of this age corrected the indecency of the vicious school introduced at the Restoration, they were deficient in force and greatness of fancy, had little real pathos or enthusiasm, and as philosophers no comprehensiveness, depth, or originality.

Cowper, at the close of the eighteenth century, had begun the work of bringing back poetry to the channels of truth and Nature.   In April, 1800, he ceased from his labors, and Wordsworth undertook to complete what he had only begun.   Wordsworth was born at Cockermouth, in Cumberland, in 1770.   His father was a solicitor in the town, and the poet received a good education.   In early life he was left an orphan.   Placed at a grammar school in the antique village of Hawkshead, he there spent nine years of his life in almost primitive seclusion, lodging in a country cottage, and " haunting the tall rock and sounding cataract " until his whole being identified itself with external Nature.   Here the inner Wordsworth was formed, and his genius here took its peculiar bent.

In 1787 Wordsworth was entered at St. John's College, Cambridge.   There he spent three years, broken by visits to Hawkshead, and by a bold, and almost literally pedestrian tour through France, Switzerland, and the district of the Italian lakes. In January, 1791, the poet took his degree at Cambridge, and evidently led by enthusiasm for the political changes then at work in France, went over to that country and remained in Orléans and Paris about fifteen months. There he witnessed the culmination of the revolutionary tumult and the beginning of the reign of bloodshed and terror. From this arena of crime and horror, so strangely contrasting with his after-life of tranquillity and repose, chance carried him back to England, though his sympathies are said still to have been with the Republican party.

Wordsworth's friends had intended him for the Church, but he showed not the least disposition to carry out their views, living now in a desultory way, either in town or country, and being at one time on the point of securing daily bread by newspaper drudgery. Happily, in his twenty-seventh year he came into possession of nine hundred pounds, — the bequest of a young friend " in the faith of the poet's vocation to literary achievement." Endowed with this modest sum, he considered himself independent, and with his sister Dorothy settled down in Somersetshire on his slender income. Though Dorothy Wordsworth did not herself " build the lofty rhyme," it is said to have been the work of her life to bring to her idolized brother the rarest " building materials " for his verse ; and he has told us that her mind, next to Coleridge's, was most operative on his own.

Here Wordsworth first met Coleridge, and it was an epoch in his life. Coleridge's highest poetic period was this of his daily intercourse with the sister and brother. One sees in imagination these three friends making their frugal pedestrian tours about the country, or taking modest journeys in cosey old wagons drawn by circumspect elderly nags, — Wordsworth and Coleridge on their very highest stilts, talking poetry together, and utterly oblivious of horse, wagon, and " refreshment for man and beast; " while Dorothy, like any common mortal, attends to such prosaic trivialities as keeping the road, feeding the horse, and procuring sublunary nourishment for two hungry poets.

In 1798 they all passed the winter in Germany. Coleridge plunged into metaphysics, and stayed on, while Wordsworth and his sister returned to England, and settled snugly down in the cottage at Grasmere. After his own profound and quiet fashion Wordsworth is said tenderly to have loved his cousin, whom he married in 1802. This exquisite sonnet on her portrait, painted many long years after their honeymoon, testifies to the depth of his affection for her. Petrarch himself never flung a fairer posy at Laura's feet.

> " Though I beheld at first with blank surprise
> This work, I now have gazed on it so long,
> I see its truth with unreluctant eyes;
> O my beloved! I have done thee wrong,
> Conscious of blessedness, but whence it springs
> Ever too heedless, as I now perceive.
> Morn into noon did pass, noon into eve,
> And the old day was welcome as the young,
> As welcome and as beautiful, — in sooth
> More beautiful, as being a thing more holy;
> Thanks to thy virtues, to the eternal youth
> Of all thy goodness, never melancholy;
> To thy large heart and humble mind, that cast
> Into one vision, future, present, past ! "

Two years after their marriage Wordsworth celebrated his Mary in those exquisite verses entitled " She was a Phantom of Delight," in which he has given us that apt couplet, —

> " A creature not too bright and good
> For human nature's daily food."

In 1803 Wordsworth and his sister made a tour in Scotland, of which we have a pleasing record. There they were honored guests of Sir Walter Scott, and formed a lifelong acquaintance with him.

In 1839 the poet received an honorary degree at Oxford, which was given in the theatre " with great acclamation." On the death of Southey, in 1843, he was made poet laureate. Once only did he sing in discharge of his office, and in 1850 ends the story of his life. A poet crowned, full of years, and ripe in goodness, he was gathered home to God. His body rests in the quiet churchyard at Grasmere.

In 1798 Wordsworth settled among his beloved lakes, in the north of England, first at Grasmere and afterward at Rydal Mount. Southey's subsequent retirement to the same beautiful country, and Coleridge's visits to his brother poets, originated the not very intelligible designation of the Lake School of poetry. Jeffrey, I think, first maliciously styled Wordsworth, Coleridge, and Southey " that school of whining and hypochondriacal poets that haunt the Lakes."

The peculiarities which are conceived to constitute what is called the Lake manner first appeared in the " Lyrical Ballads," the first volume of which was published by Wordsworth in 1798. The second volume, together with the " Ancient Mariner " of Coleridge, was published in 1800. Some of the ballads were also from the pen of Coleridge, but the greater part by Wordsworth. The ballads were designed by him as an experiment how far a simpler kind of poetry than that in use would afford permanent interest to readers.

In the Preface he describes his object to be that of " fitting to metrical arrangement a selection of the real language of men in a state of vivid sensation." This theory of poetry, which Wordsworth appears to have set

out with, is happily most thoroughly contradicted and re-
futed by the greater part of his own poetry. It maintains
that passion or strong feeling, even in the rudest natures,
has always something of poetry in it, — a truism which
nobody denies; still, it is *not* true that the real language
of men, however much excited, is usually, to any considerable extent, *poetry*. If emotion or excitement alone would
produce that idealization in which poetry consists, then we
might have poetry without *poets*, instead of poets without
poetry, as Heaven knows we too often have. " Poetry,"
it has been well observed, " belongs not to the realm of
Nature, but to the realm of art; and upon whatever principle or system of operation he may proceed, it is the poet
that makes the poetry, and without him it cannot have
birth or being. He is the bee, without whom there can be
no honey; the artist, or true creator, from whom the thing
produced, whatever be its material, takes shape and beauty
and a living soul."

The attempt of Wordsworth to destroy altogether the
fine fabric of poetic diction which the tuneful tribe had
for generations been rearing, and to substitute a style of
composition disfigured by colloquial plainness; to effect a
transition from the refined and sentimental school of verse
to such themes as the " Idiot Boy," — was too violent to
escape ridicule; and down upon his devoted head came the
hostility of reviews and the ridicule of satirists. At once,
he became notorious as one —

> " Who both by precept and example shows
> That prose is verse, and verse is merely *prose*."

Fortunately, with Wordsworth, as with many another,
theory and practice did not go hand in hand. This *theory*
of his was, after all, but the indignant protest of an earnest, truthful soul against the then prevalent vices of style

characterizing the artificial school.   An idiosyncratic tendency to exaggerate the importance of trivial things, a sort of mawkishness in imagery and sentiment, gives those ludicrous touches to some of his verses which almost overpower the simple, natural beauty and the spirit of tender humanity by which they are characterized.

Some one has remarked, and justly, that " had Wordsworth been more capable of separating by discernment his bad from his good, there would, it is likely enough, have been far less of the *bad ;* but the *good* perhaps would have been far less *good*."   Having no humor or comedy of any kind in him, it is often impossible to tell whether he means to be comic or tender, serious or ludicrous, or whether his choice of subjects and illustrations may be regarded as genuine simplicity or silliness and affectation.

In the " Idiot Boy " we find such stanzas as this : —

> " And Susan 's growing worse and worse,
>   And Betty 's in a sad quandary ;
>   And then there 's nobody to say
>   If she may go, or she must stay !
>   She 's in a sad quandary."

We too are " in a sad quandary."   We cannot tell whether such stuff as this, given under the name of poetry, is the production of a man of genius, or of the identical " boy " whose fortunes it relates !   However it may be, we are fain to exclaim, " Prithee, good Betty, wait no longer in thy ' quandary ; ' go, bring thy Johnny home, and that directly ; and (consummation most devoutly to be wished) bring *us* to the story's end."

In his famous " Rejected Addresses " the witty James Smith felicitously parodies Wordsworth's bald, colloquial style and frequent infelicity of theme.   The parody is spoken in the character of Nancy Lake, and is entitled

"The Baby's Début." This is the opening stanza of the parody : —

> " My brother Jack was nine in May,
>   And I was eight on New Year's Day ;
>   So in Kate Wilson's shop
>   Papa (he 's my papa and Jack's)
>   Bought me, last week, a doll of wax,
>   And brother Jack a top."

Fortunately, it is out of the power of the most perverse theory to spoil the true poet ; and in defiance of his crotchets, Wordsworth must ever charm and elevate mankind. The spirit of truth and poetry has redeemed from oblivion and hallowed and ennobled such homely themes as Harry Gill and the Wagoner, and even Peter Bell and his ass will go jogging down the centuries with the Tam O' Shanters, the John Gilpins, and other famous equestrian heroes. Of the poems expressing Wordsworth's most peculiar manner — that which used to be especially understood as the style of the Lake School — the " Fountain " is perhaps the best example.

In many of Wordsworth's homeliest and most hackneyed ballads we find the sweetest and tenderest humanity, as in " Goody Blake and Harry Gill," or the most profound philosophical touches, as in " We are Seven." But much, perhaps we might say the greater part, of his poetry, is in a style and manner quite different from these. His theory is as much confuted by his own poetry as it is by the universal past experience of mankind. Take, for example, his " Lonely Leech Gatherer," his " Ruth," with the exception of a few lines, his " Tintern Abbey," his " Feast of Brougham," the " Water Lily," the greater part of the " Excursion," most of the sonnets, his great " Ode on the Intimations of Immortality in Early Childhood," many of his shorter lyrical pieces, and his "Laodamia" (the last without the exception of a single line) ; these are as unexceptionable in diction as they are deep and true in feeling, judged according to existing rules or principles of art. An artist should be judged by his *best ;* for then, if ever, he touches with finger-tips the endless endeavor of his soul. Many of Wordsworth's best verses, embodying the philosophy and sentiment of our common humanity, have a completeness and impressiveness, as of texts, mottoes, and proverbs ; and we may safely affirm that no cotemporary poet has so well attained that undying beauty of expression, that harmony between thought and word, which is the condition of immortal verse. "Poetry," says a reviewer, "like science, has its final precision ; there are pieces of poetic language which, try as men will, they will simply have to recur to, and confess that it has been done before." As an example of that which, in Wordsworth's way of putting it, has attained the one form which of all others truly belongs to it, many of his shorter pieces might be quoted. Of this kind of writing this little poem is a marked example : —

> " My heart leaps up when I behold
> A rainbow in the sky :
> So was it when my life began ;
> So is it now I am a man ;
> So be it when I shall grow old,
> Or let me die !
> *The child is father of the man ;*
> And I could wish my days to be
> Bound each to each by natural piety."

These stanzas are equally characteristic : —

> " A slumber did my spirit seal ;
> I had no human fears :
> She seemed a thing that could not feel
> The touch of earthly years.

20

> " No motion has she now, no force ;
>   She neither hears nor sees,
>   Rolled round in earth's diurnal course
>   With rocks, and stones, and trees."

In the poem beginning " Three years she grew in sun and shower," the peculiar philosophy of Wordsworth is exquisitely embodied. In execution and sentiment it is one of his most perfect productions. These two stanzas are almost perfect : —

> " The floating clouds their state shall lend
>   To her ; for her the willow bend ;
>   Nor shall she fail to see
>   Even in the motions of the storm
>   Grace that shall mould the maiden's form
>   By silent sympathy.

> " The stars of midnight shall be dear
>   To her ; and she shall lean her ear
>   In many a secret place
>   Where rivulets dance their wayward round,
>   And beauty, born of murmuring sound
>   Shall pass into her face."

Wordsworth, we cannot deny, wrote over-much, and sometimes measured the result of his labor by *quantity* rather than *quality*. The art of condensation he rarely practised ; consequently, in reading many of his poems one has daintily to pick out the good bits. Sometimes we find a complete poem good throughout, and good as a *whole*. Such a poem is " Laodamia," in which Wordsworth divests himself of all local and personal associations and throws himself back upon antiquity in intensest sympathy with the persons of the historic and heroic ages of Greece. He says of this poem : " I wrote it with the hope of giving it a loftier tone than, so far as I know, has been given to it by any of the ancients who have treated of it." A more delicate and graceful homily on the wisdom of subduing the sensual to the spiritual than Wordsworth's version of this example derived from the ante-Homeric age, cannot be found in our language ; and the versification is in absolute harmony with the subject. Thus runs the story : The Delphic oracle has foretold that the first Greek who touches the Trojan strand shall die. Protesilaus, with the fleet, sets sail from Aulis ; upon the silent sea he revolves in his mind the oracle, and nobly determines —

> " If no worthier lead the way,
>   That of a thousand vessels, his shall be
>   The foremost prow in pressing to the strand,
>   His the first blood to tinge the Trojan sand."

On Laodimia, his queen, too, fondly does his memory hang. He recalls the joys they shared in mortal life, the paths which together they have trod, their fountains and their flowers ; and bitter is the pang when he thinks of *her* loss. Yet thus bravely he resolves and acts, —

> " And shall suspense permit the foe to cry,
>   ' Behold, they tremble ! Haughty their array,
>   Yet of their number no one dares to die ' ?
>
> .   .   .   .
>
> And forth he leaps upon the sandy plain,
> A self-devoted chief by Hector slain."

Her hero dead, Laodamia will not be comforted. She sends her wail through the " veiled empires of eternity." In the lonely night, " 'mid shades forlorn," she vainly implores him " from the infernal gods." Still, undaunted by failure, with sacrifice and vows she now further entreats from great Jove her lord's return.

> "O terror! What hath she perceived? O joy!
> What doth she look on? Whom doth she behold?
> Her hero slain upon the beach of Troy?
> It is — if sense deceive her not — 't is he!
> And a god leads him, winged Mercury."

Touching her with his wand, mild Hermes calms all fear, and thus addresses her, —

> "'. . . Such grace hath crowned thy prayer,
> Laodimia! that at Jove's command
> Thy husband walks the paths of upper air:
> He comes to tarry with thee three hours' space;
> Accept the gift; behold him face to face!'"

Protesilaus, cold and serene, eludes her impassioned clasp; only a phantom stands before her. In his high sphere is her love to him a thing of naught? Is there indeed a bridgeless gulf between them set? With sinking heart she thus entreats the shade of her beloved, —

> "'Confirm, I pray, the vision with thy voice:
> This is our palace; yonder is thy throne;
> Speak, and the floor thou tread'st on will rejoice.
> Not to appal me have the gods bestowed
> This precious boon, and blest a sad abode!'"

Protesilaus replies, —

> "'Great Jove, Laodamia, doth not leave
> His gifts imperfect. Spectre though I be,
> I am not sent to scare thee, or deceive;
> But in reward of thy fidelity.
> And something also did my worth obtain;
> For fearless virtue bringeth boundless gain.'"

Thus reassured, Laodamia again approaches this immaterial being with mortal love and hope: —

> "'Supreme of heroes, bravest, noblest, best!
> Thy matchless courage I bewail no more,
> Which then, when tens of thousands were depressed
> By doubt, propelled thee to the fatal shore
> Thou found'st — and I forgive thee — here thou art, —
> A nobler counsellor than my poor heart.

> "'But thou, though capable of sternest deed,
> Wert kind as resolute, and good as brave;
> And he, whose power restores thee, hath decreed
> That thou should'st cheat the malice of the grave;
> Redundant are thy locks, thy lips as fair
> As when their breath enriched Thessalian air.

> "'No spectre greets me, — no vain shadow this;
> Come, blooming hero, place thee by my side!
> Give, on this well-known couch, one nuptial kiss
> To me, this day, a second time thy bride!'"

On this impracticable "love and longing" —

> "Jove frowned in heaven; the conscious Parcæ threw
> Upon those roseate lips a Stygian hue."

And thus changed, Protesilaus admonishes his rash queen, —

> "'This visage tells thee that my doom is past:
> Know virtue were not virtue if the joys
> Of sense were able to return as fast,
> As surely, as they vanish.   Earth destroys
> These raptures duly — Erebus disdains:
> Calm pleasures there abide, — majestic pains.

> "'Be taught, O faithful consort, to control
> Rebellious passion: for the gods approve
> The depth, and not the tumult of the soul;
> A fervent, not ungovernable, love.
> Thy transports moderate; and meekly mourn
> When I depart, for brief is my sojourn.'"

Again Laodamia pleads with impassioned importunity:

" ' And wherefore ?   Did not Hercules by force
Wrest from the guardian monster of the tomb
Alcestis, a reanimated corse,
Given back to dwell on earth in vernal bloom ?
Medea's spells dispersed the weight of years,
And Æson stood a youth, 'mid youthful peers.

" ' The gods to us are merciful, — and they
Still farther may relent; for mightier far
Than strength of nerve and sinew, or the sway
Of magic potent over sun and star,
Is love, though oft to agony distrest,
And though his favorite seat be feeble woman's breast.

" ' But if thou goest, I follow ' — ' Peace ! ' he said.
She looked upon him, and was calmed and cheered.
The ghastly color from his lips had fled ;
In his deportment, shape, and mien, appeared
Elysian beauty, melancholy grace,
Brought from a pensive, though a happy place.

" He spake of love, such love as spirits feel
In worlds whose course is equable and pure ;
No fears to beat away, no strife to heal,
The past unsighed for, and the future sure."

These are his parting words, —

" ' I counsel thee by fortitude to seek
Our blest reunion in the shades below.
The invisible world with thee hath sympathized ;
Be thy affections raised and solemnized.

" ' Learn by a mortal yearning to ascend —
Seeking a higher object.   Love was given,
Encouraged, sanctioned, chiefly for that end ;
For this the passion to excess was driven,
That self might be annulled, her bondage prove
The fetters of a dream, opposed to love ! '

" Aloud she shrieked ! for Hermes reappears !
Round the dear shade she would have clung ; 't is vain ;

The hours are past, — too brief had they been years;
And him no mortal effort can detain.
Swift towards the realms that know not earthly day,
He through the portal takes his silent way.
And on the palace floor a lifeless corse she lay.

" Ah, judge her gently who so deeply loved !
Her, who in reason's spite, yet without crime,
Was in a trance of passion thus removed;
Delivered from the galling yoke of time,
And these frail elements, — to gather flowers
Of blissful quiet 'mid unfading bowers."

To accommodate the narrative to the account given by
Virgil, who places the shade of Laodamia in a mournful
region, among unhappy lovers, Wordsworth thus remod-
elled this final stanza, —

" She who, though warned, exhorted, and reproved,
Thus died, from passion desperate to a crime,
By the just gods, whom no weak pity moved,
Was doomed to wear out her appointed time
Apart from happy ghosts, who gather flowers
Of blissful quiet in unfading bowers."

The first conclusion is, I think, the most satisfactory.
The *justice* of the gods is far less admirable than their
compassion : and it would hardly have been consistent
in these mighty beings, who in their own persons, according to the myths, have given mankind many examples of intemperate passion, to doom poor Laodamia to
a place of punishment for excess of affection.

" For ages," so runs the tale, " a knot of spiry trees
grew upon the tomb of Protesilaus ; and in sympathy
with the suffering Laodamia, whenever from their tall
summits they gained a view of Ilium, they instantly withered at the top," — thus maintaining a constant under-

growth of change and blight. In "Laodamia," Wordsworth, repudiating his own theory, has ventured upon the
loftiest theme. It is a purely and richly classic poem.
Here, in calm, sustained elevation of thought and appropriate imagery, he may compete with Milton. The address
of Protesilaus to Laodamia equals the sublime strains of
the elder bard. In his "Feast of Brougham Castle"
and his "Egyptian Maid, or, The Romance of the Water
Lily," Wordsworth has shown his mastery over the most
popular of all our poetic styles, that of the old romance
in its highest and most refined forms. The "Egyptian
Maid" is his greatest poem of this kind.

In the sonnet Wordsworth has perhaps best displayed
his elevation and sustained power. The necessity for
brief and rapid thought here represses his tendency to
prolixity and diffuseness; and in this form of poetic composition he has been surpassed by Milton alone. His sonnets are characterized by a chaste and noble simplicity,
a winning sweetness, or simple grandeur. One of the
finest and most characteristic is this, entitled "The World
is Too Much with us" : —

> "The world is too much with us; late and soon,
> Getting and spending, we lay waste our powers :
> Little we see in Nature that is ours.
> We have given our hearts away, a sordid boon !
> This sea that bares her bosom to the moon,
> The winds that will be howling at all hours,
> And are up-gathered now like sleeping flowers, —
> For this, for everything, we are out of tune ;
> It moves us not. Great God ! I 'd rather be
> A pagan, suckled in a creed outworn ;
> So might I, standing on this pleasant lea,
> Have glimpses that would make me less forlorn ;
> Have sight of Proteus coming from the sea ;
> Or hear old Triton blow his wreathed horn."

"The Excursion" — a philosophical poem in blank verse — contains passages of sentiment, description, and pure eloquence not excelled by any poet of Wordsworth's time. The narrative part of the poem is a framework for a series of pictures of mountain scenery, and philosophical dissertations, tending to show how the external world is adapted to the mind of man, and good educed out of evil and suffering.

"The Excursion" is not without that incongruity which characterizes many of Wordsworth's poems. Thus, the Wanderer — a poor Scotch pedlar — is a profound moralist and dialectician, and discourses with clerk-like fluency,

"Of truth and grandeur, beauty, love, and hope."

Prolixity is the great and distinguishing fault of the poem. He who would traverse the mountains in company with the poet and the Wanderer, should have a long day before him at the start, plenty of patience, and an unfailing supply of wide-awakeness; and even then — as De Quincey humorously suggests — he will be fain to say to the long-winded Wanderer, "Now, dear old soul, if you *could* cut it short a little!" But the "dear old soul" must say his say to the bitter end. "Cut it short?" Why, the tediousness of the poem is evidently conceived by the poet as a part of its relish! It has also that inequality of diction "which," as Craik happily observes, "makes Wordsworth's productions a brittle mixture of poetical and prosaic forms, like the image of iron and clay in Nebuchadnezzar's dream." One cannot deny too that the Wanderer gives us a great deal of plain prose in the guise of verse; yet with all its faults the "Excursion" is a noble poem, conceived and executed in a lofty style of moral observation, and peculiarly consecrated by a spirit of Christian benevolence and enlightened humanity.

The "Prelude" is an unfinished poem on the growth of the author's own mind. It is a posthumous poem, though projected in his twenty-ninth year. The existence of this work in manuscript, its lofty pretension and great magnitude, had long been known to the public. Jeffrey is said to have made himself very merry in computing the probable dimension of the poem. De Quincey had read it and praised it. All that is publishable has now been published; and though so vast, it is only a fragment. It is a faithful record of the individual experience of a man of genius, and may be regarded at once as his earliest production and his latest legacy to the world. The long poem is not always the great poem. What is richest and best in Wordsworth may not, I think, be found either in the "Excursion," or in the "Prelude." Coleridge thus defines a true poem: "It should give us as much pleasure as possible in a short space." Undoubtedly "Tintern Abbey" and the "Ode on Immortality" will live long after the "Excursion" is forgotten, and the "Prelude" "dead as Cæsar." Only "a thing of beauty is a joy *forever !* " In his magnificent "Ode on the Intimations of Immortality from Recollections of Early Childhood" Wordsworth is seen at his very best.

> " Though inland far we be
> Our souls have sight of that immortal sea
> Which brought us hither," —

and can respond to every line of this exquisite poem.

To sum up this review of Wordsworth's poetry, it may be said that his characteristic power is that of raising the smallest things in Nature into sublimity, and immortalizing them by the force of sentiment, as he has done with that primrose by the river's brim. " His passion for Nature," says De Quincey, " was a necessity, like that of the mulberry leaf to the silkworm. From the truth of his love his knowledge grew ; whilst most others, being merely hypocrites in their love, have turned out mere charlatans in their knowledge. If we accept Dampier, and some few professional naturalists, he first, and he last, has looked at Nature with an eye that will neither be dazzled from without nor cheated by preconceptions from within. He, first of all, has given the true key-note of the sentiment belonging to her grand pageantry." Describing the shifting pomp of an evening sky-scene, it is, moralizes the poet, —

> " Meek Nature's evening comment on the shows,
> . . . .
> . . . the fuming vanities of Earth ! "

Critics allow Wordsworth little fancy, no wit, little or no humor ; an austere purity of language, both grammatically and logically ; a perfect harmony between word and thought ; originality and sinewy strength of diction, peculiarly exhibited in single lines and paragraphs ; perfect fidelity to Nature in his images and descriptions ; meditative but not *moving* pathos, in the contemplation of his own and man's nature ; great occasional elegance, combined with peculiar and frequent rusticity and baldness of allusion ; style natural and severe ; versification sonorous and expressive ; imagination in the highest and strictest sense of the word.

" Let me," said Wordsworth, " be a teacher, or nothing." A teacher he was, and (with the exceptions of Milton and Cowper) the intensest and most pure-minded, as he was the most unique, of our English poets, — Nature's great High-Priest who has entered into her Holy of Holies as no preceding poet had ever done ; an undaunted literary reformer, who under general unpopularity, and a weight of opprobrium that would have crushed a weaker man,

worked steadily on in his mountain retirement, giving voice
to whatever things " the Spirit said unto him *write !* "   One
who met Wordsworth at Rydal Mount in the later years
of his life thus concisely described to me his appearance :
said my friend, " He was a *sacred*-looking man." Death,
stiller and sterner than poetry, has now folded him into
his embrace, beyond —

> " . . . the fretful stir
> Unprofitable, and the fever of the world."

Behind him he has left a rich epitaph in the memory of
his private virtues.   It has, I know, been said of him
"that he stood aside from his time, hearing the tumult
afar off ; " and some one inclined to contemn the mild pre-
cepts of this rural moralist, who lifted up his life as a distant beacon-fire among his valleys, " piping a simple song
to thinking hearts," rather than listening in crowded cities
to the wild heavings of the great heart of humanity, has
derisively compared his morality to the achievements of
that celebrated French sea-captain, —

> " Who fled full soon
> On the first of June,
> But bade the rest keep fighting."

Yet Wordsworth was not a man of timid virtue, neither
had his experience lain altogether out of the road of temptation.   A young man in Paris during the heat of the first
Revolution must have seen something of the thick of
the struggle and conflict of existence.   There are poets
of life and action who must necessarily come near enough
to the sins, sufferings, and follies of their brother men to
get through experience that " fellow-feeling that makes
us wondrous kind " to the prevailing infirmities of our
race.   On the other hand, there are poets of retirement
and reflection.   Wordsworth, among the vales of Gras-

mere, on the summit of Rydal Mount, or plunging into the thick woods at noonday, kept " perpetual honeymoon with Nature." In this love, that through life haunted him like a passion, lies the source of his strength. It left him untouched by the artificial and mechanical tastes of his age, colored his thoughts, gave originality to his concep-tions, and hallowed the whole man with —

> " The consecration and the poet's dream."

Honored be the poet who brought poetry back to her own sweet self; who turned the public taste from pompous inanity to truth and simplicity, standing ever first and foremost by the forlorn hope, a sturdy and steadfast champion of truth and Nature! The battle well done, serenely upon Rydal Mount the victor wore his laureate crown; and evermore —

> " It shall be greener from the brows
> Of him who uttered nothing base."

" Though dead, he yet speaketh." Hear him : —

> ". . . Nature never did betray
> The heart that loved her."

CHAPTER XV.

COLERIDGE AND SOUTHEY.

A POET of quite another calibre was Samuel Taylor Coleridge, — the friend and associate of Wordsworth, and his most enthusiastic admirer. The logician, metaphysician, critic, and rich, imaginative poet were in this remarkable man most singularly united.

Coleridge was a native of Devonshire, and born in 1772, at Ottery-St.-Mary, of which parish his father was vicar. The principal part of the poet's education was received at Christ's Hospital, — a school originally intended by Edward VI. as a foundation for poor orphan children born in London, but which afterward extended its benefits to the middle classes as well as the lower, and where some of the first writers and scholars of England have been educated. Here he had Charles Lamb for a school-fellow, and formed for him that friendship which death alone was permanently to interrupt.

Coleridge has described himself as being from eight to fourteen " a playless day-dreamer." The child is father of the man, and such a dreamer he was to the end of his life. A stranger whom he had accidentally met one day, on the streets of London, was struck with his conversation, and made him free of a circulating library. He read greedily through the catalogue, folios and all. " At fourteen," says his biographer, " he had, like Gibbon, a stock of erudition that might have puzzled a doctor, and a degree of ignorance of which a school-boy would have been ashamed."

A fatherless boy, and — as he himself tells us — " without a spark of ambition," he had seriously thought of apprenticing himself to a shoemaker who lived near the school. This honor to the craft of St. Crispin was happily prevented by the interference of the head-master. Coleridge subsequently became head scholar, and obtained from the hospital a presentation to Jesus College, Cambridge, which he entered in his nineteenth year, and the ensuing summer, gained the gold medal for the Greek ode. Though a very considerable proficient in classical studies, he was once or twice afterward an unsuccessful candidate for college honors.

At Cambridge the poet spent two unfruitful years. His reading was desultory and capricious ; he was at any time ready to unbend his mind in conversation, and his room was a constant rendezvous of conversation-loving friends. These years, in which he accomplished nothing but the increase of an already immense heap of undigested, miscellaneous reading, seem to have been unsatisfactory to Coleridge ; and in 1793 he quitted college abruptly without taking a degree, and went to London, where, finding himself forlorn and destitute, he resolved to get bread by becoming a soldier, and accordingly enlisted under the name of " Silas Titus Cumberback."

The poet made a poor dragoon, and is said never to have advanced beyond the awkward squad ; he wrote letters, however, for all his comrades, and they, in return, attended to his horse and accoutrements. After a military career of four months, his situation became known to his friends, who had meanwhile been at a loss to account for his sudden disappearance ; and his family, with some difficulty, effected his discharge. In April, 1794, Coleridge returned to Cambridge; the adventures of the preceding six months having broken the continuity of his college life, he had now no chance of obtaining a fellowship at the university, and having shut himself out from the advantages that might have lain open to him as a member of the Established Church, by professing himself a Unitarian, he remained only till the beginning of the summer vacation.

At this period of his life Coleridge was an ardent republican and a Socinian; and now he met for the first time Southey, whose friendship through his whole life was of the intensest value to him. Full of high hopes and anticipations, — "the golden exhalations of the dawn," — Coleridge, Southey, and Lovell, another poetical enthusiast, from building air-castles came to framing commonwealths. The three friends resolved to emigrate to America, where, amid the wilds of the Susquehanna, they were to found a pantisocracy, in which beatific state of society all things were to be in common, and neither king nor priest should mar the universal felicity. This Utopian dream was never realized; it is said from a very prosaic cause, the want of funds.

From pantisocracy the three poets turned their attention to matrimony; and three fair sisters, the Misses Fricker of Bristol, became the respective wives of each. To make provision for marriage, Coleridge and Southey gave public lectures at Bristol. Coleridge lectured on political, religious, and moral subjects. Lamb says of one of these lectures, "It is the most eloquent politics that ever came in my way;" yet they seem not to have made much addition to his income, and one can scarcely imagine a more forlorn picture of "Love in a Cottage," minus kitchen and larder furnishment, than is suggested by Coleridge's letter to his friend Cottle, dated two days after marriage, from his cottage at Cleveden, near Bristol,

in which he begs him to " send down without delay, a
riddle slice, a candle-box, two ventilators, one tin dust-
pan, two glasses for the wash-hand stand, one small tin
teakettle, one pair of candlesticks, one flour dredge, three
tin extinguishers, one carpet-brush, two large tin spoons,
two mats, a pair of slippers, a cheese-toaster, a Bible, and
a keg of porter, coffee, rice, catsup, raisins, currants,
nutmegs, allspice, cinnamon, cloves, ginger, and mace."
Some one has suggested that it must have been *after* the
receipt of these trifles that Coleridge, writing to his friend,
calls it his " *Comfortable* Cot."

In April, 1796, Coleridge's volume of poems, containing
most of those pieces which have been published under
the title of " Juvenile Poems," appeared.   The volume
afforded but slight indication of the coming splendors
of " Christabel."   In the year following Coleridge went
to live at Stowey ; here, in the closest friendship with
Wordsworth, who then lived at Allfoxden, only about
two miles from Stowey, were spent two or three years,
the most felicitous and illustrious of his literary life.   Here
he wrote some of his most beautiful poetry, — the first
and finest part of " Christabel ; " the exquisite little poem
entitled " Love ; " his best tragedy, " Remorse ; " " Kubla
Khan," that consummate fragment of weird melody, so
like " a dream remembered in a dream ; " and that wonderful poem, " The Ancient Mariner."

In 1798 Coleridge officiated in the Unitarian pulpit in
the parish of Shrewsbury, in the absence of their pastor.
Hazlitt walked ten miles on a winter's day to hear the
poet preach ; thus he describes it : —

" As he gave out his text, his voice rose like a steam of rich,
distilled perfumes ; he launched into his subject like an eagle
dallying with the wind.   The idea of St. John came into my mind,
of one crying in the wilderness, who had his loins girt about,

21

and whose food was locusts and wild honey. It seemed to me
as if his prayer might have floated in solemn silence through
the universe. For myself, I could not have been more delighted
if I had heard the music of the spheres."

Coleridge now received an invitation to the Shrewsbury
pulpit. The Wedgewoods — two wealthy brothers, who
were his munificent patrons — were strongly attached to
the Established Church ; and believing that as a clergyman
of the Unitarian faith his talents would be employed in
promulgating false and pernicious doctrines, they offered
him one hundred pounds if he would reject the invitation.
This bid seems to have been too low ; it was declined, and
Coleridge assumed the pastorship. A subsequent offer
from the same source, of an annuity of a hundred and
fifty pounds a year for an indefinite series of years, was
too much for the preacher's weak virtue. His convictions
were worth more to him than a hundred pounds ; but a
hundred and fifty pounds a *year* was to be *considered!*
And after some grave deliberation " St. John " ungirt
his loins, and cried no more in the wilderness. Judge
him not too hastily ; this bribe, to a dreamy and indolent
man, was no small temptation ; and God only knows how
many possible Judases live and die St. Johns solely for
lack of the " price."

Coleridge's religious speculation was emblematic of himself, — a man of high endowment and lax purpose, having
an eye to discern the beauty of holiness, but lacking the
courage and will to attain it. Languid and irresolute, he
(to use his own words) " skirts the howling deserts of
infidelity," and is by turns Jacobin and Royalist, Unitarian
and Trinitarian. " Coleridge," says Carlyle, " knew the
sublime secret of believing by the reason what the understanding had been obliged to fling out as incredible ; and

COLERIDGE AND SOUTHEY.   323

after Hume and Voltaire had done their best and worst
with him, he could still profess himself an orthodox
Christian, and say to the Church of England, with its
singular old rubrics and surplices, at All-Hallowtide,
Esto perpetua !"

Having concluded this financial arrangement, Coleridge
was now enabled to carry out a long-cherished plan of
visiting Germany in company with Wordsworth. There
he resided fourteen months, acquiring a well-grounded
knowledge of the German language and literature, and
becoming confirmed in his bias for philosophy and metaphysics. On his return he went to live with Southey, at
Keswick, and now became a warm and devoted believer
in the Trinity. He published at this time his translation
of Schiller's "Wallenstein," and as a means of subsistence, reluctantly consented to undertake the literary and
political department of the "Morning Post." In 1804 he
became Secretary to the Governor in Malta, with an annual salary of eight hundred pounds. Disagreeing with
the Governor, he held this lucrative office but nine months,
and after a tour in Italy, returned to England to resume
his precarious labors as author and lecturer.

It is painful to follow farther the wasted years of Coleridge. His desultory and irregular habits had become
confirmed by constant addiction to that dreadful vice, self-
indulgence. He now completely surrendered himself to
opium. "At one time," says Southey, "his ordinary
consumption of laudanum was from two quarts a week to
a pint a day." He appears, even in his most contrite con-
fessions, to have solaced his conscience by imputing this
sin to morbid bodily causes ; yet medical men have uniformly ascribed the evil not to bodily disease, but altogether to indulgence.

In spite of this detestable vice, Coleridge had many

warm friends, who never deserted him. Cottle, his biographer, was one of these, and he now proposed to raise an annuity of a hundred and fifty pounds, to be held in trust for him.

" On what grounds," writes Southey to Cottle, " can such a subscription as you propose raising for Coleridge be solicited? His miseries of body and mind all arise from one accursed cause, — excess in opium. . . . Perhaps you are not aware of the costliness of this drug. In the quantity which Coleridge takes, it would consume more than the whole which you propose to raise. A frightful consumption of spirits is added. Nothing is wanted to make him in easy circumstances but to leave off opium, and to direct a certain portion of his time to the discharge of his duties. There are two Reviews, the ' Quarterly,' and the ' Eclectic,' in both of which he might have employment at ten guineas a sheet."

But to every plan proposed Coleridge was irreconcilably averse. His wife and children received from him only half of the Wedgewood annuity (one of the brothers having withdrawn *his* portion), and they now sought shelter beneath Southey's kindly roof. The health and spirits of the forsaken wife were beginning to sink under her trials, and still Coleridge sank lower and lower in the depths of that misery into which he had plunged open-eyed. For a time he placed himself under the care of a physician ; and while in his hands he thus writes : —

" I am unworthy to call any good man friend. . . . Conceive a spirit in hell employed in tracing out for others the road to that heaven from which his crimes exclude him! In short, conceive whatever is most wretched, helpless, and hopeless, and you will form as tolerable a notion of my state as it is possible for any *good* man to have."

Mentally and morally irregular, the days of Coleridge were now given up to magnificent self-deceptions and vague speculations, now filled with vain excuses for the past or weak resolutions for the future, and the whining cant of self-condemnation. Never was he a valiant-hearted victor, yet ever but half vanquished. One can scarcely conceive a thing more mournful than this " greatly sinning and greatly aspiring soul." On the 19th of April, 1816, Coleridge went to reside permanently with Mr. Gillman of Highgate, who is described as " an amiable, weak-minded man, a professed admirer of the poet, and attaching the highest importance to all that concerned him, and flattered at the notoriety which he acquired by having so distinguished an inmate in his house. There for eighteen years the poet lived, watched over by this good man and his gentle-hearted wife, who shared her husband's admiration for the poet. The quantity of opium in which he now indulged was much diminished ; and his mind had assumed a more healthy tone. Yet never did he wholly abstain from its use ; nor were his faculties ever restored to their original vigor.

After having spent a year with the Gillmans, Coleridge published what he called his " Lay Sermons." Neither Coleridge's experience nor his habits of mind fitted him to be a safe guide in weighty matters, and his tracts are of little value. Of Coleridge's lectures only fragments have been preserved, as he seldom wrote them out previous to delivery. His criticisms on Shakespeare, delivered in one of these courses, have since been collected and published. Though of very unequal value, they are distinguished by their keenness, subtlety, and discrimination, and are thought to be among the best in the language. His reputation as a poet was greatly increased at this time by the publication of the second part of " Christabel," " Kubla Khan," " The Pains of Sleep," and " Sibylline Leaves." In the autumn of 1818 " Zapoyla " was composed and published.

The principal occupation of Coleridge's later years consisted in conversation. Eminently distinguished by the power and beauty of his oral discourse, the use of unnatural stimulants enabled him to make those brilliant displays exhibited in bewitching oracular monologues, which he would, it is said, continue in an unbroken strain from hour to hour, while his hearers, as Carlyle has it, "must sit as passive buckets, and be pumped into whether they consent or not. . . . No talk," he adds, "in his century, or in any other, could be more surprising : he spoke as if preaching ; you would have said, preaching earnestly and also hopelessly the weightiest things."

Coleridge said to Lamb one day, "Charles, did you ever hear me preach?" "I never heard you do anything else," was the apt reply. "Only, now, listen to his talk," says this genial friend ; "it is as fine as an angel's."

In such scraps as are noted down in the "Table Talk," there are great inequalities, — fine thoughts finely expressed, and passages only striking for their arrogance and ignorance. Yet these reports are said to give no idea of the style of his conversation. Says Sterling, "I was in his company about three hours, and of that time he spoke during two and three quarters. It would have been delightful to listen as attentively, and certainly as easy for him to speak just as well, for the next forty-eight hours."

In 1825 Coleridge published his "Aids to Reflection ; " but as a whole his life at Highgate presents a sad picture of intellectual vagaries and decline. There he lived for eighteen gracious years, ignobly shirking the duties and responsibilities of life ; mapping out for himself great works which were never completed, if so much as begun ; entreating yearly contributions from his friends to enable him to devote himself entirely to that literary labor for which he was, in sooth, mentally incapacitated; maintaining a hazy grandeur of reputation, but to the last infirm of purpose; his age unsoothed by the pious offices of wife and children, from whom he, careless of their maintenance, had separated himself. Such is the picture of Coleridge in his later years. Who would not turn this mournful portrait to the wall and say with Charles Lamb: "Come back into my memory like as thou wert in the dayspring of thy fancies, with hope like a fiery column before thee, the dark pillar yet unturned, — Samuel Taylor Coleridge, logician, metaphysician, bard!" On the 25th of July, 1834, ended this brilliant but unfruitful life. If I have dwelt too long on these sad details, let me beg to excuse myself in Coleridge's own words: " After my death I earnestly entreat that a full and unqualified narrative of my wretchedness, and of its guilty cause, may be made public, that at least some good may be effected by my direful example." Surely in the whole range of biography, no mortal has ever so

> ". . . flung away
> The keys that might have open set
> The golden sluices of the day."

Though associated with Wordsworth as a poet and author, Coleridge has told us that he never entirely concurred with the laureate in his poetical views; and in all that constitutes artistic character his poetry is a contrast to that of Wordsworth. Coleridge, far more than Wordsworth, was a poet " of imagination all compact." His verse is pure poesy, without that alloy of prose which may be found more or less in Wordsworth's. Coleridge's poetry is remarkable too for the perfection of its execution, for the exquisite art with which its divine spirit is endowed with formal expression; Wordsworth's poetry

is more admirable for its inner spirit than for its formal
qualities. Coleridge charms and bewitches us by that
exquisite and subtle sense of beauty, that divine breath
which makes poetry what it is ; Wordsworth sustains and
instructs us by proverbial and universally applicable wisdom and by homely every-day truths. The one sings to
us. Exquisite the melody is, ear-charming and heart-
delighting the words ; yet when the song is sung, we are
but *charmed*, seldom *more*. The other elevates us while
he charms, teaching us of the beauty of holiness, " as one
having authority."

It has been observed that " quantity alone was wanting
to make Coleridge the greatest poet of his day." Might
we not say that lack of quantity is just what *has* made him
the *poet?* Quality rather than quantity is the true test of
artistic excellence. With a muse as prolific as Southey's
Coleridge could not have attained that exquisite elaboration, that perfection of execution, in which he was unmatched. The most distinguishing characteristics of his
best poetry are vividness of imagination and subtlety of
thought, combined with unrivalled beauty and expressive-
ness of diction, and the most exquisite melody of verse.

There is not, as has been remarked, enough of passion in
him to make him the poet of the multitude. There is not
in him that pulse of fire that throbs and burns in Byron,
but rather that gentle and tremblingly delicate sense of
beauty, that blossoming of thought, that belongs to Spenser, who more than any other poet may be said to have
" spoken " flowers, as the fairy did *pearls*. A critic has
happily said of Coleridge's poetry : —

" The subtly woven words, with all their sky-colors, seem to
grow out of the thought or emotion, as the flower from the stalk,
or the flame from its feeding oil. The music of his verse is as
sweet and characteristic as anything in the language, placing

him for that rare excellence in the same small band with Shakespeare and Beaumont and Fletcher in their lyrics, with Milton and Collins and Shelley and Tennyson."

Coleridge's earlier compositions have a declamatory air, and are occasionally awkward and turgid in style, — faults from which his maturer productions are entirely free; yet even these juvenile pieces are radiant with purest sunlight of poesy.   Here is a gem worthy of the ripened poet; it is entitled "Time, Real and Imaginary" : —

> "On the wide level of a mountain's head
>   (I know not where, but 't was some fairy place),
> Their pinions ostrich-like for sails outspread,
> Two lovely children ran an endless race;
>   A sister and a brother
>   That far outstripped the other;
> Yet ever runs she with reverted face,
> And looks and listens for the boy behind:
>   For he, alas! is blind!
> O'er rough and smooth with even step he passed,
> And knows not whether he be first or last."

In the "Religious Musings" and in the "Monody on the Death of Chatterton" may be found passages of great power.   The ode entitled "France," written when the author was only twenty-six, Shelley regarded as the finest ode in the language.   His "Rime of the Ancient Mariner," written about the same time, though not the best, is the most original and striking of his productions.

Wordsworth and Coleridge, at a time when their united funds were very low, agreed to defray the expense of a little tour by writing together a poem to be sent to the "New Monthly Magazine."   Much the greater part of the story was Coleridge's invention, but certain parts were suggested by Wordsworth.   They began the composition together; but their respective manners proving so widely different, the idea of making it a conjoint production was soon relinquished, and Coleridge proceeded alone. "The poem grew and grew," says Wordsworth, "till it became quite too important for our first object, which was limited to our expectation of five pounds." The germ of this story is from Shelvocke the navigator, who states that his second captain, being a melancholy man, was possessed by a fancy that some long season of foul weather was owing to an albatross which had steadily followed the ship, upon which he shot the bird, but without mending their condition. Coleridge makes the Ancient Mariner — " long and lank, and brown as is the ribbed sea-sand " — relate the imaginary consequences of this act of inhumanity to one of three wedding guests, whom he meets on his way to the marriage feast, and interrupting him in his progress to the banquet, "holds him with his glittering eye."

> "The bridegroom's doors are opened wide,
>   And he is next of kin;
> The guests are met, the feast is set,
>   He hears the merry din.
>   .   .   .   .   .   .
>   He cannot choose but hear;
>   .   .   .   .   .   .
>   And listens like a three-years' child;
>   The mariner hath his will."

" The Ancient Mariner " is a poem by itself. Nothing like it has ever been done or attempted, or can be done. The versification is irregular, in the style of the old ballads; most of the action of the piece is unnatural. The poem is full of vivid and original imagination; and the narrative is invested with touches of exquisite tenderness and energetic description. A weird wonder and mystery flows around the reader, and holds him spell-bound. The supernatural machinery of the poem is managed with consummate skill and artistic effect. The beings who lend their mysterious aid to carry out the horrible penance imposed on the Ancient Mariner for shooting the bird of ill omen are to the last degree, as the Scotch say, "eldritch." Justice cannot be done to this weird and wonderful poem by quoting it piecemeal. The narrative is too intense in its interest to bear the slightest break in its thread. To appreciate it, the reader must come under its continuous spell, held like the wedding guest by the Mariner's glittering eye until he listens like a "three-years' child." Not so with the true and beautiful bit of ethics at the conclusion of his tale. This is as perfect as a whole, as exquisite and clear-cut, as a fine antique head done in cameo.

> "Farewell, farewell; but this I tell
> To thee, thou wedding guest!
> He prayeth well who loveth well
> Both man and bird and beast.

> "He prayeth best who loveth best
> All things both great and small;
> For the dear God who loveth us,
> He made and loveth all."

In "Christabel" Coleridge further illustrates that connection which we may suppose to exist between the spiritual and the material world. This romantic poem is filled with wild imagery and the most remarkable modulation of verse. The versification is founded on Coleridge's own principle of irregular harmony, which consists in the accentuation of words instead of syllables. Scott and Byron were both charmed with it, and have imitated it.

Coleridge is said to have spent infinite labor and pains upon his metres, elaborating them to the last degree. "Christabel" is an instance of the wonderful success he achieved in this department of his art. Parts of the poem are as filmy and delicate as the mist-wreaths of an Indian summer morning; every word is light and music.

The witch Geraldine, the principal personage in the poem, is an original and highly weird conception, — a partial metamorphosis of the human into the bestial nature ; a woman with snake's blood in her veins. "There is," it has been observed, "a substratum of fact in this conception, since there are well-attested accounts of children having been nurtured by wolves until faint and scarcely discernible traces of the human being remained." That assimilation which is possible between opposite natures (that interfusion of a positive evil nature with a negative good one) is demonstrated in "Christabel," — a psychological fact not unworthy the notice of both scientist and theologian.

"Christabel" is an unfinished work. Critics have variously accounted for its incompleteness. We may perhaps impute it to Coleridge's characteristic indolence. Another reasonable supposition is that the poet found it difficult to assign a motive for Geraldine's conduct, and for this reason abandoned the attempt to complete the poem. Whatever *Coleridge's* obstacles may have been, the author of "Proverbial Philosophy," nothing daunted, felt *him*self quite equal to the completion of "Christabel." Very obliging indeed it was of Mr. Tupper to finish Mr. Coleridge's poem for us. Dr. Holmes has facetiously observed that "he could not more essentially and entirely have finished himself." The bare attempt could be no less than sacrilege, and the performance is a miserable failure !

No writing could be more gauzily delicate than some parts of "Christabel." Here is an exquisite specimen of that word-painting in which Coleridge is unrivalled : —

> "Sweet Christabel her feet doth bare,
> And, jealous of the listening air,
> They steal their way from stair to stair,
> Now in glimmer, and now in gloom,

And now they pass the Baron's room,
As still as death, with stifled breath !
And now have reached her chamber door;
And now doth Geraldine press down
The rushes of the chamber floor.

" The moon shines dim in the open air,
And not a moonbeam enters here.
But they without its light can see
The chamber carved so curiously,
Carved with figures strange and sweet,
All made out of the carver's brain,
For a lady's chamber meet :
The lamp with twofold silver chain
Is fastened to an angel's feet."

Some of Coleridge's minor poems have the same richness of coloring and perfection of finish.   It would be
difficult to find in our own or any other language a match
for those exquisite verses entitled " Love."

A popular critic says of Coleridge's " Hymn in the Vale
of Chämouni " : " It is a mere sham, made up like a cheap
panorama from engravings, as Coleridge, from the testimony of his friend Wordsworth, was never there."   If
distance *really* lends enchantment, this should not detract
from the merit of the poem ; we might, however, object to
its gorgeous diffuseness ; and though a lofty and brilliant
production, it is not in Coleridge's best vein.   In his later
poetry Coleridge gains depth and earnestness and mingles
more of the inspiration of the heart with that of the fancy ;
as in that " gem without a flaw," entitled " Love, Hope,
and Patience in Education," and in that entitled " Youth
and Age."   The concluding lines remind one of the quaint
pathos of Herrick.

" O Youth ! for years so many and sweet
'T is known that thou and I were one ;

I 'll think it but a fond conceit, —
It cannot be that thou art gone !
Thy vesper-bell hath not yet tolled : —
And thou wert aye a masker bold !
What strange disguise hast now put on,
To make believe that thou art gone ?
I see these locks in silvery slips,
This drooping gait, this altered size :
But spring-tide blossoms on thy lips,
And tears take sunshine from thine eyes !
Life is but thought : so think I will
That Youth and I are house-mates still.
Dew-drops are the gems of morning,
But the tears of mournful eve !
Where no hope is, life 's a warning
That only serves to make us grieve,
      When we are old :
That only serves to make us grieve,
With oft and tedious taking leave ;
Like some poor nigh-related guest,
That may not rudely be dismissed,
Yet hath outstayed his welcome while,
And tells the jest without the smile."

Coleridge's dramas are deficient in strong passion and rapid energy of action ; and though as works of genius, they vastly excel many popular acting plays, posterity will confirm what has already been said of them, — "beautiful but impracticable." "Remorse," as a drama intended for the closet, rather than the stage, may take its place among the standard literature of our country ; while "Zapoyla" for perfection of language and versification may be studied as a model. His translation of Schiller's "Wallenstein," said to have been executed in six weeks, has been pronounced even preferable to the original. Coleridge's rich musical numbers, the beauty of his language, and frequent amplification of the thought, make it rather a poem than a translation. These numbers, in which Wal-

lenstein, looking forth into the windy night in search of
the star of his nativity, recalls to mind the death of Max,
and bemoans his loss, affect the heart and ear like a spell.

> " He is gone, he is dust !
> He, the more fortunate ! yea, he hath finished !
> His life is bright, — bright without spot it *was*
> And cannot cease to be. No ominous hour
> Knocks at his door with tidings of mishap.
> Far off is he, above desire and fear ;
> No more submitted to the change and chance
> Of the unsteady planets. O, 't is well
> With him ! but who knows what the coming hour
> Veiled in thick darkness brings for us !
>   .   .   .   .
> . . . The bloom is vanished from my life,
> For O ! he stood beside me like my youth,
> Transformed for me the real to a dream,
> Clothing the palpable and the familiar
> With golden exhalations of the dawn.
> Whatever fortunes wait my future toils,
> The *beautiful* is vanished, and returns not ! "

In summing up the merits of Coleridge's poetry, beautiful as it is, we must admit the mournful truth that " it
indicates more than it achieves."   From childhood to age
visions of grace, tenderness, and majesty seem ever to
have haunted him.   Some of these he embodied in exquisite but often fragmentary verse.   That concentration and
steadiness of purpose necessary to him who would turn
his intellectual wealth to account he miserably lacked.
A happier destiny, which he himself might have shaped,
was wanting.   Much of his life was spent in poverty and
dependence, and in tyrannical self-indulgence that bred
for him disappointment and ill health ; and thus in days
of distasteful drudgery for the periodical press or of aim-
less, indolent lotos-eating, he wasted — to use his own
expression — " the prime and manhood of his intellect."

Holding the key to every hidden chamber of profound and subtle thought, and every ethereal conception, equally master of the wildest imagery, the airiest fancy, and the most melodious harmonies, before posterity he stands abased beside the humblest mortal who, battling with the flesh and the Devil, has obtained the mastery of himself, albeit he never —

> " On honey-dew hath fed,
> Or drank the milk of Paradise."

Robert Southey, in the commencement of his literary career the associate of Wordsworth and Coleridge, has with them been properly reckoned as one of the Lake poets.

Southey was born in 1774. Having passed with credit through Westminster School, he was entered at Oxford in 1792. His friends designed him for the Church; but the poet became a Jacobin and Socinian, and his academic career was abruptly closed. In 1795 Southey married Miss Edith Fricker of Bristol, sister of the lady whom Coleridge afterward married. He is said to have parted with his wife immediately after the ceremony, at the portico of the church, to set out on his travels in Portugal. In 1797 he returned to England, and entered himself at Gray's Inn. In the same year his " Thalaba " was published. Subsequently the poet established himself at Greta Hall, Keswick, where he spent the remainder of his life.

In 1813 Southey accepted the office of poet laureate. Subsequently he was offered a baronetcy and a seat in Parliament, both of which he prudently declined, preferring to seek fame and fortune by adhering to his solitary studies. These were, unhappily, too constant and uninterrupted. "Every day, every hour," says his biographer, "had its allotted employment, — always were there engagements to publishers imperatively requiring punctual fulfilment; always the current expenses of a large household to take anxious thought for. For although his mode of life was as simple and inexpensive as possible, his expenditure was with difficulty kept within his income, owing to his noble liberality to the distressed, and the considerable sums which were regularly drawn from him by his less successful relatives. The entire family of Coleridge had taken shelter under his kindly roof and shared his bounty. He was, too, constantly adding new purchases to his library, which at his death consisted of about fourteen thousand volumes, — probably the largest number of books ever collected by a person of such limited means. ' My ways,' he used to say, ' are as broad as the King's high-road, and my means lie in an ink-stand.' "

A thoroughly domestic man, his whole pleasure and happiness is said to have been centred in his home; yet he could not, however he might wish it, give time for the summer evening walk, or make one of a circle around the winter hearth, or even spare time for conversation after the family meals.

In personal appearance Southey is said to have been very striking, and in his early days he had been considered the beau-ideal of a poet. Lord Byron speaks of his appearance as " epic," and says, " To have his head and shoulders, I would almost have written his Sapphics." He was extremely courteous in manner, and frank and pleasant in conversation; to his intimates, wholly unreserved; disposed to give and receive pleasure, and freely pouring forth his vast stores of information upon almost every subject.

His library was his world, within which he was content to range; and his books were his most cherished and con-

stant companions. It is melancholy to reflect that for
nearly three years before his death he sat among them
in hopeless vacuity of mind.

Acutely sensitive by nature, and highly predisposed to
nervous disease, the forty years of incessant mental application which he had passed through had at length over-
clouded his great mind, and brought upon him premature
decay. His mind was beautiful even in its debility. He
was often, it is said, conscious of losing himself for a
moment in conversation, and then an expression of
pain and of touching resignation would pass over his
face. He spoke openly of his altered condition; and
though doing nothing, he would frequently anticipate a
return of his powers. His mind, while any spark of reason
remained, was busy with its old day-dreams; works which
he had projected were to be taken in hand, completed, and
new works added to these. Long after he had ceased to
compose, he took pleasure in reading, and the habit continued even after the power of comprehension was gone.
His beloved books were a pleasure to him to the end; and
when he had ceased to read them, he would walk slowly
round his library looking at them, and taking them down
mechanically.

At last no glimmering of reason appeared; the body
grew weaker; and after a short attack of fever, he died
on the 21st of March, 1843. Wordsworth — his only
intimate friend within reach — crossed the hills on a wild
March morning to follow his dear remains to their resting-place in the beautiful churchyard at Crossthwaite; and
when the April sod grew green upon his grave, all who
loved him thanked God that there he rested.

Southey's first epic, " Joan of Arc," a portion of which
was written by Coleridge, was published in 1796. In 1801
he brought out a second epic, " Thalaba, the Destroyer."

In 1804 he published a volume of metrical tales; the following year " Madoc," another epic, saw the light; and in 1810 appeared his greatest poetical work, " The Curse of Kehama."

Coleridge's recipe for an epic is *this* : " I would take," says the poet, " twenty years for the production of an epic, — ten to familiarize me with the subject chosen, to travel and gain a personal knowledge of the *locale*, and acquaint myself thoroughly with history pertaining thereto. I would wish also to be somewhat a man of science, to understand botany, geology, mineralogy, astronomy, geography, ichthyology, conchology, medicine and chemistry, mechanics, mathematics, etc., etc. I would then devote five years to the composition of the poem, and five to its revision." If such be the process requisite to the production of an epic, what shall we say of a man who turned off four in fourteen years? We must, in charity, imagine that he suffered under *what Milton calls* " the *disease* of making books." Southey wrote not wisely, but too much ; he is said to have written more than even Scott, and to have burned more verses between his twentieth and thirtieth year than he published in his whole lifetime !

A scholar, antiquary, critic, and historian ; gifted with a remarkable memory, which enabled him to command a vast supply of materials for whatever subject he was employed upon, and always, it is said, collecting for his subject an infinitely greater quantity of materials than he ever made use of; yet with all his ingenuity and fertility, lacking " the vision and the faculty divine," — Southey is not an original poet. His genius was rather imitative than creative. He could only put forth his strength while moving in a beaten track. And moreover, he lacks spontaneity. He is a poet by profession, not one by divine right, — one who carols like the bird, and —

" Knows not why nor whence he sings,
    Nor whither goes his warbled song."

In the " Curse of Kehama," his most elaborate poem,
there is much splendor and beauty, yet in parts it is both
tame and monotonous. The story is founded upon the
Hindu mythology, "which" (as Sir Walter Scott observes) "is the most gigantic, cumbrous, and extravagant
system of idolatry to which temples were ever erected."
Kehama is a Hindu rajah — an Oriental Dr. Faustus —
who obtains and sports with supernatural power. The
scene is alternately laid in the terrestrial Paradise, under
the sea, in the heaven of heavens, and in hell itself. Of
the principal actors, one is almost omnipotent, the other,
by a strange and fatal malediction, is exempted from the
ordinary laws of nature. A good genius, a sorceress, a
ghost, and Hindustan deities of various ranks, figure in
the work ; the only being that retains the usual attributes
of humanity is gifted with immortality before the curtain
drops ; surely weird invention could no farther go ! The
poem displays a wild imagination and vivid scene-paint-
ing, which has the merit of fidelity, Southey being too diligent a student to omit whatever was characteristic in the
landscape or the people. In manners, sentiment, scenery,
and costume it is distinctly and exclusively Hindu.

"The Curse of Kehama" is redundant in description,
and has the rare merit of being terrible without being
revolting. The poem is remarkable for sustained dramatic ingenuity, and evinces the hand and eye of the true
scholar. If Southey is not a great poet, he is a great
story-teller. No modern sensation novel is more enchanting to the lover of fiction ; and the moral tone of the
poem is unquestionable. Southey, both in prose and
verse, is thoroughly and unaffectedly English. His versi-

fication is sometimes abrupt and affected. His power lies chiefly in fancy and the invention of his subject. In description he is often striking and impressive; yet notwithstanding an ambition of originality which led him to Arabia and Hindustan for his models, he cannot, I think, lay claim to true creative genius. " The Curse of Kehama " embodies what is best in Southey, as well as his peculiar idiosyncrasies. There is much splendor and beauty in his description of Ereenia, the Glendoveer, or pure spirit; yet it will be seen that conciseness would have made it far more admirable. It is a fair example of Southey's style:

> " And never yet did form more beautiful,
> In dreams of night descending from on high,
> Bless the religious virgin's gifted sight,
>   Nor like a vision of delight
> Rise on the raptured poet's inward eye.
>   Of human form divine was he,
> The immortal youth of heaven who floated by,
> Even such as that divinest form shall be
>   In those blest stages of our onward race,
>   When no infirmity,
> Low thought, nor base desire, nor wasting care,
>   Deface the semblance of our heavenly sire.

> " The wings of eagle or of cherubim
>   Had seemed unworthy him;
> Angelic power and dignity and grace
> Were in his glorious pinions; from the neck
> Down to the ankle reached their swelling web,
>   Richer than robes of Tyrian dye, that deck
>   Imperial majesty:
>   Their colour like the winter's moonless sky,
>   When all the stars of midnight's canopy
> Shine forth; or like the azure steep at noon,
>   Reflecting back to heaven a brighter blue.

> " Such was their tint when closed; but when outspread,
>   The permeating light

Shed through their substance thin a varying hue;
  Now bright as when the rose,
Beauteous as fragrant, gives to scent and sight
  A like delight; now like the juice that flows
    From Douro's generous vine;
  Or ruby, when with deepest red it glows;
Or as the morning clouds refulgent shine,
When, at forthcoming of the lord of day,
  The orient, like a shrine,
Kindles as it receives the rising ray,
  And, heralding his way,
Proclaims the presence of the Power divine."

Few authors have written so much and so well, with so little real popularity, as Southey; his poetry is unsuited to the taste of the present generation, and his name and fame, with his joys and his griefs, are vanishing like a cloud from Skiddaw's top.

Some of Southey's youthful ballads — which were in their day extremely popular — and his " Battle of Blenheim " are examples of his " Lake poetry."

With " little Peterkin " in the latter poem, we are often puzzled, in view of the " thousand bodies rotting in the sun," to find —

". . . what good came of it at last ? "

CHAPTER XVI.

CAMPBELL AND SCOTT.

ABOUT the year 1799 a select circle assembled at the dinner-table of Walter Scott. A stranger had, unintroduced, taken his seat among the guests. At length, when the cloth was removed and the loyal toasts were disposed of, Scott stood up, and with a handsome and complimentary notice of the " Pleasures of Hope," proposed a bumper to the author. " The poem," he added, " is in the hands of all our friends ; the poet "— pointing to the young stranger on his right — " I have now the high honor of introducing to you as my guest." Since then Campbell's " Pleasures of Hope " has passed through nearly one hundred editions, been translated into all the chief Continental languages, and has become a model for imitation in school and college.

That precious pedigree, dear as the apple of his eye to the Scotchman's heart, was the birthright of Campbell. His father was the youngest son of a laird, and could trace his descent as far back as the first Norman lord of Loch — something ! The poet was born in the city of Glasgow, July 27, 1777. Though a partially ruined merchant, the elder Campbell had, not without effort, given to his son a careful and liberal education.

From his cradle Campbell became skilled in sweet sounds and the power of flowing numbers. His mother had a strong taste for music, and delighted in singing her favorite Scotch ballads; from her he imbibed that fondness for ballad poetry which, interwoven with the classic elegance of his verse, has made its simple grace and melody a study in our literature.

Campbell's mind was cast in no ordinary mould; when a mere child, he was familiar with classic poetry, and could recite long passages from the Greek and Latin poets. At the university he carried off all the prizes, and it was his ambition to become a ripe Greek scholar. The local celebrity arising from various early fruits of his poetic genius induced him to abandon the study of the law. Who that dates his first love of poetry as an art from the study of those poems, which still continue to delight new generations of readers, can regret that there appeared in the good city of Edinburgh, in the year of our Lord 1799, no modest shingle inscribed "Thomas Campbell, Attorney-at-Law"?

Campbell's genius was truly precocious. Even his earliest productions have the genuine stamp upon them. His "Pleasures of Hope," published at twenty-one, though in some respects juvenile in execution, in its glowing impetuosity and imposing splendor of declamation evinces the genius of a true poet as clearly as his maturest productions. The classic taste and careful artistic finish of Campbell have given this poem that hold upon the popular ear which, more than almost any other poem, it has gained by swell of sound rather than by proportion of sense. Through the conventional habits of the preceding bad school of verse-making in which he had been partly trained, and from which in his later compositions he has emerged, Campbell caught that hollowness and falseness in expression which may be found in almost every page of this once popular poem. Fine ear-charming words and sentences, with little or no meaning, readily

won applause in Queen Anne's time. A more earnest
and deep-thinking age now demands more than this in
poetry. There is also a want of connection between the
different parts of the poem. Yet after all these deduc-
tions from the excellence of the "Pleasures of Hope,"
enough remains of grace and elegance of diction, and of
pure and genuine sentiment, to suggest a *possible* immortality for the work.

"Gertrude of Wyoming," a Pennsylvania tale, in true
poetic excellence far surpasses the "Pleasures of Hope."
It is a polished and pathetic poem, in the old style of
English pathos and poetry, evincing by its delineations
of character and passion a far more luxuriant and perfect
genius. The portrait of Outalissi, the inimitable painting
of the loves of Gertrude and Waldegrave, the patriarchal
picture of Albert, and the sketches of rich, sequestered
Pennsylvanian scenery, — all display the skill and finish
of the true poetic artist. A humorous critic, while admit-
ting its poetic beauties, discovers in this poem some
strange notions on the subject of the natural history
of plants and animals. "Gertrude," he observes, "is
spoken of as reclining under a *palm-tree* in the valley
of Wyoming, and *tigers* are inventoried among the deni-
zens of our North American forest!" However, as an
English author, Campbell may be allowed any amount of
ignorance in regard to the land of the star-spangled banner; and the exquisite and touching pathos in which the
poem is conceived might make ample amends for even
more serious incongruities.

Campbell's fine lyrics are purer in execution than his
longer poems; in exquisite delicacy of touch and grace
of form they are almost perfect. No poetry of this time
is probably so deeply inscribed on the heart and memory.
The most preferable of these well-known poems are

" Lochiel's Warning," " Hohenlinden," " The Exile of
Erin," " Lord Ullin's Daughter," " Song of the Greeks,"
" The Soldier's Dream ; " the *very* best is " O'Connor's
Child." The fire and force of this poem when, near its
close, the bride of Connacht Moran, urged onward by
the fervor of her passionate love and grief, stands before
us, an inspired Pythoness, invoking the curse of Heaven
on the cruel murderers of her warrior lover, —

> " Warm in his death-wounds sepulchred,
>   Nor mass nor ulla-lulla heard
>   To soothe him in his grave," —

have perhaps never been excelled in lyric poetry.

> " The standard of O'Connor's sway
>   Was in the turret where I lay ;
>   That standard, with so dire a look,
>   As ghastly shone the moon and pale,
>   I gave, that every bosom shook
>   Beneath its iron mail.

> " And go ! (I cried) the combat seek,
>   Ye hearts that unappallèd bore
>   The anguish of a sister's shriek,
>   Go ! — and return no more !
>   For sooner guilt the ordeal brand
>   Shall grasp unhurt, than ye shall hold
>   The banner with victorious hand,
>   Beneath a sister's curse unrolled.
>   O stranger ! by my country's loss !
>   And by my love ! and by the cross !
>   I swear I never could have spoke
>   The curse that severed nature's yoke,
>   But that a spirit o'er me stood,
>   And fired me with the wrathful mood —
>   And frenzy to my heart was given,
>   To speak the malison of heaven.

> " They would have crossed themselves, all mute ;
>   They would have prayed to burst the spell ;

> But at the stamping of my foot
> Each hand down powerless fell!
> And go to Athunree! (I cried)
> High lift the banner of your pride!
> But know that where its sheet unrolls,
> The weight of blood is on your souls!
> Go where the havoc of your kerne
> Shall float as high as mountain fern!
> Men shall no more your mansion know;
> The nettles on your hearth shall grow!
> Dead, as the green oblivious flood
> That mantles by your walls, shall be
> The glory of O'Connor's blood!
> Away! away to Athunree!
> Where, downward when the sun shall fall,
> The raven's wing shall be your pall!
> And not a vassal shall unlace
> The visor from your dying face!"

Campbell, like Gray, whom in taste and genius he resembles, cannot be termed a boldly original or inventive poet. He has great elegance and elaboration of style, tolerable power and scope, both of thought and fancy; in his shorter effusions great force and animation and true lyric fire, with admirable terseness of style, and an air of tenderness and sweetness over all, like the delicate fragrance from a bed of violets. The consummate finish of his poetry, and the warm, broad, generous humanity which he evinces, will long keep his memory green; and though he has embodied in his poems no profound truths or bold originality of thought and expression, he is more sure of an enduring fame than almost any of the poets of his time. It has been well said that "a popular author has no rival so formidable as his former self." "Theodric," published twenty-five years after the "Pleasures of Hope," failed to add another wreath to Campbell's laurels. It is a domestic story, involving little incident or fervor of passion ; and though not without a tender finish both of thought and diction, as well as elegance of word and image, on the pages of "Theodric" we look in vain for those brilliant flashes of genius that illume his earlier productions.

Campbell's age and decline gave evidence of that premature decay of intellectual power so mournfully displayed by Southey and Scott, — the fearful reaction of an overworked brain ; Nature's fatal retribution for the sin of the soul against the body. Sunny days occasionally brightened his decline, but the shadows were fast creeping upon him. He who had (as Byron expresses it) "dressed to sprucery, looking as if Apollo had sent him a birthday suit or a wedding garment," became careless of his dress. He grew restless, indulged constantly in change of scene, exhibited an unfounded dread of poverty, — though his income exceeded that of most poets and literary men ; for by his industry and perseverance he had surmounted pecuniary difficulties, and by his efforts had even aided his poorer relatives. Calculating that he could live abroad in greater seclusion and at cheaper cost than in England, in 1843 Campbell left his country forever. At Boulogne, in June, 1844, after a lingering decay of mind and body, he breathed his last. His latest literary consolation was in the assurance that he "had not written one line against religion or virtue."

Notwithstanding the previous appearance of Wordsworth, Southey, Coleridge, and some other writers, it was Walter Scott who first in his day made poetry the *rage*, and with him properly commences the busy poetical production of the period which we are now reviewing. Those who had preceded him in the field he inspired with new activity, and it was after *his* appearance that they gave to the world their principal works. Before the breaking forth of Scott's bright day, neither Crabbe nor Moore had yet produced anything equal to their powers. Campbell, who, after attracting a large share of the public attention by his " Pleasures of Hope " and a few other short pieces, had laid aside his lyre for some five or six years, returned to woo the public favor by his " Gertrude of Wyoming " only after Scott had directed the public taste to narrative poetry ; and Byron, who eventually outdid Scott and forced him to seek for greener laurels " in fresh fields and pastures new," in the most taking of his earlier productions seems to have owed his inspiration to the author of the " Lay of the Last Minstrel."   It has been observed that "his ' Giaour,' ' The Bride of Abydos,' ' The Corsair,' etc., were, in reality, only Oriental lays and romances, — Turkish ' Marmions ' and ' Ladies of the Lake,' — yet containing nothing comparable to the great passages in those wonderful poems."

Walter Scott was born in Edinburgh on the 15th of August, 1771. " A Scotchman," says his biographer, " is nothing without his pedigree ; and without tracing the family line back to its illustrious stock, the ducal house of Buccleugh, one dare not pass over " all of those ancestors whom Sir Walter especially loved to commemorate. There is his great-grandfather Walter, called Beardie, a stanch old Jacobite, who swore never to cut his beard until " Jamie should have his own again ; " and as Jamie never *did* get his own again, he wore the venerable appendage till the day of his death. The portrait of Beardie, now at Abbotsford, is said strongly to resemble Sir Walter.

Then there is Beardie's grandfather, Auld Watt of Harden, a famous moss-trooper, the hero of a hundred Border songs, to whom nothing in the way of plunder came amiss that was not " *too hot* or *too heavy ;* " and there also is his wife, Mary Scott, "the Flower of Yarrow," who, when the last ox taken from English pastures was eaten, gave her liege lord an intimation of the poverty of the larder by placing on the board before him a pair of spurs in a covered dish, as a hint that he must bestir himself if he wanted to dine on the morrow.

It was this same stanch old Watt Harden who, returning with his armed retainers from a foray on the rich meadows of the south, driving a gallant herd before him, after grudgingly eying a large haystack upon the road, shook his fist at it, and rode grimly away, muttering, "By my soul, had ye but *four feet*, ye would na stan' there lang!" Then there is Auld Watt's comely son, who, riding a raid on the lands of Sir Gideon Murray, was caught by the baron and sentenced to be hanged, and cannily saved his neck by marrying the worst-looking of the baron's three unmarketable daughters, who is said to have been "precisely the ugliest girl in broad Scotland."

There too are the minstrels of his race, — rough old Walter Scott, who sang of the glories of his clan; John Scott the Lamiter, or cripple; and William the Bolt-foot, who left his deformity to Sir Walter.

Beardie himself has handed down to his descendants, as a specimen of his Latin poet-craft, a convivial chorus, which, *translated*, is, —

> "The beard shall grow, the beard shall grow
> Until the thistle again shall blow."

In strong contrast to these bold Borderers and minstrels of Clan Scott another of Sir Walter's race is pictured by his biographer: a serene old man of ninety, who rises to welcome his now illustrious nephew; tall and erect he is, with long flowing hair, whitened like

silver. Kissing Walter on both cheeks, he heartily exclaims : " God bless thee, Walter, my man ! thou hast
risen to be great, but thou wert *always* good." The
father of the poet, a writer to the signet, is said to
have been the first of his lineage who was not soldier,
sailor, or moss-trooper.

Walter Scott, when a child of eight summers, was
found on recovery from a fever to have lost the use of
his right leg. Quacks and regular physicians were alike
unsuccessful in their attempts to restore to the infant poet
his power of locomotion ; but what the doctors failed to
do, outdoor life and his own impatient desires effected ;
and after a time he began to stand a little, and by and
by to walk and run, after a lame fashion.

He passes an independent child-life, by sea-side or
among the heather, and is at length promoted from the
old corn-baillie's shoulder to a Shetland pony of his own.
Thus the time wears on till the lame boy is sent to
school. In the Edinburgh High School he is more distinguished in the yards than in the class ; for with that
resolute will which served him so well in harder pulls,
he has struggled with his natural infirmity until he can
run, jump, and " climb the kittle nine stanes " with any-
body. He is rather behind his class, both in years and
progress, and he loves " better than lear " to lie under
a high hill of leaves in the garden, reading " Ossian,"
Percy's " Reliques," and Spenser's " Faery Queen."

One of his school-fellows long remembers how he always got through his task first, and then, true to his
inborn vocation, would whisper, " Come, slink over beside me, Jamie, and I 'll tell you a story." At thirteen
he is sent to the university. Having but " little Latin,"
he resolves to have " less Greek," and is here known as
the " Greek blockhead." A severe and dangerous ill-

ness intervenes, and on returning to the university, he is found to have forgotten the very letters of the Greek alphabet. Of old ballads he knows a good stock, and has already been famous for his metrical translations at the High School. He confesses to a dislike to Latin, simply because it is classical, but having several favorite authors in this tongue, keeps up his knowledge of it, and can always read it sufficiently well. The languages of his beloved poets and romancers — French, Spanish, and Italian — he reads with facility, but never speaks them. Later in life he learns some German, but at all times his chief studies are in English. In 1786 he is apprenticed to his father's profession. It is dry work ; but whatever is to be done, reading, copying, going about, he does it with diligence. His miscellaneous readings exhaust the circulating library, and he is continually amassing new information of every kind.

He loves well to be with wood, water, and wilderness. All his holidays are spent in walking ; and his good father says, " Surely, he was born to be a pedlar." " I only wish," responds the son, " that I were as good a player on the flute as poor George Primrose, in the ' Vicar of Wakefield ; ' if I had his art, I should like nothing better than to tramp about from cottage to cottage." " I doubt," says the grave, prosaic father, — " I greatly doubt, sir, ye were born for nae better than a gangrel scraper."

In 1792 the poet puts on the advocate's robe. In his vacations, during seven successive years, the young lawyer makes " raids," as he calls them, into Liddesdale, where the rude, clannish people, still cleaving to the customs of their forefathers, have stores of moss-trooping legends. Here, at farm-house, manse, and cottage, he gathers old ballads, old tunes, and —

" A fouth of auld nicknackets,
Rusty airn caps and jinglin jackets,"—

" treasures," says his biographer, " for which he would
have renounced the lord chief-justiceship, had it been
offered him." " He was *makin* himsel a' the time," says
his shrewd Scotch guide in these excursions ; " but he
didna ken maybe what he was about until years had
passed." In 1796 appears his first publication, " Lenore "
and the " Wild Huntsman," translated from the German
of Bürger. " Upon my word," exclaims one of his lady
friends, " Walter Scott is going to turn out a poet ! "
" Lenore " is coldly received, but he determines to go
on in spite of it.

At twenty-six the poet is " sair beside himself" for Miss
Charlotte Parker. The lady is of French parentage, and
very lovely and lovable, though not his first love. He
woos and wins her, and she is his true and faithful wife for
many long years. The same year, having been appointed
sheriff of Selkirkshire, Scott is enabled to quit the drudgery
of his profession, of which he says, after the manner of
Slender in his wooing of Ann Page, " There was no great
love between us in the beginning, and it pleased Heaven to
decrease it on further acquaintance." Three years go by,
and then the first and second volumes of the " Minstrelsy
of the Scottish Border" make their appearance. They are
well received, and in the ensuing year the last volume is
published. In 1805 appears the " Lay of the Last Minstrel ; " it is enthusiastically received. And now, under
the tall old trees by the Tweed-side, or wandering away
along the wilderness through which the Yarrow creeps
from her fountains, pacing his good black steed up and
down the sands, to the " slow song of the sea,". or gal-
loping over brake, bush, and scar, reckless as his own

Lochinvar, the poet weaves his finest web of song, — "Marmion," the most magnificent of his chivalrous tales.

In 1810 the "Lady of the Lake" sails forth in handsome quarto, at two guineas per copy, and sets the good people "clean daft." The whole country rings with the praises of the poet. Every eligible house and every inn in the neighborhood is crowded with visitors, come to view the scenery of Loch Katrine; and long after, an old woman, keeping an inn at Glenross, who, poor soul! has but little custom, begs "the gentleman who had written a bonnie book about Loch Katrine, which had done the inn a muckle deal of good, to write a little about *their* lake *also*." "The Vision of Don Roderick," "Rokeby," "The Bridal of Triermain," "The Lord of the Isles," "The Field of Waterloo," and "Harold the Dauntless," are successively published.

And now Byron appears. The world, having a new idol, becomes weary of the old; and, moreover, it must be acknowledged that at the "Lady of the Lake" Scott's poetical splendor had reached its maximum. Nothing equal to that bewitching idyl ever after appeared from his pen. Dauntless and intrepid under this reverse, the poet falls back on his reserved force; and for seventeen years he pours forth those varied creations in prose upon which the world still hangs enchanted.

He works diligently this golden mine which he has discovered. He wins honors and praise of men, a baronetcy, broad acres, and a baronial residence; princes, peers, and poets, men of all ranks and grades, it delighteth to honor him. His mornings are devoted to composition, and the rest of the day is given to riding among his plantations and entertaining his guests and family. And all this is the result of his pen! Never before had literature been such a genie of the lamp to her votary! Who would not gladly

drop the curtain before this fair picture, and close the scene
while all is bright and lovely? But, alas! beside it another
picture hangs before the world, — a bowed and weary
man, his private affairs in ruin, the wife of his youth laid
low in the kirkyard, broken in health and spirits, yet
sturdily maintaining his integrity, and undertaking to liqui-
date by intellectual labors alone a debt of one hundred
and twenty thousand pounds! In four years he has realized for his creditors no less than seventy thousand! The
world cheers him on, and he shrinks not from his gigantic,
self-imposed task, till in the struggle the strong man suc-
cumbs at last. He has given his life to maintain his honor!
A helpless and almost unconscious wreck, he lingers on.
He tries to write, but his fingers will not close upon the
pen; the magician's hand is powerless; and sinking back
in his chair, the big tears roll fast and heavy down his
cheeks. " Get me to bed, friends," he murmurs, — " get
me to bed, that's the only place for me now." Gradually
he declines; his mind wanders, — old fancies are with him.
Sometimes he mutters words of comfort from the Bible or
the Prayer-Book, — old Scottish Psalms or bits of fine old
Catholic hymns; and often, from those fading lips that
long ago had chanted the old Border-songs, loving watch-
ers hear in solemn cadence the grand Dies Iræ, —

> " Broken-hearted, lone, and tearful,
> By that cross of anguish fearful,
> Stood the mother by her son."

And now the flame in the expiring lamp burns bright
and clear, and the unclouded reason returns for the solemn adieus to earth. True to his own kindly nature,
he will have only one called from sleep to receive these,
his parting words, — they should be written in letters of
gold, — "I may have but a moment to speak to you.

My dear, be a good man; be virtuous; be religious. Be a good man. Nothing else will give you any comfort when you come to lie here. God bless you all!" Again he becomes unconscious; and at noonday, on the 21st of September, 1832, the soft autumnal breeze sighed amid the foliage of Abbotsford; the Tweed rippled on its silvery way; and the warm sun, riding proudly in the zenith, shone as in mockery through the open window, where slowly and gently, "in God's own calm," a great sun was setting. When all was over, mourning children knelt beside his couch, and kissed into eternal rest the dear dead eyes that had of late known many tears. Old servants, sobbing as they went, carried the kind master to the waiting hearse; children and kinsmen bore the pall; and thousands upon thousands watched with uncovered heads the mournful procession. Thus they bore him to Dryburgh, and laid him beside his fathers, — the rarest genius in his art that all-creating Nature ever shaped; the kindliest, truest heart; the manliest knight and high-souled gentleman that ever trod on Scottish heather!

Walter Scott, by birth, education, and natural bias, was a high Tory. Let it be his excuse that he was born in a country where reverence for gentle blood is a religion. He came of an ancient equestrian race, to which clanship was as strong a feeling as filial affection and love of native land. By ties of blood he was connected with the feudal heads of his name.

It was the innate disposition of his imagination to live in the past rather than in the future. Visions of the baronial castle, the court and camp, the wild Highland chase, feud and foray, the antique blazonry and institutions of feudalism, heroic action, romantic tenderness, — all made fair and holy by thoughtful reverence for the past, —

floated forever in splendid pageantry through the chambers of his brain, mingled ever with the regretful consciousness that before the wave of democratic equality these goodly things were slowly but inevitably being swept away. To paint these olden glories in which his imagination delighted to revel became his self-elected mission. All that would have shocked and revolted our modern humanity was toned down by his idealism, or put altogether out of sight; while the devotion of his heroes, their noble valor and godlike strength of purpose, were brought into boldest relief.

We may not accept the questionable logic that affirms a man to be altogether right when he is simply consistent with himself; yet surely we cannot withhold our cordial approbation of that noble manhood that, having erected these things into principles and opinions, honestly and earnestly upheld them through a long and comparatively blameless life, — giving abundantly of his time, means, and intellect for the support of opinions by which he could gain no temporal advantage, and which, indeed, brought upon his gray hairs the only indignity his fond countrymen ever offered to that brave old Scottish knight, whose heart was wide enough to hold his neighbor, his country, and his king; and who, courted and caressed in many lands, could still cling to his own "honest gray hills," and say, "If I did not see the heather at least once a year, I think I should die."

The enemies of Scott have accused him of fondness for broad acres and over-much love of rank and titles. If the first be a weakness, it was blamelessly shared by another great and well-beloved poet: Shakespeare retired early with *his* gains, and purchasing an estate, became a rural squire. If his love of wealth is proven by his unremitting toil to obtain it, let it be remembered that

no questionable commercial shift, no untrue word, or
mean and sordid action, ever put a farthing into his
coffers ; and if abundantly he gathered golden grain, he
let fall as abundantly for the gleaners. Among his distressed friends, disabled scholars, indigent authors, and
Christ's humble poor, he scattered of his harvest with no
niggard hand. His seeming idolatry of rank was but
inborn reverence for gentle blood. A title to him was
not an empty name ; it was the symbol and sign-manual
of ancient name and lineage, the heirloom of heroic
deeds. "He had," says his biographer, "more respect
for the impoverished chief of four or five thousand kirtled
mountaineers than the mightiest magnate of the land
that ever wore orders and honors without an historical
name."

The great intellectual strength of Scott lay in the prolific richness of his fancy, that from the most minute and
barren antiquarian details could arrange the most stirring
scenes and adventures and the most romantic poetical
narrative ; and in the abundant stores of his memory,
that could collect and retain a load of fact and incident
that would have staggered old Atlas himself ; and an
unwearied creative energy, that could reanimate and en-
kindle all with a power and vividness unknown since the
days of Homer. His genius was eminently a narrative
genius, and whether in verse or prose, he groups and describes with irresistible and ever-charming effect.

A distinguishing feature of Scott is the perfect trans-
parency of his style. In expression, sentiment, and description he is so simple and direct that "he who runs
may read." His diction is not obscured by a dim and obsolete phraseology ; his meaning is not entangled among
riddling conceits ; nor is his thought enveloped in a haze
of mysticism that only the initiated can hope to penetrate.

In the present age the tide of popularity sets toward poets who (in the words of quaint old Wilson) "delight much in their own darkness, especially when none can understand what they do say." Perspicuity is consequently held cheap. Nevertheless, it has its sterling value; and some of us are still old-fashioned enough to get our conundrums legitimately — from our riddle-books — in preference to making guess-work of our poems.

In diction Scott is careless and incorrect; he looked only at broad and general effect. Making pictures with his words, rather than melody, he could perhaps afford to dispense in some degree with that finish so highly prized by less graphic and creative poets. In description he is various, powerful, and picturesque. In narrative he is *perfection itself*. We cannot claim for him profound depth and intensity of feeling. Whatever is visible and tangible he has mastered; below the surface he has less power. His intellect, potent as it was, never went out of sight of the material, — "never," as Carlyle would express it, "groped among the eternal abysses of things." Experiences were infinitely more to him than speculations, and within the whole circumference of his giant brain there was not enough transcendentalism to make a single immortal thought of Emerson. Neither was the language of the heart his familiar study; the passions do not obey his call, as with Shakespeare.

He gives us rare specimens of moral painting; as in the knightly grace of Fitz-James, the rugged virtues and savage death of Roderick Dhu, the remorse of Marmion, and the sin and suffering of Constance. Nothing could more vividly and distinctly exhibit the contrasted effect of passion and situation. Yet fine as these pictures are, the force lies in the situation, not in the thought and expression. There are no immortal words, no talismanic sentences, that by right divine go down the ages "undimmed, alone, and forever."

Yet all these defects are nobly redeemed by that element of intense life which is never wanting in his verse. This animation, fervor, enthusiasm, and earnestness, this strong athletic life engendered in Scott by that dash of wild Border blood from the old moss-trooping ancestry, goes tingling hotly through his veins, and infusing itself into all his poems, colors them with the hearty joyousness of a healthy manhood, — a manhood in which physical and intellectual culture, like "mercy and truth, have met together," and, like "righteousness and peace, have kissed each other." This it was, above all else, that took the public admiration by storm, carrying men onward with an excitement of heart as well as of head, which they had never before experienced in the perusal of modern poetry, which had chiefly, and too often exclusively, aimed at critical gratification rather than emotional. Here were poems all glowing and alive, uniting the interest and excitement of a novel with the subtler charm of verse.

Scott's first original poem, the "Lay of the Last Minstrel," was published when the author, at thirty-four, had arrived at the maturity of his powers. No living man was so well fitted by information on this subject to write this tale. Border story and romance had been the study and passion of his life. The "Lay" is a story of the sixteenth century, related by a Border minstrel, the last of his race. All the characters are finely drawn ; the gray-beard harper, the moss-trooper, the coarse Border chief, and the "ladye high," are equally vigorous portraits, and grouped with the feudal accessories of the piece, make of the olden time —

> "A picture rich and rare
> Hanging in the shadowy air" : —

"The way was long, the wind was cold,
The minstrel was infirm and old;
His withered cheek and tresses gray
Seemed to have known a better day;
The harp, his sole remaining joy,
Was carried by an orphan boy.
The last of all the bards was he,
Who sung of Border chivalry.
For, well-a-day! their date was fled,
His tuneful brethren all were dead;
And he, neglected and oppressed,
Wished to be with them, and at rest.
No more, on prancing palfrey borne,
He carolled, light as lark at morn;
No longer courted and caressed,
High placed in hall, a welcome guest,
He poured, to lord and lady gay,
The unpremeditated lay:
Old times were changed, old manners gone;
A stranger filled the Stuart's throne;
The bigots of the iron time
Had called his harmless art a crime.
A wandering harper, scorned and poor,
He begged his bread from door to door,
And tuned, to please a peasant's ear,
The harp a king had loved to hear."

"Marmion," a tale of Flodden Field, is undoubtedly Scott's greatest poem. If it does not possess the unity of the "Lay," it has more striking beauties, and also greater faults. It was received with instant enthusiasm by the world. Jeffrey slashed at it in the "Review;" but Scott, sufficiently consoled by the applause of better men, only revenged himself by asking the pugnacious critic to dinner, and treating him in his usual kind-hearted manner. In "Marmion" feudal times and manners are inimitably painted. By an oversight, which the author soon saw and regretted, the harmony of the conception is somewhat marred. The hero is made to commit the crime of

forgery, — a crime unsuited to a chivalrous and half civilized age.   The death of Marmion and the battle of
Flodden are the finest specimens of Scott's inimitable
descriptive power.   " Of all the poetical battles which
have been fought from the days of Homer," says an
eloquent critic, " there is none comparable for interest
and animation, for breadth of drawing and magnificence
of effect, with this," —

> " Of the stern strife, and carnage drear
>   Of Flodden's fatal field,
> Where shivered was fair Scotland's spear,
>   And broken was her shield! "

As a scene of tragic wildness and terror, the trial of
Constance De Beverly is unsurpassed. This picture is
drawn with the skill of the true artist.

> " Her sex a page's dress belied;
>   The cloak and doublet loosely tied,
>   Obscured her charms, but could not hide.
>   Her cap down o'er her face she drew;
>   And, on her doublet breast,
>   She tried to hide the badge of blue,
>   Lord Marmion's falcon crest.
>   But, at the Prioress' command,
>   A monk undid the silken band,
>   That tied her tresses fair,
>   And raised the bonnet from her head,
>   And down her slender form they spread,
>   In ringlets rich and rare.
>   Constance De Beverly they know,
>   Sister professed of Fontevraud,
>   Whom the church numbered with the dead,
>   For broken vows, and convent fled.
>   .   .   .   .
>   Her look composed, and steady eye,
>   Bespoke a matchless constancy.
>   And there she stood, so calm and pale,

> That, but her breathing did not fail,
> And motion slight, of eye and head,
> And of her bosom, warranted
> That neither sense nor pulse she lacks,
> You might have thought a form of wax,
> Wrought to the very life, was there;
> So still she was, so pale, so fair."

" The Lady of the Lake " is perhaps more widely popular than either " Marmion " or the " Lay." It has more domestic interest than " Marmion," is more regular and interesting in plot, and more richly picturesque, than any of Scott's poems.

This picture of Malise bearing the fiery cross, is inimitable word-painting: —

> "Then Roderick with impatient look
> From Brian's hand the symbol took:
> 'Speed, Malise, speed!' he said, and gave
> The crosslet to his henchman brave.
> 'The muster-place be Lanrick mead —
> Instant the time — speed, Malise, speed!'
> Like heath-bird when the hawks pursue
> A barge across Loch Katrine flew;
> High stood the henchman on the prow;
> So rapidly the bargemen row,
> The bubbles, where they launched the boat,
> Were all unbroken and afloat,
> Dancing in foam and ripple still
> When it had neared the mainland hill;
> And from the silver beach's side
> Still was the prow three fathoms wide,
> When lightly bounded to the land
> The messenger of blood and brand.

> "Speed, Malise, speed! the dun deer's hide
> On fleeter foot was never tied.
> Speed, Malise, speed! Such cause of haste
> Thine active sinews never braced.

Bend 'gainst the steepy hill thy breast,
Burst down like torrent from its crest;
With short and springing footstep pass
The trembling bog, and false morass;
Across the brook like roebuck bound,
And thread the brake like questing hound;
The crag is high, the scar is deep,
Yet shrink not from the desperate leap:
Parched are thy burning lips and brow,
Yet by the fountain pause not now;
Herald of battle, fate, and fear,
Stretch onward in thy fleet career!
The wounded hind thou track'st not now;
Pursuest not maid through greenwood bough,
Nor pliest thou now thy flying pace
With rivals in the mountain race;
But danger, death, and warrior deed,
Are in thy course; speed, Malise, speed!
Fast as the fatal symbol flies,
In arms the huts and hamlets rise;
From winding glen, from upland brown,
They poured each hardy tenant down.
Nor slacked the messenger his pace;
He showed the sign, he named the place,
And pressing forward like the wind,
Left clamor and surprise behind."

The funeral wail of Duncan is finely conceived and executed.   Reading it, one can fancy the dead warrior on his
torch-lit bier, and can hear "the funeral yell, the female
wail," toned down to this sad, sweet rhythm.

" He is gone on the mountain,
    He is lost to the forest,
Like a summer-dried fountain,
    When our need was the sorest.
The font, reappearing,
    From the rain-drops shall borrow,
But to us comes no cheering,
    To Duncan no morrow!

"The hand of the reaper
  Takes the ears that are hoary,
But the voice of the weeper
  Wails manhood in glory.
The autumn winds rushing
  Waft the leaves that are searest,
But our flower was in flushing
  When blighting was nearest.

" Fleet foot on the correi,
  Sage counsel in cumber,
Red hand in the foray,
  How sound is thy slumber!
Like the dew on the mountain
  Like the foam on the river,
Like the bubble on the fountain,
  Thou art gone, and forever! "

In " Rokeby " — a tale of the English Cavaliers and
Roundheads — Scott has his foot off his native heather;
and though the poem displays the utmost art and power in
the delineation of character and passion, it is considered a
failure. "Don Roderick," " Harold," and " Triermain," have
no higher degree of merit. " Bannockburn," as a tale,
has little of sustained interest. Its chief excellence consists in the truth and beauty of the descriptive passages
of the poem. " The Lord of the Isles " — a Scottish
story of the days of Bruce — has more of Scott's characteristic fire and animation. In childhood, youth, and
early manhood, the old ballad songs were to Walter Scott
" meat and drink." Before he was ten years old he had
collected and bound up several volumes of them. His
genius, indeed, has some points of resemblance to that of
the old ballad-makers themselves, who simply give the
words and actions of their heroes and heroines, and never
venture to analyze motive or character. In his lyrics he
is gay, arch, tender, warlike, or romantic; and all bear

evidence of that spontaneity which also characterizes the old songs. It has been happily observed that "there are lyrics that, however polished and fine, seem to have been made piecemeal, like the Coral Islands." Scott's are emitted rather than shaped, and given free and easy, — as the author should say, "Take it, and welcome ; there's plenty more where this came from."

The best known, and perhaps the best, is "Young Lochinvar," from "Marmion;" "Hail to the Chief," from the "Lady of the Lake," is almost equally good ; and "Pibroch of Donald Dhu" no mortal but Scott *could* have written. In another and less characteristic style is this dainty serenade of Minna Troil's pirate lover :

> "Love wakes and weeps,
>   While beauty sleeps !
> O for music's softest numbers,
>   To prompt a theme
>   For beauty's dream
> Soft as the pillow of her slumbers !
>
> "Through groves of palm
>   Sigh gales of balm ;
> Fireflies on the air are wheeling,
>   While through the gloom
>   Comes soft perfume,
> The distant beds of flowers revealing.
>
> "O wake and live !
>   No dreams can give
> A shadowed bliss the real excelling ;
>   No longer sleep,
>   From lattice peep,
> And list the tale that love is telling ! "

From poetry Scott retreated into the wider field of prose fiction. It is enough to say that there he takes his undisputed seat among the masters of the art, both British and foreign.   Modern criticism, it is true, has gone so far as to assert of Walter Scott's novels that on account of their conspicuous high Toryism, their frequent divergence from historical fact, and their extreme romanticism, they are unsafe reading for the rising generation.   However this may be, it is safe to conclude that the " Wizard of the North " will still continue to charm and elevate mankind.

CHAPTER XVII.

BYRON AND MOORE.

IN the epoch under consideration Byron and Moore alone may be especially designated as poets of the passions. Byron, at least, is eminently so; singing, as he did, from a law and necessity of his nature, he dared the heaven-reaching heights, which to Moore were unattainable. Yet Moore, on feebler wing, has soared high enough to warble catches of melody graceful and tender as the singing of birds, — strains which the world will not willingly let die. Moore's friendship for Byron appears to have been sincere and lasting; and though sneering at " little Tommy's love of lords," Byron honored him with the gift of his personal memoirs, intended for publication, but generously withdrawn from the press by Moore at the request of the family of Byron, though " Little Tommy " sustained thereby a loss of two thousand guineas which Murray had paid him for the manuscript.

Thomas Moore was a native of Dublin, and born in 1779. At fourteen he commenced rhyming. In 1793 he was sent to the university, where he distinguished himself by his classical acquirements, and at nineteen proceeded to London to study law. Moore's life affords little matter of deep interest; for the most part, it was sunny as his poetry and bright and gay as his wit. The poet was of humble and unpromising birth, his father being but a respectable grocer and liquor-dealer, and a strict Roman

Catholic at a time when that faith was comparatively
under ban in Great Britain. He owes to great talent,
industriously cultivated and exercised, to tact, prudence,
and a genial nature, that personal popularity which won
the hearts of his admiring countrymen, and the smiles
and patronage of the English aristocracy.

Leigh Hunt gives us this graphic personal description
of the little Irish poet : —

" His forehead is bony and full of character, with bumps of
wit large enough to transport a phrenologist; his eyes are as
dark and fine as you would wish to see under a set of vine-
leaves; his mouth, generous and good-humored, with dimples;
his nose, sensual and prominent, and at the same time the
reverse of aquiline, — there is a very peculiar characteristic in
it, as if it were looking forward to and scenting an orchard.

" The face, upon the whole, is Irish, not unruffled by care
and passion, but festivity is the predominant expression. His
talk is full of the wish to please and be pleased."

Moore passed pleasantly through this varying world ;
a few shadows, such as come to all, of sickness and
death, darkened the evening of his life. His slips of the
pen seem not, like those of Byron, to have been parallel
to slips in his life. He was a faithful and devoted husband, a true and loving son ; and though like a roving
butterfly " in search of delight, grazing all sweets with his
wing," he turned ever to home for his love and his rest.

Moore's poetry is perhaps more generally known than
that of any of his cotemporaries. " Lalla Rookh," his
brilliant Oriental poem, is in the hands of all readers of
poetry. Of the four tales comprised in the poem, " The
Fire Worshippers " is the finest. " Paradise and the
Peri," having the grace of moral sentiment superadded
to the charm of brilliant imagery and ornament, is most
frequently read and remembered. " The Veiled Prophet

24

of Khorassan" possesses great energy and power, but is somewhat marred by the extravagance and improbability of the fiction.   " The Feast of Roses " is sweet as a love-tale, told in flowers. Before the commencement of the work the publisher agreed to pay Moore three thousand guineas for the copyright of " Lalla Rookh ; " Hazlitt says he should not have written it even for *that* sum. The poet devoted three years of painstaking labor to this poem.

As the work was to be an Eastern tale in verse, though the subject had not been settled, it was Moore's first aim to work himself up into a proper Oriental frame of mind, — an easy thing to accomplish amid bulbuls and roses, tessellated floors, fragrant cassolets, scented fountains, and ambrosial airs, but no mean task among the fogs and snows of an English atmosphere ; yet how admirably he at length succeeded, the poem itself shows.   " Lalla Rookh " cannot be called a great poem ; but all critics allow it to be a great work of art.   The wonder is how one small brain could hold such a multifarious collection of Eastern materials.   " Moore's reading," says a great Eastern traveller, " is better than riding through those countries on the back of a camel."

"The Loves of the Angels " is another Eastern story related with graceful tenderness and passion, though Moore's angels are not *quite* after the manner of Milton, and have indeed but little of what we suppose to be the angelic air about them.   Moore's longer poems lack human interest ; they have no grand depth of passion, only a sort of " firefly sparkle," and no high and pure moral sentiment.   As a poetical artist, he has preferred beauty to strength, working in exquisite ornament of foliage, flowers, and gems, rather than in the durable and permanent materials of the art.   Though lacking simplicity and genuine passion, Moore is brilliant and gorgeous to excess ; and as honest

Jamie Hogg expresses it, " his verses are far ow'er sweet, ow'er sweet ! "

His fame rests chiefly upon his lyrical productions. Here he may rank with the great masters of English song. A passionate lover of music, possessing an exquisite ear and no mean degree of technical knowledge, with grace, tenderness, and beauty, if not *depth* of sentiment, and that exquisite tact for easy, ready adaptation which is one of the acknowledged characteristics of the sons of Erin, he is, by universal consent, the most acceptable of song-writers. " Dryden," says Moore, " has happily described music as ' inarticulate poetry ; ' and I have always felt, in adapting words to an expressive air, that I was bestowing upon it the gift of articulation, and thus enabling it to speak to others all that was conveyed by its wordless eloquence to myself." Of Wordsworth's poetry Hazlitt aptly observes, " One might think from it that there was no such thing as marrying or giving in marriage ; " of Moore's verse it might as justly be said, one would think from it that there was nothing *but* marrying and giving in marriage. Even on the pages especially consecrated to moral reflection or grave metaphor, airy little Cupids peep from sly corners, pert and bewitching as the marginal cherubs of the Sistine Madonna.

Romantic love-songs, as well as romantic *love*, have gone a little out of fashion since Moore was in his prime. The age is more worldly-wise and less romantic ; it is no longer " all for love, and the world well lost," but rather, all for the *world* and *love* well lost. What modern lover, however bold, would venture to suggest " a cot in the valley he loves," when fair maidens (in Yankee phrase) " trade " for nothing less than a " Queen Anne " or a four-story stone-front ? Yet some of us have listened to these melodies in " the days that are no more," and perchance from lips that are now mute and cold. To us they are still passion-laden and sweet, stealing upon the memory like wandering airs from the rose-gardens of our youth, where, under the dead, scented leaves, old loves and dreams lie buried. A song-writer does not need to work in heavy, durable materials, and love-songs may carry a burden of gems and flowers that would sadly cumber graver strains. Moore's songs are therefore the most excellent of his productions. If grace and melody could give immortality to a poet in this field, he surely would have won it; but the "serene creator of immortal things" must embody in his verse a deeper pathos, profounder passion, and more exalted moral sentiment than can be found on the rose-scented pages of this bard of green Erin. Of Moore's lyrics, "The Meeting of the Waters," "The Last Rose of Summer," "Rich and Rare were the Gems she wore," "Eveleen's Bower," and "Araby's Daughter," are the best; the last-named song is like the embodied soul of melody.

Moore's light, ironical pieces are in their way unrivalled. His wit is as subtle, keen, and delicate as his fancy is airy and brilliant. He never, like Byron, dips his pen in gall; and it has been prettily said of his satires, "They give delight, and hurt not." In some of them he has unfortunately trespassed upon delicacy and decorum. This, as a specimen, contains its due proportion of wit, and is perhaps as unexceptionable as any. It appeared at a time when an abundance of mawkish reminiscences and memoirs had been showered from the press, and bore the title of "Literary Advertisement":—

> "Wanted — Authors of all work to job for the season,
>   No matter which party, so faithful to neither;
> Good hacks, who, if posed for a rhyme or a reason,
>   Can manage like —— to do without either.

" If in jail, all the better for out-of-door topics ;
　Your jail is for travellers a charming retreat ;
They can take a day's rule for a trip to the tropics,
　And sail round the world at their ease, in the Fleet.

" For a dramatist, too, the most useful of schools —
　He can study high life in the King's bench community ;
Aristotle could scarce keep him more *within rules*,
　And of place, he at least must adhere to the *unity*.

" Any lady or gentleman come to an age
　To have good ' Reminiscences ' (three score or higher),
Will meet with encouragement, — so much per page,
　And the spelling and grammar both found by the buyer.

" No matter with what their remembrance is stocked,
　So they 'll only remember the *quantum* desired ;
Enough to fill handsomely two volumes *oct*,
　Price twenty-four shillings, is all that 's required.

　　.　　.　　.　　.　　.　　.　　.　　.

"Funds, Physic, Corn, Poetry, Boxing, Romance,
　All excellent subjects for turning a penny ;
To write upon all is an author's sole chance
　For attaining at last the least knowledge of any.

" Nine times out of ten, if his title is good,
　The material within of small consequence is ;
Let him only write fine, and if not understood,
　Why — that 's the concern of the reader, not *his*."

These fine stanzas from "An Irish Melody" embody
Moore's philosophical creed : —

" Ne'er tell me of glories serenely adorning
　The close of our day, the calm eve of our night ;
Give me back, give me back the wild freshness of morning,
　Her clouds and her tears are worth evening's best light.

" Oh, who would not welcome that moment's returning,
　When passion first waked a new life through his frame,
And his soul, like the wood that grows precious in burning,
　Gave out all its sweets to Love's exquisite flame ? "

To no poet of this era can we more justly apply Gray's description of the poetical character — " thoughts that breathe, and words that burn " — than to Byron; he is, in conception and expression, most intensely a poet of the passions. The blood of a passionate, uncurbed, half-mad ancestry ran like burning lava in his veins. The Gordons had for many generations been tainted with madness; the Byrons were extremely passionate and eccentric; and when, in London, January, 1788, the son of Capt. John Byron and Catherine Gordon first saw the light, would it have been reasonable to have presupposed any rare moral excellence of him? To replenish his empty coffers his dissolute father had married a woman who would now and then enact before her only son such spirited little home-scenes as tearing off her caps and ribbons in fits of passion, and boxing the ears of her servants all round. In his eleventh year this child of ill parentage succeeded to a peerage and Newstead Abbey.

The leading incidents in Byron's life are well-known. In college he was an idle and irregular scholar, and an eager devourer of all sorts of learning except that prescribed for him. In 1807 appeared his first volume of poetry, "Hours of Idleness." It was fiercely assailed in the "Quarterly Review;" and more fiercely was the assailant disarmed, if not altogether discomfited, by his vigorous satire, "English Bards and Scotch Reviewers." Then came foreign travel, and as its fruits, the first two cantos of "Childe Harold;" and thereafter the young poet "awoke one morning, and found himself famous." A rapid succession of Eastern tales followed, and Byron was now the splendid idol of the day. The whole United Kingdom raved of Byron. Not only his poems, but the man himself, became the rage. Shirt-collars were unanimously turned down, and Young England became sud-

denly bilious and misanthropic. Then came a round of
heartless pleasures for the poet, alternating with satiety
and disgust; a loveless marriage, discord, perplexity, and
a shameful separation. Miserable, reckless, sinning, and
aspiring, "contending with low wants and lofty will,"
Byron produced poem after poem, his mental energy
still gathering force.

Finally there came to this reckless nature — God knows
how! — a new and nobler mood; and in 1823 he set sail
for Greece (endeared to his recollection as the scene of his
youthful travels), to aid in the struggle for its independence. In Missolonghi, where in January, 1824, he landed,
Byron had in three months done much by his influence and
money, both of which he had generously devoted to the
work. The world beheld with joy this dawning of a truer
and better life. How much it might have become ennobled
through unselfish work we can never know; for on the
9th of April, 1824, the poet was seized with a dangerous
illness. Delirium ensued, and it proved fatal. In those
last hours he whispered incoherent messages, of which
nothing was intelligible except "my sister, my child."
About six o'clock in the evening of the 19th he murmured, "Let me sleep now," and turning upon his
pillow, fell into that slumber which ended in eternal
calm.

Looking at Byron's poetry, as we now must, at the
remove of half a century, when the cloudy smoke of the
old incense, curling away, has at last melted into thin air,
we may hope to measure with unprejudiced eye his length,
breadth, and depth, and to examine impartially the causes
of his strength and his weakness. Of true poetic inspiration perhaps no poet ever had more than Byron; and
when we come to consider what he has *done*, apart from
what he *was*, we must award to him the most brilliant and

elegant fancy, caustic wit, intensity of conception and expression, wild originality of invention, perfect command of the Anglo-Saxon tongue, and that Rubens-like facility of touch, indicating resources inexhaustible, — power and strength yet in reserve, which the most prodigal expenditure cannot bring to bankruptcy.

It has been said, and with truth, that he has left no school behind him. He neither has, nor *ever* had, a successful imitator. Neither can it be denied that the popularity of his poetry has declined ; this is, I think, solely to be attributed to the absence of any sustained moral elevation in his verse, and to the innate falsity of his sentiment. " Beauty," which is " a joy forever," he has created ; but to ugliness and deformity he has too often wedded that beauty, — a marriage unseemly and monstrous to God and man ! His art we approve ; its perversion we deplore. Far be it from me to assert that a poem must of necessity owe its immortality to the moral truth which it contains. Were this true, Pollok would go swimmingly down the " corridors of time ; " while Anacreon would be consigned to the top shelf instanter. A poem may live, and that right vigorously, by mere virtue of its artistic and æsthetic perfection. But let it be understood that if there is no profound moral strength or beauty, though it may but fill the eye, as does the bloom of the rose ; may but satisfy the ear, as does the song of a bird, charming the sense, rather than the soul ; while it contains no moral loveliness, — it should, to stand any chance of immortality, equally be free of all moral taint ; and this unhappily cannot be said of Byron's verse as a whole.

The genius of Byron was as versatile as it was energetic. Various are the styles of poetry he has tried. First came the " Hours of Idleness," preluding rather than indicating his power ; then " English Bards and Scotch

Reviewers," more original and more promising; then the
first two cantos of " Childe Harold," higher and more
finished strains; next the Oriental rhapsodies, in which
Lord Byron is served up *à la* Corsair and *à la* Giaour
done to a turn, but still the inevitable Lord Byron, who
" hath not loved the world, nor the world him." The
novelty of scene and subject, and the exaggerated tone
of passion in these tales, so intoxicated the public mind
as to make all other poetry seem spiritless and wearisome.
" Though evincing infinitely more power than anything he
had yet done, these tales," says a profound critic, " owe
their popularity mainly to a certain trickery in the writing, which takes the ear, in spite of hollowness of sentiment and extravagance of narrative and portraiture."
" Parisina," " The Siege of Corinth," " Mazeppa," and
" The Prisoner of Chillon " followed, — all more true, deep,
and beautiful than the preceding tales. " The Prisoner of
Chillon," while it is, in point of morality, the most faultless of Byron's poems, for tenderness, simplicity, and
touching pathos is perhaps unexcelled in our literature.
The highest forms of Byron's poetry may be found in the
last two cantos of " Childe Harold," in " Cain," " Manfred," and finally in " Don Juan," which, though under
ban for its levities, audacities, and indecencies, looked
at simply from an artistic point of view, without reference
to anything but the genius and power of writing which it
manifests, is allowed to be perhaps the greatest English
poem of the present century.

In writing this poem, Byron took great pains to collect
his materials. His account of the shipwreck is drawn
from narratives of actual occurrences; and his Grecian
pictures — feasts, dresses, and holiday pastimes — are
literal transcripts from life. In the character of Haidee
there is infinitely more poetical beauty than may be found

in all his other heroines put together. Aside from its artistic merit, and the genius and power of writing displayed in the poem, it has no claim upon our admiration. A more pitiable prostitution of the poetic talent than is displayed upon some of the pages of "Don Juan," the angels never wept over; a more revolting outrage upon decency the annals of English literature cannot show.

In vain are we told that the poem had a moral purpose, having been written to remove the cloak which the maxims and manners of society throw over its secret sins, and to show them to the world as they really *are*. No amount of sophistry will ever make black white; and all the vigor of this fine satire, all the beauty and truth of portraiture and description with which it abounds, cannot make the poem, as a whole, even presentable. Byron himself seems to have vaguely regretted its publication; and had he lived to have become altogether true to his nobler self, he would undoubtedly have purged its pages "as by fire."

As it is, the poem has really done less harm than many another work where licentiousness is more covertly introduced. "Vice," says the poet, "to be hated, needs but to be seen." While the rich variety of Byron's genius may be seen in "Don Juan," its greatness and power are best exhibited in "Childe Harold." There is in the poem abundance of scorn and defiance of the ordinary pursuits and ambitions of mankind; but from licentiousness it is entirely free. The portrait of the hero (Byron served up again *à la* Childe), though repulsive, from its morbid bitterness and mock desolation, looks passable in its beautiful frame.

The Childe, satiated with pleasure, contemning society, the victim of a dreary and hopeless scepticism, traverses the fair earth, gives us the most graceful and animated descriptions of scenery, with glimpses of life and manners, surveys the ruins of ancient cities, pictures their fallen glories, describes the glorious remains of ancient art, and moralizes in magnificent strains on the particular events which adorned or cursed the soil on which he trod.

Byron's intense appreciation of ideal beauty and sculptured grace, his passionate energy and ecstasy, reflected back on the glowing pages of "Childe Harold," have made it one of the noblest creations in poetry.

Over the ruins of Athens, the Childe indulges in this grand but drearily sceptical strain of philosophy. Nothing finer of its kind can be found in our language.

> " Look on this spot, — a nation's sepulchre !
> Abode of Gods, whose shrines no longer burn.
> Even gods must yield, — religions take their turn :
> ' T was Jove's, ' t is Mahomet's ; and other creeds
> Will rise with other years, till man shall learn
> Vainly his incense soars, his victim bleeds ;
> Poor child of Doubt and Death, whose hope is built on reeds.
>
>   .   .   .   .
>
> " Remove yon skull from out the scattered heaps :
> Is that a temple where a god may dwell ?
> Why, ev'n the worm at last disdains her shatter'd cell !
>
> "Look on its broken arch, its ruin'd wall,
> Its chambers desolate, and portals foul ;
> Yes, this was once Ambition's airy hall,
> The dome of Thought, the palace of the soul ;
> Behold through each lack-lustre eyeless hole,
> The gay recess of Wisdom and of Wit,
> And Passion's host, that never brook'd control :
> Can all saint, sage, or sophist ever writ,
> People this lonely tower, this tenement refit ?
>
> " Well didst thou speak, Athena's wisest son !
> ' All that we know is, nothing can be known.'
> Why should we shrink from what we cannot shun ?
> Each has his pang, but feeble sufferers groan

> With brain-born dreams of evil all their own.
> Pursue what Chance or Fate proclaimeth best ;
> Peace waits us on the shores of Acheron :
> There no forced banquet claims the sated guest,
> But Silence spreads the couch of ever-welcome rest.

> " Yet if, as holiest men have deemed, there be
> A land of souls beyond that sable shore,
> To shame the doctrine of the Sadducee
> And sophists, madly vain of dubious lore,
> How sweet it were in concert to adore
> With those who made our mortal labors light !
> To hear each voice we feared to hear no more !
> Behold each mighty shade revealed to sight,
> The Bactrian, Samian Sage, and all who taught the right."

Many of Byron's minor poems are exquisitely graceful and tender. After the separation of Lord and Lady Byron the full tide of public opinion set against him ; his most slanderous and deadly foes were those who had most coveted his friendship. Miserable, and utterly hopeless of stemming the torrent of abuse, tormented by pecuniary troubles which his own recklessness and improvidence had brought upon him, he determined to leave England. The only person with whom he parted with regret was his sister, Mrs. Leigh, and to her he penned that fine and touching tribute, " Though the Day of my Destiny's over." To Mr. Moore he addressed that well-known song, " My Boat is on the Shore ; " and to Lady Byron, " Fare thee well." These stanzas from the poem to his sister are a fair example of Byron's style in his shorter poems : —

> "Though the day of my destiny 's over,
> And the star of my fate hath declined,
> Thy soft heart refused to discover
> The faults which so many could find ;

Though thy soul with my grief was acquainted,
　　It shrunk not to share it with me,
And the love which my spirit hath painted,
　　It never hath found but in *thee*.

　　·　　·　　·　　·　　·　　·　　·

" Though human, thou didst not deceive me,
　　Though woman, thou didst not forsake,
Though loved, thou forborest to grieve me,
　　Though slandered, thou never couldst shake;
Though trusted, thou didst not disclaim me,
　　Though parted, it was not to fly,
Though watchful, 't was not to defame me,
　　Nor mute, that the world might belie.

" Yet I blame not the world, nor despise it,
　　Nor the war of the many with one.
If my soul was not fitted to prize it,
　　'T was folly not sooner to shun;
And if dearly that error hath cost me,
　　And more than I once could foresee,
I have found that, whatever it lost me,
　　It could not deprive me of *thee*.

" From the wreck of the past, which hath perished,
　　Thus much I at least may recall,
It hath taught me that what I most cherished
　　Deserved to be dearest of all:
In the desert a fountain is springing,
　　In the wide waste there still is a tree,
And a bird in the solitude singing,
　　Which speaks to my spirit of thee."

" The Dream," in which Byron has commemorated his
boyish idolatry of his Mary, is an exquisite poem and in
point of morality entirely unexceptionable. Byron's later
dramas are, for the most part, stiff, declamatory, and undramatic. "Manfred," his earliest dramatic production, is
a work of great power *as* a poem; as a drama for presentation on the stage it is excelled by many another far

inferior play.   It contains some of Byron's very best
poetry, and as a whole, it may, I think, compare with
Goethe's "Faust."   In the second scene there are passages unrivalled in dramatic poetry.   The soliloquy of
Manfred, though intensely Byronic, Shakespeare alone
has surpassed.   The time is morning; Manfred is alone
upon the cliffs of the Jungfrau.

"The spirits I have raised abandon me —
The spells which I have studied baffle me —
The remedy I reck'd of tortured me;
I lean no more on superhuman aid.
It hath no power upon the past, and for
The future, till the past be gulf'd in darkness,
It is not of my search. — My mother Earth!
And thou fresh breaking Day, and you, ye mountains,
Why are ye beautiful?   I cannot love ye.
And thou, the bright eye of the universe,
That openest over all, and unto all
Art a delight — thou shin'st not on my heart.
And you, ye crags, upon whose extreme edge
I stand, and on the torrent's brink beneath
Behold the tall pines dwindled as to shrubs
In dizziness of distance ; when a leap,
A stir, a motion, even a breath, would bring
My breast upon its rocky bosom's bed
To rest forever — wherefore do I pause ?
I feel the impulse — yet I do not plunge ;
I see the peril — yet do not recede ;
And my brain reels — and yet my foot is firm :
There is a power upon me which withholds,
And makes it my fatality to live ;
If it be life to wear within myself
This barrenness of spirit, and to be
My own soul's sepulchre, for I have ceased
To justify my deeds unto myself, —
The last infirmity of evil.   Ay,
Thou wing'd and cloud-cleaving [an eagle passes] minister,
Whose happy flight is highest into heaven,

Well may'st thou swoop so near me ; I should be
Thy prey, and gorge thine eaglets ; thou art gone
Where the eye cannot follow thee ; but thine
Yet pierces downward, onward, or above,
With a pervading vision. — Beautiful !
How beautiful is all this visible world !
How glorious in its action and itself !
But we, who name ourselves its sovereigns, we,
Half dust, half deity, alike unfit
To sink or soar, with our mixed essence make
A conflict of its elements, and breathe
The breath of degradation and of pride,
Contending with low wants, and lofty will,
Till our mortality predominates,
And men are — what they name not to themselves,
And trust not to each other.   Hark ! the note,
          [*The Shepherd's pipe in the distance is heard.*]
The natural music of the mountain reed, —
For here the patriarchal days are not
A pastoral fable, — pipes in the liberal air,
Mix'd with the sweet bells of the sauntering herd ;
My soul would drink those echoes. — Oh, that I were
The viewless spirit of a lovely sound !
A living voice, a breathing harmony,
A bodiless enjoyment — born and dying
With the blest tone which made me ! "

In no other poetry is the man and the poet so intimately
blended as in Byron.   His rank, youth, and personal fascinations, the depth of his sufferings and attachments, his
unreserved disclosure of his own feelings and passions, his
moodiness and misanthropy, all combined to throw around
him that weird enchantment which has created for the
world an illusory picture of the man.   " So various, indeed," says Moore, " were his attributes, both moral and
intellectual, that he may be pronounced to be not one but
many ; nor would it be any exaggeration of the truth to
say that out of the mere partition of the properties of his

single mind a plurality of characters, all different and all vigorous, might have been furnished."

Moore is, I think, the best and most truthful of Byron's biographers ; yet he has been accused of time-serving, and certainly he seems to have lacked courage to be invariably just and candid.

Countess Guiccioli, with too partial pen, in a work of nearly seven hundred weary pages not only undertakes to show that Byron was not a bit of a sinner, but to prove him, beyond the shadow of a doubt, the most consummate of saints.

An American authoress next tries her hand at him, and in a miserably ill-judged article hastens to informs us that he is no saint nor even *sinner* in the common acceptation of the word, but simply a monster, an incarnate fiend ! The public, in view of the enormity of her accusation, ventures upon remonstrance, and suggests *proof*. Hereupon, with the admirable consistency of a certain famous "wise" man in "Mother Goose," who, having lost both his eyes by a disastrous jump into a " brier bush," " with all his might and main jumps straight into another bush to scratch them in again," she gives us another and a " True Story of Lady Byron's Life," which only serves to bewilder us in a labyrinth of conjecture and to bring Byron into fashion again, does a little harm to Lady Byron and her cause, and a great deal to one whom we all love and admire, — its author.

And after all has been said, a wise and candid judgment which " naught extenuates, nor aught sets down in malice," must still accord to Byron a noble though faulty nature. His peculiar nervous organization made him a medium for all exquisite poetical sensibilities, for all fine and subtle harmonies of being, and all intense sensual emotions that stir this mortal frame. Such an inflammable, uncertain, fascinating creature Nature made at her own sweet will, — her beautiful and wayward child.

In no wise becoming apologists for the sins of Byron, candor still compels his critics to acknowledge his generosity, his truthfulness, his sincere attachment to the few whom he really loved, his tender solicitude for his mother, his yearning fondness for his daughter Ada, his watchful care for his illegitimate child Allegra, and his idolatrous affection for his only sister, who was, as he affirms, " the purest, the most angelic of beings, goodness itself" (and until we really have proof to the contrary, let us not violate the ashes of a dead woman by doubting him), and last, but not *least*, his kind and almost paternal care for his servants. Filial and paternal love are instinctive, and may in some degree exist in natures otherwise mean and barren; but delicate, thoughtful recognition of the claims and needs of the poor and the lowly can only emanate from a truly noble soul. To "Mr. Ruskin," he writes of his servants, "I have sent Robert home with Mr. Murray, because the country through which I am about to travel is in a state which renders it unsafe for one so young. Let every care be taken of him, and let him be sent to school. In case of my death, I have provided enough in my will to render him independent." And again to his mother, "Fletcher is well; pray take care of my boy Robert and the old man Murray. It is fortunate they returned; neither the youth of the one nor the age of the other would have suited the changes of climate and fatigues of travelling." And later he writes to her, "Pray take some notice of Robert, who will miss his master, poor boy!"

While rendering due homage to the purity and goodness of Lady Byron, one cannot fail to admit that his marriage was the great mistake of Byron's life. Eccentric to the

25

verge of insanity, his "blood all meridian," organically impatient of conventional restraint, and ever feverishly restless, small affinity (if I may use a misused word) had he with this serene, matter-of-fact Englishwoman, — lovely and perfect in her own way, no doubt, but by those very perfections rendered infinitely antagonistic to this wild, irregular nature. As well put a royal eagle in a hen-coop as such a man within the quiet paling of domestic life. Later, when years had tamed his erratic nature, when the real and nobler Byron was in the ascendant, it might have been well, — for, eminently tender and affectionate where he really loved, he *could* have rarely blest where he only wounded and outraged; but as it was, all was wrong from beginning to end, and the fatal result of this marriage was foreseen by all who understood him.

To sum up this estimate of Byron's character, we must accord to him rare virtues and glaring vices; yet let us ever remember that whatever he was, he was at least no hypocrite. Not only was it his fixed purpose ever to disavow his virtues, but morbidly to delight in the imputation to himself of imaginary crimes.

> " This should have been a noble creature : he
> Hath all the energy which might have made
> A goodly frame of glorious elements,
> Had they been wisely mingled; as it is,
> It is an awful chaos, — light and darkness,
> And mind and dust, and passions and pure thoughts,
> Mixed, and contending without end or order,
> All dormant or destructive."

In view of the disgraceful controversy which has disturbed the ashes of one of England's greatest poets, it can only be said that Byron asked of life as its final boon, " sleep." Let him then sleep, accusing world!

" It is enough ; for him there are
  No fruits to pluck, no palms for winning,
  No triumph, and no labor, and no lust,
  Only dead yew-leaves, and a little dust.
  O quiet eyes wherein the light saith naught,
  Whereto the day is dumb, nor any night
  With obscure finger silences your sight ;
  Nor in your speech the sudden soul speaks thought,
  Sleep, and have sleep for light ! "

CHAPTER XVIII.

MINOR POETS OF HUMBLE BIRTH.

WORDSWORTH, Coleridge, Southey, Scott, Campbell, Moore, and Byron, whatever discordance there may have been in public opinion in regard to their relative or absolute merits, were oracles to whom all listened, whose inspiration all men acknowledged; yet many other voices there were from which divine words were now heard.

To the humbler bards of this time, —

> ". . . humming their lowly dreams
> Far in the shade where poverty retires," —

we owe that reverence and admiration which our Longfellow has thus beautifully expressed, —

> " Read from some humbler poet,
> Whose songs gushed from his heart,
> As showers from the clouds of summer,
> Or tears from the eyelids start;
>
> " Who through long days of labor,
> And nights devoid of ease,
> Still heard in his soul the music
> Of wonderful melodies.
>
> " Such songs have power to quiet
> The restless pulse of care,
> And come like the benediction
> That follows after prayer."

Leaving awhile the proud "corridors of time," where distant footsteps of more famous children of song still grandly echo, let us now follow these lowlier paths where poetry and poverty have walked hand in hand.

Wandering about Edinburgh in search of old volumes, Bishop Heber, early in the present century, dropped often into the little shop of Constable, — afterward the eminent publisher; here, perched like Dominie Sampson on a ladder, where with a huge folio in his hand he would remain for hours, he frequently found a queer, uncouth-looking personage. Entering into conversation with this unshorn stranger, he discovered him to be somewhat acquainted with everything in the way of literature, and especially a master of legend and tradition, and an enthusiast for Border ballads. This singular person was John Leyden, born in a peasant's cottage in one of the wildest valleys of Roxburghshire.

To this extraordinary man poverty was no barrier to learning. Give him bread and water and books, it is said, and he was happy. His whole life was one eager study, and his rude, savage manners mingled with his learning are said to have placed him "somewhere between the schoolman and the moss-trooper."

His parents, seeing his desire for instruction, determined to educate him at Edinburgh College, where he was entered in the fifteenth year of his age. He made rapid progress, was an excellent Latin and Greek scholar, and acquired also the French, Spanish, Italian, and German, besides studying the Hebrew, Arabic, and Persian. He became no mean proficient in mathematics and various branches of science. Before his commanding talents, his retentive memory, and robust application, every difficulty vanished. His college vacations were spent at home; and as his father's cottage afforded him little opportunity for quiet and seclusion, he looked out for accommodation abroad.

The kirk (except during divine service) is rather a place of terror to the Scottish rustic; and the parish church of Cavers, a gloomy and ancient building, was generally believed in the neighborhood to be haunted. Leyden, partly to indulge his humor, and partly to secure his retirement, contrived to make some modern additions to the old tales of ghosts and witchcraft. To this well-chosen spot of seclusion, usually locked during week-days, he made entrance by means of a window, read there for many hours in the day, and deposited his books and specimens in a retired pew. The nature of his abstruse studies, some specimens of natural history, as toads and adders left exposed in their spirit-vials, and a few practical jests played off upon the curious, rendered this gloomy haunt sacred from intrusion. From this singular and romantic place of study Leyden sallied forth with his curious and various stores to astonish his college associates.

At the expiration of his university studies, he became tutor to the young Campbells, whom he subsequently accompanied to college, where he still pursued his own researches connected with Oriental learning, publishing his translations from the Northern and Oriental tongues in the "Edinburgh Magazine."

In 1800 Leyden was ordained for the Church. He still continued to study and compose, ardently assisting Scott (whom with many other distinguished literary and scientific men he numbered among his friends) in his "Minstrelsy of the Border." On one occasion Scott had an interesting fragment of a ballad, but it had been hitherto found impossible to recover the rest of the poem. For the sole purpose of visiting an old person who possessed this ancient historical ballad, Leyden walked between forty and fifty miles and back again!

He performed successfully a variety of literary work. His strong desire to visit foreign countries induced his friends to apply to Government for some appointment for him connected with the languages and learning of the East. The only situation they could procure was that of surgeon's assistant; and in five or six months, by incredible labor, Leyden qualified himself, and obtained his diploma. In 1802 he left Scotland forever. He afterward became a professor in the Bengal College and was appointed a judge in Calcutta. Here he still devoted his spare time to Oriental manuscripts and antiquities, and soon acquired the reputation of the most extraordinary of Orientalists. After seven years' labor he became affected with the fatal sickness peculiar to the climate, and died in the midst of his hopes, having reached the same age that Burns and Byron lived to see, — thirty-six.

As a poet Leyden is elegant rather than forcible. His ballads are greatly superior to his " Scenes of Infancy," — a poem descriptive of his native vale. His versification is soft and musical. The opening of his ballad entitled " The Mermaid " " exhibits," says Sir Walter Scott, " a power of numbers which for mere melody of sound has seldom been excelled in English poetry."

This one poem proves Leyden among his various endowments to have been not meanly gifted with the genuine power of the poet. These stanzas are from the " Mermaid," and are an example of his rhythmic grace. The story is too long for insertion. It is well conceived and interesting.

> " On Jura's heath how sweetly swell
>   The murmurs of the mountain bee !
> How softly mourns the writhed shell
>   Of Jura's shore, its parent sea !
>
> " But softer floating o'er the deep,
>   The Mermaid's sweet sea-soothing lay,
> That charmed the dancing waves to sleep
>   Before the bark of Colonsay."

Walter Scott honored Leyden's memory with a notice of his life and genius; and in his "Lord of the Isles" he thus touchingly alludes to his untimely death: —

> "Scarba's Isle, whose tortured shore
> Still rings to Corrievreckan's roar,
>   And lonely Colonsay;
> Scenes sung by him who sings no more.
> His bright and brief career is o'er,
>   And mute his tuneful strains;
> Quenched is his lamp of varied lore,
> That loved the light of song to pour:
> A distant and a deadly shore
>   Has Leyden's cold remains."

Robert Bloomfield, the self-taught author of the "Farmer's Boy," born in 1766, was the son of a tailor, and was himself brought up to the craft of St. Crispin. His poetry was chiefly composed in a shoemaker's garret. Bloomfield was literally one of the poets who sang —

> "Through long days of pain,
> And nights devoid of ease."

He was thirty-two years of age, married, and the father of three children before the world acknowledged his merit.

The Duke of Grafton now patronized the poet, and through his influence he was appointed to a situation in the Seal Office. Here his situation was irksome and laborious, and he was forced to resign it from ill health. He engaged in the bookselling business, but was unsuccessful. In his later years he resorted to making Æolian harps, which he sold among his friends. Southey took much interest in his welfare, and Rogers kindly exerted himself to procure for him a pension; but his last days were embittered by poverty, and so severe were his sufferings from continual headache and nervous irritability that fears were entertained for his reason.   In 1823 death came to release him from "this poor world's strife."

Bloomfield is a descriptive realist.   Like Crabbe, he pictures rural life in its hardest and least inviting forms. In his tales he embodies moral feeling, is equally faithful in painting, but far more cheerful in tone, and his incidents are more agreeable than Crabbe's.   A remarkable feature in his poetry is the easy smoothness and correctness of his versification.   His ear was attuned to harmony by nature before he had learned anything of the art, and his taste for the beauties of expression was innate.

Bloomfield is one of the most characteristic and faithful of our poets.   The humility of his themes, joined to the want of vigor and passion in his verse, is perhaps the cause of his being now little read.   His "Farmer's Boy" is remarkable for freshness and reality of description, and was exceedingly popular.   He subsequently published a collection of "Rural Tales," which fully supported his reputation ; and to these were afterward added "Wild Flowers" and "Hazlewood Hall," a village drama ; and in the year of his death he published his "May-day with the Muses."

George Crabbe, born in 1754, takes precedence of Bloomfield for originality and force.   His father was a salt-master, in humble circumstances ; yet out of his poverty he managed to give his son a superior education. At seventeen Crabbe was apprenticed to a surgeon.   Coming into practice, he found his prospects so gloomy that he abandoned his profession, and with only three pounds in his pocket, proceeded to London as a literary adventurer.   His poetical wares were rejected by the publishers, and he was plunged into great perplexity and want.   In this desperate state of his affairs he applied to Sir Edmund Burke, who kindly became his friend and patron ; and while under his hospitable roof, and enjoying the society of the statesman's distinguished friends, he published his poem, "The Library," which was favorably noticed by the critics. Lord Thurlow now patronizes the poet, invites him to breakfast, and with pompous generosity presents him with a bank-note for a hundred pounds. He enters into sacred orders and becomes curate of Aldborough, — his native parish. Burke procures him the situation of chaplain to the Duke of Rutland, and he is nevermore in perplexity in regard to his bread and butter.

In 1783 appears his "Village," corrected by Johnson and Burke; its success is instant and complete. Lord Thurlow swears that he "is as like Parson Adams as twelve to a dozen," and presents him with two livings on the spot! He marries his early love, — a young lady who, as Mr. Swiveller would have phrased it, had been "saving up for him" for a long time, — settles down upon his curacy in humble retirement, and is silent as a poet for many years.

In the mean time his capacious mind was ever employed. Out of doors, says his biographer, he had ever some object in view, a flower, a pebble, or his note-book in hand; often reading aloud while walking, or making little excursions in his heavy one-horse chaise that, judging from its description, must have been as logically constructed as that immortal Yankee vehicle which our poet has sung. From the management of this substantial conveyance his good wife, in their journeys, used prudently to relieve her absent-minded spouse. Indoors, Crabbe is said to have been almost equally industrious, "always reading or writing."

In 1807, after a silence of twenty years, came forth his "Parish Register." Its success was unprecedented. He continued writing in the same narrative style; and his fine

delineations of life and character were received by the
public with the greatest favor.   In 1814 he was appointed
to the living of Trowbridge.   His income now amounted
to about eight hundred pounds, a large portion of which
he spent in charity.   In 1819 Mr. Murray published his
last great work, "Tales of the Hall," and gave for them
and the remaining copyright of all Crabbe's previous
poems the munificent sum of three thousand pounds!
This sum, in bills, Crabbe is said to have carried loosely
in his waistcoat pocket from London to Trowbridge;
and when Moore, Rogers, Everett, the banker, and other
friends advised its immediate safe deposit, the good old
man replied with characteristic simplicity: "No, there's
no fear of my losing them; I must take them to Trowbridge and show them to my son John.   They will hardly
believe in my good luck at home if they do not see the
bills."

Crabbe's tales have now taken their place among our
standard national literature.   His "Village," "Parish
Register," and shorter tales are his best productions.   As
a painter of English scenery he possesses high merit.
His delineations of character are equally meritorious.

Crabbe (if that is not a misnomer) is not a poetical
poet.   His poetry, without the rhyme and feet, would
differ but little from prose.   His muse was matter-of-
fact to a degree that would quite have charmed our old
friend Mr. Gradgrind.   He is, like Wordsworth, the poet
of the poor; yet he does not invest his characters with
"the consecration and the poet's dream."   Wordsworth
puts quantities of his own wisdom and imagination into the
pack of his pedlar; his "Wagoner" is a sort of classic
Phaeton; and all his characters come before us in their
Sunday clothes.   Crabbe, on the other hand, while he is
as faithful in dramatic representation, brings upon the

stage his poachers, smugglers, gypsies, and gamblers in their every-day attire, dowdy, out-at-elbows, and disinvested of all romance or imagination, — pictures made shocking by their very fidelity, and, as anatomical exhibitions of character and passion, exhibiting a naked reality that makes us blush for our humanity. Crabbe is also too generally a gloomy painter of life, fond of depicting the unlovely and the unamiable. He does not appear to believe that it is the poet's mission to "turn the sunny side of things to human eyes."

The distinguishing and redeeming feature of Crabbe's genius is its fidelity to Nature in its minutest details. "His pictures," it has been aptly said, "have all the force of dramatic representation." Heaven allotted him an old age of kindly length. In 1832 he died. After his death this touching stanza from his pen was found wrapped round his wife's wedding-ring. It is far more graceful than most of his efforts.

> "The ring so worn, as you behold,
>   So thin, so pale, is yet of gold:
>   The passion such it was to prove;
>   Worn with life's cares, *love yet was love.*"

In the present age Crabbe's poetical popularity would have been simply an impossibility; and yet in his day this matter-of-fact poet, whose verse barely escaped being downright prose, carried in his pocket three thousand pounds earned at his craft! Shade of Milton, forgive the sordid world that doled thee five paltry pounds for thy divine epic!

The best passages from Crabbe's "Tales" — such as the "Real Mourner," the "Story of Phebe Dawson," etc. — are familiarly known. This song of the Crazed Maiden, from "Tales of the Hall," is a specimen containing less prosaic alloy than the above-mentioned popular quotations, yet still ghastly enough in parts to have merited the approval of Amine herself, — that lady of the Arabian tale whose ghoulish proclivities have forever endeared her to the youthful heart.

> "Let me not have this gloomy view
>   About my room, about my bed;
> But morning roses wet with dew,
>   To cool my burning brow instead;
> As flowers that once in Eden grew,
>   Let them their fragrant spirits shed
> And every day their sweets renew
>   Till I, a fading flower, am dead.
>
> "O let the herbs I loved to rear
>   Give to my sense their perfumed breath!
> Let them be placed about my bier
>   And grace the gloomy house of death.
> I'll have my grave beneath a hill
>   Where only Lucy's self shall know
> Where runs the pure pellucid rill
>   Upon its gravelly bed below.
> There violets on the borders blow,
>   And insects their soft light display,
> Till, as the morning sunbeams glow,
>   The cold phosphoric fires decay.
>
> "I will not have the churchyard ground,
>   With bones all black and ugly grown,
> To press my shivering body round,
>   Or on my wasted limbs be thrown.
> With ribs and skulls I will not sleep
>   In clammy beds of cold blue clay,
> Through which the ringed earth-worms creep,
>   And on the shrouded bosom prey.
>
> "I will not have the bell proclaim
>   When those sad marriage rites begin,
> And boys, without regard or shame,
>   Press the vile mouldering masses in.

Raise not a turf, nor set a stone,
    That man a maiden's grave may trace
But thou, my Lucy, come alone,
    And let affection find the place."

The thought contained in the second stanza quoted has
been honored by a repetition in that exquisite poem,
"June," by our own Bryant.

James Hogg, the Ettrick Shepherd, as he was commonly called, made himself known by a volume of poems
published in 1801, and continued to put forth both verse
and prose as long as he lived. Hogg was descended from
a family of shepherds, and born, as he alleged (though
the point was often disputed), on the 25th of January
(Burns's birthday), in the year 1772. When a mere child
he was put out to service, acting first as cowherd until
capable of taking care of a flock of sheep.

Hogg had in all his life but a half-year's schooling. As
he lay watching his flock on the hillside, he taught himself
to write by copying the printed letters of a book. He subscribed to a circulating library, and was an eager reader
of poetry and romances. His mother was, like Burns's,
a famous reciter of legends and ballads, and "when doors
were barred, and darkness fell," his lonely days on Ettrick's wildest hills were exchanged for evenings of listening to the —

"Mystic lore sublime
Of fairy tales of ancient time."

At eighteen, with his light-brown hair curled up under
his blue bonnet, Jamie Hogg is said to have been the
bonniest of shepherd laddies. A severe illness, we are
told, subsequently destroyed all his beauty. He had
already published in a small volume his first literary
efforts in song-writing, when William Ludlow, his mas-

ter's son, introduced him to Sir Walter Scott, who, with ready discernment, found under his rude, uncultivated exterior a loving, generous heart and a soul full of genius. Hogg, like Leyden, assisted Scott in the collection of old ballads for the "Border Minstrelsy."

As his efforts were warmly praised by his illustrious friend, he came down from the forest to pay him a visit, and with William Ludlow and others was asked to dinner. The worthy shepherd appeared in his ordinary herdsman's dress, with his hands well tarred by a recent shearing. Not being accustomed to the society of "grand folk," he had, it is said, communed with himself how he should act, and had come to the conclusion to copy the lady of the house in all things. Mrs. Scott, being quite unwell, received her guests reclining on a sofa. Jamie, true to his principle, had no sooner made his best bow than he crossed the room and stretched himself out at full length upon another!

Hogg now published another volume of songs and poems, under the title of "The Mountain Bard," in which the style of the ancient ballads was imitated with great felicity. Embarking in sheep-farming, he lost in the enterprise all he had saved as a shepherd, and at this crisis of his fortunes, repaired to Edinburgh, and endeavored to subsist by his pen. "The Forest Minstrel," a collection of songs, was his first effort; his second a periodical called "The Spy;" but it was not until 1813 that the shepherd, by the publication of the "Queen's Wake," established his reputation as an author. "The Queen's Wake" is a legendary poem consisting of a collection of tales and ballads, supposed to be sung to Mary, Queen of Scots, by the native bards of Scotland, assembled at a wake at Holyrood, in order that the fair queen might prove "the wondrous powers of Scottish song." The work in design and execution exhibits at once the delicacy and the genius of the author. The thread of narrative by which the different productions of the native minstrels are strung together is written with exquisite grace.

Hogg has the same abstract beauty and wealth of gorgeous splendor that characterizes Spenser. He loved, like "Eliza's golden poet," to picture scenes of supernatural beauty and magnificence. Painter or poet never woke to life a lovelier fairy vision than his "Kilmeny;" it is too long to quote entire, and almost too fine to mutilate.

> "Bonny Kilmeny gaed up the glen ;
> But it wasna to meet Duniera's men,
> Nor the rosy monk of the isle to see,
> For Kilmeny was pure as pure could be.
> It was only to hear the yorlin sing,
> And put the cress-flower round the spring ;
> The scarlet hypp, and the hindberrye,
> And the nut that hangs frae the hazel tree.
> For Kilmeny was pure as pure could be.
> But lang may her minny look o'er the wa',
> And lang may she seek i' the greenwood shaw ;
> Lang the laird of Duniera blame,
> And lang, lang greet or Kilmeny come hame.
>
> When many a day had come and fled,
> When grief grew calm, and hope was dead,
> When mass for Kilmeny's soul had been sung,
> When the beadsman had prayed, and the dead-bell rung,
> Late, late in a gloamin', when all was still,
> When the fringe was red on the westlin hill,
> The wood was sere, the moon i' the wane,
> The reek o' the cot hung over the plain
> Like a little wee cloud in the world its lane ;
> When the ingle lowed with an eiry leme
> Late, late in the gloamin', Kilmeny came hame !
> Kilmeny, Kilmeny, where have you been ?
>
> Kilmeny looked up with a lovely grace,
> But nae smile was seen on Kilmeny's face ;

As still was her look, and as still was her ee,
As the stillness that lay on the emerant lea,
Or the mist that sleeps on a waveless sea.
For Kilmeny had been she knew not where,
And Kilmeny had seen what she could not declare;
. . . .
In that green wene Kilmeny lay,
Her bosom happed wi' the flowrets gay;
But the air was soft, and the silence deep,
And bonny Kilmeny fell sound asleep.
She kend nae mair, nor opened her ee,
Till waked by the hymns of a far countrye,
She wakened on couch of the silk sae slim,
All striped wi' bars of the rainbow's rim;
And lovely beings round were rife,
Who erst had travelled mortal life.
. . . .
They lifted Kilmeny, they led her away,
And she walked in the light of a sunless day;
The emerald fields were of dazzling glow,
And the flowers were of everlasting blow.
Then deep in the stream her body they laid,
That her youth and beauty never might fade;
And they smiled in heaven when they saw her lie
In the stream of life that wandered by.
The sun that shines on the world so bright,
A borrowed gleid frae the fountain of light;
And the moon that sleeks the sky sae dun,
Like a gowden bow, or a beamless sun,
Shall wear away, and be seen nae mair,
And the angels shall miss them travelling the air.
But lang, lang after baith night and day,
When the sun and the world have elyed away;
When the sinner has gane to his waesome doom,
Kilmeny shall smile in eternal bloom!"

Hogg had not Burns's strength of passion or peculiar
grasp of intellect; neither was his song, like Burns's,
linked to the joys and sorrows of actual existence. He
was more prone to commit himself to aerial phantoms of
supernatural beauty and splendor than Burns, whose vis-

ions had always in them a preponderance of good tangible flesh and blood. He lacked art to construct a fable, and that taste which gives due effect to imagery and conception; and though the most imaginative and creative of the uneducated poets, his taste was sadly defective.

Blackwood wanted some very dark passage in his " Pilgrims of the Sun" omitted or elucidated; Hogg was immovable. " But, man," said the publisher, " I do not know what you mean in this passage." " Hout tout, mon," quo' Jamie, " I dinna ken what I mean *mysel*."

One can imagine the poet who propounded to us the riddle of the " red slayer " to have conceived his poem in a vein of sophistry not unlike this of the honest shepherd; and here it may be recorded that among the favorite poetry of Emerson was Hogg's " Kilmeny."

Hogg's worldly schemes were unsuccessful enough to have proved him a true brother of the precariously sustained minstrels of the " North Countree." For the latter years of his life his sole support was the remuneration afforded by his literary labors. These days were spent in his moorland cottage, where he divided his time between the labors of the pen, and angling and hunting, of which he was passionately fond. Generous, kind-hearted, and charitable far beyond his means, notwithstanding his personal foibles, he was beloved throughout the vale of Ettrick, and all rejoiced in his fame. Deeply lamented, in the autumn of 1835 the shepherd minstrel, after weary days of suffering, succeeded by a long, death-like trance, fell asleep as quietly as when, wrapped in his plaid, he rested through the summer noon among the lonely Ettrick glens. Few poets have been more largely endowed with that direct inspiration which proves poetry in the abstract to be indeed an art unteachable and untaught.

His songs have a wild lyrical flow, inexpressibly sweet

and musical, — a rhythm whose fall is as soft as the sigh of an Æolian harp, as is seen in this exquisite lyric, "The Skylark" : —

> "Bird of the wilderness,
> Blithesome and cumberless,
> Sweet be thy matin o'er moorland and lea!
> Emblem of happiness,
> Blest is thy dwelling-place —
> O to abide in the desert with thee!
> Wild is thy lay and loud,
> Far in the downy cloud,
> Love gives it energy, love gave it birth,
> Where on thy dewy wing,
> Where art thou journeying?
> Thy lay is in heaven, thy love is on earth.
>
> "O'er fell and fountain sheen,
> O'er moor and mountain green,
> O'er the red streamer that heralds the day,
> Over the cloudlet dim,
> Over the rainbow's rim,
> Musical cherub, soar singing away!
> Then, when the gloaming comes,
> Low in the heather blooms,
> Sweet will thy welcome and bed of love be!
> Emblem of happiness,
> Blest is thy dwelling-place —
> O to abide in the desert with thee!"

Allan Cunningham, a happy imitator of the old Scottish ballads, was born at Blackwood in 1784. His life affords a fine example of successful original talent, integrity, and perseverance.

Cunningham was of humble parentage, his father (like Burns's) being a gardener; and he was himself but a mason's apprentice, when, impelled by that Destiny that shapes our rough-hewn ends, in 1810 he abandoned his trade, and removed to London to connect himself with the newspaper press. There he was engaged as clerk, or superintendent, to Chantrey, the eminent sculptor, in whose establishment he continued till his death, which took place in 1842. Besides being the author of many clever songs, he was an expert and voluminous writer in prose. All his literary labors were performed in the intervals of his stated avocations in Chantrey's studio, which most men would have considered ample employment.

As a poet Cunningham may be considered as imitative rather than creative. His lyrics abound in traits of Scottish rural life and primitive manners, are characterized by grace and tenderness, and though less popular than those of Ramsay, are replete with rich Doric simplicity and fervor. Cunningham was an indefatigable writer. His last prose work — " Life of Wilkie the Artist " — was completed just two days before his death. One of his most popular songs is " A Wet Sheet and a Flowing Sea."

This lyric of Cunningham is arch, graceful, and tender : —

> " Red rows the Nith 'tween bank and brae,
>   Mirk is the night and rainy O,
> Though heaven and earth should mix in storm,
>   I 'll gang and see my Nanie O ;
> My Nanie O, my Nanie O ;
>   My kind and winsome Nanie O,
> She holds my heart in love's dear bands,
>   And none can do 't but Nanie O.
>
> " In preaching time sae meek she stands,
>   Sae saintly and sae bonnie O,
> I cannot get ae glimpse of grace,
>   For thieving looks at Nanie O ;
> My Nanie O, my Nanie O ;
>   The world 's in love with Nanie O :
> That heart is hardly worth the wear
>   That wadna love my Nanie O.

"My breast can scarce contain my heart,
    When dancing she moves finely O;
I guess what heaven is by her eyes —
    They sparkle sae divinely O;
My Nanie O, my Nanie O.
    The flower O Nithsdale's Nanie O;
Love looks frae 'neath her long brown hair,
    And says, 'I dwell with Nanie O.'

"Tell not, thou star, at gray daylight,
    O'er Tinwald's top sae bonnie O,
My footsteps mang the morning dew
    When coming frae my Nanie O;
My Nanie O, my Nanie O;
    Nane ken o' me and Nanie O;
The stars and moon may tell 't aboon
    They winna wrang my Nanie O!"

John Clare, one of the most truly uneducated of our English poets, and one of the best of our rural describers, affords another fine example of the struggles of youthful genius. He was born at Helpstone in 1793. His parents were peasants, his father a helpless cripple and a pauper.

Working as a ploughboy, John acquired from the labor of eight weeks as many pence as paid for a month's schooling. At thirteen, he met with Thomson's "Seasons," and hoarding up a shilling to purchase a copy, at daybreak, on a spring morning, he walked six or seven miles to obtain the coveted treasure. Returning to his native village with the precious purchase, Clare composed his first piece of poetry, which he called the "Morning Walk." This was soon followed by the "Evening Walk," and some other pieces.

A benevolent exciseman had meantime taught him writing and arithmetic. "Most of his poems," says his biographer, "were composed under the immediate impressions of his feelings in the fields or on the roadsides."

He wrote them down with a pencil on the spot, his hat serving him for a desk. He could not always decipher these imperfect memorials; and from this cause many of his poems exist only in fragments. From a hole in the wall of his room, where he deposited his manuscripts, a bit of paper was often taken to hold the kettle with, or light the fire; thus many of his early pieces were entirely destroyed.

In 1817 Clare resolved to "see himself in print." By hard working, day and night, he had got a pound saved that he might have a prospectus printed. This was accordingly done, and as the result, only seven subscribers came forward. One of these prospectuses brought Clare into notice with a kindly bookseller, and through him the poems were purchased by a publisher for twenty pounds.

His poems, bearing the title of "Poems descriptive of Rural Life and Scenery," were published in 1820. The public interest was awakened. The magazines and reviews were unanimous in his favor, and many noblemen and gentlemen now contributed from their abundance; and in a short time Clare was in possession of a little fortune. With a permanent allowance of thirty pounds per annum, he married his "Patty of the Vale," — the daughter of a neighboring farmer; and in his native cottage at Helpstone, with his aged and infirm parents and his young wife by his side, Clare basked for a time in the sunshine of successful and rewarded genius. In 1821 he published the "Village Minstrel, and other Poems." He afterward contributed short pieces to the Annuals and other periodicals, marked by a more choice and refined diction. Though he now enjoyed the reputation of a true poet, his prosperity, alas! came to an end. His discretion was not equal to his genius. Speculating in farming, he wasted his little hoard, and amid accumulating difficulties, sank into despondency and despair, and became a hopeless maniac; and the life whose morning was so bright was doomed to close in a private insane asylum.

> " We poets in our youth begin in gladness;
>   But thereof comes in the end despondency and madness."

Literature has at no time exhibited a more striking instance of patient and persevering talent, existing and enduring through poverty and privation.

Clare's chief excellence consists in his minute and faithful painting of rustic scenes and occupations. Careful finish he does not give to his pictures. He wrote of Nature out of the fulness of a lover's heart; and in his picturesque catalogue of her charms he has included all her beauties, weeds as well as flowers. In these happy microscopic views of Nature, Grahame, the poet of the Sabbath, can alone come into competition with Clare. In sentiment Clare is delicate and true. This poem, entitled " First Love's Recollections," is in his best vein: —

> " First love will with the heart remain,
>   When its hopes are all gone by;
> As frail rose-blossoms still retain
>   Their fragrance when they die:
> And joy's first dreams will haunt the mind,
>   With the shades 'mid which they sprung,
> As summer leaves the stems behind,
>   On which spring's blossoms hung.
>   .   .   .   .
> " How loath to part, how fond to meet,
>   Had we too used to be;
> At sunset with what eager feet
>   I hastened unto thee!
> Scarce nine days past us ere we met
>   In spring, nay, wintry weather;
> Now nine years' suns have risen and set,
>   Nor found us once together.

" Thy face was so familiar grown,
 Thyself so often nigh,
A moment's memory when alone
 Would bring thee in mine eye;
But now my very dreams forget
 That witching look to trace;
Though there thy beauty lingers yet,
 It wears a stranger's face.

" When last that gentle cheek I prest,
 And heard thee feign adieu,
I little thought that seeming jest
 Would prove a word so true!
A fate like this hath oft befell
 Even loftier hopes than ours;
Spring bids full many buds to swell,
 That ne'er can grow to flowers."

Robert Tannahill, a lyrical poet of a superior order, followed the occupation of a weaver. His education was limited, but he was a diligent reader and student. Smith, a musical . composer, set some of Tannahill's songs to original and appropriate airs, and in 1807 he ventured on the publication of a volume of poems and songs, of which the first impression, consisting of nine hundred copies, was sold in a few weeks.

Tannahill was an ill-starred son of genius. He had prepared a new edition of his poems for the press; the publisher to whom he sent it, not having time to publish it that season, returned the manuscript. This disappointment preyed on his sensitive mind ; he burned all his manuscripts, sank into mental derangement, and in May, 1810, put an end to his weary mortal existence. His lyrics are rich and original, both in sentiment and description, and in them his diction is copious and luxuriant, and he is often tender and pathetic.

This stanza from Tannahill's lyric, " The Flower of Dumblane," may compare with Burns : —

"The sun has gane down o'er the lofty Ben-Lomond,
   And left the red clouds to preside o'er the scene,
While lanely I stray in the calm summer gloamin,
   To muse on sweet Jessie, the flower o' Dumblane.
How sweet is the brier, wi' its sauft fauldin' blossom!
   And sweet is the birk, wi' its mantle o' green;
Yet sweeter and fairer, and dear to this bosom,
   Is lovely young Jessie, the flower o' Dumblane."

Tannahill's poems are far inferior to his songs. He did not write well in English; and they are often commonplace and artificial.

Ebenezer Elliott, the Corn-Law Rhymer, born in 1781, sprung from the manufacturing poor of England, and was early accustomed to toil and privation, though eventually he won ease and comparative affluence. Elliott writes from genuine feeling and impulse. Against the laws relating to the importation of corn he especially inveighed; hence his title. In depicting the social and political wrongs of the poor he has committed many errors of taste which his genius has fortunately redeemed. Elliott is said to have approved of " equal division of unequal earnings." As a poet he often rises into pure sentiment and real eloquence.

This, entitled " A Poet's Prayer," shows Elliott at his best.

"Almighty Father! let thy lowly child,
   Strong in his love of truth, be wisely bold —
A patriot bard by sycophants reviled,
   Let him live usefully, and not die old!
Let poor men's children, pleased to read his lays,
   Love for his sake the scenes where he hath been.
And when he ends his pilgrimage of days,
   Let him be buried where the grass is green,
Where daisies, blooming earliest, linger late
   To hear the bee his busy note prolong;

> There let him slumber, and in peace await
> The dawning morn, far from the sensual throng,
> Who scorn the wind-flower's blush, the redbreast's lovely song."

One more poet of this time, who amid poverty and discouragement struggled valiantly for a place among the "lords of song," claims our notice. "The battle of his life was brief," and at twenty-five the over-tasked body of Robert Nicoll surrendered to —

> "The mild herald by our fate allotted
> To lead us with a gentle hand
> Into the Silent Land."

Nicoll had steadily cultivated his mind by reading and writing, and his poems, especially the short occasional pieces and songs, display happy rural imagery and fancy. Some of his poetry was written when, far gone in consumption, like poor Keats, he "felt the daisies growing over him."

This, from a poem entitled "Thoughts of Heaven," may serve as a specimen of Nicoll's style : —

> "High thoughts!
>   They come and go,
> Like the soft breathings of a listening maiden,
>   While round me flow
> The winds, from woods and fields with gladness laden:
> When the corn's rustle on the ear doth come,
> When the eve's beetle sounds its drowsy hum,
> When the stars, dewdrops of the summer sky,
> Watch over all with soft and loving eye ;
>   While the leaves quiver
>   By the lone river,
>   And the quiet heart
>   From depths doth call,
>   And garners all ;
>   Earth grows a shadow
>   Forgotten whole,
> And Heaven lives in the blessed soul."

Among the poets here reviewed we have not the marvellous workmanship that reveals the master-hand, — sometimes only simple poetic utterances, — yet they sang as one sings who believes what he is singing; and though we cannot look to them for

"Poems round and perfect as a star,"

let us still honor the valiant souls who, amid "want and poortith cold," have kept the heaven-kindled flame of poesy alight, and while learning in suffering, have taught in song.

CHAPTER XIX.

"FEMALE POETRY."

JEFFREY, that doughty Scot before whose critical bludgeon many a poor poet has shaken in his shoes, in a review of 1829 has been pleased to accord to the metrical composition of our sex the name of " Female Poetry ; " and, not without grave doubts as to its elegance and propriety, I have used his appellative as the designation of this chapter.

Of women as artists this has been encouragingly said : " In their finished performances they accomplish perhaps more completely than men all the ends at which they aim ; and the pure specimens of feminine art exhibit a fine and penetrating spirit of observation, soft-handed delicacy of touch, and unerring truth of delineation," and it might be added (though these are the exception, not the general rule), rugged masculine strength and power, — as in the painting of Rosa Bonheur, the prose of George Eliot, and the poetry of Elizabeth Barrett Browning. It cannot be denied that woman, since the downfall of Eve, has had compulsory and especial training in the hard school of patience ; and although "patience is" *not*, as has been asserted, "genius," by the cultivation of this humble virtue she has not only attained to an important condition of artistic success, but has obtained a positive advantage over the bolder but less all-enduring artisans of the other sex.

To the inherent and inevitable necessities of her life, rather than to the sparsity of her education or the tyranny of her social position, must, I think, be attributed the fact that woman has seldom taken the highest rank as a creative artist. The sacred duties of wifehood and motherhood alone, involving as they do an endless round of attention to petty detail, have tended rather to make woman " careful and troubled about many things " than to foster and develop in her any latent artistic power. But a discussion of woman's duties and capabilities leads far afield ; and the question of the equality of the sexes — as unprofitable as it is much vexed — has been so ably and thoroughly discussed that I need but say, with Dennis, that prudent " double," " so much has been said, and so well said, etc.," and wisely return to my own especial subject.

Of purely feminine art, without the slightest masculine admixture, our literature affords no fairer specimen than the poetry of Felicia Hemans, born at Liverpool, 1793. Her father was a native of Ireland, her mother of mingled Italian and German descent. To compound a poet Nature could not more happily have chosen her elements, — easy spontaneous mental facility from Ireland, intellectual insight from Germany, and sensuous fervor from Italy.

From her cradle Felicia Browne was distinguished for beauty and precocity. Her father, a merchant of considerable eminence in Liverpool, on account of commercial reverses was obliged to break up his establishment in that city before his daughter had attained her seventh year. He removed with his family into Wales, and there, among the most picturesque mountain scenery, in a large old mansion beside the " ever-sounding sea," her poetic genius was nursed. There she imbibed that romantic love of Nature which became to her an intense passion.

The " green land of Wales," with its hoary ruins and

old traditions, till the latest day of her existence was cherished in her heart of hearts; and when parted from it, she seems to have had for this beloved soil a fond yearning not unlike the Swiss homesickness. In her fifteenth year Felicia Browne published her first volume of poetry, which naturally met but little encouragement beyond the circle of her partial friends. Another small volume, entitled "The Domestic Affections, and Other Poems," was given to the world in 1812, and in the summer of the same year Felicia Browne became Mrs. Hemans.

At fifteen, in the full glow of her radiant beauty, when she is said irresistibly to have suggested Wordsworth's

> " . . . phantom of delight
> A dancing shape, an image gay,
> To haunt, to startle, and waylay,"

this romantic girl first met Captain Hemans, whose impassioned admiration awoke in her artless and enthusiastic nature a return to his professed devotion; and to this ardent soldier-lover ("by no means," it is said, destitute of advantages either of person or education) she gave her heart, and easily invested him with all the attributes of the heroes of her dreams. After six years this marriage came to that untoward separation which ended in permanent alienation. Uncongeniality, indifference on the part of Captain Hemans, and jealous dislike to those quiet mental pursuits that to this gifted woman were the necessities of life, have been assigned as causes for this unhappy separation, that to so exquisitely moulded a nature as Mrs. Hemans's, endowed with the rarest capabilities for loving and suffering, must have been a deadly blow. Though ever delicately reticent in regard to her desertion, its effect may be distinctly seen in Mrs. Hemans's poems; and this it was, no doubt, that gave to them that peculiar

strain of sentimental sadness which is one of their almost
morbid defects. A brighter destiny might have made
them as hearty and wholesome as they are genuine and
beautiful, but —

> "Unto *her*, Earth's gift was fame."

Whatever may have been the cause of the alienation of
Captain Hemans from his wife, it cannot have been that
essential unfitness of the poetess for domestic life which
shallow minds have predicated of genius. By her brothers
and sisters she seems to have been regarded with little
less than idolatry; and to her boys she was ever the truest and most devoted of mothers. The sympathy of the
children in the pursuits of their mother was singularly
deep and touching. When the prize of the Royal Literary Society was awarded to her poem of "Dartmoor,"
she thus writes: "Would that you had but seen the
children when the prize was announced! Their accla-
mations were deafening; and George said that the excess
of his pleasure had really given him a headache." And
again she says in a private letter: "Of all things, never
may I become that despicable thing, a woman living upon
admiration! The village matron, *tidying-up* for her husband and children at evening, is far, far more enviable
and respectable. . . . Those whom the multitude believe
to be rejoicing in their own fame, strong in their own
resources, beyond all others," she writes, "have most
need of true hearts to rest upon." Said Wordsworth,
with his clear and simple insight, "It is not because
women possess *genius* that they make unhappy homes,
but because they do not possess *enough;* a higher order
of mind would enable them to see and feel all the beauty
of domestic life." And amid all the adulation awakened
by her genius and loveliness Mrs. Hemans, it is said,

turned ever from " the wide world " to " sing to her nest."

And now this " widowed wife," still corresponding with her husband in Italy, and referring to him in all things relative to the disposal of her boys, yet for the last seventeen years of her life never once meeting him, devoted the remainder of her days to poetic composition and the education of her children. Her reputation increased. Jeffrey applauded, Byron admired, her verse; Scott and Wordsworth extended to her their cordial appreciation and sincere friendship; the gifted of her own sex — Mary Mitford, Joanna Baillie, Hannah More, Mary Howitt, and others — gave her their warmest sympathy and approbation; and now, while strong claims were urging her to incessant literary labor, the fatal effect of constant poetical composition upon a frame naturally delicate began to appear. She suffered often from pain and alarming palpitations after intellectual toil; and in the autumn of 1834 a severe cold told fearfully upon a constitution already enfeebled, sapped too, no doubt, of its strength by that ceaseless inward bleeding known only to the breaking heart. Pulmonary symptoms soon appeared, ending in hopeless decline. On Sunday, the 26th of April, calmed and sustained by a beautiful faith, and serene in hope, Mrs. Hemans dictated her last poem, this beautiful " Sabbath Sonnet " : —

> " How many blessed groups this hour are bending
> Through England's primrose meadow-paths their way
> Toward spire and tower, 'midst shadowy elms ascending,
> Whence the sweet chimes proclaim the hallow'd day!
> The halls, from old heroic ages gray,
> Pour their fair children forth; and hamlets low,
> With whose thick orchard blooms the soft winds play,
> Send out their inmates in a happy flow,
> Like a freed vernal stream; *I* may not tread
> With them these pathways — to the feverish bed

Of sickness bound; yet, O my God! I bless
Thy mercy, that with Sabbath peace hath filled
My chasten'd heart, and all its throbbings stilled
To one deep calm of lowliest thankfulness."

When May with blossoms and singing-birds made glad the hours, God took this weary singer to his eternal peace. The period under consideration has, with the single exception of Mrs. Browning, produced no poetess as eminent as Mrs. Hemans. She was by birth, training, and profession a poet, publishing her first verses at fifteen, and until her death, at forty-one, scarcely allowing her pen to rest. "Poor soul! poor soul!" said Wordsworth of her, "she wrote too much;" and Dr. Holmes has aptly compared her poetic growth to "a bed of asparagus, cut every morning." Both have found the key-note to her weakness. That fine frenzy in which the poet works his miracles is not perpetual, an unfailing celestial afflatus turned on at will like water from a well-ordered conduit. As the wind, inspiration cometh and goeth where it listeth, but with no mortal doth it abide continually; and the poet who seeks Parnassus as regularly as he winds his watch, cannot invariably —

"Drink deep of the Pierian spring."

Though highly popular during her lifetime, and still valued and admired, Mrs. Hemans's poetry, with a few exceptions, is not likely to go down the ages with that of some of her cotemporaries. "The Graves of a Household," "Bernardo Del Carpio," "Casabianca," and "The Landing of the Pilgrim Fathers," touching, as they do, with masterly skill and power, chords existent in our common humanity, bid fair for immortality. Higher and more passionate strains may be found in the "Records of Woman;" and her "Forest Sanctuary" has been consid-

27

ered the best of her longer poems. Beauty enough there is in her poems; chivalrous and romantic imagination they do not lack, nor melody of versification. Her verse abounds in glittering imagery, polished words, grace, sweetness of conception, and passionate fervor; yet we look in vain to her for that bold originality of thought and style which characterizes immortal poetry. Though hers was not the highest and most commanding genius, her poems are infinitely sweet, elegant, and tender, and finished with exquisite delicacy of execution; and the rare purity of her mind is displayed in all her works.

In tragedy she has not been successful. Some of her longer poems are " linked sweetness long drawn out," and often wearisome from their sameness. Not so with her "Records of Woman." Here we have Mrs. Hemans's best and most sustained effort. In these poems she engages our attention by the interest of her narrative, and wins and holds our admiration by the passionate fervor and ornate diction of her verse. Her "Women" are, it is true, somewhat old-fashioned in type; they seem to accept without a pang of discontent the limitations of their sex, and are never observed to be in a pother about their "sphere." Gloriously loyal to love they are, and content with the opportunities that lie close at hand, yet when occasion presents, falling into heroic places as naturally and easily as grass grows, or water runs down-hill. As mothers they are religiously devoted to their children; and they are so emphatically out of date as to be romantically in love with their lovers and husbands, and to think it worth their while to do and dare, and at a pinch, even to *die* for them. Such are the women whose deeds and fortunes are related in Mrs. Hemans's "Records." "The Indian City" is perhaps one of the finest of these tales. This passage does indeed appeal to "thousands" : —

" Are there no words for that common woe?
Ask of the thousands, its depth that know!
The boy had breathed, in his dreaming rest,
Like a low-voiced dove, on her gentle breast:
He had stood, when she sorrow'd, beside her knee,
Painfully stilling his quick heart's glee;
He had kiss'd from her cheek the widow's tears,
With the loving lip of his infant years;
He had smiled o'er her path like a bright spring day —
Now in his blood on the earth he lay!
Murder'd! — Alas! and we love so well
In a world where anguish like this can dwell!"

In the epistle from " Lady Arabella Stuart" she has
finely displayed her power, and in " Properzia Rossi" she
has expressed her very self. Properzia, a celebrated
female sculptor of Bologna, possessed also of talents for
poetry and music, died in consequence of an unrequited
attachment. A fine painting represents her as showing
her last work, a basso-relievo of Ariadne, to a Roman
knight, the object of her affection, who regards it with
indifference. Properzia, notwithstanding, would still

". . . leave enshrined
Something immortal of her heart and mind."

And as she shapes her ideal, she thus soliloquizes: —

". . . Awake! not yet within me die,
Under the burden and the agony
Of this vain tenderness, — my spirit, wake!
Ev'n for thy sorrowful affection's sake,
Live! in thy work breathe out! that he may yet,
Feeling sad mastery there, perchance regret
Thine unrequited gift.
                    It comes; the power
Within me born, flows back; my fruitless dower,
That could not win me love. Yet once again
I greet it proudly, with its rushing train
Of glorious images. They throng, they press;

A sudden joy lights up my loneliness, —
I shall not perish all!
             The bright work grows
Beneath my hand, unfolding, as a rose,
Leaf after leaf, to beauty; line by line,
I fix my thought, heart, soul, to burn, to shine,
Thro' the pale marble's veins. It grows; and now
I give my own life's history to thy brow,
Forsaken Ariadne! . . .
     .   .   .   .
Thou shalt have fame! Oh, mockery! give the reed
From storms a shelter; give the drooping vine
Something round which its tendrils may entwine;
Give the parch'd flower a rain-drop, and the meed
Of love's kind words to woman!"

Lady Arabella Stuart, — a possible heir to the English throne, — having alarmed the cabinet of James I. by a secret marriage with William Seymour, the wedded lovers were immediately imprisoned. Seymour eventually escaped, but Arabella remained in her dungeon until death released her. The imagined fluctuations of the prisoner's thought and feelings during that dreadful imprisonment in which she finally lost her reason are touchingly and graphically expressed in the poem from which the following extract is taken: —

" Ye are from dingle and fresh glade, ye flowers!
  By some kind hand to cheer my dungeon sent;
O'er you the oak shed down the summer showers,
  And the lark's nest was where your bright cups bent,
Quivering to breeze and rain-drop, like the sheen
Of twilight stars. On you Heaven's eye hath been,
Thro' the leaves, pouring its dark sultry blue
Into your glowing hearts; the bee to you
Hath murmur'd, and the rill. — My soul grows faint
With passionate yearning, as its quick dreams paint
Your haunts by dell and stream, — the green, the free,
The full of all sweet sound, the shut from me!
   .   .   .   .

There went a swift bird singing past my cell.
O Love and Freedom! ye are lovely things!
With you the peasant on the hills may dwell,
  And by the streams; but I — the blood of kings,
A proud unmingling river, thro' my veins
Flows in lone brightness, and its gifts are chains!
  .   .   .   .

Death! — what, is death a lock'd and treasured thing,
Guarded by swords of fire? A hidden spring,
A fabled fruit, that I should thus endure,
As if the world within me held no cure?
Wherefore not spread free wings — Heaven, Heaven
Control these thoughts. . . .
                    . . . Give strength to pray,
So shall their dark hosts pass.
                    The storm is still'd,
Father in Heaven! Thou, only thou, canst sound
The heart's great deep, with floods of anguish filled,
  For human line too fearfully profound.
Therefore, forgive, my Father! if Thy child
Rock'd on its heaving darkness, hath grown wild,
And sinn'd in her despair!"

The story of the "Sicilian Captive" is told with great
force and sweetness, and is perhaps the best example of
that blending of graceful narrative, pathetic description,
and beautiful imagery in which Mrs. Hemans was so singularly felicitous. The tale is of the rude Norsemen, who,
having taken with the spoils of war a beautiful Southern
maiden, after the Scalds have chanted at their feast in
Runic rhyme, have summoned her to sing to them. "At
the warrior's call," the homesick captive stands forth in
the midst of that frowning hall, and holding her lyre with
"trembling hand," she thus sings for her rude captors
her "Swan-song" of that beloved and foregone Sicily:

"'They bid me sing of thee, mine own, my sunny land! of thee!
Am I not parted from thy shores by the mournful sounding sea?
Doth not thy shadow wrap my soul? in silence let me die,
In a voiceless dream of thy silvery founts, and thy pure, deep sapphire
    sky;

How should thy lyre give *here* its wealth of buried sweetness forth ?
Its tones of summer's breathings born, to the wild winds of the
  north ?

" ' Yet thus it shall be once, once more ! my spirit shall awake,
And through the mists of death shine out, my country, for thy sake !
That I may make thee known, with all the beauty and the light,
And the glory never more to bless thy daughter's yearning sight !
Thy woods shall whisper in my song, thy bright streams warble by,
Thy soul flow o'er my lips again — yet once, my Sicily !

" ' There are blue heavens — far hence, far hence ! but, oh ! their glo-
  rious blue !
Its very night is beautiful, with the hyacinth's deep hue !
It is above my own fair land, and round my laughing home,
And arching o'er my vintage hills, they hang their cloudless dome ;
And making all the waves as gems, that melt along the shore,
And steeping happy hearts in joy, that now is mine no more.

" ' And there are haunts in that green land ; oh ! who may dream or
  tell
Of all the shaded loveliness it hides in grot and dell ?
By fountains flinging rainbow-spray on dark and glossy leaves,
And bowers wherein the forest dove her nest untroubled weaves ;
The myrtle dwells there, sending round the richness of its breath,
And the violets gleam like amethysts, from the dewy moss beneath !

" ' And there are floating sounds that fill the skies through night and
  day, —
Sweet sounds ! the soul to hear them faint in dreams of heaven
  away !
They wander through the olive woods, and o'er the shining seas ;
They mingle with the orange-scents that load the sleepy breeze ;
Lute, voice, and bird are blending there ; — it were a bliss to die,
As dies a leaf thy groves among, my flowery Sicily !

" ' I may not thus depart — farewell ! yet no, my country ! no !
Is not love stronger than the grave ?   I feel it must be so !
My fleeting spirit shall o'ersweep the mountains and the main,
And in thy tender starlight rove, and through thy woods again.
Its passion deepens — it prevails ! I break my chain — I come
To dwell a viewless thing, yet blest, in thy sweet air, my home ! '

" And her pale arms dropp'd the ringing lyre;
    There came a mist o'er her eye's wild fire,
    And her dark rich tresses in many a fold,
    Loosed from their braids, down her bosom rolled.
    ·Her head sank back on the rugged wall,
    A silence fell o'er the warrior hall;
    She had poured out her soul with her song's last tone;
    The lyre was broken, the minstrel gone! "

In endeavoring to show Mrs. Hemans at her best, I
have quoted from her poems perhaps too freely, but must
still make room for an extract from an epitaph written in
good-humored raillery on Mr. W——, a celebrated mineralogist, who at the time made one of a party of visitors
at the house of a friend where the poetess was staying:

" His fossils, flints, and spars of every hue,
    With him, good reader, here lie buried too.
    Sweet specimens! which, toiling to obtain,
    He split huge cliffs, like so much wood, in twain.
    We knew, so great the fuss he made about them,
    Alive or dead, he ne'er could do without them,
    So, to secure soft slumber for his bones,
    We paved his grave with all his favourite stones.
    His much-loved hammer 's resting by his side;
    Each hand contains a shell-fish petrified :
    His mouth a piece of pudding-stone incloses,
    And at his feet a lump of coal reposes;
    Sure he was born beneath some lucky planet, —
    His very coffin-plate is made of granite."

Mrs. Hemans's easy facility in this lively style of composition, as displayed in this epitaph, and in one equally
humorous, on " The Hammer of the Same Mineralogist,"
shows her genuine Irish wit; and we regret that she has
not seen fit to give us more work of the same kind.   These
epitaphs and her " Sheet of Forgeries" (scarcely surpassed,
in its way, by the famous " Rejected Addresses") are not

included in her printed poems, and were only given us by her biographer.

In conclusion, it must be said of Mrs. Hemans that if she had not been great as a poet, she would still take high rank as a gifted woman. Her memory is said to have been phenomenal; her acquirements were large and various. In English, French, German, Italian, and Spanish literature she was equally at home, and thoroughly read in history, essay, and fiction. Her taste for music amounted to an absolute passion; and on both harp and piano she was a finished performer. She evinced decided talent for drawing; and it was no flattery when Walter Scott said to her, after listening to her music: " I should say you had *too many* gifts, Mrs. Hemans, were they not all made to give pleasure to those around you." Though gifted with a quick sense of the ludicrous and quite equal to the keenest sarcasm, such was the gentleness of her sweet nature that it was said " no sharp or scornful speech is on record against her." One who knew her long and well, thus enthusiastically bears testimony to the moral beauty of her character: " In her nature there were no faults that were not better in themselves, and more engaging, than the virtues or merits, whatever people choose to call them, of most others."

After Mrs. Hemans the age produced no very eminent poetess before Mrs. Browning, though many respectable writers of verse among our sex appeared, and had in their day their meed of praise. Cotemporary with her was Joanna Baillie, who in the drama achieved a high if not an enduring reputation. Hannah More, Mrs. Tighe, Mrs. Hunter, Mrs. Opie, and Mrs. Barbauld have all given us poems, some of them carefully written and highly finished pieces; but though the hymns of Mrs. Barbauld are still valued and admired, and will not soon be consigned to oblivion, and Miss Baillie's tragedies have been by the critics pronounced the best ever written by a woman (which after all is but faint praise), in the highest sense to none of them can the name of poet be awarded.

Mrs. Norton has more of true poetic genius than is to be found in all these writers put together, and in our own day and in our own land women have written poems that not only exceed theirs in merit, but may proudly compare with those of Mrs. Hemans and Mrs. Browning (but, however, of *living* poets I do not propose to write). Of Miss Landon, generally known as L. E. L., in consequence of having first published with her initials only, it may safely be said that had length of days been granted her she might have attained a secure place among poets. As it was, she but sang a few mournful and incomplete strains and then —

> " Through the door of opal
> Toward the heavenly people,
> Floated on a minor fine
> Into the full chant divine."

In the "Improvisatrice" Miss Landon displays much of that intensity, rich exuberance, and passionate fervor of style characteristic of Byron, as may be seen in this fragment : —

> "I loved him as young genius loves,
>   When its own wild and radiant heaven
> Of starry thought burns with the light,
>   The love, the life, by passion given.
> I loved him too as woman loves,
>   Reckless of sorrow, sin, or scorn ;
> Life had no evil destiny
>   That, with him, I could not have borne !
> I had been nursed in palaces ;
>   Yet earth had not a spot so drear
> That I should not have thought a home
>   In Paradise, had he been near !"

The advent of Elizabeth Barrett (Mrs. Browning) about the year 1809 seems to have settled the question as to the essential masculineness of genius. This woman, so delicate and diminutive that her poet-husband is said to have drawn her portrait when, in the " Flight of the Duchess," he sketched " the smallest lady alive," was not only of genius " all compact," but as remarkable for rugged strength of intellect, force of expression, and scholarly ability as she was for sweetness of temper, tenderness of heart, depth of feeling, and purity of spirit. She is aptly described as " a soul of fire enclosed in a shell of pearl."

In early life Elizabeth Barrett became an invalid, and in 1838 was suddenly brought to the very brink of the grave by lung-disease. In 1840, while slowly recovering, she was again prostrated by a sudden catastrophe, — the death by drowning of a beloved brother, who had accompanied her to the seaside, and of whose death therefore she persisted in considering herself the cause. Not until a full year after this sad event had she recovered strength to be transported to London, where in her father's house she remained for five long years a prisoner, and a helpless, almost hopeless invalid, seeing no one but her own family, restricted to a darkened room, and eagerly reading almost everything worth reading in almost every language. In such circumstances inherent, morbid tendencies would naturally strengthen, and a many-sided, enlarged view of life could not have been gained; but a more favorable condition for the growth of the spiritual side of our nature cannot be imagined. It was during these years of feebleness and suffering that some of her best work was done.

Here Robert Browning first saw her, his —

> " Lyric love, half angel, and half bird,
> And all a wonder and a wild desire."

And in the autumn of 1846, in defiance of the wishes of her devoted father (who is said never after to have suffered her name to be mentioned in his presence, and who died unrelenting and unforgiving), Elizabeth Barrett rose from her sick bed to become the beloved wife of Robert Browning.

"Love really is the wizard the poets have called him," said Miss Mitford, on hearing how the invalid had borne the fatigue of the honeymoon journey to Italy, and was not only improved by the rash effort, but completely "transformed." "Love" had not only "justified itself to love," but had proved itself wiser than prudence. A union more true and perfect than that of these "poets twain" it is not possible to imagine, — he a noble type of manly power, she of noble, sensitive womanhood. In those exquisite love-songs which have been given to the world in the delicate disguise of "Portuguese Sonnets," the story of this love has been told. Juliet, that liberal maiden, exclaims, —

> "My bounty is as boundless as the sea
> My love as deep, . . .
>   . . . And both are infinite."

Mrs. Browning, assuming, on the contrary, that love can be *measured*, is equally " a lavish giver," as this exquisite sonnet will show. It is the finest of all the " Portuguese Sonnets."

> "How do I love thee ?   Let me count the ways.
> I love thee to the depth and breadth and height
> My soul can reach, when feeling out of sight
> For the ends of being and ideal grace.
> I love thee to the level of every day's
> Most quiet need, by sun and candle-light.
> I love thee freely, as men strive for right.
> I love thee purely, as they turn from praise.
> I love thee with the passion put to use

In my old griefs, and with my childhood's faith.
I love thee with a love I seemed to lose
With my lost saints.   I love thee with the breath,
Smiles, tears, of all my life; and, if God choose,
I shall but love thee better after death."

These " English thrushes " now built their nest in the
land of song, art, and romance; and for fourteen years
Mrs. Browning lived in Florence in one house, looking
out from Casa Guidi windows upon that " clime where
gray old shadows of the past still haunt the garish sunshine of the present."   There she is pictured for us: " A
slight delicate figure, with a shower of dark curls falling
on either side of a most expressive face; large tender
eyes, fringed with dark lashes, and a smile like a sunbeam. . . . Books and humanity, and great deeds and
the grand questions of the day, were ever foremost in her
thoughts and oftenest on her lips.   She never made an
insignificant remark.   One never dreamed of frivolities in
her presence, and gossip felt itself here out of place."
And now she heard " the nations praising her far off;"
every book showed an increase of power.   Her life had
been crowned with motherhood; " the mother of the beautiful child" was the sweet Italian name given her.   And
thus in Casa Guidi windows, tender and serious as the
Madonna folding in her arms the sinless Child, she is enshrined forever.   But, alas! this poet-soul " kept up too
much light under its eyelids " for *our* "night;" and at
last, when summer danced over the vine-clad hills, and
morn was lifting her drowsy lids, she lay fading from
the dear arms of that love whose tender ministration had
made her

" Dying bed feel soft as downy pillows are."

Her soul saw the far day breaking over the " jasper
sea."   " It is beautiful!" she said, and softly —

"Passed through glory's morning gate
To walk in Paradise!"

Her going home was but six days of suffering, bravely
borne; and now, "listening down the heart of things,"
we hear her singing still, and —

"Glory to God — to God! she saith,
Knowledge by suffering entereth,
And life is perfected by Death!"

By high authority Mrs. Browning has been termed the
greatest of English "female poets," and some have even
boldly placed her side by side with the laureate. Whatever may be the justness of these claims, we must admit
her to be the great genius, if not the great poet. Her
inspiration is almost painfully intense; and if she has not
attained to highest excellence in poetic art, it is rather
to be imputed to her odd views in regard to the techni-
calities of verse, and to the one-sided development of her
nature, than to the paucity of her genius. The artist
who would create for all time should cultivate form no
less than spirit, and should touch life at every point,
and thus be enabled to give to the world healthy out-door
growth rather than hot-bed miracles. A poet's song,
while it may accord with the subtlest harmonies of the
seraphim, should still be sweet as the singing of birds
with earth-born cadences.

Mrs. Browning was born in 1809; she became a writer
in 1819, and a publisher in 1826. Her first volume, an
"Essay on Mind," written in the style of Pope's "Essay
on Man," she afterward withdrew from print. Her next
work, "Prometheus Bound," translated from Æschylus,
shared a like fate with her first venture in authorship.
Her subjects were various; and she seldom reproduces
her thought, as Mrs. Hemans too often does. "The Lay

of the Brown Rosary," "Isobel's Child," and "Bertha in the Lane," are perhaps the most widely popular of her poems. "The Rhyme of Duchess May" may be considered one of her very best. Ruskin considers her Duchess "the finest female character brought into literature since Shakespeare's day." "The Cry of the Children," "The Ragged School," and "The Runaway Slave at Pilgrim's Point" are the most humanitarian and the most pathetic of her poems. "The Vision of Poets" is eminently characteristic, and deserves a high place in the catalogue of her verse. "Lady Geraldine," a poem covering thirty printed pages, is remarkable for the rapidity of its production, having, it is said, been written in the almost incredibly short space of twelve hours! Some of its characters are not quite truthfully conceived; and Geraldine, at the conclusion, poses too long "'twixt the purple lattice-curtains," and "smiles in slow silence" until she becomes quite trying, as she approaches her lover at a pace altogether too measured and ghostly for a mere mortal. The poem is but little marred by Mrs. Browning's peculiar infelicities of taste, and is interesting in narrative, and altogether one of her most pleasing productions. "The Lost Bower" is full of life, perfume, and color. "Casa Guidi Windows" is one of her more vigorous works. It is neither romantic nor idyllic, but teeming with earnest matter, and instinct with marvellous clearness of logical insight in its treatment of the political problems of the day.

Some of Mrs. Browning's sonnets have scarcely been equalled since Milton's; and her Eve in the "Drama of Exile," has been pronounced "superior to the Eve in 'Paradise Lost.'" This, however, is exaggerated praise. Fancy the first woman talking in this fashion, —

> "By my percipiency of sin and fall
> In melancholy of humiliant thoughts," —

or discoursing of the "precedence of earth's adjusted uses," "the visionary stairs of time," the "steep generations," and "supernatural thunders!" The later poems of Mrs. Browning, though they exhibit an increase of power, are by no means her best.

"Aurora Leigh," a modern novel in blank verse, discussing many of the social questions of the day, and revealing the writer's experience of life, has a particular application to the questions which have been started in regard to the nature and position of woman. It expresses the complete development of the life of a woman and an artist, and illustrates the theory that the largest mental culture does not unfit woman for the tenderest relations of life ; that the highest possible intellectual development results in the highest possible social happiness. Aurora, though true artist, is not the less true woman, and "very womanly" at last. She lays the poet's crown from off her brow, and chooses the love that is sweeter than fame.

"Aurora Leigh" — as far as perfection of internal structure goes — is Mrs. Browning's greatest poem. It abounds in striking and graphic description, in trenchant portraiture of persons, and evinces throughout that strength of thought and terseness of expression which have sometimes been thought peculiar to man. Yet, great poem as it is, "Aurora Leigh" is notoriously rife with the blemishes to which allusion has already been made. Taste is barbarously sacrificed to truth of description. The figures are often taken from objects which excite our loathing. Lady Waldemar is a ghoul-like exaggeration. The story of Marian Erle — more improbable than anything out of Munchausen — is so thoroughly heart-sickening that even the fair, skyey poet-thought cannot make it presentable. As an artistic work the poem is a failure. The story abounds in contradictions.

The figures are sometimes absurd and are often repeated, especially those which are repugnant. The style is frequently diffuse and occasionally stilted, as in this passage : —

> "Shall I hope
> To speak my poems in mysterious tune
> With man and Nature, — with the lava-lymph
> That trickles from successive galaxies
> Still drop by drop adown the finger of God,
> In still new worlds ? "

Her figures too are often bad and far-fetched ; as here :

> "The goats whose beards grow sprouting down towards
> Hell, against God's separative judgment hour."

There is in the poem a shockingly inartistic mixture of the prosaic and poetic, as comparing a disappointed lover devoting his life to purposes of philanthropy to "a man drowning a dog." Verbal finish, though far less important than internal structure, is one of the acknowledged conditions of immortal verse ; and "Aurora Leigh" has been happily compared to "the century plant, — beautiful for the thought that the entire age has been needed for its production, and no less enjoyable for the certainty that it yet will very shortly wither before our eyes !" In these four lines there is a world of suggestion to the rough-handed reformist : —

> "Disturb our nature never, for our work,
> Nor count our right hands stronger for being hoofs.
> The man most man, with tenderest human hands,
> Works best for men, — as Christ in Nazareth."

Another though far less considerable blemish in Mrs. Browning's poetry is the frequent recurrence in her diction of obsolete words. The English of the nineteenth century is in many respects a different language from that of the fourteenth, or even of the sixteenth century; and no writer, however much he may lean toward the olden-time, should use a vocabulary that, having ceased to fall from our lips, is not obvious to ordinary readers. Old poet-words there be, that, though by common consent they have dropped out of prose, should *never* "leave off *singing.*" Yet "geste," "blee," "eke," "certes," "natheless," and "wis," are but musty old words, and let us leave them where they belong, in the cobwebbed garret of the Past. One can afford to read Chaucer and Spenser with a glossary; but let nineteenth-century thought be dressed in nineteenth-century costume.

Admiring Mrs. Browning as a woman, and glorying in her genius, fidelity to art still demands of us a protest against her inelegances. By no means insisting upon that fastidious nicety which weakens poetic diction by rejecting every word or expression that is not powdered and perfumed to suit the "curled darlings" of literary and critical "upper-ten-dom," we cannot hold that poetry gains enough in force to balance its loss in propriety, by such passages as these from "Aurora Leigh":—

> "I'd rather take the wind-side of the stews
> Than touch such a woman with my finger-ends."

> ". . . She lied and stole
> And spat into my love's pure pyx
> The rank saliva of her soul."

> "Cheek to cheek with him
> Who stinks since Friday."

> "That's coarse; you'll say
> I'm talking garlic."

If, as Dr. Holmes asserts, "Poetry is the description of the beautiful in language which harmonizes with the

28

beautiful," the above lines are not poetry. They are the mishaps of the poet, — blots on her pages which we long to erase, and leave the poems clean as her own white soul.

For that fantastic strain of imagination which sometimes unwittingly grazes the absurd, the forced seclusion and introversion of Mrs. Browning's maidenhood is no doubt answerable. Had her mind been shaped in the stir and bustle of human action, she would doubtless have spent less strength on the psychological and the mystical, and would have chosen her themes differently. Her errors of judgment are to be excused by her natural impulsiveness and that strength of will which led to her insistent use of forced rhymes of two syllables in the face of all remonstrance ; as, —

> " You have done a
> Consecrated little Una."

The frequent harshness of her more orthodox rhymes, and that grating use of the adjective, — as " God's divine," " your human," — are to be excused by her innate lack of " ear," as deplorable and as insurmountable as " color-blindness." She had no possible perception of these harsh prosaic lapses. In character she does not distinctly individualize. In depicting type she is far more successful. In " Aurora Leigh " we have, to start with, Mrs. Browning as Aurora. Then, all the good characters in the book are more or less repetitions of Aurora. Marian Erle, the daughter of a tramping poacher, talks and behaves as high-flown and properly as, in the same situation, Aurora would have talked and behaved. Lord Howe, Vincent Carrington, and even that ubiquitous person, Mr. Smith, have each a dash of Aurora ; and Romney himself is but another Aurora in male attire, and with

other ends and purposes. Lady Waldemar, who misses
being either a woman or a fiend, having been painted too
cold-bloodedly diabolical for the one, and too contemptibly
human for the other, is nevertheless often a mouth-piece
for Aurora's own fine-spun sentences. Aurora's aunt
who "liked instructed piety" and

> ". . . thanked God (and sighed) that
> English women were models to the universe,"

being but the typical matter-of-fact English lady, though
perhaps slightly exaggerated, is life-like and fine.

And now, with all these hindrances to her poetical perfection, no one can deny that Mrs. Browning has done
more in poetry than any woman, living or dead. She
has even surpassed, with one exception, English cotemporary poets of the other sex. Her best poems — in
conception and spirit, if not always in execution — are in
the highest rank of art. They are marked by strength of
passion, by intensity of feeling, and sometimes by felicity
of expression. In her verse she often displays vigorous
condensation of thought and forceful imagination. If she
has in her style great faults, she has greater merits. If
her figures are sometimes too bald and grotesque, we often
forgive their singularity for the sake of their aptitude. In
exquisite word-painting she is almost unrivalled ; her meta-
phors are rich, pointed, and abundant. Nature, art, mythology, history, literature, holy writ, and every-day life
furnish her illustrations. Her satire is keen, but, as has
been happily remarked, "it is like wormwood, whole-
somely bitter." She is the first poet of her sex, — the
Milton among women !

Mrs. Browning has been designated as embodying more
intensely than any of her compeers the Spirit of the

Present. May we not rather say of the *Future?* Was she not ever —

> "Stretching past the known and seen, to reach
> The archetypal beauty out of sight" ?

Her verse throbs with " the still, sad music of humanity." The suffering and the happy, the sinning and aspiring, share alike her sympathy. Her theology was not learned in the schools. Though nominally of the (so-called) evangelical faith, in spirit she belonged only to that mystic Church which has no head but the Infinite God. With her there was always "open vision;" and seeing God face to face, she needed not the meagre go-betweens of form and creed to put her at one with him.

To Mrs. Browning poetry was the grand business of life, — a religion. "As serious a thing to me as life," were her own words : thus she confesses, —

> ". . . If heads
> That hold a rhythmic thought must ache perforce,
> For my part, I choose headaches."

Every poem is wrought to an intense white heat in the glowing forge of her soul. Her verses ache with thought, — "swept as angels do their wings, with cadence up the blue." She realizes her own description of a poet :

> ". . . Broadly spreading
> The golden immortalities of his soul
> On natures lorn and poor of such."

No wonder that the frail body refused at last to bear the burden of the great brain ! And now, on earth, her singing is " all done."

> " She has seen the mystery hid
> Under Egypt's pyramid
> By those eyelids pale and close
> Now she knows what Rhamses knows."

"Aurora Leigh," faulty as it is, is richly studded with gems. Here is a fragment that in its way is perfect: —

> "Nor would you find within a rosier flushed
>   Pomegranate. . . .
>   . . . There he lay upon his back,
>   The yearling creature, warm and moist with life
>   To the bottom of his dimples, — to the ends
>   Of the lovely tumbled curls about his face;
>   For since he had been covered over-much
>   To keep him from the light-glare, both his cheeks
>   Were hot and scarlet as the first live rose
>   The shepherd's heart ebbed away into
>   The faster for his love.   And love was here
>   As instant: in the pretty baby-mouth,
>   Shut close; . . .
>   The little naked feet drawn up the way
>   Of nestled birdlings; everything so soft
>   And tender, — to the tiny holdfast hands
>   Which, closing on a finger into sleep,
>   Had kept the mould of 't. . . .
>   .   .   .   .
>   The light upon his eyelids pricked them wide.
>   .   .   .   .
>   He saw his mother's face, accepting it
>   In change for heaven itself with such a smile
>   As might have well been learned there, never moved
>   But smiled on in a drowse of ecstasy,
>   So happy (half with her, and half with heaven)
>   He could not have the trouble to be stirred,
>   But smiled and lay there.   Like a rose I said?
>   As red and still indeed as any rose,
>   That blows in all the silence of its leaves,
>   Content, in blowing, to fulfil its life."

And here is another passage fine and true enough to be set beside some of Shakespeare's: —

> " . . . 'T is too easy to go mad
>   And ape a Bourbon in a crown of straws:

The thing 's too common.
                          Many fervent souls
Strike rhyme on rhyme, who would strike steel on steel,
If steel had offered, in a restless heat
Of doing something.   Many tender souls
Have strung their losses on a rhyming thread
As children cowslips: the more pains they take
The work more withers.   Young men, ay, and maids,
Too often sow their wild oats in tame verse,
Before they sit down under their own vine,
And live for use.   Alas! near all the birds
Will sing at dawn; and yet we do not take
The chaffering swallow for the holy lark."

Of Mrs. Browning's shorter poems, apart from the
" Sonnets," the verses on Cowper's grave are the most
perfect.   They were written before the poetess had ventured on her later bold departure from established critical
rules; and the diction is, consequently, in beautiful accord
with the sentiment.   A few stanzas of this admirable piece
are subjoined : —

" It is a place where poets crowned may feel the heart's decaying.
  It is a place where happy saints may weep amid their praying.
  Yet let the grief and humbleness as low as silence languish ;
  Earth surely now may give her calm to whom she gave her anguish.

" O poets, from a maniac's tongue was poured the deathless singing!
  O Christians, at your cross of hope a hopeless soul was clinging!
  O men, this man, in brotherhood your weary paths beguiling,
  Groaned inly while he taught you peace, and died while ye were
      smiling!

" And now, what time ye all may read through dimming tears his
      story,
  How discord on the music fell, and darkness on the glory,
  And how when, one by one, sweet sounds and wandering lights
      departed,
  He wore no less a loving face because so broken-hearted.

" He shall be strong to sanctify the poet's high vocation,
And bow the meekest Christian down in meeker adoration.
Nor ever shall he be, in praise, by wise or good forsaken,
Named softly as the household name of one whom God hath taken."

In front of the house in Florence where Mrs. Browning wrote and died, a marble tablet has been erected by the Italians as a grateful memorial of one who " by her song, created a golden link between Italy and England."

CHAPTER XX.

LEIGH HUNT AND KEATS.

THE poetry of the period under consideration discovers great variety, both in thought and style. Different schools had arisen, each representing peculiar characteristics of sentiment and diction. All appear to have agreed in rejecting that enslavement of ideas to rhythm and metre enounced by the schools of which Pope and Goldsmith were representatives; yet each sought to refine and elevate by widely diverging methods.

Of the new generation of poets Lord Byron rose first. For a while he assumed the dictatorship of poetry, was alternately flattered and condemned, and at length superseded by the Lake poets, who, going back to the Elizabethan era for precedent, opened a new path for poetic inspiration by disregarding established metrical rules.

While this school was slowly overcoming critical prejudices, and gaining " by inches," as it were, popular esteem, a third school appeared, derisively called by its cotemporary enemies the " Cockney School," — poets who not only rejected the ancient models of poetry, but were radical reformists in morals, society, and government.

Of this school, Keats has been termed the martyr, Shelley the hope, and Hunt is said to have proposed to himself the glory of heralding this approaching era which should eclipse the fairest periods of poetical history; for long before the appearance of either Shelley or Keats, Leigh Hunt had, by both verse and prose, established his claim to the attention of the world. For more than half a century he occupied a conspicuous, if not a foremost, rank among the literati of England.

As the descendant of American parentage, and a lifelong consistent adherent to what we call liberal principles, — what in England are called radical, — he has no slight claim to our consideration. His admirable " Autobiography," presenting a perfect key to his feelings and prejudices, and illustrating the weakness and strength of his character as no posthumous memoir could have done, was issued within a year of the close of his life. It has made him more widely known on this side of the Atlantic, giving, as it does, a true impression of the actual man, who is in perfect harmony with the conception one forms of him through his works.

The poet was born at Southgate, 1784. His ancestors for several generations were natives of Barbadoes. His great-grandfather, grandfather, and father were all clergymen of the Established Church of England. His mother was of Quaker descent, — a daughter of a wealthy Philadelphia merchant. Hunt was a sickly child, and the village doctor sagely predicted that he would die an idiot before he was fifteen. In spite of this cheerful prophecy the poet, through the watchful care and solicitude of his good mother, grew to a fine healthy boyhood, and in 1792 was admitted a student at Christ's Hospital, where his school-days were passed with Coleridge and Lamb.

After leaving school, Hunt turned his attention to the unsubstantial profession which he had determined to follow, — poetry and literature. In 1802 appeared his first volume of verses, published by his father, which he agrees with every one else in calling wretched. Next appeared his prose essays, mainly confined to theatrical criticism ; and though little better than his verses, they gained for him a species of popularity, and he became quite a lion among the English literati.

He now devoted himself earnestly to books ; and from Voltaire, whom he warmly admired, he imbibed those revolutionary ideas which lost him favor with the leading literary celebrities, and brought the Government about his ears. For a printed libel on the Prince Regent — which would, it has been asserted, in Elizabeth's day have brought his head to the block — the poet, after a careful trial at the judicial bar, along with his brother, was sent to prison for two years. A finer picture of adversity sweetened by the devices of a blithe, beauty-loving soul has never been drawn than in this description of Hunt's prison-life, taken from his " Autobiography."

" I papered the walls," he says (referring to his room in the Prison Infirmary, where, owing to ill health, he was fortunately domiciled), — " I papered the walls with a trellis of roses; I had the ceiling covered with clouds and sky; the barred windows were screened with Venetian blinds; and when my bookcases were set up, with their busts and flowers, and a pianoforte made its appearance, perhaps there was not a handsomer room on that side the water. Charles Lamb used to declare that there was no other such room except in a fairy tale.

" There was a little yard outside, belonging to a neighboring yard.

" This yard I shut in with green palings, adorned it with a trellis, bordered it with a thick bed of earth from a nursery, and even contrived to have a grass-plot.

" The earth I filled with flowers and young trees. There was an apple-tree from which I managed to get a pudding the second year. As to my flowers, they were allowed to be perfect. A poet from Derbyshire [Mr. Moore] told me he had seen no such heart's-ease."

Happy poet, who could grow heart's-ease where a less sunny-hearted and more prosaic captive would have planted rue or nightshade. Here the sensuous artist, with that warm runlet of West Indian blood keeping perpetual holiday in his veins, his fine taste, romantic fancy, and child-love of flowers, spirited away from the Babelish world and its " carking cares," was perhaps for the only time in his life in his true element.

Hunt was born rather to nurse poetical fancies than to apply himself steadily to worldly business; and in the rough battle of life he was ever discomfited. His friends, failing in their efforts to obtain for him a pension, resorted to amateur theatrical performances, as another method of relieving his poverty. Dickens and Jerrold were among the actors; and the result was pecuniarily a success.

In 1859 Leigh Hunt passed forever from these weary buffetings of misfortune, — let us hope to a region where the adverse gales, even here "tempered to the shorn lamb," are lulled to an eternal calm.

The character of Hunt, notwithstanding its alloy of self-conceit and eccentricity, is one toward which we are irresistibly attracted. His enthusiasm, love of humor, and kindly temper, the genial friendliness of his nature, and (above *all*) his warm, loving heart, contrast finely with the cold, sarcastic, and worldly-minded nature of Byron, — at one time his closest friend.

Mrs. Carlyle speaks of Leigh Hunt with enthusiasm in her "Letters," though her Scotch thrift and prudence seem to have been deeply outraged by the " waste and mismanagement" going on in his household. Thus she writes: " Still prettier were Leigh Hunt's little nights with us; he has the figure and bearing of the man of a perfectly graceful, spontaneously original, dignified, and attractive kind." One feels in her description of his attire that it must have been not unlike his poetry. " He came," she tells us, "always rather scrupulously, though most simply and modestly dressed." Carlyle himself grimly accorded to him the name of "Kind of Talking Nightingale."

Leigh Hunt's affectionate nature was alive almost in death. He spent his last breath in asking of the welfare of his beloved ones, and in sending love and messages to the absent. He died at the age of seventy-five, the survivor, by many years, of the two poets with whom he is associated. To the last he is said, even in outward form, "to have forcibly recalled Shelley's fine picture of him in his 'Elegy on Keats,' written nearly forty years before":

> "What softer voice is hushed over the dead?
>   Athwart what brow is that dark mantle thrown?
> What form leans sadly o'er the white death-bed,
>   In mockery of monumental stone,
> The heavy heart heavy without a moan?
>   If it be he, who, gentlest of the wise,
> Taught, soothed, loved, honoured the departed one;
>   Let me not vex with inharmonious sighs
> The silence of that heart's accepted sacrifice."

The characteristics of his poetry are sprightly fancy, animated description, and quaint originality, in a style which he has made his own, and in which, with many imitators, he has been pronounced "without a rival." His two greatest works are the "Legend of Florence" and the "Story of Rimini." The latter poem, published in 1816, has given him a place of his own as distinct as that of any other poetical writer of his day; and much that he has produced is brilliant either with wit and humor or with tenderness and beauty.

Critics have praised Leigh Hunt's modernizations of Chaucer, and have said of him that "no modern poet has so entered into the true spirit of the father of our poetry." We have unhappily fallen upon a time when that mental calisthenics by which the *meaning* of a poet is wrenched from his verse is far more attractive to the multitude than the poem *itself*. By this fad of the hour the appetite for poetry proper is no doubt vitiated; and Leigh Hunt, " piping but as the linnet sings," his verse in structure almost perfect, but clear and simple and without the least spice of riddle or conceit, seems but a tame poet beside the " maker and moulder" of this involved song. It cannot be denied that his themes are often simple, and having no higher purpose than that of a moment's entertainment; but sometimes, as a moral teacher, he has forcibly appealed to the universal heart and conscience. We could ill spare from our literature his " Abou Ben Adhem," which contains " in a nut-shell " the entire creed of social ethics. Custom cannot stale a thing so perfect in structure and so divine in sentiment.

> " Abou Ben Adhem (may his tribe increase!)
> Awoke one night from a deep dream of peace,
> And saw, within the moonlight in his room,
> Making it rich, and like a lily in bloom,
> An angel writing in a book of gold.
>
> " Exceeding peace had made Ben Adhem bold,
> And to the presence in the room he said,
> ' What writest thou ? ' The vision raised its head,
> And with a voice made all of sweet accord
> Answered, ' The names of those who love the Lord.'
> ' And is mine one ? ' said Abou. ' Nay, not so,'
> Replied the angel.
>
>   " Abou spoke more low,
> But cheerly still; and said, ' I pray thee, then,
> Write me as one who loves his fellow-men.'
> The angel wrote, and vanished. The next night,
> It came again with a great wakening light
> And showed the names whom love of God had blest,
> And, lo, Ben Adhem's name led all the rest ! "

Craik has happily said of Leigh Hunt, " Into whatever he has written he has put a living soul ; " and in some of his best pieces we find not only perfection of versification, but originality of genius.   He has at least given us to drink of the " well of English undefiled."   In his prose he is, in his own way, only excelled by Charles Lamb ; and as a true poet his claim is beyond dispute.   Here is an unpretentious sonnet ; but who, in fourteen lines, has better suggested the wisdom of prizing our " blessings " *ere* " they take their flight " ?   It is entitled " An Angel in the House " : —

> " How sweet it were, if without feeble fright,
>   Or dying of the dreadful beauteous sight,
>   An angel came to us, and we could bear
>   To see him issue from the silent air
>   At evening in our room, and bend on ours
>   His divine eyes, and bring us from his bowers
>   News of dear friends, and children who have never
>   Been dead indeed — as we shall know forever.
>   Alas ! we think not what we daily see
>   About our hearths, angels that *are* to be
>   Or may be if they will, and we prepare
>   Their souls and ours to meet in happy air ;
>   A child, a friend, a wife whose soft heart sings
>   In unison with ours, breeding its future wings."

John Keats, whom Mrs. Browning has distinguished as,

> " The man who never stepped
>   In gradual process like another man,
>   But, turning grandly on his central self,
>   Ensphered himself in twenty perfect years,
>   And died, not young (the life of a long life
>   Distilled to a mere drop, falling like a tear
>   Upon the world's cold cheek to make it burn
>   Forever),"

was in his life, in his literary progress, and in his " sad decline," intimately associated with Leigh Hunt, — his steadfast friend.

" Nature," as some one has observed, " often makes apparent mistakes in casting nativities ; " and it cannot but be seen that though in the main exact, she does now and then put a poor passenger of time in the wrong coach. Had John Keats been ushered into the Elizabethan age, when the singing-birds each made his own song in his own way (rich, varied, and fresh, yet, mayhap, with many quaint little trills and quavers ; sweet and winsome withal, but not distinctly included in any score), and no bloodthirsty reviewer was at hand to aim his cruel arrows among the song-tipsy warblers, crying, " Wretches, how dare you ? Take that, and that, and that ! Sing by note, or die ! " — had Keats, with his wild, rich, tropical growth of song, the fine poetic madness burning in his brain, and the wanton, turbulent melody thrilling his whole being, been put in these pleasant places of song, it is impossible to say what he might have done. Unhappily for himself and mankind, he came into this workaday world in 1795, in the house of a London livery-stable keeper, who was no less than his own grandfather. He may be supposed to have eaten his beef and pudding, to have thumbed his school-books and played his cricket, like any ordinary English lad ; and at fifteen he was, like a mere matter-o'-fact mortal, apprenticed to a surgeon, and it is not even recorded of him that over the gallipots of the apothecary he dreamed of —

" Emptying some dull opiate to the drains."

Most of his time was, however, devoted to the cultivation of his literary talents. During his apprenticeship he made and carefully wrote out a translation of Virgil's Æneid, and instructed himself in Greek and Italian. Leigh Hunt, being shown some of his verses, was struck with their exuberant promise and with the fine, fervid countenance of the writer, and became his first critic and one of his earliest and latest friends.

In 1818 Keats published his first, longest, and most defective poem, "Endymion." The poem fell into the hands of Gifford, — a critic organically coarse and rough, and as incapable, both mentally and physically, of analyzing the sky-colored, flower-scented fancies of Keats as an oyster would be to write an essay on the song of an oriole. A young and sensitive poet, flattered by partial friends, and ardently panting for distinction, the seeds of a fatal malady already sown in his fragile constitution were fearfully ripened by the savage onslaught of this brutal critic on the first-born of his brain. The agony of his sufferings is said to have resembled insanity, and suicide was only prevented by assiduous watching. The rupture of a blood-vessel ensued; and the fatal disease which cut short his embittered existence began its deadly work.

Keats did not abandon poetry. As well try to smother the song of a robin among the apple-boughs of May as to silence by a critique the singing of a true poet, who gravitates to song by a law as inevitable as that which sends a smoke-wreath curling up into the ether or a silvery runlet down a hill-slope. In 1820 he brought out his second volume, "Lamia, Isabella, The Eve of St. Agnes, and other Poems." These verses met with a just appreciation which amply atoned for previous injustice. Jeffrey (we kiss reverently the hem of his garment for the kindliness that soothed the wounded pride of poor Keats) in the "Edinburgh Review" eloquently reviewed the volume. This favorable judgment, which was confirmed by the

readers of poetry, came too late to save the poet. Far
gone in consumption, he sought, as a last resource, beneath the kindlier skies of Italy to replenish the wasted
lamp of his young life. From Naples he made his last mortal journey, to Rome, and there he died. " He suffered so
much in lingering," says Leigh Hunt, who tended him
lovingly to the last, " that he used to watch the countenance of his physician for the favorable and fatal sentence, and express his regret when he found it delayed."
A little before he died he said that he " felt the daisies
growing over him." His last words were, " I am dying.
I shall die easy; don't be frightened. Be firm, and thank
God that it has come!" In February, 1821, they laid
him in the Protestant burying-ground; and there, under
the same sweet coverlet ('broidered the livelong year with
violets and daisies) where amid his ashes lies the Phœnix-
heart of the " Eternal Child," he sleeps well.

Since Spenser we have had no poet so abstractly poetical as Keats. Morals, politics, metaphysics, and all kindred dulness he leaves to common mortals. His very
philosophy is æsthetic: " A thing of beauty is a joy forever." " Beauty is truth; truth beauty." It has been
happily observed of his poetry that it is like a tangled
forest, beautiful, indeed, with many a majestic oak and
sunny glade, but still with the unpruned, untamed sav-
agery everywhere, — the rankness of a tropic vegetation,
coming of too rich a soil and too much light and heat.

Keats has shown much of that power over words which
characterizes our greatest poets. He was a student and an
intense admirer of the Elizabethan poetry, and we can look
with indulgence upon his obsolete syllabification, knowing that the excess of his love and reverence led him into
the affectation of mimicry. Whatever his faults may be
(and their name is legion), they are amply redeemed by

his beauties. His most wanton sins against art have a relish of goodness in them. His sickliest nonsense scarcely nauseates you ; like the pills he moulded in the surgeon's mortar, it is sugar-coated, and for sake of the sweetness you swallow it contentedly, and, mayhap, like those mythical children of "Sherman lozenge" notoriety, "cry for more."

Keats seems to have been altogether enamoured of "the fair humanities of old religions." The classic myths of antiquity are lovingly embodied in his verse. "Endymion" is an old, old fable, and the story of "Hyperion," as some one has remarked, "is older than antiquity itself."

"Keats's Hyperion," says De Quincey, "presents the majesty, the austere beauty, and the simplicity of Grecian temples, adorned with Grecian sculpture." This is high praise, for the Opium-eater is not an admirer of Keats, being exceedingly harrowed up in his Anglo-Saxon soul by the young poet's sins against the syntax, prosody, and idiom of the mother-tongue. For easy, finished, statuesque beauty and classic expression, the picture of Saturn and Thea in "Hyperion" is perhaps unequalled in modern poetry. A similarity of thought between Coleridge's "Christabel" and Keats's "Lamia" has been observed ; but whether he took the idea from that poem, from the story in Burton's "Anatomy of Melancholy," or from the old classic fable, is not known.

"Isabella," a story of love and grief, from Boccaccio, and somewhat revolting in detail, in Keats's hands reminds one of a flower-strewn corpse, — the ghastliness and decay put out of sight by odor and color. The odes to autumn and to a nightingale are the finest of Keats's lyrics. This latter poem, though not without his characteristic manner, as a creation is simply exquisite : —

ODE TO A NIGHTINGALE.

My heart aches, and a drowsy numbness pains
　My sense, as though of hemlock I had drunk,
Or emptied some dull opiate to the drains
　One minute past, and Lethe-ward had sunk:
'T is not through envy of thy happy lot,
　But being too happy in thy happiness,
　　That thou, light-winged Dryad of the trees,
　　　In some melodious plot
　Of beechen green, and shadows numberless,
　Singest of summer in full-throated ease.

O for a draught of vintage that hath been
　Cool'd a long age in the deep-delved earth,
Tasting of Flora and the country-green,
　Dance, and Provençal song, and sunburnt mirth !
O for a beaker full of the warm south,
　Full of the true, the blushful Hippocrene,
　　With beaded bubbles winking at the brim,
　　　And purple-stained mouth ;
　That I might drink, and leave the world unseen,
　And with thee, fade away into the forest dim :

Fade far away, dissolve, and quite forget
　What thou among the leaves hast never known,
The weariness, the fever, and the fret
　Here, where men sit and hear each other groan :
Where palsy shakes a few, sad, last gray hairs,
　Where youth grows pale and spectre-thin, and dies;
　　Where but to think is to be full of sorrow
　　　And leaden-eyed despairs ;
　Where beauty cannot keep her lustrous eyes,
　Or new Love pine at them beyond to-morrow.

Away ! away ! for I will fly to thee,
　Not charioted by Bacchus and his pards,

But on the viewless wings of Poesy,
  Though the dull brain perplexes and retards :
Already with thee ! tender is the night,
    And haply the Queen-Moon is on her throne,
      Clustered around by all her starry fays ;
        But here there is no light,
      Save what from heaven is with the breezes blown
        Through verdurous glooms, and winding mossy ways.

I cannot see what flowers are at my feet,
  Nor what soft incense hangs upon the boughs,
But, in embalmed darkness, guess each sweet
  Wherewith the seasonable month endows
The grass, the thicket, and the fruit-tree wild ;
    White hawthorn, and the pastoral eglantine ;
      Fast-fading violets covered up in leaves ;
        And mid-May's eldest child,
  The coming musk-rose full of dewy wine,
    The murmurous haunt of flies on summer eves.

Darkling I listen ; and for many a time
  I have been half in love with easeful Death,
Called him soft names in many a mused rhyme,
  To take into the air my quiet breath ;
Now more than ever seems it rich to die,
  To cease upon the midnight with no pain,
    While thou art pouring forth thy soul abroad
      In such an ecstasy !
  Still wouldst thou sing, and I have ears in vain —
    To thy high requiem become a sod.

Thou wast not born for Death, immortal bird !
  No hungry generations tread thee down ;
The voice I hear this passing night was heard
  In ancient days by emperor and clown ;
Perhaps the self-same song that found a path
  Through the sad heart of Ruth, when sick for home

She stood in tears amid the alien corn.
  The same that oft-times hath
Charmed magic casements, opening on the foam
  Of perilous seas, in faery lands forlorn.

Forlorn! the very word is like a bell
  To toll me back from thee to my sole self!
Adieu! the fancy cannot cheat so well
  As she is famed to do, deceiving elf.
Adieu! adieu! thy plaintive anthem fades
  Past the near meadows, over the still stream,
    Up the hillside; and now 't is buried deep
      In the next valley-glades:
Was it a vision, or a waking dream?
Fled is that music, — Do I wake or sleep?

"The Eve of St. Agnes" is so beautiful that one can
scarcely bear to talk about it in mere common words.
The poem is all aglow with light, perfume, color, and a
delicious warmth that might have made the old "Beadsman's" benumbed fingers tingle to their tips, if he could
but have read the verses, instead of stupidly mumbling
his rosary with frosty breath in that icy chapel. The poem
is no less rich with the charm of picture than of music, —
"golden-tongued, and yearning like a god in pain."
Out of Spenser, there is nothing daintier than this piece
of description; in parts it even surpasses the elder poet:

  "A casement high and triple-arch'd there was,
    All garlanded with carven imageries
  Of fruits, and flowers, and bunches of knot-grass,
    And diamonded with panes of quaint device,
    Innumerable of stains and splendid dyes
  As are the tiger-moth's deep damask wings;
  And in the midst, 'mong thousand heraldries,
  And twilight saints, and dim emblazonings,
  A shielded scutcheon blushed with blood of queens and kings.

> " Full on this casement shone the wintry moon,
>   And threw warm gules on Madeline's fair breast,
>   As down she knelt for Heaven's grace and boon;
>   Rose-bloom fell on her hands, together prest,
>   And on her silver cross soft amethyst,
>   And on her hair a glory, like a saint :
>   She seemed a splendid angel, newly drest,
>   Save wings, for heaven : Porphyro grew faint :
>   She knelt, so pure a thing, so free from mortal taint."

Apart from all its sweetness and beauty, there is in the poem the rarest vividness of painting. The description of Madeline, " by the poppied warmth of sleep oppress'd," is like a draught of mandragora. You may hear the floor creak as Porphyro steals out to set his charmed table ; may see in the dim twilight of the chamber that gorgeous " cloth of woven crimson, gold, and jet." The candied fruits, the jellies " soother than the creamy curd," the " lucent syrups tinct with cinnamon, the manna, dates, and spiced dainties, every one," heaped in their golden dishes and baskets bright, are as appetizing as a confectioner's bow-window. In fancy you may smell the clean lavender-scented linen that lines the " soft and chilly nest" of Madeline ; may mark the very coverlet rise and fall with her gentle breath. And when at last the poet breaks the enchantment, and tells you that these lovers fled away into the night and storm ages ago ; that Angela the old is dead ; that the Beadsman has told his thousand Aves, and gone to Paradise, — it is like waking from a vivid dream that still haunts the broad, wakeful sunshine.

All of worth in the present has its archetype in the past. Thus it is in poetry. Wordsworth, grave, reverent, and oracular, is moulded after the ancient Scalds, whose province it was to instruct and inform, as well as to entertain, by their song. Keats, on the other hand, — like the merry minstrels, who in *their* song had no higher

purpose than to soothe and delight, — came not into the
world to *teach*, but to *charm*.   In a brief, sweet spring-
tide the joys of all his life were said and sung; all his
yearning passion-songs, — his " lays of love and longing," — sweet with the breath of violets and the warble
of pairing birds, warm with the ardent kisses of the sun,
wild with the turbulence of brimming rills, and fair with
dewy greenery and virgin bloom.   To him there came no
affluent summer-time, no mellow autumn with its ripened
fruitage ; for in his young May-time he —

> " Wept away this life of care
> Which we have borne, and yet must bear."

" In these bad days," says the author of " Obiter
Dicta," " it is thought more educationally useful to know
the principles of the common pump than Keats's ' Ode on
a Grecian Urn.' "   In view of this state of things, it surely
behooves us, in the cause of that admirable poem, to take
sides with the " Urn " against the " Pump."   We cannot
afford to pander to a too material age by letting any pure
poetry pass into nothingness.   Let us therefore come
promptly to the rescue, and boldly — if somewhat rashly
— assert with Keats in that matchless ode that —

> " Beauty is truth, truth beauty, that is all
> Ye know on earth, and all ye need to know."

CHAPTER XXI.

SHELLEY.

EVERY incident in the life of Percy Bysshe Shelley wears a romantic interest. Born at Sussex, Aug. 4, 1792, the son and heir of a wealthy English baronet, Destiny gave him from the cradle that " world's gear" which she has too often withheld from the tuneful souls ; yet sad and strange was his brief, troubled existence. Sorrow and he seem to have so early met as to have been playfellows ; for he tells us that when a mere lad at school he walked forth upon the glittering grass, in the fresh May-dawn, weeping, he knew not why. At Oxford he studied hard but irregularly, made chemical experiments for diversion, and ever through all, thought and speculated, till thought became misery, and speculation mere midsummer madness.

At seventeen, glowing with youthful ardor, and loving with a martyr's passion what he mistook for truth, Shelley foolishly challenged the authorities of Oxford to deny in public controversy his unanswerable arguments for atheism. The most sage authorities not only properly refused to measure swords with so bold an enthusiast, but in the same spirit of dogmatical intolerance that a few centuries earlier might have consigned him to the stake, hastened to expel him with opprobrium, as an atheist, from the university.

The friends of the rash, misguided boy turned from him in disgust; and he seems upon the whole to have met from the world that very treatment which of all others was most calculated to nourish the very evil it professed to cure.

Infidel by intellect, but Christian by the tendencies of his heart, God knows how different Shelley's after-life might have been had the lines fallen to him in more liberal places, where his doubts and difficulties had been met with the kindness and tolerance born of broader theological perception and that divine charity too often ignored by blind and over-zealous religionists. Fragile in health and frame, organically sceptical, metaphysical to a degree next to insanity, and continually poring over unwholesome French philosophy, his brain had suspended all healthy action; and for the time being he should have been treated for incipient lunacy rather than reviled for infidelity. Who that reads " Queen Mab " can doubt it?

Shortly after his expulsion from college Shelley married a beautiful girl for whom he seems at the time to have had a kind of school-boy attachment as unstable as it was ill-judged. Harriet Westbrooke was the daughter of a retired coffee-house keeper; and proud Sir Timothy Shelley never forgave his infidel son this insult to the ancestral dignity. Such flagrant disloyalty to his patrician creed, overlapping his retrograde from the lineal faith, was to him that " last feather " which is supposed to " break the camel's back." This marriage seems to have added but little to the happiness of the poet. Feuds arose between the boy-husband and his child-wife; and after the birth of two children, incompatibility of mind parted the lovers forever. Young, beautiful, and unprotected, stung, it is said, by the calumny of the world, and no doubt a prey to temporary delirium, the young wife threw herself into a pond, and met, like poor Ophelia, "a muddy death." After this dreadful event Shelley is said to have been for some time deranged. It is generally supposed that he could not have had to reproach himself for contributing by his harshness or neglect to this fearful tragedy.

A chancery decree depriving the father of the guardianship of his children on the ground of his immorality and atheism was the superfluous drop in a cup already brimming with misery. Shelley's opinions upon marriage were notoriously erroneous; and although his practice was far better than his theory, — for not only was he lawfully married to both his wives, but in the case of his first marriage the ceremony was twice performed, — still his most partial eulogists cannot altogether commend his disregard of a social tie which, however irksome, it would have been more to his credit to have respected. In a second and better-assorted marriage, with the talented daughter of Godwin and Mary Wollstonecraft, the poet seems at last to have realized the love-dream of his youth. A short, sweet dream it was, ending too soon in that sleep that neither dreams nor loves.

In 1818 Shelley and his Mary left England for Italy, hoping that a milder climate might improve his health, for he had long been a martyr to intense physical suffering. It was in July, 1822, that the cruel waves of the bay of Spezia flung like senseless driftwood upon the sands all that mortality might claim of Shelley.

The poet was drowned on his homeward passage from Leghorn, whither he had gone to welcome Leigh Hunt to Italy. The body, having lain in the water eight days, was so much decomposed as to render removal difficult; and accordingly it was reduced to ashes by fire. Lord Byron, Leigh Hunt, Trelawney, and Captain Shenley, on the seashore watched mournfully beside the classic pyre, while it consumed all that could perish of this noble being. It is affirmed that the heart of Shelley — by some marvellous fortuity — remained undestroyed amid his ashes. That gentle heart which love and suffering had already made pure enough for immortality the devouring element forbore to harm!

They buried his ashes at Rome in that cemetery where Keats is laid, and which Shelley himself has thus described: "An open space among the ruins of ancient Rome, covered in winter with violets and daisies, — it might make one in love with death to think that one should be buried in so sweet a place." And there he is made one with Nature, and has won from her sweet grace the boon to become a —

"Portion of the loveliness which once he made more lovely."

A poet possessing a more genuine poetic impulse and inspiration than Shelley has not sung in England since the time of Shakespeare. If to his vital heat, his fusing, shaping power of imagination, had been superadded a profounder insight, a calmer temperament, and a broader, truer philosophy, Shelley's song might have been such as mortal never sang before; for he had indeed —

"... Bathed in the Thespian springs,
And had in him those brave translunary things
That the first poets had."

And moreover, he was by divine election a seer, — the poet of the hereafter, "the herald of the golden year," the prophet of universal religious freedom and universal human brotherhood! In him culminated the great tendencies of our time, — its democracy, its socialism, its scepticism, and its pantheism. Impelled by mental gravitation to the most daring heights of speculation, like the bird of Jove, he "soared too high, too boldly gazed;" and the light that might have warmed and fructified, blinded and seared.

However deplorable was Shelley's scepticism, his life is affirmed to have been one of singular purity, elevation, and martyr-like devotion to principle; and surely honest unbelief is less condemnable than dead, unfruitful faith. The pitying angels only know which sight was saddest before high Heaven, — Shelley in his desolate unbelief, rudderless and unpiloted, and drifting mournfully away from the "infinite haven of our souls;" or Coleridge, securely lapped in Lethean dreams, and mouthing prayers with drugged lips, devoutly subscribing to the "Thirty-Nine Articles," while roundly denying God and truth by a selfish and unsanctified life! Shelley died at twenty-nine. Ten years was the brief time allotted him to sing on earth; and though his vernal time was rife with immortal bloom, he was not permitted to bring his full ripe sheaf into the eternal garner of song.

His "Queen Mab," written at eighteen, is crude and defective, and unworthy to be classed with the productions of his riper years; yet it has been considered as the richest promise ever given at so early an age, of high poetic power. In sentiment, the poem outrages every institution and ordinance of God or man; and so insanely atheistic a production has perhaps never been born among poets. Though bringing a heavy weight of obloquy and censure upon Shelley, "Queen Mab" has done but little harm to Christianity. One takes always into consideration the frame of mind in which it was written; for no impartial reader could consider it the sane production of a healthful intellect, yet, as some one observes, "as in the ravings of a maniac there is much that is clear and sweet, with much that is but mere gibberish and incoherence, so it is with this singular poem."

" Alastor, or, The Spirit of Solitude," was the next production of the poet. In " Alastor" Shelley draws from his own experience, and its descriptive passages are excelled in none of his previous works. From the date of " Alastor " to his death was not quite seven years. In this brief Maytime of song, " The Revolt of Islam," the dramas of " Prometheus Unbound," " The Cenci," and " Hellas," " The Tale of Rosalind and Helen," " The Masque of Anarchy," " The Sensitive Plant," " Julian and Maddalo," " The Witch of Atlas," " Epipsychidion," " Adonais," " The Triumph of Life," his translations and shorter poems were produced. " So much poetry," observes a careful critic, " so rich in various beauty, was never poured forth with so rapid a flow from any other mind."

Shelley, with all his abundance and facility, was a fastidious writer, and accustomed to elaborate to the utmost whatever he wrote. It has been justly said that " all that can be properly called unripeness in his composition had ceased with the ' Revolt of Islam.' That haziness of thought and uncertainty of expression which may be found in almost all his subsequent works is not to be confounded with rawness ; it is but the dreamy ecstasy, too high for speech, in which his subtle, sensitive, and poetically voluptuous nature delighted to dissolve and lose itself."

Shelley's most predominant characteristic is ideality. As has been happily observed, —

" Thought, with him, is in fact the reality, while outward things are but its shadow ; hence the remote, abstract character of his poetry, and its lack of reality and tangibility.

" He was at once pure and impassioned, sensuous and spiritual ; from form, color, and sound he could draw a keener and more intense enjoyment than the gross, animal sensations of more earthy natures."

Add to all this that in his "heart of hearts" he hungered after absolute ideal perfection with an intenseness that only a poet, freighted with "golden immortalities of being," may know. No poet more sincerely reverenced his art. "Poetry," he says in one of his essays, "is the record of the best and happiest moments of the happiest and best minds;" and again, "Poetry redeems from decay the visitations of the divinity in man."

The abstract, mystic idealism of Shelley's poetry will always render it less widely popular than it deserves to be. To the realist he is sometimes fearfully obscure. His imagery is often accumulated, and he has an incorrigible tendency to become purely metaphysical when he should be purely poetical. His imagination is rich and fertile, and his diction singularly classical and imposing in sound and structure. "The Revolt of Islam" is a poem of great beauty and of great faults. The description of the river-voyage at the end of the poem is among the most finished of Shelley's productions.

"Prometheus Unbound" — a sequel to the "Prometheus Bound" of the Greek — is a remarkable poem. Here the poet and his subject are in perfect harmony. A remarkable feature in the poem is that constant personification of inanimate objects which is a striking characteristic of Shelley's style. This fine description of the flight of the Hours, makes a picture vivid as Titian himself could have painted.

> "Behold!
> The rocks are cloven, and through the purple night
> I see cars drawn by rainbow-winged steeds,
> Which trample the dim winds : in each there stands
> A wild-eyed charioteer urging their flight.
> Some look behind, as fiends pursued them there,
> And yet I see no shapes but the keen stars :
> Others, with burning eyes, lean forth, and drink

With eager lips the wind of their own speed,
As if the thing they loved fled on before,
And now, even now, they clasped it. Their bright locks
Stream like a comet's flashing hair : they all
Sweep onward.
            These are the immortal hours,
Of whom thou didst demand. One waits for thee."

"The Cenci," a tragedy, was published in 1819. In a dedication to Leigh Hunt the author remarks, —

" Those writings which I have hitherto published have been little else than visions which impersonate my own apprehensions of the beautiful and the just. I can also perceive in them the literary defects incidental to youth and impatience; they are dreams of what ought to be or may be. The drama which I now present to you is a sad reality."

As an effort of intellectual strength "The Cenci" is incomparably the best of Shelley's productions ; as a tragedy it is one of the best of modern times. In selecting for his plot the revolting story of the Cenci, the poet has been accused of a ghoul-like appetite for the horrible and shocking. Against this unfounded assertion De Quincey thus happily protests : —

" The true motive of the selection of such a story was, not its darkness, but the light which fights with the darkness. Shelley found the whole attraction of this dreadful tale in the angelic nature of Beatrice, as revealed in the portrait of her by Guido. The fine relief; the light upon a background of darkness, giving the artistic effect; the touching beauty of Beatrice; her remorse in the midst of real innocence; her weakness, and her inexpressible affliction; and even the murder, which is but the embodiment of her noble aspirations after deliverance, throwing into fuller revelation the glory of the suffering face, — were alike the dream of the painter and the poet, and both have made them immortal."

This outbreak of Beatrice, in view of her execution, is not unlike the soliloquy in "Hamlet." Shakespeare, however (divinely beautiful as some of his fancies are), keeps always a firm foot on Mother Earth. He never "hitches his wagon to a star." Shelley, on the other hand, is quite at home among the nebulæ, and his habitual tethering-post is somewhere in the Milky Way.

BEATRICE (*wildly*).

                                        Oh,
My God! can it be possible I have
To die so suddenly?   So young to go
Under the obscure, cold, rotting, wormy ground!
To be nailed down into a narrow place;
To see no more sweet sunshine; hear no more
Blithe voice of living thing; muse not again
Upon familiar thoughts, sad, yet thus lost!
How fearful! to be nothing!   Or to be —
What?   O, where am I?   Let me not go mad!
Sweet Heaven, forgive weak thoughts!   If there should be
No God, no Heaven, no Earth in the void world!
The wide, gray, lampless, deep, unpeopled world!
If all things then should be — my father's spirit,
His eye, his voice, his touch surrounding me;
The atmosphere and breath of my dead life!
If sometimes, as a shape more like himself,
Even the form which tortured me on earth,
Masked in gray hairs and wrinkles, he should come,
And wind me in his hellish arms, and fix
His eyes on mine, and drag me down, down, down!
For was he not alone omnipotent
On Earth, and ever present?   even though dead,
Does not his spirit live in all that breathe,
And work for me and mine still the same ruin,
Scorn, pain, despair?   Who ever yet returned
To teach the laws of death's untrodden realm?
Unjust perhaps as those which drive us now,
O, whither, whither?

LUCRETIA.

                    Trust in God's sweet love,
The tender promises of Christ : ere night
Think we shall be in Paradise.

BEATRICE.

                         'T is past !
Whatever comes, my heart shall sink no more.
And yet, I know not why, your words strike chill :
How tedious, false, and cold seem all things ! I
Have met with much injustice in this world ;
No difference has been made by God or man,
Or any power moulding my wretched lot,
' Twixt good or evil, as regarded me,
I am cut off from the only world I know,
From light, and life, and love, in youth's sweet prime.
You do well telling me to trust in God;
I hope I do trust in him.   In whom else
Can any trust ? And yet my heart is cold.

That morbid misery in which Beatrice reproduces
prospectively the ghastly phantom of her mortal fear —
the loathed shape of the monster who called her " child " —
is intensely characteristic of Shelley. The putting into the
mouth of Beatrice — a Catholic of the sixteenth century
— his own dreary speculative atheism is an oversight
which somewhat mars the consistency of characterization
in this tragedy.   The natural and universal interest which
the story of the Cenci has produced for two centuries, and
among all ranks of people in Rome, suggested to Shelley
its fitness for a dramatic purpose.

To increase the ideal, and diminish the actual horror
of the events, so that the pleasure which arises from
the poetry, existing in tempestuous crimes and sufferings,
may mitigate the pain of the contemplation of that moral
deformity from which they spring, has been the avowed
object of the poet.   The highest moral purpose of the

drama — the teaching of the human heart the knowledge of itself, by reproducing the various interests, passions, and opinions of mankind in its characters — is, I think, eminently attained in this tragedy; and the failure of Beatrice to accomplish by crime a happy release from suffering, has its moral lesson, enforcing, as it does, the wisdom of that old maxim, "It is better to suffer wrong than to do wrong."

Shelley's "Adonais" is to me the most purely classical, tender, and divinely beautiful of poems. It has been observed that the three elegiac poems most remarkable in our language are Milton's "Lycidas," Shelley's "Adonais," and Tennyson's "In Memoriam."

"Adonais" — an elegy in memory of Keats — has the same classic elegance that has immortalized "Lycidas." The poem opens with a wail, mournful as the moaning sea, and tender as the soughing of the April wind among wet, resinous pines. Then the poet's imagination, groping — as is its wont — among the tombs, is consoled with the drearily beautiful thought that his dead Adonais still lives as a portion of the universe; out of this comfortless speculation, this dismal absorption into Nature, which is scarcely an improvement upon annihilation, the poet is carried, in spite of himself, by an instinctive God-given belief in individual life beyond the grave; and in conclusion he rises into this grand and true accord : —

> " The inheritors of unfulfilled renown
> Rose from their thrones, built beyond mortal thought,
> Far in the Unapparent.   Chatterton
> Rose pale; his solemn agony had not
> Yet faded from him ; Sidney as he fought
> And as he fell, and as he lived and loved,
> Sublimely mild, a spirit without spot,

Arose; and Lucan. by his death approved :
Oblivion as they rose shrank like a thing reproved.

"And many more, whose names on earth are dark
But whose transmitted effluence cannot die
So long as fire outlives the parent spark,
Rose, robed in dazzling immortality.
'Thou art become as one of us,' they cry ;
'It was for thee yon kingless sphere has long
Swung blind in unascended majesty,
Silent, alone amid a Heaven of song.
Assume thy winged throne, thou Vesper of our throng!'"

"Epipsychidion," written in the last year of the poet's
life, for its wealth and fusion of imagination, of expression
and of music, has been pronounced "the greatest miracle
ever wrought in verse." It is too purely fanciful and filmy
in texture to attain a wide popularity. To float with the
poet through this "nebulous ether of moonlit fancies" is
like supping on hashish.

"It is an isle under Ionian skies,
Beautiful as a wreck of Paradise,
  .   .   .   .
The blue Ægean girds this chosen home,
With ever-changing sound, and light and foam,
Kissing the sifted sands and caverns hoar;
And all the winds wandering along the shore
Undulate with the undulating tide.
  .   .   .   .
            . . . the waterfalls,
Illumining with sound that never fails,
Accompany the noon-day nightingales ;
And all the place is peopled with sweet airs,
The light clear element which the isle wears
Is heavy with the scent of lemon-flowers,
Which floats like mist laden with unseen showers
And falls upon the eyelids like faint sleep.
And from the moss violets and jonquils peep,

> And dart their arrowy odor through the brain,
> Till you might faint with that delicious pain.
> And every motion, odor, beam, and tone
> With that deep music is in unison:
> Which is a soul within the soul — they seem
> Like echoes of an antenatal dream."

The odes to the cloud and the skylark are the most brilliant and characteristic of Shelley's shorter poems, and with perhaps *one* exception (" Adonais ") are more purely poetical than any other of his productions.

Shelley has produced nothing richer in true poetic warmth of color than this little poem entitled " Lines to an Indian Air " : —

> " I arise from dreams of thee,
>   In the first sweet sleep of night,
> When the winds are breathing low,
>   And the stars are shining bright;
> I arise from dreams of thee,
>   And a spirit in my feet
> Has led me — who knows how ? —
>   To thy chamber window, sweet.

> " The wandering airs they faint
>   On the dark and silent stream,
> The Champak odours fail
>   Like sweet thoughts in a dream;
> The nightingale's complaint,
>   It dies upon her heart,
> As I must do on thine,
>   O, beloved as thou art ! "

Shelley was a lineal descendant of the ancient house of Sir Philip Sidney, — " the spirit without spot," to whom in character he bears some resemblance. He lived like a hermit, took neither meat nor wine, rose early, and passed the greater part of the day in reading and studying, or walking. He read particularly Plato, Homer, the

Greek tragedians, and the Bible. The books of Isaiah and Job he especially admired.

He was a blessing to the poor. He visited the sick in their beds, — for he had studied medicine that he might be able to practise on occasion. He inquired personally into their wants, and kept a regular list of industrious poor, whom he assisted with small sums to make up their accounts ; and out of his income of a thousand pounds a year he bestowed a pension of one hundred upon a needy literary man.

In person Shelley was the beau-ideal of a poet. He is described as looking " like an elegant and slender flower, whose head drooped from being overcharged with rain." In mind he was singularly free from all sickly sentimentalism.

" Many persons," says De Quincey, "remarked something seraphic in the expression of his features; and something seraphic there was in his nature. He would from his earliest manhood have sacrificed all that he possessed to any comprehensive purpose of good to the race of man. He looked upon the evils of existing institutions, and the vices of old societies, through the distorted media of that cruelty and injustice which had been a portion of his own bitter experience, and which had roused in him that bitter indignation against Christianity that colored his whole crusade against revealed religion."

In summing up this estimate of Shelley's poetry, what has already been quoted in another chapter may be here again applied, — " it lacks flesh and blood ; " and for that reason it is less widely popular than it deserves to be. Of the poet's obscurity (which has been often censured) it should be distinctly observed that it is not at all an unintelligibility purposely planned to give relish to his thought, — as in other verse, — but the inherent haziness of a being never quite at home on *terra firma*.

Shelley was not only intensely psychological, but like Spenser and Sidney, organically ethereal. At his steadiest poise, he has a tendency to soar; like the sweet-pea ever —

> " On tiptoe for a flight,"

he easily escapes into regions where lower-thoughted mortals cannot follow him and his sky-born fancies. Had he but lived to gain the wisdom and experience that comes with riper years, instead of leaving us before his brown locks had known their earliest frost, he might have attained to even higher structural perfection. His matured judgment would have better regulated the selection of his themes, and would undoubtedly have corrected the rashness of his sentiment; but to the last, his poetry would have been above the grasp of minds that chiefly commerce with the actual and the real, and eschew fancies and ideals, for —

> " Native to the sky,
> Downward he could not hie."

CHAPTER XXII.

HOOD, MACAULAY, AND LANDOR.

OUR poetical literature at this time was brightened by many lively and agreeable versifiers who display among themselves refinement, taste, and classic elegance rather than force, or originality of invention, and by two poets of really creative energy. Hood has produced poems that appeal to the universal heart, and have wrought themselves into the memory of all readers of verse ; and we may safely place him among distinguished poets. And independent of his high reputation in prose, Macaulay's masterly ballads will long hold their distinct place in English literature. No poet has more forcibly illustrated the lamentable truth that

> "Laughter to sadness is so near allied,
> But thin partitions do their bounds divide,"

than Thomas Hood, who has given to the world more puns and levities than any cotemporary author, and has written some of the most powerfully pathetic song that our literature affords.

This "poet of melancholy and of mirth" was the son of a bookseller, and born in London, 1798. Hood was educated for the counting-house ; but his health being found unequal to the confinement and close application of the merchant's desk, he went to Dundee to reside with the relatives of his father, and there destiny most fortunately led his steps to the first round of that ladder which he afterward so successfully mounted : he became a contributor to the local newspapers and to the " Dundee Magazine." His modest judgment of his own abilities deterred him at this time from literature as a profession, and on his return to London he applied himself assiduously to the art of engraving, in which he acquired a skill that enabled him in after-years to illustrate his humors and fancies by those quaint devices which have given rare effect to his drolleries.

About the year 1821 Hood adopted literature as a profession, and was installed as regular assistant to the " London Magazine." In this congenial work he became the associate of the best literary men of the time, and in that happy, genial intercourse gradually developed his own intellectual powers. Poor Tom Hood! his life was one of incessant exertion, embittered by ill health, straitened circumstances, and all the disquiets and uncertainties pertaining to literary bread-getting; and when one thinks of all he suffered while playing the merry harlequin for the gaping world, his puns seem sorrowful as sighs, and his jests sadder than tears! When almost prostrated with disease, the British Government, whose moderation in rewarding the national services of authors is " known unto all men," came tardily to the rescue with a niggardly pension. It came too late for the toil-worn poet ; and in May, 1845, his kindly heart, with all its sadness and its mirth, was forever stilled.

Though Hood has chiefly appeared before the world in the character of a humorist, he possessed a rich imaginative fancy, poetic insight, wonderful power over the higher passions and emotions, and a pathos that has seldom been surpassed. His productions are in various styles and forms. His first work, " Whims and Oddities," attained to great popularity. " National Tales," and " Tilney Hall," a novel, followed. Hood's prose was less attractive than his verse ; and his novel was a decided failure. He next gave to the world his " Midsummer Fairies," — a rich, imaginative poem, superior to any of his former productions.

As editor of the " Comic Annual," and also of some of the " Literary Annuals," Hood increased his reputation for sportive humor and poetical fancy. In the " Comic Annual," which he undertook and continued, almost unassisted, for several years, Hood treated all the leading events of the day in a fine spirit of caricature, and in a style which (like the delineation of Hogarth) will be identified by posterity as peculiarly his own.

The most original feature in Hood's humorous productions is the abundant use of puns, generally considered too contemptible for literature, but in his plastic hands made graceful and poetical, often becoming the basis of genuine humor or purest pathos, and sometimes uniting the serious and mournful in strangely effective combination, — as in this description of the birth of Miss Kilmansegg.

> " What different dooms our birthdays bring !
> For instance, one little manikin thing
>   Survives to wear many a wrinkle ;
> While death forbids another to wake,
> And a son that it took nine moons to make
>   Expires without even a twinkle !

> " Into this world we come like ships,
> Launched from the docks, and stocks, and slips,
>   For fortune fair or fatal ;
> And one little craft is cast away
> In its very first trip in Babbicome Bay,
>   While another rides safe at Port Natal.

"What different lots our stars accord!
This babe to be hailed and woo'd as a lord,
    And that to be shunn'd like a leper!
One, to the world's wine, honey, and corn,
Another, like Colchester native, born
        To its vinegar, only, and pepper.

"One is littered under a roof
Neither wind nor water proof, —
        That's the prose of Love in a Cottage, —
A puny, naked, shivering wretch,
The whole of whose birthright would not fetch,
Though Robins himself drew up the sketch,
        The bid of a mess of pottage.

"Born of Fortunatus's kin
Another comes tenderly ushered in
        To a prospect all bright and burnished:
No tenant he for life's back slums, —
He comes to the world as a gentleman comes
        To a lodging ready furnish'd.

"And the other sex — the tender — the fair —
What wide reverses of fate are there!
Whilst Margaret, charmed by the Bulbul rare,
        In a garden of Gul reposes,
Poor Peggy hawks nosegays from street to street,
Till — think of that! who find life so sweet! —
        She *hates* the smell of roses!

"Not so with the infant Kilmansegg!
She was not born to steal or beg,
        Or gather cresses in ditches;
To plait the straw, or bind the shoe,
Or sit all day to hem and sew,
As women must — and not a few —
        To fill their insides with stitches!

"She was not doomed for bread to eat,
To be put to her hands as well as her feet,
        To carry home linen from mangles,

Or heavy-hearted and weary-limbed,
To dance on a rope in a jacket trimm'd
    With as many blows as spangles.

" She was one of those who by Fortune's boon
Are born, as they say, with a silver spoon
    In her mouth, not a wooden ladle :
To speak according to poet's wont,
Plutus as sponsor stood at her font,
    And Midas rocked the cradle.

" At her first debut she found her head
On a pillow of down, in a downy bed,
    With a damask canopy over.

.   .   .   .

" Her very first draught of vital air
It was not the common chameleon fare
    Of plebeian lungs and noses.
     No   her earliest sniff
      Of this world was a whiff
Of the genuine Ottar of Roses ! "

Immediate success was important to Hood, and his
originality being most apparent in the humorous and grotesque, he sought popularity in the gayeties of mirth and
fancy. He has, however, given us verses in a grave,
lofty, and sustained style, purely poetical and imaginative, and rich and musical enough in diction to recall
some of the finest flights of the Elizabethan poets, as in
these stanzas from his admirable ode entitled " Autumn."

" I saw old Autumn in the misty morn
Stand shadowless like silence, listening
To silence, for no lonely bird would sing
Into his hollow ear from woods forlorn,
Nor lowly hedge nor solitary thorn ; —
Shaking his languid locks all dewy bright
With tangled gossamer that fell by night,
    Pearling his coronet of golden corn.

"The squirrel gloats on his accomplished hoard,
  The ants have brimmed their garners with ripe grain,
      And honey-bees have stored
  The sweets of summer in their luscious cells ;
  The swallows all have winged across the main ;
  But here the Autumn melancholy dwells,
      And sighs her tearful spells
  Among the sunless shadows of the plain.
      Alone, alone,
        Upon a mossy stone,
  She sits and reckons up the dead and gone,
  With the last leaves for a rosary,
  Whilst all the withered world looks drearily,
  Like a dim picture of the drowned past
  In the hushed mind's mysterious far away,
  Doubtful what ghastly thing will steal the last
  Into that distance, gray upon the gray.

"O go and sit with her, and be o'ershaded
  Under the languid downfall of her hair :
  She wears a coronal of flowers faded
  Upon her forehead, and a face of care ; —
  There is enough of withered everywhere
  To make her bower, — and enough of gloom ;
  There is enough of sadness to invite,
  If only for the rose that died, — whose doom
  Is Beauty's."

Hood has written but few sonnets, yet enough, I think,
to display his mastery over that form of poetic composition, — as in this : —

  "Love, dearest Lady, such as I would speak,
    Lives not within the humor of the eye, —
    Not being but an outward phantasy,
    That skims the surface of a tinted cheek —
    Else it would wane with beauty, and grow weak,
    As if the rose made summer, — and so lie
    Amongst the perishable things that die,
    Unlike the love which I would give and seek
    Whose health is of no hue — to feel decay

> With cheeks' decay, that have a rosy prime,
> Love is its own great loveliness alway,
> And takes new lustre from the touch of time;
> Its bough owns no December, and no May,
> But bears its blossom into winter's clime."

The poem on the story of "Eugene Aram" first manifested the full extent of that poetical vigor which advanced as the health of the poet declined. From a sick bed, from which he never rose, Hood conducted with marvellous energy the magazine which he had started in his own name; and there he composed those two poems which have taken their place among the

> "jewels . . .
> That on the stretched forefinger of all time
> Sparkle forever," —

the "Song of the Shirt," and the "Bridge of Sighs." In these wonderful poems Hood has taken homely, prosaic human interests from the low level of fact, and lifting them to the skyey region of imagination, has hung them — masterly "pictures rich and rare" — where they appeal eternally to the human heart. "The Bridge of Sighs" combines eloquence and poetry with a metrical energy scarcely excelled in our language; and hardened indeed must be the heart that can read it and still look with "Levite eyes" on the slipping sinners "of Eve's family." Though the use of the sewing-machine may have impaired the literal pathos of that "stitch, stitch, stitch" in the "Song of the Shirt," we must still wear our tucks and furbelows and exquisitely made shirts with a sad consciousness that "all this white satin" has not been put within ordinary reach without its proximate wear of "flesh and blood."

It is perhaps to be regretted that an author possessing

such undoubted command over the passions and emotions as has been displayed by Hood in " Eugene Aram," " The Song of the Shirt," and " The Bridge of Sighs," should have given us so little in this vein; yet even in his puns and jests there is always a savor of good. They are entirely free from that grossness and vulgarity which unhappily abounds in the compositions of many humorists of our day. Hood's satire is without a spark of personal malice; there is always in him an under-current of beautiful Christian humanity; and as has been observed, " those who come to laugh at folly remain to sympathize with want and suffering." Among his lofty and graver productions are many fine and finished poems that may compare with the very best in our literature; as the " Ode to Autumn," " The Haunted House," " The Death-Bed," and " I remember, I remember." His " Fair Inez" is one of our finest poems. This sonnet is good enough to have been the work of Shakespeare himself : —

> "It is not death that sometimes in a sigh
> This eloquent breath shall take its speechless flight;
> That sometime these bright stars, that now reply
> In sunlight to the sun, shall set in night;
> That this warm conscious flesh shall perish quite,
> And all life's ruddy springs forget to flow;
> That thought shall cease, and the immortal sprite
> Be lapp'd in alien clay and laid below;
> It is not death to know this, but to know
> That pious thoughts, which visit at new graves
> In tender pilgrimage, will cease to go
> So duly and so oft; and when grass waves
> Over the past-away, there may be then
> No resurrection in the minds of men."

Let these stanzas from our own Lowell's beautiful tribute to Hood's memory assure us that the " resurrection in

the minds of men " craved by this noble, kindly heart has
not been denied him.

> " Let laurelled marbles weigh on other tombs,
>   Let anthems peal for other dead,
> Rustling the bannered depths of minster-glooms
>   With their exulting spread.
>
> " His epitaph shall mock the short-lived stone,
>   No lichen shall its lines efface,
> He needs these few and simple lines alone
>   To mark his resting-place :
>
> " Here lies a Poet.   Stranger, if to thee
>   His claim to memory be obscure,
> If thou would'st learn how truly great was he,
>   Go, ask it of the poor."

In 1842 Thomas B. Macaulay, a brilliant prose-writer,
surprised the world with his " Lays of Ancient Rome."
Selecting as themes for his verse four of the heroic and
romantic incidents related by Livy of the early history
of Rome, he identifies himself with the plebeians and trib-
unes, and makes them chant these ancient stories.   The
style is homely, energetic, and abrupt.   His pictures of
local scenery and manners are strikingly graphic.   The
interest of the narrative is rapid and progressive, and
the true Roman spirit animates the whole.   A popular
critic has observed of these " Lays": " The man who
can read them without feeling a thrill at his heart *is
not fit to serve in the militia.*"

Macaulay's " Lays " are characterized by the same
abounding strong athletic life which in Scott's poetry
carries by storm everything before it.   His heroes are
not done in marble ; they are warm, palpitating flesh
and blood, and one seems verily to witness their deeds
of prowess and, courage.   Our poetical literature affords

us nothing finer in the way of graphic and spirited narrative than the "Keeping of the Bridge." It cannot admit of mutilation, and though perhaps already familiar, must be quoted entire as an example of his style.

> " Out spake the Consul roundly :
>   ' The bridge must straight go down ;
>   For since Janiculum is lost,
>   Naught else can save the town.'
>   .   .   .   .   .
>
> " Then out spake brave Horatius,
>   The Captain of the gate :
>   ' To every man upon this earth
>   Death cometh soon or late.
>   And how can man die better
>   Than facing fearful odds,
>   For the ashes of his fathers,
>   And the temples of his gods ?
>   .   .   .   .   .
>
> " ' Hew down the bridge, Sir Consul,
>   With all the speed you may ;
>   I, with two more to help me,
>   Will hold the foe in play.
>   In yon straight path a thousand
>   May well be stopped by three.
>   Now, who will stand on either hand,
>   And keep the bridge with me ? '
>
> " Then out spake Spurius Lartius, —
>   A Ramnian proud was he :
>   ' Lo, I will stand on thy right hand,
>   And keep the bridge with thee.'
>   And out spake strong Herminius, —
>   Of Tatian blood was he : —
>   ' I will abide on thy left side,
>   And keep the bridge with thee.'
>
> " ' Horatius,' quoth the Consul,
>   ' As thou say'st, so let it be.'
>   And straight against that great array
>   Forth went the dauntless three.

For Romans, in Rome's quarrel,
　　Spared neither land nor gold,
Nor son nor wife, nor limb nor life,
　　In the brave days of old.

" The three stood calm and silent,
　　And looked upon the foes,
And a great shout of laughter
　　From all the vanguard rose.
But soon Etruria's noblest
　　Felt their hearts sink to see
On the earth the bloody corpses,
　　In the path the dauntless three !

" Meanwhile the ax and lever
　　Have manfully been plied,
And now the bridge hangs tottering
　　Above the boiling tide.
' Come back, come back, Horatius ! '
　　Loud cried the Fathers all ;
' Back, Lartius ! back, Herminius !
　　Back, ere the ruin fall ! '

" Back darted Spurius Lartius ;
　　Herminius darted back ;
And, as they passed, beneath their feet
　　They felt the timbers crack.
But when they turned their faces,
　　And on the further shore
Saw brave Horatius stand alone,
　　They would have crossed once more.

" But, with a crash like thunder,
　　Fell every loosened beam,
And, like a dam, the mighty wreck
　　Lay right athwart the stream ;
And a long shout of triumph
　　Rose from the walls of Rome,
As to the highest turret-tops
　　Was splashed the yellow foam.

31

" Alone stood brave Horatius,
  But constant still in mind;
Thrice thirty thousand foes before,
  And the broad flood behind.
' Down with him! ' cried false Sextus,
  With a smile on his pale face.
' Now yield thee! ' cried Lars Porsena,
  ' Now yield thee to our grace.'

" Round turned he, as not deigning
  Those craven ranks to see;
Naught spake he to Lars Porsena,
  To Sextus naught spake he;
But he saw on Palatinus,
  The white porch of his home;
And he spake to the noble river
  That rolls by the towers of Rome:

" ' O Tiber! Father Tiber!
  To whom the Romans pray!
A Roman's life, a Roman's arms,
  Take thou in charge this day!'
So he spake, and, speaking, sheathed
  The good sword by his side,
And, with his harness on his back,
  Plunged headlong in the tide.

" No sound of joy or sorrow
  Was heard from either bank;
But friends and foes, in dumb surprise,
  With parted lips and straining eyes,
Stood gazing where he sank;
  And when above the surges
  They saw his crest appear,
All Rome sent forth a rapturous cry,
  And even the ranks of Tuscany
  Could scarce forbear to cheer.

" ' Out on him! ' quoth false Sextus;
  ' Will not the villain drown ?

> But for this stay, ere close of day
>   We should have sacked the town!'
> 'Heaven help him!' quoth Lars Porsena,
>   'And bring him safe to shore;
> For such a gallant feat of arms
>   Was never seen before!'
>
> "And now the ground he touches,
>   Now on dry earth he stands;
> Now round him throng the Fathers,
>   To press his gory hands;
> And now, with shouts and clapping,
>   And noise of weeping loud,
> He enters through the River-Gate,
>   Borne by the joyous crowd."

Walter Savage Landor, born 1775, will be remembered as a prose-writer rather than a poet; yet his first publication was a small volume of poems, dated as far back as 1795. He is also the author of "Gebir" and several dramas. The boyhood of Landor was spent at Rugby School; from thence he was transferred to Trinity College. Having imbibed Republican sentiments, he declined entering the army, for which he was intended.

His father then offered him an allowance of five hundred pounds per annum, on condition that he should study the law; if he refused, his income was to be restricted to one third of the sum. Landor chose the pursuit of literature, with the smaller sum. He subsequently, however, succeeded to the family estate, and about the year 1815, left England for Italy, where for the remainder of his days he chiefly resided. He died in 1864. As a ripe scholar, imbued with the spirit of antiquity, Landor transcended most of his cotemporaries. Notwithstanding his high intellectual endowments and proud social standing, he was in his old age subjected to the indignity of a trial for defamation, and was convicted of having grossly and indecently slandered a lady in one of his publications, and he afterward left England poor and dishonored. His friends seem to have come somewhat tardily to his rescue ; but he was finally established comfortably at Florence, with an annuity of two hundred pounds, which Robert Browning is said to have kindly seen " duly employed so long as he remained in Florence."

Though deaf and ailing, Landor still solaced himself by writing and publishing verses ; and at his ninetieth year, when death ended his labors, he was still engaged in working at new " Conversations," in which it is said " the old fire burned not dimly." Landor's poetry is far inferior to his prose. " Gebir " — his principal poem — has not been widely appreciated. Southey warmly admired the work ; De Quincey extolled it, and said of it that it had for some time the sublime distinction of having enjoyed only two readers — Southey and himself. The poem was originally written in Latin (Gebirus). Unprejudiced critics have pronounced its chief fault to be its obscurity. Landor was a deep and fluent thinker, but in his verse he does not always clothe his ideas in clear, forcible, and direct terms, and is often unintelligible to his readers. This fine passage, which has been amplified by Wordsworth in his " Excursion," is from " Gebir " :

> " But I have sinuous shells of pearly hue
>   Within, and they that lustre have imbibed
>   In the sun's palace-porch, where when unyoked
>   His chariot-wheel stands midway in the wave :
>   Shake one, and it awakens, then apply
>   Its polished lips to your attentive ear,
>   And it remembers its august abodes
>   And murmurs as the ocean murmurs there."

Landor's " Imaginary Conversations" are written in pure, nervous English. A series of dialogues published at intervals, they number in all one hundred and twenty-five; and it has been aptly said of them that they " range over all history, all time, and almost all subjects."

In character Landor was moody, egotistic, and full of crotchets and prejudices which he liberally expressed, regardless of others, and often in language offensive to good taste. He was somewhat visionary in his philosophy; and Mr. John Bull has esteemed him an unsound politician.   In an appeal to Lord Brougham — in 1850, I think — respecting the claims of literary men upon the nation, he suggests that " a portion of the sum expended in building stables for a prince not tall enough to mount a donkey, be appropriated to the reward of the chief living geniuses who have adorned and exalted their age."   In his aphorisms Landor is often apt and forcible, as in this : " The happy man is he who distinguishes the boundary between desire and delight."

CHAPTER XXIII.

ROGERS, LAMB, POLLOK, AND MINOR POETS OF THE TIME.

EMINENT in that school whose verse is relished only by the intellectual classes, and has no deep pathos or kindling energy to touch the soul or fire the imagination, is Samuel Rogers, born at Stoke Newington, near London, 1763. Rogers can in no sense claim to have "learned in suffering what he taught in song." His life was as calm and felicitous as his poetry.

The son of a wealthy banker, he received a careful private education, and was subsequently made a partner in the paternal establishment, where he continued to his death. Rogers's life emphatically gives the lie to that dispiriting asseveration of the Man of Uz, "Man is born unto trouble as the sparks fly upward." An accomplished traveller, a lover of the fair and good and great, and enabled by kindly fortune to cultivate his favorite tastes and to follow his favorite pursuits ; to enrich his home with rare pictures, fine busts, choice books, and whatsoever delighteth a poet's heart ; to choose and entertain his friends with generous hospitality, and to soothe and relieve with noble bounty suffering worth and unfriended talent ; at ninety years still retaining his passion for the beautiful, and dying painlessly by slow decay, — who would not rejoice to behold so gracious a mortal lot?

Rogers's reign in London literary society was long and brilliant. An invitation to his dinners was much coveted,

and his ten o'clock breakfasts were so distinguished that
it was considered something even to have seen such men
as had breakfasted with Rogers.   In his long life he was
a cotemporary of many men of genius.   As a young man he
was the friend of Fox, Sheridan, and Adam Smith; later,
an intimate of Moore, Byron, Wordsworth, and Sir Walter
Scott; and in his old age Tennyson, Dickens, and Ruskin
were welcomed at his table, where " the feast of reason and
the flow of soul " even exceeded the ample grosser supply.   There Coleridge in his wonderful monologue talked
poetry to the guests; Wordsworth discoursed of his own
particular poetry; Walter Scott told capital stories; and
Sydney Smith's sharp wit seasoned the feast.

Rogers, on the death of his friend Wordsworth, was asked
to succeed him as poet laureate.   He is said to have written
to Prince Albert, in declining the honor, at eighty-seven:
" Nothing remains of me but my shadow, — a shadow
soon to depart."   His pungent wit, and his well-known
propensity to exercise it, made him a terror to his foes;
and in early life he is said sometimes to have indulged
it even at the expense of his friends.   He became more
gentle in character as age drew on; but it has been
aptly said of him that " no one ever said severer things
or did kinder deeds."

Rogers's elegance and polish as a poet half atones for
his lack of power and originality.   In his published " Table
Talk " he says: " I was engaged on the ' Pleasures of
Memory ' for nine years; on ' Human Life ' for nearly
the same space of time, and ' Italy ' was not completed in
less than sixteen years."   Here surely was time enough
for the poet to have " appealed from Philip drunk to
Philip sober; " but unfortunately *this* " Philip " was
never " drunk " at all!   His allowance of the divine afflatus was, alas! but a safe teaspoonful or so.   His verse

is chiefly characterized by elegant finish and pensive tenderness of the soberest kind.   His best poems are the three above-named.   In " Italy " his tale of Ginevra is embraced;   this poem gives to the reader delightful glimpses of Italian life and scenery and traditional lore. " Human Life" possesses deeper feeling than may be found in " Italy," or even in the " Pleasures of Memory." " Italy " was published in a form so highly ornate as to captivate by its mere externals.   Dr. Holmes has aptly remarked of this poem: " 'T is a pity that all poets are not rich bankers, one's children look so much better dressed in point-lace than in plain muslin."

" The Pleasures of Memory " is Rogers's most popular poem.   It has been happily remarked that he was " more fortunate in his choice of a subject than Campbell or Akenside, since Hope and Imagination we may outlive ; but Memory passes away only with the heart wherein it dwells."   Rogers was a laggard votary of the school of Pope ; and this fragment is not without its spice of the bard of Twickenham.

TO THE BUTTERFLY.

CHILD of the sun! pursue thy rapturous flight,
Mingling with her thou lovest in fields of light ;
And, where the flowers of Paradise unfold,
Quaff fragrant nectar from their cups of gold.
There shall thy wings, rich as an evening sky,
Expand and shut with silent ecstasy!
Yet wert thou once a worm, a thing that crept
On the bare earth, there wrought a tomb and slept.
And such is man ; soon from this cell of clay
To burst a seraph in the blaze of day.

Rogers was thoroughly in love with his muse, and assiduously cultivated his poetical talent to the very end of life. Heaven rest the poet to whom Nature denied the divine consecration, but gave him, as he tells us in " Italy,"—

> " A passionate love for music, sculpture, painting,
>   For poetry, the language of the gods,
>   For all things here, or grand or beautiful,
>   A setting sun, a lake among the mountains,
>   The light of an ingenuous countenance,
>   And, what transcends them all, a noble action."

Charles Lamb, whose poetical pieces barely indicate those powers which were displayed in his fine prose essays, published his early verses along with those of his two friends, Coleridge and Loyd. Lamb was of humble parentage, his father being servant and friend to a bencher of the Inner Temple. He was born in London, on the 10th of February, 1775, and was, from his seventh to his fifteenth year, an inmate of Christ's Hospital, where he was educated with a view to his entering the Church. An impediment in his speech proved an insuperable objection, and decided against a college admission ; and in 1792 he obtained an appointment in the accountant's office of the East India Company. The principal traits in his character and the leading events of his life are well known ; his filial tenderness, his genial love of friends, and his almost martyr-like devotion to his poor, crazed Mary, — the beloved sister who had watched over him from infancy, and whose solicitude he repaid by dedicating his whole existence to her, nobly resolving to form no tie which could interfere with her supremacy in his affections, or impair his ability to sustain and comfort her.

In 1834 this genial heart, with all its whims and prejudices, its playful humor, and its faithful love, had ceased to beat. In the churchyard at Edmonton they laid him, the brave, affectionate, and pure-souled poet, wept and regretted by many friends.

Lamb was a true Londoner, and as much enamoured of Fleet Street and the Strand as Dr. Johnson himself. Clambering to the top of Skiddaw with Coleridge, and deeply struck with the solitary grandeur and beauty of the lakes, he said to his friend, "I could spend a year, two or three years, among them; but I must have a prospect of seeing Fleet Street at the end of that time, or I should mope and pine away."

Social life, its habits, courtesies, and observances, was to Lamb as vitally necessary as the air he breathed. From it he drew his mental inspiration; and if sometimes, drunk with the new wine of poetry, he floated skyward in dreams, his affinity was still properly with earth, and soon drew him back to his familiar and well-beloved home.

In spirit, if not in form, Lamb was a poet, and may claim his place among poets. Among English essayists he is ranked as a genuine and original master. For his style he is indebted to the old English writers, who were his constant study and lifelong admiration; and he has liberally grafted upon it the fine sayings, noble thoughts, and quaint conceits of his favorites. His writings are marked by strong individuality; they display original thought and fancy, curious reading, nice observation, and fine poetical conceptions. Though carefully elaborated, they are altogether in defiance of the conventional pomp and style.

In the drama Lamb failed. His tragedy, "John Woodvil," was handled roughly in the "Edinburgh Review." His two plays are meagre in plot, apparently affected in style, yet containing much that is exquisite, both in sentiment and expression. This fragment from one of Lamb's essays ("Dream Children") is a specimen of his prose-poetry; it has been often quoted, but is not yet staled by repetition.

"The children prayed me to tell them some stories about their pretty, dead mother. Then I told how, for seven long years, in hope sometimes, sometimes in despair, yet persisting ever, I courted the fair Alice W —— n; and as much as children could understand, I explained to them what coyness and difficulty and denial meant in maidens. When, suddenly turning to Alice, the soul of the first Alice looked out at her eyes with such a reality of re-presentment that I became in doubt which of them stood before me, or whose that bright hair was; and while I stood gazing, both the children gradually grew fainter to my view, receding, and still receding, till nothing at last but two mournful features were seen in the uttermost distance, which, without speech, strangely impressed upon me the effects of speech: 'We are not of Alice, nor of thee; nor are we children at all. The children of Alice call Bartram father. We are nothing, less than nothing, and dreams. We are only what might have been, and must wait upon the tedious shores of Lethe millions of ages before we have existence and a name;' and immediately awaking, I found myself quietly seated in my bachelor armchair, where I had fallen asleep."

Lamb's quaint humor may be seen in his verses entitled "A Farewell to Tobacco." The poem is too long to quote. "The Old Familiar Faces" is full of touching pathos; but his best poetry (so to speak) is his prose. His essays signed Elia were originally printed in the "London Magazine;" and upon them his fame chiefly rests.

Robert Pollok, author of the "Course of Time," was a clergyman of the Scottish kirk, born in 1799. He studied divinity five years under Dr. Dick. Intense mental application brought on pulmonary symptoms, and what with

Calvinism and ill health, he became as gloomily pious as possible ; and after embodying in this long religious poem his morbid theological tenets, he died of consumption in 1827. The same year witnessed Pollok's advent as a preacher and a poet, and his untimely death.

"The subject of his poem" (which is written in blank verse), as has been observed, "is the grandest that can be conceived, and embraces within itself almost every possible theme of the philosopher, the moralist, and the poet." In style the work is a composite imitation of Milton, Blair, and Young. The object of the poet is to describe the spiritual life and destiny of man. The religious speculations of the author are varied with episodical pictures and narratives, illustrating the effects of virtue and vice. Many splendid passages and images are scattered through the work ; but the poet is often harsh, turgid, vehement, and repulsive. His morbid fancy delights most in describing the woe and wailing of that future world of despair which his cheerful theology has graciously appropriated to the "non-elect." In design and in diction the work indicates remarkable power, which taste, refinement, and a better creed might have more happily developed. The work attained to great popularity, and Pollok was at the time even honored with the name of "the Scotch Dante." It went through eighteen editions, and still holds its own among very devout but not over-fastidious readers.

Pollok ended his mortal course at the early age of twenty-eight. His piety was ardent and sincere ; and we may hope that now he sees no longer "as through a glass darkly," and has learned that God is not vengeance, but love. His description of a miser is a fair specimen of Pollok's style, which is often prolix beyond endurance : —

"But there was one in folly further gone;
  With eye awry, incurable, and wild,
  The laughing-stock of devils and of men,
  And by his guardian Angel quite given up, —
  The Miser, who with dust inanimate
  Held wedded intercourse.
                . . . Of all God made upright,
  And in their nostrils breathed a living soul,
  Most fallen, most prone, most earthy, most debased,
  Of all that sold Eternity for Time
  None bargained on so easy terms with death.
  Illustrious fool!   Nay, most inhuman wretch!
  He sat among his bags, and, with a look
  Which hell might be ashamed of
  Drove the poor away unalmsed; and midst abundance died —
  Sorest of evils — died of utter want!"

Bernard Barton, the Quaker poet, belongs to this period. His verses appeared in 1820, and though not of a striking character, they possess warmth of feeling, and are not without grace of manner.

Henry Kirke White, who died in 1806, at the early age of twenty-one, has left us, among a few other pieces, that fine and forcible hymn in which occurs this beautiful and impressive stanza : —

"Howl, winds of night! your force combine;
  Without his high behest,
  Ye shall not in the mountain pine
  Disturb the sparrow's nest."

The promise of his blossoming-time was fair and large, but long before the season of fruitage he was gathered by the "Reaper."

Bishop Heber, born in 1783, takes his rank among the minor poets of this time.   Though deficient in passion and imagination, Heber has much elegance of diction; and the sentiment of his verse is often strikingly beautiful.   His

piety was as unaffected as it was deep, and " his comparatively short life was, " says his biographer, " till the day
of his death like one unbroken track of light."

Heber is best known by his hymns. Some of them
are the best in our language, as his missionary hymn,
"From Greenland's Icy Mountains''; and that beginning
thus, "Brightest and best of the Sons of the Morning."
The "Lines written to a March," show his mastery over a
livelier kind of verse.

> "I see them on their winding way,
> About their ranks the moonbeams play."

This song was once highly popular, but like many
another fine old song, it has been superseded by less
meritorious productions.

James Grahame, born in Glasgow, 1765, and dying in
1811, is placed among the minor poets of this period. He
was a curate in the Church of England, until ill health
obliged him to resign his position. Of the several works
that he published, "The Sabbath" is the best. This
pleasing anecdote is related in connection with its publication : "Grahame had not prefixed his name to the work,
nor acquainted his family with the secret of its composition, and taking a copy of the volume home with him one
day, he left it on the table. His wife began reading it
while the sensitive author walked up and down the room ;
and at length she broke out into praise of the poem, adding, 'Ah, James, if you could but produce a poem like
this !' The joyful acknowledgment of its authorship was
then made."

Grahame is not a forceful poet. Like Cowper, he excels in the power of close and happy observation ; but he
has no humor or satire to enliven his verse, which is, on

the whole, rather dull and prosaic, though faithful in description. His poem is recommended to the Scotsman by its distinct and accurate portrayal of the ordinary features of a Scottish landscape; and its prevailing tone of pious trust in God commends it to all.

Charles Wolfe, a Dublin clergyman, was born in 1791, and died in 1823. He gained literary immortality by one short, perfect poem, and that copied with some closeness from a prose account of the incident. His ode entitled "The Burial of Sir John Moore" was anonymously published in an Irish newspaper, in 1817, and was ascribed to various authors. Shelley considered it not unlike a first draught of Campbell. In 1841 the poem was claimed by a Scottish student and teacher. "Fame, like wealth, has its covetous and unprincipled pursuers." Wolfe's right is now, however, established beyond any further question or controversy. Wolfe's incessant attention to his duties in a wild and scattered parish hurried him to an untimely grave.

Though far less popularly known than the ode, that little song which Wolfe composed to a certain Irish melody, when it is said, "after singing the air over and over, he had burst into a flood of tears," is full of the sweetest pathos, as may be seen by this fragment : —

> "If thou wouldst stay e'en as *thou* art,
>   All cold, and all serene,
> I still might press thy silent heart,
>   And where thy smiles have been !
> While e'en thy chill bleak corse I have,
>   Thou seemest still mine own ;
> But there I lay thee in thy grave —
>   And I am now alone !
>
> "I do not think where'er thou art,
>   Thou hast forgotten me ;

And I, perhaps, may soothe this heart
  In thinking too of thee :
Yet there was round thee such a dawn
  Of light ne'er seen before,
As fancy never could have drawn,
  And never can restore ! "

Wolfe is the author of that once popular but now almost obsolete song, " Go, Forget Me." His versification is melody itself.

In 1812 the famous " Rejected Addresses " — the joint production of the witty brothers, James and Horace Smith — was given to the world. The directors of the Drury Lane Theatre had offered a premium for the best poetical address to be spoken at the opening of the new edifice. A casual hint from the secretary of the theatre suggested to them the composition of a series of humorous addresses, professedly composed by the principal authors of the day. They were jointly engaged for six weeks in the work, which was ready by the opening of the theatre.

Its success was almost unexampled. Eighteen editions have been sold ; and the copyright, after the sixteenth edition, sold for one hundred and thirty pounds. The articles written by James Smith are some of them inimitable. The parodies on Cobbett and Crabbe are most praised. Of Horace Smith's parodies, that of Walter Scott is thought to be most felicitous. A very amusing one is that on Wordsworth, noticed in the chapter on that poet.

James Smith was a fascinating companion, a professed joker and diner out ; of extensive information and refined manners, joined to an inexhaustible fund of liveliness and humor, and a happy, uniform temper. He was a true lover of London, and used to quote Dr. Johnson's dogma, " Sir,

the man that is tired of London is tired of existence."
Lady Blessington has said of him, "If James Smith were
not a *witty* man, he would still be a *great* man."

The "Address to the Mummy in Belzoni's Exhibition"
is one of Horace Smith's best productions. It is too long
to quote entire; but here are some of its best stanzas:

" And thou hast walked about (how strange a story!)
　In Thebes's streets, three thousand years ago,
When the Memnonium was in all its glory,
　And time had not begun to overthrow
Those temples, palaces, and piles stupendous,
Of which the very ruins are tremendous!

" Speak! for thou long enough hast acted dummy;
　Thou hast a tongue, come, let us hear its tune;
Thou 'rt standing on thy legs above ground, mummy!
　Revisiting the glimpses of the moon.
Not like thin ghosts, or disembodied creatures,
But with thy bones and flesh, and limbs and features.

" Tell us — for doubtless thou canst recollect —
　To whom should we assign the Sphinx's fame?
Was Cheops or Cephrenes architect
　Of either pyramid that bears his name?
Is Pompey's pillar really a misnomer?
Had Thebes a hundred gates, as sung by Homer?

" Perhaps thou wert a mason, and forbidden
　By oath to tell the secrets of thy trade, —
Then say, what secret melody was hidden
　In Memnon's statue, which at sunrise played?
Perhaps thou wert a priest — if so, my struggles
Are vain, for priestcraft never owns its juggles.

" Perchance that very hand, now pinioned flat,
　Has hob-a-nobbed with Pharaoh, glass to glass;
Or dropped a half-penny in Homer's hat,
　Or doffed thine own to let Queen Dido pass,

32

> Or held, by Solomon's own invitation,
> A torch at the great temple's dedication.
>
> .   .   .   .
>
> "Why should this worthless tegument endure,
>   If its undying guest be lost forever?
> Oh! let us keep the soul embalmed and pure
>   In living virtue, that, when both must sever,
> Although corruption may our frame consume,
> The immortal spirit in the skies may bloom."

Horace Smith was a stockbroker, and made a fortune at his business. Shelley said of him: "Is it not odd that the only truly generous person I ever knew, who had money to be generous with, should be a stockbroker? And he writes poetry too, and pastoral dramas, and yet knows how to make money, and does make it, and is still generous!" Says Leigh Hunt: "A finer nature than Horace Smith's, except in the single instance of Shelley, I never met with in man." Shelley has thus summed up his merits in verse: —

> "Wit and sense,
> Virtue and human knowledge, all that might
> Make this dull world a business of delight,
> Are all combined in Horace Smith."

Nature unhappily broke the die after Horace Smith, and now produces stockbrokers of quite another mould.

James Montgomery, a religious poet, born in 1771, and dying in 1854, was with a large class of readers one of the most acceptable poets of his time. His father was a Moravian missionary, and the poet was educated at a Moravian school, but declined the honor of being a priest; and after being grocer's apprentice, and shop-boy, he carried his early poems to London, but failing to obtain a publisher, took a situation in a newspaper office as clerk, and subsequently, with the aid of his friends, established a weekly journal which he conducted with marked ability, though its course did not always run smooth. His first volume of poetry, entitled "The Wanderer of Switzerland, and other Poems," appeared in 1806. It had already gone through two editions, and his publishers had just issued a third when the "Edinburgh Review" attacked the poor volume with a brutal insolence that mortal verse could scarcely hope to survive. The reviewer predicted that "in less than three years nobody would know the name of the 'Wanderer of Switzerland' or of any other of the poems in the collection;" but let the author, "crushed to earth" by a critique, take courage and "rise again;" for in spite of this friendly oracle, edition after edition of the condemned volume has been issued, and it had, years ago, reached to nearly twenty of them!

Of Montgomery's longer poems "The Pelican Island" is thought to be the best. It is characterized by his own felicity of diction, and by a minute and delicate description of natural phenomena. Though he is most popularly known by his sacred lyrics, Montgomery has given ample proof that his powers were not restricted to purely spiritual themes. Thoughtfulness and simple grace, combined with a musical flow, are the especial characteristics of his hymns, which among the serious have attained a popularity almost equal to the verses of Moore among the lovers of lighter song. This beautiful lyric is a fair specimen of Montgomery's style : —

> "Friend after friend departs :
>   Who hath not lost a friend ?
> There is no union here of hearts
>   That finds not here an end :
> Were this frail world our final rest,
> Living or dying, none were blest.
>
> "Beyond the flight of time,
>   Beyond the reign of death,

There surely is some blessed clime
  Where life is not a breath,
Nor life's affections transient fire,
Whose sparks fly upward and expire.

.   .   .   .

" Thus star by star declines
  Till all are passed away,
As morning high and higher shines
  To pure and perfect day ;
Nor sink those stars in empty night,
But lose themselves in heaven's own light."

LIST OF POEMS QUOTED OR MENTIONED.